Here's What People Are Saying . . .

"Women are no longer at a disadvantage in business. These 307 Awesome Money-Making Strategies will ignite thousands of sizzling ideas for success-bound business owners. If you're ready to increase your profits, get this book!"
—Tami DePalma, partner, MarketAbility, Inc.;
coauthor, *Maximum Exposure Marketing System*

"*Brazen Hussies* translates into 'women in the trenches tell all.' That's what makes this a read worth your time and money. It's from the gals who do it, and do it well every single business day."
—Danielle Kennedy, author, *Seven Figure Selling*
and *Balancing Acts—An Inspirational Guide for
Working Mothers*; speaker; actress

"Marilyn Ross is right! This book is a must for all women starting and building businesses. Wish I had it as I began! Buy a bunch for your friends and daughters."
—Dottie Walters, author, *Speak & Grow Rich,
Selling Women* and *Never Underestimate the
Selling Power of a Woman*; www.walters-intl.com

"Ross offers strategies from the get-go of starting a business, choosing a name, creating a business identity, choosing a business location (including operating out of the home), quick and easy marketing ideas, media tips, evaluating the demographics of your customers . . . you name it, she addresses it!"
—SOHO America
Small Office Home Office

"Marilyn Ross answers the 'Who, me?' bewilderment felt by many women entrepreneurs with a powerful 'Here's how.' In peppy prose, with scores of illuminating examples, she takes you step by step to successful business building and self-promotion. What a winner!"
—Marcia Yudkin, author, *Six Steps to Free Publicity*
and other books

"*Shameless Marketing for Brazen Hussies™* has an eye-popping life lesson on every page. Marilyn Ross covers all the bases as they've never before been covered. It's fun to read, shockingly incisive, and extremely enlightening—whatever your gender. Mandatory reading for any entrepreneur who wants to see for herself how little traffic there is on the extra mile. I've never seen a better roadmap for that mile than the shameless map in the pages of this book."
—Jay Conrad Levinson, author, *Guerrilla Marketing*
series of books

"Why would you even think about marketing a business without a recipe when you wouldn't cook without one? Consider this book your foolproof recipe to business success."

—Raleigh Pinskey, author, *101 Ways To Promote Yourself*; www.promoteyourself.com

"Successful solo entrepreneurs know you can't be shy when it comes to marketing, and Marilyn Ross shows how to go from bashful to brazen with a dose of humor, insight, and get-it-done practicality. Whether you're a startup or an experienced business pro, this book will entertain, inspire, and guide you all the way to reaching your business goals."

—Terri Lonier, author, *Working Solo* and *The Frugal Entrepreneur*

"*Shameless Marketing for Brazen Hussies*™ belongs on every woman's (and man's) desk...if they want to be wildly successful. This gem delivers the new new thing in marketing smarts. It's a terrific blueprint of what to do and what not to do. Get your Hi-Liter and Post-its...you will need them."

—Judith Briles, Ph.D., author, *Woman to Woman 2000*, *10 Smart Money Moves for Women* and 23 other books; speaker; columnist; spokesperson

"This book will benefit every female entrepreneur who has talent, creativity, and drive. I wish this was available when I started my business. I am excited to implement many of the 307 great ideas."

—Marjorie Brody, MA, CSP, CMC; president, Brody Communications Ltd., Jenkintown, PA; author, *Professional Impressions . . . Etiquette for Everyone, Every Day*

"The ultimate marketing book of resources for women in the business world. If you are interested in starting your own company, but have no idea where to turn, this book is truly a gem. If you currently run your own business—or work in a nonprofit—and are continually looking for ideas to improve, this book offers a wonderful opportunity to learn and grow as a professional in today's business world."

—Lisa Wood Wilkinson, businesswoman, Charlotte, North Carolina

"Garnering bold marketing strategies from Marilyn Ross—Queen of the Brazen Hussies—should be your next step in growing a successful business. Female entrepreneurs will find her advice well organized, easy to apply, ready to be acted upon—even inspiring."

—Kim Dushinski, partner, MarketAbility, Inc.; coauthor, *Maximum Exposure Marketing*

307 Awesome Marketing Strategies
For Savvy Entrepreneurs

Marilyn Ross

Illustrations by Curtis Killorn

COMMUNICATION CREATIVITY
Buena Vista, Colorado

First printing 2000
Second printing 2000

Library of Congress Cataloging-in-Publication Data
Ross, Marilyn Heimberg.
   Shameless marketing for brazen hussies : 307 awesome marketing strategies for savvy entrepreneurs / Marilyn Ross ; illustrations by Curtis Killorn.
      p. cm.
   Includes bibliographical references and index.
   ISBN 0-918880-44-0
      1. Marketing. 2. Professions—Marketing. 3. Women-owned business enterprises. I. Title.

HF5415 .R5798 2000
658.8—dc21

                                                        00-030334

ABOUT THE AUTHOR

Marilyn Ross, who has been called a "trend tracker" by *Entrepreneur* magazine, has written or co-authored twelve books. Her *Big Ideas for Small Service Businesses* was selected as one of the 30 best business books of the year by Soundview Executive Book Summaries. In *Shameless Marketing for Brazen Hussies™* she again preaches about what she practices.

In addition to writing award-winning books, articles, and newsletters, Marilyn is in demand as a professional speaker. A member of the National Speakers Association, she presents seminars and training workshops for associations, organizations, and corporations. She speaks about marketing, writing, publishing, and entrepreneurship.

Marilyn—and her husband and business partner, Tom—has been noted and quoted in publications across the land: *The Wall Street Journal, U.S. News & World Report, The Los Angeles Times,* and *The New York Times* have all written about them and their work. Additionally, they've been featured twice on NPR's "All Things Considered," on hundreds of radio stations, and dozens of TV shows from coast to coast. Recently Marilyn was also spotlighted in a lead story on CNN financial news on the Internet.

Bitten early by the entrepreneurial bug, at nine years old she was making and selling potholders door-to-door. By 18 she was managing a women's ready-to-wear store. This led to her being the first woman ever hired by the Mervyn's Department Store chain to be a night/Sunday manager. Marilyn has also owned and operated a hotel and restaurant, and previously headed her own advertising/PR agency. Since 1978 this savvy business leader has focused her energies on the publishing industry.

Through their consulting firm, About Books, Inc., Marilyn and Tom offer turnkey help to professionals who want to package their specialized knowledge in book form. These clients gain greater visibility and credibility with an expertly-produced book from the Rosses' company.

She was a founding member on the board of directors for San Diego Women in Business and served her local Rotary Club as president. Currently she sits on the editorial advisory board for *ForeWord* magazine. Marilyn is a Senior Fellow of the Center for the New West, a Colorado-based think tank. Her areas of specialization are rural entrepreneurship and home-based businesses. She is a contributor to the National Foundation for Women Business Owners and a member of the Authors Guild, the American Society of Journalists and Authors, the National Association of Female Executives (NAFE), and the National Association of Women Business Owners (NAWBO).

In 1996 she and Tom launched a nonprofit trade association for authors and publishers. The Small Publishers Association of North America (SPAN) has since become the second largest such organization in the world.

Marilyn is listed in the 23rd edition of *Who's Who in the West; Who's Who of American Women; Men and Women of Distinction; Working Press of the Nation; Who's Who in U.S. Writers, Editors & Poets; Contemporary Authors;* and *The International Authors and Writers Who's Who.*

The Rosses—along with a Samoyed husky named Peaches and a Siamese cat who answers to Pookey—have traded southern California for a small Colorado mountain town surrounded by 14,000-foot peaks.

OTHER BOOKS BY THE AUTHOR

The Complete Guide to Self-Publishing
Jump Start Your Book Sales
Country Bound!
Big Ideas for Small Service Businesses
How to Make Big Profits Publishing City & Regional Books
National Directory of Newspaper Op-Ed Pages
Marketing Your Books
Discover Your Roots
The Encyclopedia of Self-Publishing
Be Tough or Be Gone
Creative Loafing

Want a dynamic speaker?

Marilyn Ross has been delighting and informing audiences nationwide for more than two decades. She speaks about business startup secrets, unabashed creative marketing, and awesome PR and promotions. To discuss hiring her for your next conference, fund-raiser, or special event, see the contact information below.

Want to Join the Brazen Hussies Network?

You get Marilyn's ongoing irreverent advice and inspiration in her monthly e-mail newsletter, *The Brazen Hussies Network News,* when you become a member. The institute also offers many cost-saving member benefits. To get full details on how membership can benefit you, visit online at http://www.BrazenHussiesNetwork.com.

Need more marketing help?

Marilyn occasionally accepts consultation clients who need customized on-site help in launching or growing their businesses. Her individualized coaching kicks in where *Shameless Marketing for Brazen Hussies*™ leaves off. For more details about how she can mentor you to become a money-making marketing mogul, reach her below:

Marilyn Ross
About Books, Inc.
P. O. Box 1500-BH, Buena Vista, CO 81211-1500
phone: 719-395-2459; fax: 719-395-8374
e-mail: MarilynRoss@BrazenHussiesNetwork.com

ACKNOWLEDGMENTS

This book couldn't have been birthed without our wonderful staff. My deep appreciation goes to Cathy Bowman, who designed and typeset a book that is both reader-friendly and fun. To Sue Collier and Kate Deubert for their editing expertise. To Marcy Alfred for her patience as we went through version after version—and for her fact checking skills.

To Deb Ellis who spent what must have seemed like a lifetime researching on the Internet and being my special brainstorming partner. Especially to Gloria Brown and Curtis Killorn whose talent made the cover special—also thanks to you, Curtis, for your deft and playful pen. Your whimsical illustrations add a lot. I'm indebted to Susan Doherty and Liza Wilkinson for their generosity in taking time to read and critique the whole manuscript. And to Lurina Thieman, and Orpha Paape for their back up efforts.

I'm so appreciative of the parents I was fortunate to have. Both entrepreneurs themselves, they bequeathed me a "can do" legacy that has helped me excel all my life. Last, but far from least, I want to thank my wonderful husband, Tom. Your wise advice and unending support has made this a distinctive book

Many people contributed their knowledge, stories, advice, and experiences to enrich this manuscript. I thank each of you.

TABLE OF CONTENTS

Table of Contents

Part IV: Mission Possible— Unstoppable Direct Marketing

Part V: Maximize Your Strengths— More Gutsy Strategies for Wonder Women

Part VI. Sources & Resources Packed With More Power Than a Protein Bar

List of Sidebars and Visuals

You Go, Girl—Capitalize on Your Gender!

It isn't a fad. It isn't a trend. It's a revolution. If the 19th century is considered the "Industrial Age," then the turn of the 21st century may go down in history as the "Entrepreneurial Age." From the rubble of contemporary corporate life, entrepreneurship has emerged as the single most dramatic consequence since the desktop computer.

No longer does "small business" necessarily connote a mom and pop establishment or a store on Main Street. Today, it's just as likely to be a Web site with a global reach. Entrepreneurship has captured the country's imagination.

It especially appeals to the driven, "go the extra mile" Boomers who are taking charge of their lives in record numbers. They have expertise gained from a lifetime of working for others; now they're hungering to cash in on this knowledge for themselves.

Even more poised to dive into entrepreneurial waters are Generation Xers. An amazing 87 percent of these young people want to work for themselves. Personal and creative fulfillment, coupled with the desire for freedom to innovate, are the driving forces behind Xers' migration to entrepreneurship. Many are tired of the label "slackers." They are also tired of endless meetings, paperwork dungeons, and overbearing bosses. They're out to prove themselves the hardest-working, most independent-minded generation in our country's history.

Twentysomethings are also going back to school for MBAs. Not to become corporate bigwigs, however, but to start their own companies. The University of Michigan recently conducted a study finding that 25- to 34-year-olds are launching businesses at three times the rate of 35- to 55-year-olds. These young turks, many of whom have been weaned on computers, are becoming overnight millionaires from participating in high-tech startups. The number of households headed by someone under 35 with assets of more than $1 million has risen 250 percent since 1989.

Creating Your Own Financial Independence

And who is leading this revolution? Women-owned firms are transforming the business culture of yesteryear. Female entrepreneurs are already an acknowledged force fueling today's economic prosperity. Perhaps you're one of them. As of 1999, there were 9.1 million women-owned businesses in the U.S. employing over 27.5 million people and generating a whopping $3.6 *trillion* in sales.

We girls are finally learning how to kick butt. Disgusted by the enormous pay gap in corporate America where women are paid 75¢ on the dollar compared to men (losing approximately $420,000 over a lifetime because of unequal salary practices), we're jumping ship in record numbers. We've stopped whining and started winning, learned to capture the best and leave the rest, and begun taking control of our own destiny.

Sassy lassies are starting new companies at twice the rate of macho males. It's estimated that by 2005, 50 percent of all American businesses will be owned by women. It's a gender bender of huge proportions and far-reaching ramifications.

Mixing Estrogen and Entrepreneurship

To fully succeed in today's competitive and complicated business environment, however, we must be clever. Gutsy. Dedicated. Technologically savvy. Service oriented. We must develop a business mind-set that capitalizes on our femininity; one that allows estrogen and entrepreneurship to mix—and create excellence. Fortunately, we are innately qualified to do this.

Woman is blessed with a nurturing nature. We're the care takers, the care givers. We've been emotionally supporting our husbands and lovers since the beginning of time. And we'll be nurturing our children from infancy through adulthood. These same traits translate beautifully into the business world. They are what allow us to take customer service to extraordinary levels. And they help us build relationships that are destined to be the underpinnings of success in this new century.

We are good listeners, not only hearing what is said but also what is implied. We've listened to mothers, fathers, spouses, lovers, children. In so doing we've discovered their needs, then addressed how to fill them. This is exactly what business requires.

Additionally, we're intuitive. We sense what will and won't work. When to back off, when to ask for the sale. We have true vision.

Organizational skills are another bit of magic in our bag of tricks. Running a house, raising a family, juggling a career: Many of us are like a street performer with three balls constantly in the air. It's shopping, chauffeuring, sympathizing—or cleaning, cooking, and cajoling. We learned early to write lists, make every minute count, prioritize tasks.

Of necessity, we think holistically. How will this impact that? What is the most well-rounded approach that tunes into the needs of all? How can we get everyone to buy into our ideas?

And we're as tenacious as pit bulls. Determined, even relentless. Many of us still feel we have something to prove. We'll put in the necessary hours, energy, and commitment to turn our passion into profit.

Lastly, we're endowed with a sensuality that gives us a powerful weapon to conquer our male counterparts in the world of work. Sensuality (not *sexuality*) allows you to employ your feminine wiles and at the same time remain businesslike. Coquettish charm can put magic in the moment. Tune in to the three "Fs": Be friendly, focused, and fascinating. In the *Ladies Home Journal* Third Annual American Woman Survey, 98 percent of participants said it's okay for women, even in positions of authority, to show their feminine side.

We definitely need an advantage. We don't have the omnipotent Old Boy Network—with its tradition, layers of important contacts, and infinite opportunities—working for us. Many of us didn't grow up in the world of sports. So we lack the understanding of teamwork and supporting each other for the common good. Too often we end up being adversaries and sabotaging each other instead of pulling together.

Yet our only limitation is our own expectations. We needn't be dominated by "alpha male" leaders brimming with testosterone. Businesswomen with intelligence, perspective, and backbone have no boundaries. As women, we can be confident, powerful, bold, prosperous, spunky, self-assured, irreverent, empowered, and sensational. We can have just as much "juice" as the guys and can play hardball to the max. As stewards of our own talents and gifts, we need to be possibility thinkers. When doing so, we can make an invaluable contribution: to ourselves, our families, our community, our world.

The application of knowledge is power. Many of the previously mentioned survey respondents said women will join and even replace men as the movers and shakers of the world. And for good reason: They'll be better educated. Already women are getting 55 percent of all bachelor's and master's degrees. By 2007, the U.S. Department of Education predicts that 9.2 million women will be enrolled in college.

Compare that to only 6.9 million men. This will spark an explosion of female power. In the next decade respondents expect that most of us will have a female doctor, lawyer, accountant, or stockbroker. And 88 percent think the great scientists of this century are just as likely to be women as men. It's going to be a woman's world!

Maybe you're one of the 47 percent of women who told the U.S. Junior Chamber of Commerce that "entrepreneur" would be their favored occupation. If you aspire to own your own business, or currently operate one, there is an area that will make you or break you: mastering the marketing mind-set.

Developing Marketing Moxie

Marketing does *not* mean going to the grocery store. It means getting behind your service, product, practice, organization, or store with creative branding, publicity, promotion, advertising, and sales strategies. It starts the minute you conceive a business idea—and it never ends! That is what this book is about. I'll show you how to level the playing field. To succeed in business without a penis. To renew your marketing energy and swim with the dolphins.

This book is for new startups that need guidance on how to push the envelope all the way to the top. It's also for established businesses and professional practices that seek fresh ideas and innovative ways to recharge their batteries. Many of these ideas are bootstrap concepts. So what you lack in money you can make up for in moxie. Female executives climbing the corporate ladder, or those who yearn to do so, will also glean insight here into powerful personal promotional strategies.

And although this message is primarily slanted for women, it also applies to men—men of quality who respect women's *equality*. Yes, we'll enjoy a joke at your expense from time to time, just as you've been doing at ours for eons. But males who are turned off by the title or flavor of this book might well realize that by overlooking occasional offensive verbiage, they can access information to make themselves more effective in the business world.

It's sort of like the Oklahoma Land Rush. Except that instead of hardy pioneers racing to claim homesteads, today we have canny businesspeople sprinting to capture customers or clients. So if you're a woman with an entrepreneurial fire raging in your gut, or a lady just entertaining the idea of going into business for herself, *Shameless Marketing for Brazen Hussies™* will show you how to be a triumphant revolutionary. Read on to learn. To be inspired. To change your life.

Part 1

Empowering
Marketing
Maneuvers

CHAPTER 1

Setting the Stage
for Success

New small businesses are starting at the rate of one million a year. According to a recent study released by three prominent women's business organizations—Catalyst, the National Foundation for Women Business Owners (NFWBO), and the Committee of 200—the primary reason women are launching new businesses is that they are inspired by an entrepreneurial idea. The next most frequently stated reason is frustration with their previous work environments. It seems the glass ceiling, rather than being shattered, has turned into a concrete barrier for many corporate females.

But before you can find your entrepreneurial soul mate and effectively grapple with all the elements of going into business, there must be a backdrop of research, knowledge, and planning. That's what this chapter deals with. Market research—learning who your competition is, positioning yourself and establishing your niche, developing a marketing plan, budgeting and pricing properly, plus unleashing your creativity—will help you steal the show.

Business is a contact sport. I'm going to give you tons of hands-on cheeky tips to jolt your thinking, transform your vision, and fast forward your career.

But before we embark on this adventure, allow me to offer one primary piece of advice: Have a *passion* for your profession! If you're not excited about what you do, how can you expect others to be? Enthusiasm is catching. It's the bedrock of business success. Know what you care about, what you do well. Then follow your flair to turn that passion into profits!

Quick and Easy Market Research

Market research is simply an orderly, objective way to learn about people—those who deal with you now or might deal with you in the future. It allows you to put or keep your ear to the marketplace. It can be expensive and sophisticated. It can also be economical, nonscientific, and effective if done creatively. You need to know the potential market risks and consumer biases to avoid nasty surprises. Market research is a wonderful tool to help you hedge your business bet. Digging for facts is infinitely smarter than jumping to conclusions.

Historically, research has rewarded those who do it well and heed what it reveals. It must, however, be correctly interpreted. Coca-Cola proved that even huge corporations can go astray. They interpreted consumer taste tests too literally a while back and replaced their traditional drink with a new, supposedly improved, one. It was a poor understudy. Within a matter of months they were forced to eat crow—and truckloads of product—and rescind their decision.

Research begins with tough questions. We might call it market intelligence. My aim is to suggest innovative, inexpensive ways you can accomplish this so someone else doesn't mine the gold while you get the shaft.

There are two ways to conduct market research. One is using secondary data—information accumulated by others. The other is primary data—information gathered yourself. Either can be accomplished by a variety of different forms of investigation and surveillance.

Perhaps the most obvious approach is to talk to people. Not just selected people, but anyone and everyone who might have an informed opinion on industry influences and issues that could affect your idea. When deciding whom to approach, think about salespeople. They love to talk and can give you tremendous insights about a company and its direction. Also consider support personnel from companies with complementary services. What about chatting with past employees of these companies or alumni of your competitors? Talk to distributors, dealers, and franchisees serving your potential customer/client base. How about key industry vendors, plus associations that serve your industry?

Another idea is to check in with your allies. Scott Fiore, a natural pharmacy owner, talked to businesses in the same shopping mall he was considering. Additionally he queried people in his same industry—but in different geographical locations—about what worked for them.

Anne-Marie specializes in helping large corporations relocate their employees from other countries to the Atlanta area. Before going into business for herself several years ago, however, she checked out other relocation companies in Atlanta, talking with them and their clients; read trade publications; and got government statistics. She ultimately learned how many competitors she would have, what she could offer that they did not, how many prospects would realistically turn into clients, even what her fees should be.

If you're really serious, step up your research and seek to interview investment banking and security analysts from large financial institutions, industry fund and portfolio managers, consultants, and other industry luminaries. These people will have done their homework and can offer a better perspective on the viability of your proposed idea.

No doubt you could benefit by talking directly with consumers. Ask them what they need and want—and what they're willing to pay for it. There is a way to do this. It is called "focus groups." It's relatively easy to set up sessions at local shopping malls. However, because a typical focus group session lasts about two hours, business customers are understandably reluctant to take time from their day to participate.

If you were to hire a firm to arrange and direct a focus group, the cost would be around $3,000. With planning and chutzpah, you can conduct one yourself. One enterprising soul used her church congregation as a test audience. Remember, however, it is almost mandatory to provide some sort of financial incentive or gift for participation.

The Internet can also be used to pull together a focus group. Securing attendance takes a bit of persuasion. You might invite 25 people and only six or eight attend, so figure that into your initial estimate. Recruitment is typically done via a list of questions on the Web. Online groups are susceptible to TV as a distraction so schedule around such events as award shows, big sporting events, or the last episode of a popular program. The best days are Monday through Wednesday.

An additional option is to interview prospects by phone. Although this eliminates the group dynamics, people are often more candid. They may not speak freely in a group because of the perceived "pecking or-

Research: Fact Finding on the Net

■ **Seeking demographic data to target a marketing plan?** This site may be especially intriguing to regional businesses as it covers up-to-date economic data and analysis at metro, state, as well as national, levels. There are also fascinating overviews, forecasts, and trend perspectives that might be helpful as you develop projects. Go to http://www.dismal.com.

■ **SBA's small business profiles available free.** The latest one-stop reference source for state-by-state economic statistics on small businesses is contained in *Small Business Profiles*. Published by the Small Business Administration's Office of Advocacy, it is a collection of 51 three-page statistical briefs for each of the 50 states and the District of Columbia. If you're debating where to locate your business, this could be a treasure. Find it at www.sba.gov/ADVO/stats/profiles/.

■ **More federal statistics available.** You don't have to be in government to use Fedstats, located on the Web at www.fedstats.gov. With data from more than 70 government agencies, this site lets you search for the Consumer Price Index, employment trends, vital statistics, and more.

(continued on next page)

der." Do bear in mind you miss the high and low ends of the economic spectrum when using the telephone. Often well-to-do consumers have unlisted numbers; many low-income families are without a phone.

A third way to glean customer input is via mail interviews. The smallest sample to consider is around 2,000 names. The more people you test, the higher the probability your results will be accurate. Here again, some incentive is called for. Be sure to include a self-addressed, stamped envelope (SASE) or a postage-paid business reply card.

Colleges and universities are another prime resource. Not only do their libraries contain useful information, but professors are a knowledgeable resource. Interview university faculty who specialize in your field. What about working through the marketing department professor? Perhaps she or he will make your research needs part of a course. Students can work on questionnaires, service development, market evaluations, etc. This approach can save you a small fortune compared to hiring outside professional research companies.

There is a wealth of information tucked away in doctoral dissertations all over the United States. I recently discovered a way to access them! Bell & Howell Information & Learning (www.bellhowell.infolearning.com) offers a free subject catalog of more than 6 million dissertations available for purchase. Much of this information has never been printed elsewhere. A further creative way to use this bonanza is to contact the dissertation's author to get your questions answered.

Speaking of getting questions answered, don't overlook a source of local information available in any town or city: the chamber of commerce. Their mission is to represent the businesses in the area and promote the area's economy. To accomplish this job, most have facts and figures that will prove useful to you. Since most cities now have their own Web sites, looking up chambers of commerce in any area is just a click or two away.

What about trade and professional associations? In many cases they set the standards for their fields, take surveys, and offer assistance in research. To find out which ones operate in your specialty, contact the American Society of Association Executives, 1575 I Street NW, Washington, DC 20005; 202-626-2723; www.asaenet.org. For an even more complete list, check the *Encyclopedia of Associations*.

A large local library will also have answers. In addition to the normal books and periodicals, there are reference works, maps, charts, audiovisual aids, and a vertical file with pamphlets and brochures covering countless subjects. A library near us has a Colorado Room where a myriad of worthwhile documents and facts are stored. Your local library may provide similar re-

RESEARCH: FACT FINDING
ON THE NET (continued)

■ **Want an expert for research purposes?** Members of the National Speakers Association can be reached on the Web at http://www.nsaspeaker.org. These folks are typically up-to-the-minute on facts and trends within their subject areas. And they love publicity! If you're seeking data about customer service, gender issues, diversity, change, negotiation, humor, health, networking, relationships, technology, team building—and a variety of other subjects—you can find experts (even celebrities) here. Simply hit "topic" and browse to your heart's content.

■ **Experts Searchable Database** can be found at http://www.experts.com/. It's a global online directory of experts with a search engine to make your job easier.

■ **BznetUSA** is another possibility. It is designed to connect the nation's business press to academic, government, and think tank information sources nationwide. Find them at http://top.monad.net/~gehrung/.

■ **Company Sleuth helps you detect information.** This free tracking service provides SEC filings, earnings estimates, financial reports, and news items on up to 10 companies for you. You'll receive daily e-mail reports as well as "Scoop Alerts" when big news breaks about your selected companies. It all happens

(continued on next page)

at www.companysleuth..com. Although they currently only track public companies, private businesses are expected to be added shortly.

■ **Tricks for conducting competitive intelligence.** HotBot (www.hotbot.com) is a useful search engine. Although it doesn't have the largest database, it does have Boolean search capabilities. What that means is you can type in the words "and," "or," or "not" to refine and narrow your search and receive more relevant information about your competitors.

■ **Find an Expert** is the Web site of Matthew Lesko. It deals solely with government resources but covers a wide range: sewing machines to eggs, fishnets to hemorrhoids. To tap into this free expert service go to http://www.lesko.com/.

■ **Federal Reserve's Beige Book now free online.** Formally known as the *Summary of Commentary on Current Economic Conditions* (now you know why it's called the "beige book"), this wealth of economic data is issued eight times a year for the Fed's 12 districts. It provides detailed statistics and opinions on the sentiments of the local business community, the strength of various business sectors, and other useful information. Here you can take the pulse of a region or of the nation. Go to

(continued on next page)

sources. Some larger libraries also serve as depositories for government documents. Did you know the U.S. government is the largest publisher in the world?

Of course, government agencies at the local, state, and federal levels can provide an abundance of useful information for little or no cost. The Department of Commerce oversees the research and distribution of economic information. Their *Survey of Current Business and Census Bureau Reports* covers changes in the nation's economy, population statistics, and other demographic data. Again, much of this information can be accessed via the Web.

Many communities also have Economic Development Offices. Here you can find current statistical data regarding the economy, building activity, sales trends, community services, etc. Don't overlook the Superintendent of Documents, U.S. Government Printing Office, Washington DC 20402, http://www.gpo.gov. They have books, reports, and government documents on a variety of subjects.

Then there's the Small Business Administration. Although their literature is typically general in nature, they have a consulting arm called SCORE (Service Corps of Retired Executives). It consists of thousands of talented women and men—one of whom might be a boon to your market research project. You can reach them online at http://www.score.org.

In its first year of operation the site got 7 million hits from small businesses interested in taking advantage of their professional guidance.

If fast facts on competitor reconnaissance is a vital strategy for you, going online puts global information at your fingertips. For more guidance, see the sidebar called Research: Fact Finding on the Net. It's packed with irresistible sites.

The Web is also wonderful for studying industry trends and prospecting. A keyword or key-phrase search of trade magazines, government publications, professional journals, consumer magazines, or association surveys can yield an enormous return. And you can scout for new clients among the computerized special interest groups, forums, discussion groups, and electronic bulletin boards.

When Marcia Layton—who operates out of her home in Rochester, New York—wants new clients, she simply logs on to her computer! Layton produces business plans. She finds potential customers through an online special interest group for entrepreneurs. By auditing the mail messages posted there, she can pinpoint startups who seek guidance. Then she goes online and suggests ideas and software. Should the individual need more expert help, guess who's available to save the day? She also tests new ideas by conducting electronic surveys.

Nothing beats these tools of the computer generation. They are in-

---

RESEARCH: FACT FINDING
ON THE NET (continued)

www.federalreserve.gov/FOMC/BeigeBook/2000.

■ **Directory of news sources** is the online site of the National Press Club. Access it at http://npc.press.org/who/sources.htm. You can search it three different ways.

■ *Yearbook of Experts, Authorities & Spokespersons* is also available online at http://www.yearbook.com/search.html. You can search for a specific individual or organization, or do a topic list search to click your way to a group that meets your criteria. Unlike many of the above sites, this one contains more diversity of entities, so you may be more likely to find the expert you want.

■ **Rely on Uncle Sam for strategic planning data.** By hopping over to http://www.census.gov you can tap into an abundance of current U.S. statistics that may be useful in planning and marketing. Tap into population projections, current economic indicators, what the top industries are in each region or country—all sorts of goodies. You can also do a "word search" of their ever-expanding online library of documents and files or a "place search" for data on local areas by place names or zip codes.

■ **More sophisticated data** awaits you at www.econdata.net. It's chockful of demographics and

(continued on next page)

---

economics, plus links to government, private, and academic sources you could spend hours with. Register free with EconData.net and you'll receive updates on new information available on the Web and other goings-on in the world of socio-economic data.

■ **Polls that could put you in the driver's seat.** The PollingReport.com serves up important trends in business and society in general. You can find polls on consumer confidence, business issues, and investing. This can add rich depth to your decision-making process. Go to http://www.pollingreport.com/.

■ **Need professional help with online research, competitive intelligence, etc?** The Association of Independent Information Professionals is an international organization of owners of information businesses. You can hire their expertise. Members provide such information as online database searching, market and industry surveys, document delivery, library services, general research, public records research, indexing and abstracting services, and a variety of specialized research services in specific subject areas. Member listings include full contact details as well as when their business was founded, the services offered, and subject specialties. If this site sounds interesting to you, saunter over to http://www.aiip.org/.

credibly helpful for small businesses, not only in the initial research stages but for future marketing decisions as well. Says one user, "Research that used to take me all day now takes me 20 minutes."

Sometimes phone books prove useful. The Yellow Pages will tell you how much competition you have. By studying the white pages in smaller towns, you can pick up on such things as the ethnic mix. For a small fee, you can order any phone directory published in this country by calling Pacific Bell Directory at 800-848-8000.

Suppose you need a more sophisticated measuring stick. *Findex: The Directory of Market Research Reports, Studies and Surveys* is a treasure trove of information. It contains references to approximately 11,000 studies, surveys, and reports on market and business research. They are arranged in 12 general industry classifications, then divided further into subcategories to allow quick scanning. For instance, if you are involved in banking, financial services, plumbing, industrial cleaning, or computer and information systems, there are sections devoted to market research in each of these areas. Report costs range from a low of $13 to a whopping $12,000.

Who's Your Competition?

No matter what business you're in, it makes sense to mind your competitors' business. By employing ingenious "intelligence-gathering" techniques, you can monitor their activity. This gives you direction and helps you focus on what to do to keep one step ahead. There are a multitude of ways to probe what—and how—your rivals are doing. Let's start with some of the elementary techniques, then graduate to more innovative strategies.

Call or write and request information. Ask them to mail you a brochure, a company history, and letters from some satisfied customers or clients. If appropriate, you might also ask for an annual report and a copy of any newsletter they publish. Analyze this literature to discover their strategic plans.

Now look them up in the Yellow Pages. Ads often reveal such things as date founded, additional locations, hours of business, membership in national associations, etc. You can also get a feel for what they emphasize. Are they touting price, service, quality, or some unique characteristic?

Once again, the chamber of commerce can come to your aid for local or regional competitors. If they are members, the chamber typically can tell you who the principals are, as well as shed some light on their reputation, history, and civic involvement.

Don't overlook the area Better Business Bureau. They frequently have company histories on file that show the date of incorporation, who the owners are, and what the company does. Additionally, they will know if any consumer complaints have been received and whether a satisfactory settlement was reached.

What's the ideal way to glean first-hand information? Use their service yourself! Make every second count while you're on the premises. What image is projected—is the atmosphere conservative or avant-garde, friendly or formal? Are there plaques, awards, or framed letters on the walls that give clues about their reputation? Is the environment organized and sparkling or messy and dirty? What kind of reading material is in the lobby? How do employees act toward each other—and you?

Now think about how the product or service is delivered. Is it timely? Of superior quality? Are any value-added extras included? Did the person who worked with you make an effort to sell you something additional? Noticing what they do poorly (and well) gives you a mighty weapon for your marketing arsenal.

A trip to the biggest library in the area will also net information to help you outmaneuver the competition. For large corporations, look in the *Dun & Bradstreet Directory* or *Standard & Poor's Registry*. Firms with a net worth from $500,000 to $1,000,000 are listed in *D & B's Middle Market*. Those topping $1 million are in the—you guessed it—*Million Dollar Directory*. You can also access Dun & Bradstreet via the Internet at http://www.dnb.com.

Here you will learn when and where incorporation took place, subsidiary details, names and functions of corporate officers and directors, annual sales volume, plus the number of employees. The Standard & Poor's reference set is even more complete. It probes capitalization, corporate background, finances, and recent dividends.

If you weren't able to get an annual report yourself, major libraries often have copies for heavyweight area businesses. During your research safari, look up the CEO in *Who's Who in America* or one of the other who's who directories. These biographical references reveal such tidbits as alma mater, accomplishments, books authored, community involvement, hobbies, and personal data.

One more library assignment: Research local news stories. Many libraries index the local newspaper or clip articles and place them in filing cabinets. By scouring these you can harvest pertinent competitor information, plus get a feel for their advertising budgets. Many newspaper Web sites have search engines that allow you to enter the company's name and access recent articles or mentions about them.

Word-of-mouth can be more revealing than a sheer blouse. Talk with friends, relatives, business colleagues, vendors, sales representatives, even strangers. Listen carefully. One daring damsel I know puts herself within close physical proximity to her competitor's location in the hope of overhearing useful information. She eavesdrops in nearby neighborhood restaurants, bars, and on buses to catch snatches of conversation.

If you don't have that much moxie (and most of us don't), consider attending trade shows and conferences. By visiting your competitors' booths, you can collect available literature, tune in to industry gossip, and perhaps get a leg up by discovering their future expansion plans.

Always have your antennae out. Help-wanted ads, for instance, can yield information on your opponent's activities. Are they adding to their staff? Looking to hire a branch manager? Another place to scrutinize is trade journals in your field. Tune in to them for articles about your opponents. Specific magazine sections—such as personnel announcements, calendar listings, or news and notes—can also provide ammunition.

It may be wise to hire a clipping service. You can instruct them to pull all magazine or newspaper articles on any company, clip industry trend pieces, watch for Internet mentions, and cover virtually anything you want to track. (If you hire one, be sure to add your own company name so they provide an overview of what is appearing in print about you.) Should radio and TV play a major role in your adversary's plan, they also audit electronic media.

There is yet another way to tune in to a competitor's advertising activity. Space Analysis Systems, Inc., (2300 Computer Avenue, Suite B12, Willow Grove, PA 19090, 215-784-0404) monitors ads in over 525 publications. For a minimum of $30, they can check their database and determine which publications your competitors use for advertising.

Last, but far from least, you can read your way to a hot career. Yes, there are books, magazines, newsletters, and newspapers to help you stay abreast of trends and create exciting new business opportunities. For trend tracking, one of the best publications I've found is *American Demographics* magazine. Primarily a tool for advertising agencies, it forecasts consumer trends and provides revealing statistics.

Positioning Yourself for Profits

When times turn tough, there's great temptation to cut the marketing budget and work harder. I'd like to suggest you work easier...and more ingeniously. How?

By "positioning" yourself for greater success. What does this term really mean? Positioning is simply looking for the hole—then plugging it. Finding ways to differentiate yourself from the pack. And many of these strategies cost little or nothing. Using traditional techniques to fight for market share makes about as much sense as mice banding together to build a cat. Take a leadership posture rather than being a look-alike.

The twin sister of positioning is named Unique Selling Proposition (USP). You develop this by discovering what you do better, faster, more compellingly than your competition: what is distinctly "you." Businesses position themselves and capitalize on USPs in different ways:

Gratzi's, a high-end Italian restaurant located near an industrial complex in Colorado Springs, Colorado, launched Fax-A-Meal using modern technology to appeal to the rushed business crowd. All people have to do is fax in their order and the time it is to be ready. Presto. They can arrive and eat in—or send a gofer to pick up antipasto, tortellini, or crispy calamari. Another positioning trend is for restaurants to deliver elaborate feasts to your doorstep. Harried two-career couples can wait until the kids are down, add candles and wine, then dine.

The Blue Frog Bar & Grill's owner, Mim Witschy, got frustrated working for someone else. So she bought a little hole-in-the-wall bistro. But how to attract customers? She and a partner came up with the idea of offering children's games to their adult patrons. Bar sales zoomed to $500,000. Both businesspeople and yuppies love the games—for ages three to 12!

What you're reading right now is a prime example of developing a distinguishing USP. When I got the idea to write a marketing guide for small businesses, I did my homework. A trip to the library and an hour or so poring over *Books in Print* revealed what was already available. What a blow! There was page after page of titles on advertising, promotion, sales, and publicity. After studying them more carefully, however, it became evident hardly any of these books targeted female entrepreneurs. And most were hopelessly dull. So a book concept that hip businesswomen would enjoy and benefit from was a natural.

How do you find your special stance for success? As I said before, know the competition. Before you can possibly position yourself ideally you must evaluate what your rivals do well—and poorly. Then you can differentiate yourself from them, turning their anorexic weaknesses into your robust strengths.

According to Valerie Wiener, author of *Power Positioning: Advancing Yourself as THE Expert,* you must "stay focused and take action steps to *sidestep* the other players. Be *first...the leader...*at what you do. Be first in the prospect's mind. Once the potential customer learns about your expertise—and that you were the pioneer in your area—you will have secured your position with that prospect. Others who follow with that expertise or anything similar will not be able to replace you."

Next you need to understand *your* operation. What do you do better, faster, more innovatively than others? Is quality, exclusivity, or snob appeal your ticket? Or do you offer a downright cheap alternative? Is your selection huge? Your service extra speedy? Perhaps convenience is your drawing card. Just what is your special gift? Focus on your real power. Don't try to be all things to all people. Rather make the most of your unique resources.

The key point in positioning is to know what your goals are and be sure they're consistent with your morals and ethics. Then everything that flashes across your life relates. Ask of everything you read, everything you see, every experience you have: How does this fit with my goal? By doing that you're constantly looking for "hooks"—ways to position yourself.

Then get out of *your* head and into your prospects' minds. "What's in it for me?" is all they care about. If you put more in it for them, they'll put more in your coffers in return.

That's what happened at a Chicago travel agency. They came up with a different twist: a discount travel club that offers short-notice vacations. Discovering that traveling on short notice was the preferred mode for a fast-growing group of people, they cater to young professionals looking for exotic vacations within their budget. Retirees who consider travel an important part of their lifestyle are another large segment of their clientele. Their drawing card? Economical pricing. Members save several hundred dollars per trip.

Speaking of travel, Mighty Eagle Travel, Inc., moved their agency into a former bank building with a drive-through window. Quips owner Christopher Hinn, "If McDonalds can do it, why can't I?" This new twist on an old concept allows customers to pick up tickets in a more convenient way. One woman drives in wearing her robe and slippers. A corporate executive sends a driver over for tickets while she's conducting a meeting. And because the agency is situated between downtown and the airport, customers can get their tickets on the way to catch their flights.

A forward-thinking Massachusetts woman by the name of Susan Berk set up sightseeing tours called Uncommon Boston, Ltd. Berk quickly built her business into a quarter-million dollar venture. "People want to feel like an insider. They want to get unusual questions answered and see unique places," she observes. Berk's firm customizes each program for the client—be it a spouse tour, reunion, retirement party, or dinner for the chairman of the board.

She has amazing resources and can pull off exceptional events. Rather than hitting the usual tourist spots, Uncommon Boston gives people an insider's view of the city. A cadre of guides whisks clients off on a tour of a chocolate factory (to learn its history, how it's made, and to indulge in a tasting party). Or perhaps a college tour for students and parents making alma mater selections is in order. Even private home tours for cooking lessons with renowned chefs and visits to famous area artists' studios to watch them work can be arranged. Uncommon Boston, Ltd., gives the typical tours servicing the city a real run for their money. Susan Berk has created something special. Different. Imaginative. She constantly proves small is spectacular—and profitable too.

There are countless strategies for positioning your business. Perhaps you should investigate the hours or days you are open. One store that closed Sundays found it was their second busiest day when they opted to remain open. Or maybe an outlandish guarantee could be your claim to fame. Chances are, offering pick-up and delivery service will capture new business.

Today time is currency. But how do you "buy" time? By purchasing convenience. In our harried world, people are especially receptive to anyone or any place that saves them time or makes their lives easier. Most women perceive their lives as a decathlon: a set schedule of unending events. Ease that pressure by doing her grocery shopping, providing video rental delivery, offering a chauffeuring service, and you've made a friend as well as a customer.

A Vista, California, entrepreneur decided to piggyback two businesses. Dubbed Clean & Lean, the concept consists of a laundromat in conjunction with a fitness facility. People seem to like Clean & Lean's personalized service and the opportunity to make new acquaintances. It is very different from a big, impersonal gym where you have to sign an expensive, long-term contract. Here you choose from a menu of four options: coin laundry only, a visit to the fitness center, fitness sessions on a monthly basis, or a combination laundry and fitness deal.

Partially due to tremendous publicity (they've been interviewed by CBS World News, ABC, CNN, BBC, Japanese TV, the Japanese Wall Street Journal, Sports Illustrated, Time, Glamour, and People), things are looking anything but lean. In fact, they're "cleaning up." Several franchises are in operation now and many more are in the works.

Positioning comes in as many varieties as Madonna has outfits. Capitalizing on age to set itself apart, a Denver bank specializes in kids doing grown-up business. Junior patrons open checking accounts and take out loans while the bank makes a name for itself—and long-term customers. A doctor makes house calls from her fully equipped medical vehicle. An enterprising masseuse makes "office calls" to loosen the stressed neck muscles of secretaries and executives.

When burgeoning entrepreneur Joann Malizia of Craig, Colorado, lost her job teaching sign language to students at the local elementary school because of cutbacks, she went into business for herself selling sign language posters. In her work with the hearing impaired, she was always disappointed at the lack of fun, modern tools with which to teach. So she hired a talented artist fresh out of college who charged very little and went about designing beautiful full-color posters, each of which depicts a different concept, such as "friendship" and "believe." Now they are being sold all over the country.

The list is endless. Women all across America are discovering practical, profitable ways to make themselves uniquely competitive.

While it's true the only person who really likes change is a wet baby, to survive and thrive in today's economy we must be willing to change—to innovate—to supply the solution. You can try to do business as usual, or you can do business unusually well. Positioning and creating your special USP often makes the difference.

Niches Spell Riches

A close cousin to positioning is niche marketing/segmentation. Think of it this way: rather than deluging everybody with a fire hose, you bring thirsty people a cup of water. Perhaps using a military analogy will also help you understand what I mean. For thousands of years military leaders have used the strategy of maneuvering *around* strength, rather than *confronting* it, to win victories. They exploit their adversaries' weaknesses. It's the old "divide and conquer" theory.

You can carve out a niche just for yourself, doing something different or better or faster than your competition. This way you identify and serve a segment all your own, instead of tackling the major competition head on.

Let's use cookies to understand how it works. Cookie manufacturers tailor their approaches to appeal to very different segments of the population. Thus some cookies are *chewy*. Others are *crunchy*. There are those "like Grandma used to make" for nostalgia buffs. And what about *nutritious* cookies pitched to the health-conscious, or *low fat* ones? Then there are *gourmet* cookies for those poised on the cutting edge of cuisine. And don't forget *gigantic* cookies—or *bite-sized* miniatures—or the just plain *fun* ones we learned to unscrew and devour (centers first) as toddlers. Get the picture? These manufacturers are definitely *not* into cookie-cutter marketing! Smart cookies go after their own sweet section of the market.

That's what Rebecca Mathias did almost 20 years ago when she realized pregnant women wanted to end their long exile from fashion. She birthed a $300 million publicly traded company called Motherswork, which has more than 600 stores today. Bellying up to the bassinet more recently, Cherie Serota and Jody Kozlow Gardner have also found this to be a fertile market. They merchandise their top-selling Pregnancy Survival Kit to none less than Bloomingdale's. It's a mother-to-be wardrobe in a box consisting of four key pieces: a dress, skirt, tunic, and leggings.

In the service sector, hospitals and health-care facilities are becoming very innovative at carving out special niches for themselves. They've aborted their attempts to reach every health- care patient and are dissecting and refining health-care markets, focusing on specialty care. The primary objective of these niche programs is to increase market share. It's working handsomely. In an annual diversification survey by *Hospitals* magazine, the results show overall hospital segmentation strategies add to profitability.

To court mothers-to-be, Women's Hospital in Houston offers a special "cameo" package. It features a private room, lobster dinner, and a limousine ride home. Other hospitals concentrate on physical rehabilitation, senior care, oncology, corporate wellness, even eating disorders. They specialize to help them stand out from the crowd, selecting only those services that blend with their community or regional demographics.

Futurist Edith Weiner, president of New York-based Weiner, Edrich & Brown, noted at the American Marketing Association's 50th Anniversary World Marketing Conference and Exhibition that niche marketing will soon become the rule rather than the exception.

Two collection agencies have taken different approaches to deconstructing convention in the collection field. Michelle Dunn, owner of M.A.D. Collection Agency specializes in getting money out of accounts her competitors refuse to touch because they are too old to collect. To further sweeten the pot for her clients, she also includes her fee, along with any applicable court costs or interest, right into the debtor's bill. "When I was using collection agencies, they never offered me that perk," Dunn explains. She has lowered the past due accounts receivable for countless companies.

Another collection agency decided to focus on prodding reluctant library patrons to pay fines on overdue books. They've been rounding up recalcitrant library users since 1994 by using a "gentle nudge" approach to motivate procrastinators. Apparently, they've found a receptive niche: If a library loses 10 percent of their collection, it could run into $1 million.

Clever bed and breakfast inns also specialize. Some cater to pet owners, gay couples, or vegetarians. And more and more serve businesspeople, providing in-room telephones, convenient computer hookups, and fax machines. Others are putting together package deals to give them a competitive edge. Fifteen B&Bs in Virginia's Shenandoah Valley tied in with a vineyard to promote a new line of wines via mid-winter getaways.

Give this concept careful thought: Perhaps you could get a toehold in your industry by appealing to the price conscious—or the well-heeled. A maid service, for instance, might put together a luxury package for affluent consumers that includes such amenities as regularly polishing the silver. Or a whirlwind budget package for those who want someone to just come in once a month could attract working mothers or retirees who can't afford weekly professional cleaning.

Advertising agencies are finding ways to set themselves apart from the competition. New York–based Trout & Ries, Inc., is extolling a "second-opinion service." Says Ries, "You wouldn't have major surgery without getting a second opinion. So why spend $10 million…or $50 million on advertising without getting one?"

Niching can also be directed to certain age or ethnic groups. Many savvy marketers today are searching for the mountain of youth. These kids have more play dough (and I don't mean the toy) than ever before. A recent allowance study revealed youngsters are living the lush live. The median amount of allowance and cash kids get from parents and guardians is $50 a week. That translates into about $1 billion expendable income a week! Yes, kids are hot. And by 2010 their ranks will swell to 35 million, eclipsing even the baby boomers. Can you sell to them?

Another hot group is Hispanics. Their buying power will grow nearly three times as fast as inflation, which demonstrates the growing importance of Latino consumers. As early as 2005, some 25.5 percent of Hispanic households will earn more than $50,000 a year, up from about 17 percent today. Can you target your products or services to this fast-growing population?

Certainly from all these examples you have gained fresh perspective on how to slant your business to a specific niche, position yourself, and maximize your potential.

Crafting a Vigorous Marketing Plan

One of the best ways to prepare for developing a dynamite marketing plan is to first create a Vision Statement. This pinpoints your long-range goals and objectives. Next comes your Mission Statement.

Startup Checklist

- ✔ Accounting/Bookkeeping/ Tax Preparation
- ✔ Advertising/PR Plan
- ✔ Alarms/Security Systems
- ✔ Auto Leasing/Purchase
- ✔ Banking Services
- ✔ Business Consulting Plan
- ✔ Chamber of Commerce/ Other Memberships
- ✔ Computer Consulting
- ✔ Computer Equipment/ Software/Supplies
- ✔ Computer Repair/Service
- ✔ Copy Machine
- ✔ Data Processing
- ✔ Delivery/Messenger Service
- ✔ Equipment
- ✔ Fax Machine
- ✔ Federal ID Tax Number
- ✔ Graphic Design/Desktop Publishing/Typesetting
- ✔ Insurance
- ✔ Janitorial Service
- ✔ Leasing Space
- ✔ Legal Services/Lawyers
- ✔ Licensing Requirements
- ✔ Loans/Startup Capital
- ✔ Meeting Facilities/Conference Room
- ✔ Mission Statement
- ✔ Name Registration: Doing Business as…(dba)
- ✔ Office Furniture
- ✔ Office Machines/Computers
- ✔ Office Supplies/Business Forms

(continued on next page)

It needn't be long. In 20 to 40 words capture the essence of your business. Who is it for? How will it assist them? In what major way can you meet their needs? Writing this Mission Statement will help you get—and keep—focused.

Also be sure your employees know what it is. Steven Covey, in his keynote address to the 16th annual *Inc.* 500 conference, suggested: "As a regular exercise, ask people to name your company's purpose. The answers will shock you." Everybody needs to be marching to the same drummer. If people on your team aren't aware of where you're headed, how can you possibly expect to get there?

If you intend to sculpt yourself a dominant position in your industry or community, a forceful marketing plan is a must. Not to have one is like going bear hunting with a switch. A plan consists of two elements: *goals*— which is what you want to achieve, and *strategies*—which is how you expect to achieve them.

There are many things to take into consideration. You must analyze your customers or clients (assuming you are an already established organization) and evaluate your competition. What sort of growth trends might you logically anticipate? If you're in the information industry, for instance, spiraling opportunities are predicted in this millennium. What are your company's capabilities and capacity? Temper enthusiasm with realism. Although you might like to take on the world, success often evades those who use no common sense in their business dealings.

Obstacles accompany opportunities! Have you thought about potential threats? How can you keep a rival firm from eroding your market share? Can you preempt the disastrous consequences that could result from a shift in the economy?

For long-term success, you will ideally construct a five-year marketing plan. Of course, you'll concentrate on drafting a dynamic annual plan, which is a detailed version of the first year of your longer-range blueprint. The foundation of your plan will be a marketing mix of such traditional elements as publicity, promotion, sales literature, direct mail, and advertis-

STARTUP CHECKLIST (continued)
✔ Printing
✔ Sales Tax Permit
✔ Secretarial Service/Word Processing
✔ Shipping & Mailing Supplies/ Service
✔ Signage
✔ Space Planning & Design
✔ Telephone Equipment/Pager/ Cell Phone
✔ Trademark/Service Mark/ Copyright Registration
✔ Transportation & Moving
✔ Trash Removal/Recycling Plan
✔ Voice Mail/Answering Machine
✔ Web Site/E-mail

ing—plus the newer element of the Internet—not to mention pricing and customer service. Each is a vital building block. Don't fall into the trap of many neophyte marketers who feel if they've placed a few ads, they have a marketing plan.

To maximize your dollars, be sure PR efforts and advertising reinforce each other. (More about that later.) They should be engineered to build on one another, establishing a cohesive, forceful image in the prospect's eyes. PR creates excitement. Ads contribute drama. Sales presentations reinforce enthusiasm. Together, the elements culminate in a big bang. Individually, they can be diluted and ineffective.

Quantify your goals. Do you want to increase your market share by 10 percent this year? Twenty-five percent? If you are an upstart startup, what is your target annual revenue? One hundred thousand dollars? A quarter million? Five million?

A marketing plan isn't an academic exercise. It should be a living, dynamic tool. The good news is that to develop such a road map you don't have to visit a channeling medium or take a course in reading tea leaves. The process needn't be intimidating. (Specific guidelines are included in Chapter 17.) A sound marketing plan helps you kick yourself in the assets. And it's a wonderful tool to audit your progress because it makes you really think. Although it's vital to have this road map, remain flexible. As on vacation, so in business: Sometimes it's the side roads that are the most exciting and memorable. Perhaps an unforseen opportunity will arise that ordains action to alter previous expectations.

Don't assume if something worked in 1999 it will work today. Rubber-stamping last year's plan will likely pound another nail in the coffin of success. Backward thinking can be deadly; competition continually escalates. Invest in the future instead of trying to redesign the past. A recent *Wall Street Journal* career poll revealed the majority of people said their dream job was to "head my own business." Today more than ever before, women (and to a lesser degree, men) are turning that dream into reality. To stay competitive you need sound marketing goals and strategies. *If you fail to plan, plan to fail.*

Have an ongoing strategy. It's no accident financial planner Albert B. Woodward, Jr., CFP, stays visible in the Denver metropolitan area. He meets with his wife and partner, Marilyn, on a regular basis to go over a Marketing Matrix they've developed. "I believe in structure," says Woodward. "We look at the things already scheduled, those that need to be worked on, plus future possibilities we're thinking about."

Herein lies one of the prime tenets of marketing: To establish a presence in the community and develop a successful practice, you need *consistent, ongoing effort!* Creating a flurry of activity one month, then doing nothing for the next year is a formula for disaster. You need exposure. Repetition. Momentum.

"People have to know who you are and what your capabilities are," advises Woodward. His four-week planning matrix includes public speaking to civic and business groups, conducting in-house seminars, writing articles and columns, promoting referrals by phone and by mail, and a miscellaneous column.

A Web site you may want to check out is located at www.bplans.com. It contains business and marketing plans plus related advice. There is even a spreadsheet glossary to look up vexing business terms. Visitors can also pose questions to experts and find local small business development centers.

If you want to call the tune instead of paying the fiddler, always follow-up! Be prepared to monitor the progress of your projects. While diligent follow-through increases your odds for success in all aspects of business, it's especially crucial in marketing. Many sound marketing plans flounder for lack of follow-up.

26

The squeaky wheel gets more attention. I encourage clients to be politely persistent, to never give up. Stopping before you get results— or a firm "no"—is like ordering an ice cream cone, then letting it melt onto the floor. In the words of Mary Kay Ash, "Whenever a task seems most impossible, I simply repeat the words my mother would say to me: 'You can do it, Mary Kay. You can do it.'" Now "You can do it!" is her company's mantra. Using this and the Golden Rule, she has become the largest direct seller of skin company products with more than 500,000 Independent Beauty Consultants in 29 markets worldwide.

Prudent Budgeting

Is there a way to keep a modest budget from cramping your style? Yes and no. If you try to whittle costs too much you may end up watching your whole business being sacrificed at the altar of fiscal restraint. Typically marketing is not the place to cut back. That said, let me offer some suggestions for those of you with budgets tighter than fiddle strings.

When they think marketing, most people automatically think advertising. That can be a fatal mistake. If you're the new midget on the block, publicity and promotion are the mainstays that can help you skyrocket to success. You must outsmart, not outspend, the competition.

Depending on the type of business you're in, there are many free or very inexpensive ways to promote. A music teacher, plumber, or day-care center might do well by posting index cards on supermarket and laundromat bulletin boards. A business card can be handed out to spur word-of-mouth. Well-written news releases focus attention on your establishment.

A professional who gives talks to civic organizations often sees her practice take off. Providing a free weekly column to the local newspaper can have a similar effect. A computer consultant who offers free computer lessons for city hall employees could turn this good deed into a publicity stunt of interest to the local TV stations. These are just a few of the hundreds of ideas you'll find in the following chapters.

Marketing budgets are as individual as snowflakes. One company will only spend 1 percent of gross sales, whereas another will boldly allocate 12 percent. A further determining factor is whether you are a new or established organization. Startups require more financial commitment in the beginning. Ten percent is a wise amount for the first year. This extra investment helps lay a solid foundation. There is a logo to be designed, stationery to be printed, a brochure to be created and produced, signs to be fashioned and erected, a Web site to be built, perhaps a direct mail package to be developed, etc. Many choose to hire public relations or advertising professionals to accomplish these tasks and initially devise a convincing overall plan. (More about that later.)

The majority of established firms spend 2 to 5 percent of their gross sales on marketing. Perhaps that's why many of them fail. Spending money on marketing is a lot like tending a fire. If you want it to roar warmly, what do you do? You stoke it! Otherwise, you shiver in a semi-frigid state—perhaps not freezing to death but never being comfy and content either.

What you spend is dependent on many factors. If you're lucky enough to be in a position where there are few competitors, you needn't allocate as much as someone who is going head-to-head with several already-entrenched opponents. On the other hand, in a saturated market, it may behoove you to match what your main competitor spends to keep your portion of the market share—or enjoy increased market penetration.

One of the questions that always comes up in the seminars and lectures I give around the country is, "Shouldn't I cut back when times are bad?" Absolutely not! Slicing your marketing budget during an economic slump is like handing your assailant a gun. If you do that, instead of being on the leading edge…you'll be on the bleeding edge.

A recent issue of *Business Marketing* tells of a new study that proves the fallacy of this theory. Research conducted with some 600 companies by McGraw-Hill, Inc., of New York indicated those that didn't reduce their advertising during recessions had significantly more sales growth—both during and *after* the recession—than those who cut back.

The Price Is Right…or Is It?

According to the July/August 1999 issue of *Working Woman* magazine, "One problem is that women sell themselves cheap…. The vast majority of women do not price their skills at market value." If we undervalue ourselves, how can we expect our prospects, customers, and clients to value us?

Price is a result of three factors: 1) customer perception of what they should pay, 2) where you are relative to the competition, and 3) the margins you must maintain to be profitable.

When I talk to groups about margins, there is often a blank look on the faces of some. If you are manufacturing a product, you must factor in not only the costs to create the item, but also the middleman costs for getting it into the marketplace. If you're selling through a sporting goods store, for instance, they will expect to mark it up about 50 percent. So if you have $5 invested in the manufacturing and expect to sell it for $9.95, you are in trouble unless you can sell direct to the consumer. Work the numbers *before* you embark on producing your goods!

Also be wary of pricing your goods too low for another reason: It could cut you out of viable channels of distribution. If you hope to sell to catalogs, for example (a subject covered in depth in Chapter 9), they typically charge about $5 for shipping and handling. If your item is only $4.95, catalog buyers will balk that the shipping and handling costs as much as the item itself.

What should you ask for your product or service? We've all heard the phrase, "Charge what the market will bear." Although it sounds crude, there is wisdom here. If you are targeting a luxury clientele, the people aren't price sensitive. They are more interested in quality, convenience, and reputation. At the other extreme is the person who is highly price conscious and makes buying decisions based exclusively on that criterion. Think about your operation, channels of distribution, and your prospect. Then you will make well-informed decisions rather than simply embarking on a witch hunt for profits.

Location, Location, Location

Where you place your business can dramatically influence your success.

The most important aspect of a restaurant, for instance, is where it's located. This also plays a crucial role with most brick-and-mortar retail stores. If you depend on foot traffic to generate customers, be sure you locate in a well-traveled area. I know of a TV repair shop that moved from a dying downtown district to a thriving strip mall and tripled its business in a matter of weeks. Also consider making your business portable. If this appeals to you, read the section called "Take Your Business on the Road" in Chapter 14.

Home-based entrepreneurs

Many businesses begin in the owner's home. That's how I started many years ago. In fact, 60 percent of all women-owned businesses begin as home office operations. Examining the *Inc.* 500 magazine class of 1999 divulges that a whopping 48.5 percent reported starting their companies in their homes. And now they're the *crème de la crème*.

Small Office/Home Office (SOHO) businesses continue to dominate the small business arena. Today's vast free-agent workforce toils largely from home. The SBA reports that home-based businesses represent over 53 percent of all businesses. Home is no longer just where the heart is, it's also where the paycheck resides. Home working has grown 15 percent annually since 1995. These entrepreneurs earn an average of $50,000 a year, twice the national average of outside-the-home workers. And many of them make considerably more.

Independent Professionals (IPs) lead the growth area. Many of these individuals have traded the corporate culture for building a solo high-tech business. This at-home workforce pursues services that are creative or business-related. They are free agents, gurus, e-lancers, e-builders, e-tailers. It's easy for startups to transform themselves into Internet "*click*-and-mortar" operations in the comfort and convenience of their own residences.

With the dot.com-ing of America, the online revolution and its vanguard economy have matured into mainstream respectability. E-commerce is bigger than the invention of the printing press and many savvy younger women are climbing on this high-tech bandwagon.

It was interesting to note that when *Fortune* magazine chose the 50 most powerful women in American business in 1999, they started with the previous year's list—and replaced a third of the names. "It shocked us to see such turnover," said senior writer, Patricia Sellers. She attributes it to "a major shift in the economy and a new superhighway to success: the Internet." You go, girl!

Because it keeps overhead to a minimum, operating from home is very desirable for fledgling companies. In fact, some entrepreneurs run substantial enterprises out of their residences. So whether your goal is to be on the cutting edge of the workforce—or to weave a more satisfying and traditional life around your family needs, there's never been a better time to take inventory of your professional assets and channel them into a home career.

More options

Professionals just starting out sometimes find sharing an office a simple and effective solution to office space needs. Not only does this keep overhead down, you can provide client referrals to each other. This works especially well when the two consulting disciplines are complementary. An architect and an interior designer are a natural match; so is a management consultant and a marketing expert. What about a chiropractor and a massage therapist? Or a physical fitness specialist and a nutritionist?

If you're looking for office, store, or manufacturing space, here's an innovative resource: Go to the area where you would like to locate and talk to the mail carrier! These folks know exactly what is available and how long it's been empty. One company I know of now rents a spacious office/warehouse facility at a bargain price in an out-of-the-way location…all thanks to helpful advice from a knowledgeable mailman.

Another option is called an incubator. No, it's not a toasty warm environment for hatching baby chicks. Incubators are facilities for bringing up baby businesses. They give a startup a head start. And they're out there in record numbers. While only 12 existed in 1980, today there are more than 600, according to the National Business Incubation Association (www.nbia.org). A business incubator houses from two to over 100 separate businesses. Although each has its own unit, they share a common reception area, conference room, plus clerical and support services.

These support services can spell the difference between success and failure. Most small businesses are started by technicians. These people know their service inside and out—what they lack is experience in the day-to-day task of running a business. The Small Business Administration estimates that although nine out of 11 new firms fail during their first year, businesses that start in incubators have an 80 percent success rate.

That is because they are given management and marketing guidance, and often help in finding financing assistance. This professional guidance is what nurtures them to success. Costs of photocopiers, fax machines, and postage machines are usually shared. There are also excellent networking possibilities with other tenants.

As we're talking about location, let me mention a word about interior design. For some professional practices, this can have a huge impact. Take the case of a Denver, Colorado, children's dentist. Says Dr. Tim Adams, "Our patients seem to love this place as much as we do. We frequently have children who do not want to leave the office at the end of their visit."

Why are his young patients so enamored of Dr. Adams? His whimsical dental office is presided over by three-dimensional penguins. The reception area is a playhouse. To promote a sense of security, the treatment areas are open to the waiting room. Everything is carefully crafted to be comfortable, educational, and fun. (Now if we could just get *parents* to find dentistry an enjoyable experience!)

Retail outlets on the cheap

Suppose your financial resources are about as deep as a puddle and you don't have the bucks to lease an expensive storefront in a shopping mall or a busy enclosed strip mall. Is all lost? Not unless you're a quitter. Consider a kiosk. These stores without doors, perhaps 10-foot by 10-foot stands or attractive carts, parade down the aisles of shopping malls. Their proprietors sell everything from handcrafted items to micro-aquariums, aromatherapy candles to diet supplements, calendars to butterfly barrettes.

And if you're willing to work really hard the four months surrounding the holiday season (16-hour days are typical), you can kick back the rest of the year. That's not to say kiosks won't work year-round, but most do 80 percent of their business in the holiday period.

This retailing approach is attracting established giants too. Hickory Farms used to have 500 permanent stores. Today, they have only 39 such outlets—plus nearly 1,200 temporary stores in mall aisles.

Of course, you may come up with a more innovative take on this idea. That's what Vivian Jimenex, Lorraine Brennan O'Neil, and Karen Janson did. They are negotiating for kiosks in airports! Their concept is to offer travelers fast manicures for $15 each. "It's such a simple idea. That's why it's going to work," says Janson. Their business model calls for installing relatively inexpensive kiosks near high-traffic areas in airports, hiring $7-an-hour nail technicians, and attracting at least five customers every hour. The founders calculate that just a single airport contract with three or four outlets would be profitable. If they manage to get 13 kiosks in four locations, they could reach $3.2 million in annual revenues. Simple indeed!

Using these retailing hot spots is also ideal to test market a product. People literally stumble over kiosks. You can't avoid them. It's ideal for impulse or fad items. And this is one-on-one selling, perfect for anything that needs to be demonstrated.

Hiring Professional Help

If you're a novice at all this, you may want to enlist the help of professionals. Although most large agencies won't be interested in dealing with you unless you have a sizeable marketing budget, that's no reason for disappointment. It could even be a blessing in disguise. Most small businesses do best working with a smaller agency or a well-qualified individual PR/advertising practitioner. Smaller agencies typically respond more quickly and take a more personal interest in your future because they aren't trying to juggle 50 clients at once.

The first person you meet will normally be a key individual in the firm, rather than an "account executive" (a salesperson or customer service rep assigned to specific accounts) for a large agency. One of the most important elements in any client/PR relationship is for you to like one another. This compatibility lays the groundwork for harmony and can lead to great things. In a healthy collaboration, the CEO or vice president of marketing, and the prime agency person initially spend a lot of time together. They explore the business' strengths and weaknesses, hammer out the marketing goals, and get a sense of each other's style and pace.

If there are wide differences, beware. If your organization prides itself on being formal and sophisticated you will quickly become disenchanted by the zany creativity of an unpretentious agency run by Gen Xers. If the chemistry isn't good, the results won't be either.

At our company, About Books, Inc., my husband and business partner Tom and I refuse to accept a client with whom we don't feel comfortable. Life is too short to work with people you don't enjoy. (If you're already in such a situation, see Chapter 14 for "Pulling the Plug on Obnoxious Clients.")

If you have a small fixed budget, don't play guessing games. State up front what you can spend. If we know a client has only $10,000 to work with the first year, we take that into consideration when doing hourly consulting and making recommendations on how they should proceed. Obviously, large space ads and extensive direct mail are out of the question; our challenge is to devise low-cost, high-impact creative strategies. You want a marketing coach who will spend your money as if it is her own.

Just as there is etiquette for how to handle yourself at elegant dinner parties, there is a protocol when dealing with PR/ad agencies. Don't, for instance, expect them to put together a complicated presentation on "speculation." Many have been burned by companies that did not hire them but stole their ideas to implement themselves. The "products" of advertising and PR experts are their ideas—their creative genius. You wouldn't go into a store and ask for a free suit so you could decide if you liked the store and wanted to shop there again. So don't expect

PR professionals to give you their ideas and guidance until you have drawn up an agreement and bought a ticket to the show.

What will it cost? Fees vary as much as people. Most larger agencies prefer putting their clients on a monthly retainer basis: probably $3,000 or $4,000 a month, plus ad costs and out-of-pocket expenses. The commitment is always for several months.

We customize total startup marketing packages for new businesses and professional firms. The one-time cost typically runs from $4,000 to $15,000, depending on whether the campaign is regional or national, if travel is required, and what is included. Another option is hourly phone consulting. Costs here are $300 per hour. I've coached entrepreneurs from coast to coast—all from our Buena Vista, Colorado, location.

When you begin working with an advertising/PR professional, don't expect instant results. It will take them a while to grasp what your business is about, to learn the industry politics, and plant the necessary seeds for your campaign. Magazine placements, for instance, take about six months to jell. Although it may seem to happen about as fast as getting your teeth straightened, effective PR will be generated if you choose an agency carefully, then give them the tools and time to do their job.

There are many things you can do to make the relationship go more smoothly. First, show your own enthusiasm. If you don't give a damn about your company or industry, how can you expect them to care? Next, respect your agency's time. Don't insist on a rush job when it isn't necessary. Avoid phoning constantly over trivial things. When a person is involved in a creative pursuit, an untimely interruption can put them back to square one.

Lastly, when you are shown a new ad, direct mail campaign, or other print piece, remember creative types have sensitive personalities. Evaluate thoroughly. Praise well. Criticize constructively. State what you like before you go into what you don't like. Try to assist them in understanding why you feel something won't work in your community or industry. By helping these creative team members learn from this experience, you groom them for pleasing you more in the future.

Methods for Measurement

Of course, before you know if you've reached your destination, you have to know where you're going. Simple, right? Not necessarily. When a marketing expert begins to work with you she or he will create a plan customized to your needs and goals. This will serve as a future measurement tool. It must be compared with baseline figures that quantify the status quo.

It is much easier to access success in advertising than it is in PR. When ads are coded, replies tracked, and sales logged, the hard numbers tell the tale. This isn't the case in PR. Publicity and promotion have a cumulative effect. They cannot be tangibly quantified and easily monitored.

You have every right to expect some form of reporting. In this way you can document success and learn from failure. Major projects should be summarized and critiqued. Was the objective met? Did the return on investment match initial expectations? When you are sizing up the results your PR firm generated, don't just look at the big coups. Although our business clients love to be featured in the *Wall Street Journal*, *Fortune*, or CNN online, we know from personal experience little placements can add up to big dollars.

At our firm we practice what we preach. We have a regular program of offering complimentary articles to appropriate publications. One of our biggest clients found us as a result of a piece placed in an obscure newsletter with a circulation of less than 5,000.

Brainstorming to Flood Your Mind With Creativity

Don't just compete—create! To excel in your business or professional practice you need to think creatively—be an innovator—dare to be

Brainstorming Guidelines

■ *Appoint someone to serve as a facilitator.* It is this person's job to ensure that everyone gets a chance to discuss their ideas. It helps when the facilitator summarizes the previous participant's contributions before the next person speaks. Use a blackboard or flip chart to record what's said so it is visible to everyone.

■ *Reinforce and encourage all suggestions.* Don't worry about details at this point. Concentrate on producing as many ideas as possible. Encourage people to participate quickly without evaluating their own or others' thoughts.

■ *There are no wrong ideas.* Don't be judgmental. If you must comment, limit your remarks to how a proposal might be improved.

■ *Listen to the full explanation of an idea.* Don't interrupt others—wait until they're finished talking.

■ *Nobody has all the answers.* Group success depends on every member sharing opinions and observations. Encourage all to contribute and avoid promoting your personal agenda.

■ *Sort out the best suggestions.* At the end of the time, have the participants divide the ideas into three groups: 1) those

(continued on next page)

with excellent potential, 2) 50-50 options, 3) unacceptable suggestions.

■ *Focus attention on the most promising in group 1.* Refine these ideas. Further brainstorm why they're a good match for you and how they might be implemented. Look for ways to put a more profitable spin on them.

■ *Bank the best of the rest.* Keep an inventory of other potentially useable possibilities. This might take the form of 3-inch x 5-inch cards, notes jotted on scraps of paper, etc. Deposit them in a manila folder, large envelope, shoe box, computer file, or whatever makes sense for you. But keep them so if times turn sour, you have a waiting account from which you can withdraw inspiration. One of them will serve as a catalyst to again mobilize your creative thinking.

different. When it comes to innovation, the question is not so much how to innovate, but how to invite ideas. How do you prompt your brain to encounter thoughts you might not otherwise have? Innovation often comes from unexpected juxtapositions, from connecting things that aren't usually connected.

I love to look at something from as many sides as possible, lifting up an observation and shaking it until a revelation falls out. Being creative doesn't necessarily mean concocting something new. It can be the rearrangement of something old or seeing ordinary things in an extraordinary way. One of the secrets of true originality is to determine what everybody else is doing, then *don't* do it. Woman, liberate thyself from mediocrity!

Is there a way you can magnify or minify what you do? One caterer looking for expansion found it by *compressing* her business. Instead of going head-to-head with her competition to get the big banquets and cocktail parties, she specialized in catering smaller affairs. Banks celebrating new services had her prepare cookies, punch, and coffee for customers. She was on hand to do a little decorating, be gracious, and give refills.

Soon other businesses that previously felt they couldn't afford a catered function were calling for bids on their special activities. She even developed a variety of "packaged celebrations" for birthdays, anniversaries, special dates, etc.

The computer field gives us a perfect example of how minimizing has led to new profit centers. From computers that took up huge rooms, they invented PCs that sat on our desks, then went down to laptops, and now to PalmPilots. Small is beautiful.

So is big. Our aging population, for instance, will increase demand for large print books in the years to come. Can you capitalize on less or more? Some upscale beauty salons are now converting to mini-spas where a woman can be pampered from head to toe for a day. One enterprising Texan took the carwash concept and expanded it. He established a service that washes and cleans airplanes. Many private jets are kept spotless by his company.

Maybe you can excel by using a combining technique. An example of this is the laundromat mentioned earlier with exercise equipment. Another is a law firm that also sponsored seminars on how their corporate clients could avoid workplace discrimination problems.

Many successful new ventures offer only a slight variation on a proven market leader—just enough to establish an identity and a profitable market niche. Look how overnight delivery services flourished once Federal Express proved it was possible.

When searching for a new idea, look from all angles. Successful businesses are often simply a different application of an existing concept. Can you reverse something? (Look at the huge industry of fragrances for men. Twenty-five years ago guys wouldn't touch perfume.) When using "reverse" psychology, think about not only the opposite sex, but young to old, right-handed to left-handed, etc.

Rather than beginning from scratch try to improve on something for which there is already an established market when inventing your own business. Reverse it. Minimize it. Maximize it. Combine it. Examine the possibilities from every perspective.

Creativity may be the catalyst for a winning company slogan or jingle as well. Remember the reverse twist used in the following TV commercial: "Listerine has the taste people *hate*…twice a day." How about the Marriott hotel chain's push for their two-for-breakfast weekend: "For the price of a pair of sneakers, you can be a pair of loafers." Set your imagination free and see what you can come up with.

What's a great approach for getting from the itch to the idea? One of the best ways to generate a whole host of possibilities is to invite a group of people to help you think of ideas for a business opportunity. Set an initial time period, maybe two or three hours, and explain the procedures. (See the Brainstorming Guidelines.) Set a positive tone. You might start by reminding everyone that, "No *one* of us is as powerful as *all* of us."

In a brainstorming session, each participant generates as many options as possible. All ideas are welcome, even if they sound kooky, impractical, or wild. Remember that opinions are like belly buttons: Everybody has one. The point of this exercise is to explore a range of possibilities, not to settle on any one perspective. Brainstorming stretches the imagination and produces acres of ideas from which you can harvest the best.

It isn't necessary to have a roomful of people to accomplish wondrous acts though. You can take other approaches by yourself with a pencil and paper or computer keyboard. One method is called *free writing*. Sit down for 15 minutes and write anything and everything that comes into your head. No fair stopping or crossing out words. And don't worry about spelling or punctuation. The object is to lose control, to reach your intense inner thoughts so you can harness that energy.

Another dynamite doorway to your mind is called *clustering*. This is a magic key for getting in touch with your secret reserves of imaginative power. Clustering is a nonlinear personal brainstorming process similar to free association. It's like writing a map of ideas, beginning with a core word or statement, then branching out with associated ideas in many directions.

Starting with the main idea in the center, give your mind free reign to radiate thoughts and images out from this nucleus. Write new ideas in circles, which, in turn, are connected by lines to other circles. Ideas spill out with lightning speed. They form associations that allow patterns and solutions to emerge. Chaos becomes order as ideas surface in a gradual map that accesses our interior landscape of thoughts. It's an easy, flowing process. There's no right or wrong place to start; nothing is forced. While this is an excellent solo exercise, it can also be effective in a group.

But whether you do it individually or in tandem with others, brainstorming is sure to unleash your creativity. Now let's proceed. The next chapter deals with how you can develop an image and brand recognition that could make you so rich you could help Bill Gates recoup his losses.

Web Sites, Wisdom, and Whimsey

Brainstorming 101: Putting Creativity to Work is a "workshop" that will teach you to develop new ideas for products, better service, and greater productivity. The workshop can be conducted online, in print, or as part of a live class. Find out more at http://www.brainstorming.org/.

Looking for your perfect work? Now you can do so from the comfort of your own phone with the help of a personal coach! Discover your purpose and passion, and orient your life and career around what brings you joy. Check out http://coachfederation.org to find a coach or for more information on knocking down your own barriers to success. Take a self-assessment quiz at personal coach Lucinda Kerschensteiner's Web site at http://www.lucindak.com.

●●●●●●●

*Calling women the weaker sex makes about
as much sense as calling men the stronger one.*

●●●●●●●

If you're a new entrepreneur or if you just want to run your business better, the Online Women's Business Center has information and resources to help. This one-stop shopping site, which combines the expertise and resources of the U.S. Small Business Administration with several major corporate sponsors, has goodies about everything from how to start your business to how to operate in the global marketplace. It even has information from more than 80 SBA-affiliated women's centers from across the country. You'll find the latest on business principles and practices, management technique, mentoring, networking, and business resources at http://onlinewbc.org.

Debating whether entrepreneurship is for you? If you're thinking about leaving your corporate job and becoming your own boss, consider the 25 tips listed by eight female entrepreneurial members on iVillage Network. This impressive checklist helps to see if you've got what it takes. Find it at http://www.ivillage.com/workingdiva/entrepreneur. (By the way, if it's impractical to use a long extension address like this, simply enter the base URL—through the .com, .net, or .org—then look on their menu of listing to find the right page.)

●●●●●●●

"You must do the thing you think you cannot do."

—Eleanor Roosevelt

●●●●●●●

Is there an independent contractor in your future? Hiring freelancers to accomplish various tasks is often a practical way to get the job done. Outsourcing allows you to keep your ongoing payroll lean (or nonexistent!) and avoid providing expensive employee benefits, while still having qualified people to create and market your products or services. It's a growing trend. Although outsourcing used to be the solution for large corporations, today more and more smaller companies use this personnel tool. Two cautions: 1) You may want independent contractors to carry their own liability insurance. Otherwise, you can find yourself embroiled in a lawsuit because of their actions while working on your project. 2) For certain jobs, getting a "Work for Hire" agreement is advised. It would be disastrous, for instance, to plan an additional ad campaign around a piece of graphic art, only to learn the rights remained with the artist for something he or she was paid to create for you. Independent contractors can be a wonderful management tool to handle the ebb and flow of business needs. Just be sure you practice good skill hunting and use them wisely.

Perhaps an intern is your answer. In today's tight job market, finding a motivated, enthusiastic employee for little or no pay is a real blessing. So check out bright high school or college students. They're as anxious to get hands-on job experience as you are to find cheap help. You must be willing to invest time in training them, however. That's their payback. We've found this "work for learning" premise benefits both sides. While located in California, we hired two interns when they graduated. They were known quantities and already schooled in how we wanted things done. To get started, access your company needs and create a job description. Then get the word out to college internship and job placement offices, post notices on bulletin boards, and run an ad in the college newspaper.

●●●●●●●

Quote of the Month: Our society is moving so fast these days that the man who says it can't be done is being interrupted by the woman doing it.

●●●●●●●

Web site that specializes in SOHO topics. If you're self-employed, a home-based business owner, free agent, e-lancer, telecommuter, consultant, or other independent professional (or you dream of being one), then visit http://www.workingsolo.com/. Here you'll find tips for starting a business, plus free resources to build your company. SOHO expert Terri Lonier also makes available a free monthly e-newsletter full of good advice.

Hire wisely and save on taxes! If you hire welfare recipients, teens from low-income families, disabled workers, and some veterans you can qualify to receive tax credits. These are credits, a dollar-for-dollar reduction in your tax bill, not deductions. Get details by calling toll-free to 888-872-5621 or log onto their Web site at www.welfaretowork.org.

If you seek to establish the market viability of a new product, simply go to http://edge.lowe.org/resource/document/htmldocs/6357.HTM. (Well, not really so simple, is it?) But your reward will be an article on market planning that shows how to prepare a market analysis. It reviews the most important questions to ask at the start, plus lists a variety of secondary source materials and databases for gathering business trend and demographic data. You can find pointers on how to conduct a focus group as well.

●●●●●●●

Perception is reality: Did you hear about the guy who stayed up all night to see where the sun went? It finally dawned on him.

●●●●●●●

Looking to pinpoint trends before they're common knowledge? *American Demographics* may well become your best online buddy. The magazine covers consumer trends and presents tons of useful statistics. Targeted to advertising types who want to be on the cutting edge, you'll find the offerings here tantalizing. Reach them at http://www.marketingtools.com.

Metasearches yield greater results than normal Web search engines. A fascinating survey released last summer by an NEC Research Institute found that search engines can't keep pace with the Web's expansion. The mushrooming growth curve is outpacing the ability of search engines to index their content. Examining 11 search engines, the study found that no single engine indexed more than 16 percent of the Web. Yahoo only got 7.4 percent, Excite 5.6 percent, and Lycos a mere 2.5 percent, for instance. Additionally, indexing of new or modified pages by just one major engine can now take months. In spite of this, 85 percent of surfers continue to use search engines to find information. To help fill the gap the next time you're seeking information, use one of the more comprehensive *metasearch* sites. Go to www.dogpile.com, www.ProFusion.com, www.find.com, or www.metacrawler.com. Happy hunting!

●●●●●●●

"Doing the best at this moment puts you in the best place for the next moment."

—Oprah Winfrey

●●●●●●●

Are you tempted to self-sabotage? Some women can't seem to escape their inner traps. They are victims of their own limitations. It's time to take responsibility, to get—and stay—in the drivers seat. *You* have the sole responsibility to change yourself and your environment. Only then can you combine your daring dream with the audacity to make it happen.

Small Business Administration a treasure trove of information. One of the best online places you can land begins at http://www.sba.gov. From this home page, the SBA's site branches out in dozens of directions. You can learn about starting a business, financing it, and expanding it—not to mention access laws and regulations, publications, forms, and local resources. The site also has a "Help Desk" that covers many various topics and a search engine that permits you to access online library reading rooms.

Another wonderful site awaits you at http://onlinewbc.org/docs/market/mk_what_is.html. This is an internal link in the Online Women's Business Center site that is lavish with articles, definitions, and all things marketing-related. You can even read in depth about how PR differs from advertising, and vice versa. Highly recommended.

Remember The Little Engine That Could? This classic book, released in 1937, provides one of the all-time best lessons in positive attitude and achievement. What about you? Are you a "YES" thinker? If you think and talk in terms of "no," that's likely the results you'll get: no-thing. If you think you can, you'll know you can get over the top.

CHAPTER 2

Image-Building and Branding: Creating Personal and Professional Charisma

The personal image you project—and the reputation your business, nonprofit group, or firm cultivates—can spell the difference between success and failure. Image building must be *proactive*, not reactive. Are you just starting a new business? Or perhaps you want to change a soft-shoe, tippy-toe image into a position of power.

In either case, the tangible things you can do to become a van-guard in your field are the subjects of this chapter. Personal power and credibility will be addressed, as well as how to influence your clients'/customers' perception of your organization. We will also discuss the trappings of business: creating a pleasing facility; becoming a presence; telephone goodwill; choosing a name, logo, and slogan; designing your stationery and business cards; and developing your "brand." And I'll show you how to manage the image you project to the world.

Your Business Attitude and Manner

The philosophy of the owner, manager, or CEO sets the tone for the whole organization. How will you posture your enterprise? What means can you employ to foster an attitude of caring? A home-based accountant picks up and delivers the books for her clients. Dentists provide earphones with soothing music and interesting graphics on the ceiling of treatment cubicles. Banks offer drive-up service, stay open weekends, and make their meeting rooms available free to nonprofit groups. Real estate agents provide "get acquainted" packages to folks considering a move into the area. The list could go on and on. Some places have a knack for making you feel more like a guest than a customer.

No matter what business you're in, there are ways to show your constituents you consider them special. In the process, you become special to them. You provide a lasting value and build a genuine relationship. As you become more prominent, the resulting awareness of your existence and what you do will produce more business.

Every organization is the sum of the people who work there. Employee attitude plays a big role. When you're considering your external image, be sure you consider the image your associates have about your organization as well. They could differ. If they do, it's like trying to mix oil and water. It's imperative personnel buy into the same image you intend to portray to the world. Otherwise the disparity fosters mixed signals.

Employees impact your success in other ways too. Inattention, improper dress, and rudeness are quick ways to turn off a potential patron. Such negative impressions are hard to live down. Another thing to consider: Avoid hiring personnel who are considerably above or below the educational level of most of your clientele.

Now let's look at your business or practice through the eyes of your clients/customers. Is the image you want to present the one being received? If not, it's opening doors to show people out instead of welcoming them in. Tour your own organization, both physically and on paper. In one hotel complex, conference rooms were hard to find. This quickly became obvious when the manager toured her own facility as a guest. Pay attention to details. You may be in for some unpleasant surprises. For instance, are the restrooms clean? Properly equipped with toilet tissue, soap, and towels? Are all light bulbs burning brightly?

What kind of paper trail do you leave? Are letters being sent on suitable stationery, or is a ream with out-of-date information being used? We gain revealing insights when we perceive what others receive.

While we're talking about business attitude and manner, there is one other aspect you'd do well to consider: practicing the rules of privacy. While you'd never intentionally reveal any proprietary information about your firm, products, or clients, this can be done quite innocently in our high-tech society. Cell phones used indiscriminately are easily overheard. Laptops operated on an airplane can educate seat mates about topics they have no business knowing. Misdirected faxes or e-mails can be disastrous. Talking shop in public where a competitor might overhear—such as restaurants, bars, trade shows, and conferences—can be poor form. Such confidential "leaks" constitute lip *dis*service.

Developing Personal Power and Credibility

Locally rendered services rely heavily on the personalities performing the services. Many of us choose a mechanic, family doctor, or neighborhood hairdresser simply because we like the person. Although the 21st century will see more national franchises and chains for such things as muffler repair, teeth cleaning, and quickie divorces, individual service providers will still play a key role. Consequently, the entrepreneur, professional, or CEO will continue to have high visibility.

Whether we mean to or not, we constantly send messages to others. We're judged by how we dress, walk, speak, interact, and so on. In real estate, property buyers are said to build equity as they pay off their mortgages. Building equity can apply to people as well. Let's look at things we can do to increase our individual net worth in the business world.

We are appraised long before we're given an opportunity to perform. Thus it's wise to understand the rules of the contest. Be comfortable in the role you project. Be yourself. This doesn't mean you can't change or grow…it simply means make sure the image is *you*.

We have all encountered folks who seem artificial, a bit phony. They appear as actors in a bad role. So be the best, most polished, most sincere, and most friendly *you* that can be managed with comfort.

Most impressions are formed within the first 30 seconds of meeting someone. A firm, warm handshake makes for a good beginning. Grab hold, girls! You don't want to come off limp as old celery—these dead fish handclasps are the sign of a passive person with lousy energy. (Frankly, I've encountered pitiful paws from men as often as women.) On the other hand—pun intended—exchanges so strong the recipient needs a chiropractic adjustment afterward aren't welcomed either.) Ideally, women should extend their hands to men first. Pump the other's hand firmly a couple of times and look them in the eye.

How we dress is a large part of our image. "People take what you wear as information," says Judith Waters, Ph.D., a New Jersey psychology professor and management consultant. That is not to say you must wear tailored designer ensembles. Dress for the job. A cosmetologist will be clothed differently than a physician. There is no excuse, however, for the hairdresser to wear ripped jeans. If she is that careless about her own appearance, customers will have little confidence in her ability to cut and style their hair. Especially in the service sector, wherever you go, a picture of your firm is being conveyed.

We had a big problem with one client who had written an excellent book about power and gave lectures on the subject. Her verbal message was penetrating, perceptive, and right on target. Her physical message was something else. She looked more like an unkempt stay-at-home frump than an influential executive. Her unprofessional dress code made attendees question their own judgment in making her their guru.

It's necessary to wear attire appropriate to the occasion, especially when you're in the limelight. It may be conservatively corporate or uninhibitedly creative (if you're an artist, advertising exec, or design consultant, for instance). You must feel good in it. Then you can forget your appearance and concentrate on the important matters at hand.

Consider accessories as well. Polished, well-heeled shoes; carefully groomed fingernails; and a good haircut speak well of a person. Also think about jewelry. Dangling earrings are distracting. So are clanging bracelets. Contemplate whether you want to flaunt your expensive jewelry for business or save it for after-hours activities.

It may be you do want to impress clients. Perhaps the trappings of wealth and elegance are called for in your business. If so, don't just talk the talk: walk the walk. When showing a million-dollar property, pick up a prospective buyer in a Lexus, Cadillac, or Mercedes rather than a 1996 Ford. Wear your suede jacket and carry your alligator briefcase. When dealing with a clientele that has money and power, it is wise to project such an image yourself.

A smart, well-outfitted briefcase is the sign of a professional woman. Not only does it state you mean business, it also ensures you're prepared for most business situations. A pad in a leather case gives a touch of class, as does a nice pen for signing those important contracts.

Be aware of how you sound. We've all talked with someone on the phone and formed our very own mental picture of what that individual is like. It's sometimes disappointing to meet them in person, isn't it?

The voice is a wonderful tool. If yours is too shrill, people will shy away from you. As women, we need to work on lowering the tone of our voice to a more pleasant level. And try to avoid a breathy quality; this tends to make us sound like a little girl and not get taken seriously. If your accent is very pronounced, this may pose a problem for people to understand you. Also consider the pace at which you speak. It's ideal to match your rate to that of the person you're trying to influence. Fast talkers quickly become annoyed by those who drag out a conversation. On the contrary, you may lose slow talkers if you whiz by them in high gear.

Speaking of whizzing by, there is one occasion in particular you do not want to hurry through. That is self-introductions. This is a great opportunity to create a favorable impression, not to mention educate others about what you do. Create a 30-second introduction of yourself and your work. Your identity hook is important. If your name is the same or similar to someone famous, come up with a clever line to capitalize on it and cement the name in your new acquaintance's mind. If your name is unusual, offer a brief explanation of its background; if it's difficult to pronounce, give folks a rhyming word as a guide.

Practice your delivery. Test it out on some acquaintances who do not know about your professional life. Be sure your remarks make crystal clear what you do for people. With slight modification this introduction works whether you're introducing yourself at a cocktail party or informally before a club or committee.

It's no secret that our body language says a lot about us. Our movements signal all sorts of nonverbal communication. There are 600,000 physical human gestures. This is in comparison to 400,000 words in the English language. An astute observer can tell if someone is uneasy, defensive, or smug. There are many fine books on this subject. In conjunction with reading them, videotape yourself. It's a revealing experience.

If you must make your mark in the more educated and refined circles, be sure your table manners are impeccable. Learn proper etiquette and protocol. You can find etiquette courses in the Yellow Pages under Schools or Motivational and Self Improvement training. Use good grammar and correct English. It certainly won't hurt to be grounded in the arts. A liberal arts education will put you on comfortable footing with most CEOs. You can also raise your own cultural level by going to museums, art galleries, operas, and reading classic and current good books.

Are you a one-woman show trying to look big? Then stifle pygmy thinking. Think BIG. Imagine yourself as an international conglomerate in the formative stages. Make up business cards with your name and several different titles: CEO, Director of Marketing, Chief Financial Officer, etc. Consider tacking the phrase "International Headquarters" on your cards and letterhead. Have initial letters go out under the name and signature of someone else. Add a suite number to your address, such as Suite 324. (Sounds like you're on the third flour of an office building, doesn't it?) On your voice mail, use extension like 233 or 347 instead of 1 or 2, thus giving the impression you're in a large organization with a long queue of extensions. When making a presentation, be sure it is top-drawer. If you can't create attractive materials on the computer yourself, hire help. Especially if you're introducing a new product, a dazzling presentation is crucial.

For in-person meetings, arrange to rent a conference room in a nice location or do a meal at a swank restaurant. You might even have your subcontractors (read mom, sister, best friend) meet with them. This "assistant" can work out logistics on your behalf; then you come in to close the deal.

Power—the ability to make things happen and to control events—is often the currency of business success. It can be formal or informal. Being named a partner in a law firm or asked to chair an important local committee represents formal power. Informal power, although harder to detect, is often more influential. It centers around such things as your taking the initiative and understanding how we differ from men.

Most men have a different decision-making style. Understanding this helps us to deal more effectively with them. Men prefer left-brain thinking, which is characterized by logic, hierarchy, and facts. Women, on the other hand, are more likely to favor intuition, values, and relationships—characteristics represented by right-brain thinking.

There are advantages to being female in a man's world. Nina DiSesa is the creative force behind the turnaround of the world's largest ad agency, McCann-Erickson. Says DiSesa, "Competing in a man's world is what I want to do. I'm very much in touch with my male side. I'm really competitive and I find confrontation stimulating. But I keep those qualities in check. I use my feminine traits: empathy and collaboration." When you're dealing with big egos these are fragile, high-maintenance people, she contends. If she didn't have a strong nurturing component, she couldn't do it.

I was fascinated by an article that appeared on the front page of the February 7, 2000, *Wall Street Journal*. It was titled "Deportment Gap: Feminization of the Workplace." "A whole lot has changed in the workplace in a very short time," Ellen Joan Pollack reported. She went on to say that an earlier generation of women marched to work covering up their sexuality, but today women are far more relaxed and less inhibited about using the personal tools at their disposal to get ahead professionally.

After all, if a man has money, he uses it; if he is smart, he plays on that intelligence to get ahead. So why shouldn't an attractive woman also be flirtatious? What's wrong with using our looks (should we be so blessed) to leverage what else we've got? Dressing in an eye-catching way, making jokes and light-hearted comments, smiling and sometimes being sarcastic—these are natural ways women behave off the job. Isn't it about time we challenged the traditional stereotypes and gave ourselves permission to be ourselves *on the job*?

The Telephone as Goodwill Ambassador

The telephone is a crucial member of the sales team in many business environments. It is an extension of your operation. Phone line connections served up with warmth and exuberance can turn lukewarm inquiries into best customers—and strengthen your grip on this lifeline to the outside business world. In a few cases, the only contact people have with a company is through the telephone. Be sure your primary phone receptionist is pleasant and well-informed about routing calls. Such things as answering promptly and not leaving people stuck on hold contribute to the image callers retain. And audit your own voice mail. Can callers easily access a real person to have unusual questions answered?

Having a separate business phone line is important. Although the cost may seem high for a brand new home-based business, it is certainly more professional than answering your personal line with "hello." Additionally, it allows you to get your business listed with the information operator and in the phone book. Paying extra for a business line is also worth it so your company name will show up on Caller IDs. Not only does it put your business name out there, but it adds credibility to your "at-home" business.

If you don't want to install a business line, consider installing a second residential line (for grandma or the teenagers perhaps?). Or investigate the feature that allows one phone to have different sounding rings. Because you've already established credit as a residential user, they probably won't ask you to post another deposit. Then you can answer this second line in any way you wish. In some locations, you can have several distinctive rings on one telephone, so you can even assign one for your fax machine. Some other considerations: Putting the call-waiting feature on your phone will help absorb overflow until you can afford a second business line. But be aware it aggravates callers who are interrupted, and frequent busy signals tell callers you are small and/or a novice.

If you find yourself surfing the Net frequently, you want to have a separate phone line for your modem. Or if you don't, be sure to use your telephone company's voice mail feature so callers will not get a busy signal when they call but can simply leave a message when you're online.

Suppose you are a one-person shop and you must leave to conduct business? Then hook up your answering machine or sign up for voice mail. You do have one or the other, don't you? Agreed—many people hate talking to a machine, but it's better than an unanswered phone. You might also want to give your Web URL so callers can immediately access more information about your firm.

That brings us to an important point. Don't you get aggravated when you leave a message and the person doesn't get back to you? This is the height of rudeness. Some professionals—certain attorneys and physicians in particular—have honed this to an art. I was particularly impressed the other day when my doctor's nurse called to say he was in surgery but would get back to me as soon as he finished. Sure enough, a few hours later, he called. That's great image building!

What's in a Name?

Christening a new company needn't make you feel as uncomfortable as a eunuch in a locker room. Sure coming up with just the right name presents a challenge. But I've lots of ideas to help you find just the right moniker. Renaming an existing firm is even more complicated. We'll talk about that shortly.

You want something clear and concise—something with presence—a real slam dunk. It should stir customer interest. Project the proper image. Rally spectators to cheer you. Choosing a name is showing your face to the world. You want something that reflects what you are and what you will do. Think five or ten years out and decide on something that doesn't limit you.

How do you go about blazing this trail? First, think about what you are naming. A health-care facility would differ considerably from a Web site, as would a dance studio from an engineering firm. Cheeky irreverence works for some, dignified conservatism is called for in others. To cut a clear path, ponder your main features. What is your competitive edge—your special niche?

Who are your customers/clients? If they are mature and conservative, you will want a very different sounding name than if they are teenagers or successful Gen Xers. Identify their likes and dislikes, and think about their lifestyle.

Depending on what field you're in, it may make sense to develop a name that falls very early in the alphabet. This is especially shrewd strategy for local companies that depend heavily on the telephone Yellow Pages to generate business. Secretarial services, plumbers, and repair facilities, for instance, could benefit from such planning. Look in the phone directory to see what you are up against, however. A previous entrepreneur may already have AAA Auto Repair.

Also consider whether you'll be doing business in a foreign country. If so, beta test possible names to be sure they don't have a negative connotation in a different language. You don't need a *repeat* of Chevy's "Nova," which got slaughtered in Latin America where the Spanish translation means "doesn't go."

Another factor to ponder is visual appeal. We will be talking about logos, a readily identifiable symbol linked to your company name, in the next section. It is important, however, to think about whether a name candidate would easily translate into a logo at this point.

Now it's time to do some brainstorming. Jot down every idea that comes to mind (or use a tape recorder if you can't write that fast). Capture every word and phrase. Don't be judgmental now. Selection comes later. During this creative stage, hunker over a dictionary and thesaurus, or use those on your computer. Let one thought trigger another in a rippling circle of ideas.

Consider linguistic devices such as rhyme or alliteration. The kids' game retailer Zany Brainy and Rice-a-Roni are examples of such word play. A Chicago entrepreneur, Jodi Janich came up with Galloping Gourmutts for her combination bakery and health food store for animals.

Next begin to pick and choose. Discard those with harsh sounds. The Book of Lists tells us that "crunch," "gripe," "jazz," "sap," and "treachery" are among the 10 worst-sounding English words. On the other hand, people like "dawn," "golden," "melody," and "murmuring." Try combining different words and syllables to form new names. With a little ingenuity you can come up with hundreds of distinctive phrases and permutations. Use all the skill at your command to generate winning ideas.

Now develop a list of alternatives. Prioritize it with your favorite name on top. Be sure to check on your competition—you don't want to select something too similar. It's a good idea to do a little market research at this stage. Solicit feedback from others, especially your potential constituents. You might even want to conduct a focus group to incorporate a wider range of opinions.

Next comes the frustrating part. If you anticipate going national, you probably want to consider getting a trademark. To learn more about trademarks and patents, go to www.uspto.gov or call 800-786-9199. The Fed's Web site now features a searchable database of names so you can quickly see if your baby is taken. From there, most entrepreneurs contact a trademark attorney to do the actual filing. It can be quite complicated with registration possible in hundreds of different categories and business names often needing to be registered in multiple classifications.

Be aware that while a trademark license entitles you to hang a shingle just about anywhere, the Internet is an exception. Web domain names (URLs) are a separate arrangement. They can be researched at www.register.com or www.networksolutions.com. The current going rate to register a domain name is $70 for two years.

Dot-com names represent a new challenge. If you thought naming your kids was tough, wait 'til you try to name your Web site. Although there's no limit to the number or Ashleys and Austins walking around, there can only be one www.yourcompany.com. Most short, easy names are already taken. (Not only the .com, but also the .net and .org.) Consider combining two or three words, such as traveltogo. If that is taken, try travel.to.go, travel-to-go, or travel2go. Another option is to visit the site and see if it is actually a functioning Web site. If not, they might be willing to sell you the domain name. If you find most good names have been claimed, well—that's why you listed several alternatives to begin with.

Taking advantage of humor might also lead to a snappy name for your business. Consider the owner of a medieval entertainment agency who dubbed his firm Peasants Under Glass. Then there is the previous administrative assistant who started a data processing company, which she called Blackstone Data Publishing. The firm is named after the street where the owner lives, but people often think she has so much clout she got the city to name a street after her company!

A fascinating Web site called The Name Stormers offers free guidance, software tools, and consulting services. By going to http://

www.namestormers.com you can download their Naming Guide, which offers free tips and advice on do-it-yourself naming. And for just $15 a session, you can use Name Wave, which is a service designed to demonstrate some of the more sophisticated Name Pro's ($495) capabilities while helping you come up with name ideas for your products, services, Web sites, and companies. You simply choose from a list of categories and they use those categories to create suitable name ideas for you. If you don't see anything you like, you can resubmit and get up to 200 printable name ideas. This will also indicate if your favorites are available as domain names.

To give you a further boost in the name game, we've included a list of possibilities that may be helpful. Also consider acronyms. We live in an MTV culture. Kentucky Fried Chicken became KFC to get away from the negative "fried" label. Studies reveal, however, that unless you're a bigwig like IBM or AT&T, consumers are 30 percent less likely to remember initials than names. Still the search to find unique, positive names has reached such desperate levels that many companies now coin meaningless words or rely on acronyms or initials.

Like the nicknames we get as children, some companies eventually outgrow their identities. They need something that more precisely communicates the firm's purpose. Such was the case when Sickroom Services Company evolved into the more upbeat Healthcall, Inc., several years ago.

Perhaps *you* have an established company that requires a name change. A new name can send a powerful message to stockbrokers, portray a company's business or mission more accurately, and generate media attention. It also has a downside. You risk losing instant recognition among customers, investors, and other audiences. In one swoop you can reduce awareness back to zero.

With the current flood of mergers, divestitures, and acquisitions, however, renaming is sometimes the only sensible option. On the road to prosperity, companies are outgrowing their names at a record pace in the wake of technological advances and globalization. The most common reason for a name change today is that the nature of the business has so fundamentally changed maybe it's time to either remove a limiting descriptor or change the description completely.

When choosing a new moniker, many firms encourage employee participation. Including personnel in the decision gives them "ownership" in the process. The search is often carried out in a democratic fashion with input from the entire staff, who are sometimes plied with

Naming Notions

Agency	Mall
Annex	Management
Associates	Market
Association	Mart
Bazaar	Maxi
Beat	Mini
Browser	Mobile
Bureau	Net
Cache	Outlet
Call	Park
Camp	Partnership
Carrier	Peddler
Cellar	Place
Center	Plaza
Channel	Plus
Clearinghouse	Portable
Clinic	Practitioner
Communications	Productions
Company	Products
Connection	Provider
Consultant	Rental
Corner	Repair
Corporation	Salon
Cottage	Shelf
Cyber	Shop
Deals	Shoppe
Design	Source
Emporium	Society
Enterprise	Specialist
Equipment	Stall
Exchange	Store
Expeditions	Supply
Federation	Systems
Forum	Trader
Foundation	Trading Post
Inn	Training
Institute	Tours
Junction	Vendor
Gallery	Villa
Group	Village
Incorporated	Web
Institute	Wagon
Internet	Wares
Lodge	Warehouse
Loft	Works
Lounge	

prizes or the promise of brief notoriety. When International Harvester changed their corporate home and identity to Navistar they reportedly spent $13 million. Datsun topped that amount to become Nissan.

Logos and Slogans

There are many subtle nuances in creating a logo that effectively depicts your company, nonprofit group, or firm identity. Sometimes the symbol is the picture of an object, such as the apple missing a bite that personifies Apple Computers. Other times it is an unusual combination of the partners' or owners' initials. Although the actual job of fashioning your unique symbol should be left to a professional graphic designer, you need some understanding of good design yourself. Only then can you provide her with guidance. Your logo contributes a great deal to your overall image. It gives you muscle; it must feel right to you.

A logo has four basic components: color, type, content, and size. Let's investigate each of these elements.

Strong colors—such as red, yellow, and bright blue—are attention grabbers. They particularly appeal to younger people. (Note the spectrum of bright pigments in Apple's logo, then recall Apple was initially positioned as the computer for schools.) Political organizations, bands, or athletic clubs might opt for bright colors. On the other hand, pale pastels and soft hues elicit feelings of restfulness and tenderness. A psychotherapist or hospice could use such colors. Metallic gold and silver connote elegance and richness. One of them—in combination with another color—might be used by private schools, health spas, or yacht clubs wanting to appeal to an elite clientele. Have you noticed that Campbell's line of more expensive soups carries gold labels?

Different type styles have different personalities. The Levi Strauss Company, for instance, uses a strong, square type style that looks as tough as its pants. Script, which resembles handwriting, would be a natural for a graphologist (handwriting analyst). A circus could get extra mileage by using a typeface called P. T. Barnum. If you're a data-processing service, consider computer typeface. Kartoon works ideally for clowns; Wedding Text, for bridal consultants. A theater might do its logo in Broadway. Attorneys should stick with more traditional styles, whereas a high-tech company wants a contemporary, avant-garde feeling.

To discuss content let's go back to Apple's symbol, because most people are familiar with it. The missing bite could be interpreted as a "byte." Do you suppose the apple also connotes knowledge? Didn't kids used to take an apple to the teacher? Does the bright apple suggest a savvy, enthusiastic firm to you? There are several subtleties here.

Other well-known examples of content are depicted by the insurance industry. Prudential has its rock; Travelers uses an umbrella; Allstate's good hands promise to take care of us. An architect might use circles and straight lines to create a structural design. A law firm or financial consultancy frequently employs the principal's initials in some way. This can apply to other types of enterprises as well. Suppose a construction company was named Johnson and Sons. A clever designer might create a child's building block with a "J," an "&" and an "S." These would be placed on two sides and the top of the building block, giving it a three-dimensional look and tying in graphically with the construction idea.

Some names cry out for movement. This can be accomplished with lines that imply speed. Next time you get a delivery from Federal Express, notice their logo. The words slant up as though representing a plane taking off. Ocean Spray's logo has a rocking sensation and a wave curling over the right side.

Now let's look at size. A large, bold logo makes a statement in itself. It says the company is aggressive, a pacesetter in the industry. Smaller-size logos are used by firms that want to characterize quiet distinction.

If a professionally crafted logo is out of your immediate budget, talk with your local printer about using generic emblems. You can also purchase clip-art for your computer. There are houses for builders, computers for secretarial services, and horses for horse trainers. These universally adopted symbols are easily recognized.

Akin to logos are slogans. A slogan is a tag line or catchy phrase used in advertising and promotion. Just as a picture is worth 1,000 words, some examples will immediately give you the idea. A florist uses a play on Budweiser's "This Bud's for You." A clever shoe repairer advertises: "I doctor shoes, heel them, attend to their dyeing, and save their soles." Another sports a sign reading "Time Wounds All Heels."

PowerMark Publishing's tag line reads "Helping High-Visibility Professionals Position Themselves for Profit and Success." Lead Dog Communications reminds us "If you're not the lead dog...the view never changes."

The tourist industry relies heavily on slogans. A Colorado ski resort's ad campaign taunts "Snow Ahead, Make My Day!" Dallas Pest & Termite Services, Inc., twists words to get their tag line: "No if's, ants or bugs about it."

If you decide to coin a slogan, re-read the previous sections on creativity and naming to get your imaginative juices flowing. You might also find a rhyming dictionary and a thesaurus useful. These tag lines can also be used on bumper stickers, road signs, or marquees.

And revisit http://www.namestormers.com. They have a free report called The Word Twist that shows how to write winning headlines...many of which could be slogans. They also sell a software program called Headliner that helps you create unique and memorable tag lines.

Additionally consider a seasonal slogan for timely advertising. Over the holidays a gym used this greeting: "Merry Fitness and a Happy New Rear." On the cover of their January-March 2000 catalog Harry and David reminded customers, "Call your sweetheart on February 14 (but call *us* today)!"

Designing Letterhead That Grabs Their Attention

Once you've decided on a name and a logo, it's time to have a graphic artist orchestrate your letterhead, envelopes, and business card. Creating a contemporary visual personality is important for your corporate identity. An effective public image means a modern, integrated, and recognizable "look" to all your business collateral materials. This includes stationery, cards, invoices, mailing labels, brochures, ads, even signage. (I explore the latter elements in future chapters.)

Sometimes people forget to include important information, such as the telephone area code and the full zip code. These days be sure to also list your e-mail address and Web site URL. And if you operate primarily with a post office box, also include a street address for shipments, such as FedEx and UPS deliveries. It makes you appear more substantial and permanent.

Another consideration is paper. Although it will boost your costs considerably to use a higher-grade paper, it's money well spent. Why go to all the trouble of creating a snappy name and stunning logo and then print it on cheap 20-pound bond? Ask your printer for advice on a better quality paper stock. Speaking of paper, if you frequently do two-page letters, order an extra ream of matching paper to use as plain second sheets. Also consider something other than white. There are pale shades in several hues that create nice business effects.

Business Cards as Mini-Billboards

There are more than 45 billion business cards printed in the U.S. each year. These tiny advertising wonders first appeared in Europe in the 1600s, were called "tradesmen's cards," and circulated primarily among the rich.

Today, a business card is your goodwill ambassador within the community or across the sea. Your first contact with a prospective client or customer is often a handshake, a few words, and a business card. A card is the perfect networking tool, setting the tone for your entire relationship. Yet it always amazes me how many entrepreneurs don't have one. If you fall into this category, please do yourself a favor and remedy that tomorrow!

Back when I was doing a lot of freelance article writing, I always tucked a card in every query letter. A year after getting a negative response from one editor, he called and asked if I would cover a story for him. How did he happen to think of me? He had kept my business card on file.

Not only can you dispense cards to prospects, but you can also use them socially, post them on bulletin boards as tiny advertisements, and tuck them into correspondence. Carry them wherever you go. We've handed them out on airplanes, in the market, even at gas stations. I have a friend who takes them in a fanny pack to the spa and in her backpack when she hikes. One graceful technique when meeting some-one new is to ask for their card first. Normally an exchange follows.

If this is someone you particularly want to remember, or something you've promised to do, flip the card over and jot down a couple of key phrases to remind yourself. If this new acquaintance is more social than business, you may want to note your home phone on the card. When exchanging cards with prime contacts, give out two—one for the individual and a second for her assistant.

How do you create a memorable card—one that will fix you and your company firmly in the mind of the other person? There are several ways to make yourself unforgettable. Use an 80-pound or heavier paper stock. Flimsy cards connote a weak company.

Consider switching from the traditional rectangular shape. Many businesses lend themselves ideally to particular outlines. If you're a pi-ano teacher, an open grand piano would be perfect. Anyone working in the computer field could use the shape of a monitor with attached key-board. Women with surnames like Post, Sea, King, Spear, or Church have wonderful visual opportunities. There are two drawbacks to un-usually shaped cards, however. The die-cuts required to produce them are expensive, and people sometimes resent odd-shaped ones that don't fit conveniently into their Rolodex. A less drastic alternative might be to run your copy vertically instead of the normal horizontal way. This works well for law or CPA firms where several individual names must be listed.

Size is another way to distinguish yourself. You might deviate from the normal 2 inches high by designing yours 4 inches high, then fold-ing it like a tent. That way you actually have four tiny surfaces.

You can use such business cards in one of two ways: 1) To include more selling information about your services or to list several locations. In effect your card becomes a tiny, portable billboard. (Put all contact info on one surface, however.) 2) To provide some sort of useful freebie. A home economist printed a handy fabric conversion chart on the back of her cards, then laminated them. Political candidates include the phone numbers of public services. You might make up a list of special events in your particular industry, do a mini-directory of useful num-bers, or print a map or a calendar. A business card with a calendar often finds its way into people's wallets or under the glass on their desks.

I designed the card for a women's retail clothing store in a tent format, then added a mini-chart inside where ladies could list their clothing sizes. That way, husbands, sons, and lovers were helped with gift giving. Any of these devices encourage the recipient to keep the card and remember you.

Speaking of size, give your proposed card the "safe sight" test: Can you read it easily at arms length? Using tiny 8-point type will utterly frustrate more mature prospects who no longer enjoy 20/20 vision. And avoid using all capitals. They are more difficult for anyone to read.

Of course, there are other ways to set yourself apart. How about a full-color card? Or one that contains your photo? This works well if you do business long-distance; people like to see what the folks they are dealing with look like. (See my adjacent sample card.) Cards designed to fit in Rolodexes are another alternative.

manuscript critiques • editing
typesetting • design • printing
marketing • publicity • coaching
consulting • seminars

p.o. box 1500, 425 cedar street
buena vista, co 81211-1500
e-mail: marilyn@about-books.com
www.about-books.com

about books inc.

marilyn ross
(719) 395-2459
fax: (719) 395-8374

Is your name Black, Green, Grey, or Brown? Certainly some play on this color angle would be appropriate. Color association enhances in other ways. Certain services can be promoted with wildly bright flourescent cards. A small appliance repair shop might produce a flashy, distinctive card using a hot-pink background with black lettering. A florist, garden shop, or landscaper might go for a green background. Earth tones work well for ecology-oriented enterprises. For the conservative professions, think a palette of navy blue or burgundy with white lettering, or grey, or beige.

To cultivate a higher-quality look, many professionals prefer embossed cards. This is often done with blind embossing where the surface of the card is raised to show just a letter, word, or symbol. And some companies use a rubberized magnet material to keep their message and phone number visible on refrigerator doors, or laminate them to give a more special touch—and durability.

If you expect to do business in a foreign country, print the reverse side of your card in the language of the place you're visiting. Although many will understand English, your thoughtful gesture will be noticed and appreciated.

Be leery of including *too much*. In our high-tech world, where people often have cell phones and pagers besides a regular phone number and fax, the urge to merge all is strong. Clutter then becomes a culprit.

One final bit of advice regarding business cards: Don't pass out dog-eared ones; they give the impression you never do any business. Get a quality card holder. Also, don't try to correct old information; print new ones with the right data. Don't use your cards as scratch pads. If you don't value them, can you expect others to do so?

Branding Sets You Apart From the Herd

Nope, we're not talking about round-ups and cattle branding. We're discussing a form of recognition. Branding is the synergistic effect created by a happy combination of all the image-building techniques discussed here. It's company or product or personal comprehension before the sale; the connection of an idea, an approach, and a physical design in the minds of your audience. Branding is the act of creating specific impressions that contribute to an overall attitude among a target group of prospects. Building expectations through consistency so that eventually your reputation precedes you like a red carpet. But it's not something you can necessarily impose. Acceptance of a brand is bestowed by the consumer, who recognizes certain traits as inherent—quality, longevity, image, purpose, trust, identity.

Having a recognizable brand is an intangible asset. Famous female brands include Liz Claiborne, Mrs. Fields, Jenny Craig, Anne Klein, and Martha Stewart. Stewart—once a model, then a stockbroker, then a caterer—has become the queen of self-branding. Her $200 million empire includes a line of store products, a catalog, a magazine, books, a Web site, and TV show…so far.

Businesswomen seeking to make a career change can also create a brand for themselves. The cut of your suit, the food you eat, how you answer your e-mail and handle phone calls—all of these reflect on you and your values. They project a sense of self, a vision. You can cultivate certain consistent characteristics to launch a "me" marketing campaign.

Typically, a company or product brand is a combination of several elements: a name, a logo, and a set of attributes and associations, expectations, and perceptions. It's a covenant with the consumer. In other words, your image. It dates back to ancient Egypt where craftsmen placed a unique mark on bricks they produced to identify their authenticity.

Why is branding suddenly such a hot topic? The marketplace is becoming more complex and more competitive at an exponential rate. There is great confusion over tangible differences between one product and another, one company and another. By successfully branding its products or services, a company makes its offerings stand apart from the competition in ways that matter to buyers. It's a method to differentiate yourself. And companies with strong off-line brands also benefit from a "halo effect" in trying to establish a presence on the Web.

In an interesting poll conducted by The Conference Board, U.S. consumers were asked what matters most when forming an impression of a company. Brand quality, image, and reputation topped the list at 54.6 percent. A corporate brand draws from a wider context and rich history to create positive imagery. Hewlett-Packard, for instance, is known for precision and scientific leadership.

Perhaps one of the most universally recognized examples of successful branding is the Dummies series of books. Although they started out in the computer field, they've now branched out to *Birdwatching for Dummies, Wine for Dummies*, etc. Everyone readily recognizes their bright yellow and black covers and the stick man with rolling eyes. The whole package has become legendary. You immediately know the consistent approach, the level, the layout. Another successful series is The Complete Idiot's Guides. IDG now has over 200 titles out in 16 languages. Of course, the Chicken Soup books have taken off like a rocket and are easy to spot anywhere.

Marcia Yudkin, publisher of the weekly e-mail newsletter, The Marketing Minute (http://www.yudkin.com/marketing.htm), tells an interesting story about a firm called Zebra Design of Rockland, Massachusetts. Although they had been in business awhile, they needed a fresh look. Yet it was important to retain elements from their old identity to keep current and former clients comfortable.

To do this, Zebra Design morphed a black and white color scheme into a more sophisticated combination of black zebra stripes with beige, plum, and olive green. Their new logo included a zebra tail and striping. The former galloping zebra that was the lone image on old stationery and business cards now shows up as one graphic element on visually imaginative postcards. New slogans contain a prominent "Z" treatment: "gadZooks! RevolutioniZe your look." The old tag line, "We make graphics as simple as black & white" has been replaced with "Graphics to drive you wild."

Branding will be increasingly important in the online world. In real life you can walk into a boutique and try on a dress or "kick the tires" of a vehicle you're considering. Dot-coms don't have that advantage. In the virtual world, people buy names they trust. That's why you must work to build your brand and inspire confidence.

Are you ready for "the brand called you"? There's a Web site that explores how to make yourself a brand name and how to create your own distinctive marketing position. *Fast Company* magazine carried a recent cover story by Tom Peters on this topic. Those who want to build long-term name recognition should visit http://www. brandyou.com. There's even a Personal Brand Equity Evaluation you can take.

Another excellent site covers such topics as what is a brand, do they have life cycles like most products, what's the difference between a product and a corporate brand, isn't branding all about advertising, is it applicable to all industries/categories, is it possible to determine the financial value of a brand? To saturate your brain on the topic, go to http://www.brandconsult.com/FAQFrames/frmain04.htm.

And if you really want to understand the full impact of this technique, investigate the magazine *Brandweek*. It gives insights into what consumers are thinking, how they're acting, and why.

Now that you know how to really be a class act, let's move on to the advertising chapter. There you'll discover how to make a splash without much cash.

Web Sites, *Wisdom,* and Whimsey

Called yourself lately? If you're a home-based business, what do other people hear when your number is called? Remember, the phone you've listed on letterhead, in catalogs, and on order forms is a *business* telephone number. When it's answered "hello," it hardly sets the tone for a business relationship. The same is true when your adorable three-year-old gushes over the telephone. Businesses use answering machines and voice mail: some effectively, some dismally. Let's think about this: Isn't it obvious you're "either away from your desk or on another line" when you don't answer? Rather than this well-worn phrase, why not tell callers approximately when someone will be in the *office* (not "at home!") and promise to return their call promptly. For many of us, the telephone is our lifeline to the world. The image we project there can make us sound like a large, progressive, customer-oriented business organization—or like a hokey mom-and-pop operation. Call yourself. See if your company passes the test.

Business cards can be a value-added part of your marketing campaign. How so, you wonder? They don't always have to take the form of a paper greeting. I just received an *audio* business card for a financial service with the suggestion I pop in the tape and listen when driving. Not only did this separate the sender from the competition, it also provided valuable information I found useful. Could you apply this tactic to reaching your prospects? Any two-cassette boom box will do for copying cassettes, or Radio Shack has low-priced "dubbing" machines if you want to make lots of copies. When recording a cassette, speak with lots of energy in your voice. Since prospects can't see your face, your voice and message have to do all the work. And be sure the label is attractive. Besides a business card, tapes can be used as a give-away premium, for training, and to introduce a new product when accompanied by a price sheet.

●●●●●●●

The real bottom-line of image was captured by Emerson: "What you are speaks so loud I cannot hear what you say."

●●●●●●●

Incredible site provides multiple guidance for women. The Business Women's Network Interactive offers a sumptuous array of ingredients to make you more financially successful. They have major sections covering: enhancing your business, enhancing your career, enhancing your finances (it's a downright "enhanced" site, I'll tell you!), marketing, women's networking and diversity, women on the Web, guide to government contracting, financing a small business, even an e-commerce guide with links to articles and sites to establish and improve your e-commerce venture. Find it all at http://www.bwni.com.

●●●●●●●

Three Wise Women: You know what would have happened if it had been three wise women instead of men, don't you? They would have asked for directions, arrived on time, helped deliver the baby, cleaned the stable, made a casserole, and brought practical gifts!

●●●●●●●

What's in a name? L-O-T-S! Ever heard of ComputerLiteracy.com? How about Fatbrain.com? They are one and the same, but with a name makeover! Feeling that business was lagging because of its dull, unmemorable name, the online technical bookselling company assumed a hip new identity last spring when they relaunched as Fatbrain.com. Results were immediate. Within hours, stock prices soared 36 percent and business boomed. A study before the name change revealed that only 8 percent of those in the company's demographic customer base knew who they were. Four months after the name change that number leaped to 30 percent. What a difference a couple of words can make.

●●●●●●●

The other day, I felt so confused that I signed up
for reincarnation life insurance.

●●●●●●●

Register with WOWFactor.com to get lots of information on how to run your business successfully. Joining is easy and can be done right online. You'll receive discounts on products and services, free e-mail, a personal research assistant, access to the WOWFactor's database of women-owned businesses (over 1 million strong!), and admission into programs such as their event calendar, online classes mentioning program, and links into your local chamber of commerce. Click on http://www.wowfactor.com.

●●●●●●●

If the name fits...
Sometimes we don't have a lot of choice in naming. Take, for instance, the surgeons that medical librarians turned up named Drs. Slaughter, Butcher, Hacker, and Kutteroff. Or chiropractors Drs. Bones and Bender. Then there are the podiatrists: Drs. Foote, Cornfield, Shoemaker, and Smellsey.

●●●●●●●

Set yourself apart with the REAL thing. Occasional fruit pits are purposely left in Larry's Italian Fruit Ices during the manufacturing process. Then the owner points out, "It's so fresh and fruity, it even has pits." This same practice is used by restaurants that leave a few lumps in their mashed potatoes to subtly remind diners they are getting the real thing.

Looking for help with slogans or names? A couple of Web sites might be just the answer. Try www.quoteland.com and www.starlingtech.com/quotes. You just may find the right words for the occasion here. Don't miss Humorous Quotes at the first site for memorable movie, TV, and song lines—along with stupid things said by famous people. Add a twist and you can come up with the perfect tag line or naming inspiration.

Using logos in strange ways. We know of one man who trekked up Mount Everest and took several client's baseball caps with logos on the adventure. Wearing each hat, he had pictures taken at base camp with the mountain in the background. Clients then used the photo to proclaim in PR and advertising "We have a presence everywhere, even Mount Everest!"

●●●●●●●

Positioning motto: "You either have to be first, best,
or different."
—Loretta Lynn

●●●●●●●

CHAPTER 3

Advertising's Many Faces: Who's the Fairest of Them All?

We are bombarded by an estimated 15,000 commercial messages every day. The sell goes on with print advertising in newspapers, magazines, and Yellow Pages; radio and TV commercials; billboards; Internet banners; even such subtle things as matchbook covers and bumper stickers. Some of it is good advertising; most is "badvertising." My job is to show you how to create a demand for your product or service without a Madison Avenue budget. And to create the ooh-la-la without the blah-blah-blah.

Rather than your just "doing something creative," this chapter gives you the tools to achieve your advertising objectives and investigates the options. We'll explore print advertising in-depth—not to mention using commercials, telemarketing, exhibiting at trade shows, and dozens of other innovative ad concepts.

Advertising revolves in two different arenas: One centers around business-to-business marketing. That is where one company (such as a bank) sells to another company (such as a building contractor). The other form most of us know more about. It is companies selling directly to the consumer.

Awaken Desire with Gain or Pain

Whether you sell to consumers or to businesspeople you will always motivate people to action faster when you push their "Gain and Pain" hot buttons. Here is a sampling of vivid words and phrases to awaken desires.

Gain

- Imagine having prospective clients calling YOU to do business!
- Picture your mailbox stuffed with more checks than you could ever imagine!
- What would it feel like if you could _____?
- Have you ever dreamed of becoming a _____?
- Can you see yourself as a respected marketing consultant in your community?
- If you could paint a picture of your future, what would it look like 10 years from now?
- Discover the fortune that lies hidden in your business.
- Now you can achieve your wildest dreams!
- Tired of just getting by?
- These 10 financial rules will change your life forever!
- What are the secrets of looking your best every day?
- Can you really make sales while you sleep? You bet you can!

(continued on next page)

Writing Copy From a "Benefit" Perspective

There are a few individuals on this earth who could sell sand to a sheik. Most of us, however, have to work at being strong saleswomen. Any time you write—whether it's an ad, a brochure, or a news release—you're much more apt to seduce prospects with a "you" approach rather than "me" or "we" or "I." All of us like personalized copy that addresses our individual needs.

When you emphasize benefits, you tell the customer/client what she or he will get: not what your service or product is but what it *does*. Features tell what it is. Benefits tell prospects what's in it for them. You give people tangible reasons to buy because you offer solutions to their problems.

Create a list of the features that make your service, product, or store unique or better than the competition. Suppose, for instance, you have a custom-made, wooden lawn chair for sale with the following **features:**

1. Hand-crafted
2. Made of teak and brass
3. Curved back
4. Adjustable back angle
5. Natural teak finish

Now determine the **benefit** of each of these. Translate the lawn chair features into benefits (things that meet your customer's needs) like this:

1. Heirloom quality
2. Strong, durable, maintenance-free, naturally resistant to weather
3. Excellent back support
4. Comfortable, perfect for a nap in the afternoon sun
5. More in harmony with the natural landscape than a plastic or aluminum chair

Let's look at an example. Suppose you run a catering service. Instead of listing what goes into planning a dinner party, tell prospects why their dinner party will be a smashing success. That's the result they want.

According to Yale University researchers, the 12 most persuasive words in the English language are: discover, easy, guarantee, health, love, money, new, proven, results, safety, save, and you.

One significant writing technique is to speak in specifics rather than generalities. Instead of saying you offer low prices, say "Haircuts $8." Rather than telling prospective guests your bed and breakfast is homey, tell them there's a warm crackling fire, homemade cookies, and fresh flowers awaiting them. Those are specific amenities folks can identify with.

AWAKEN DESIRE WITH GAIN OR PAIN (continued)

Pain

- Imagine being broke in your "golden years" if Uncle Sam wipes out your retirement accounts.
- It was awful.
- Jimmy was up with the bases loaded and the video battery died…again.
- Are you paying too much for your life insurance?
- I was embarrassed to be the heaviest guy at my 10th high school reunion.
- If I hit one more traffic jam, I'll explode!
- Could I have prevented these outrageously expensive cracks in my new deck?
- Do you hate wasting money on mediocre marketing methods?

Contributed by Dan McComas, an author, public speaker, and corporate trainer who delivers keynote speeches and seminars on marketing, sales, persuasive writing skills, generating free publicity, and sustaining self-motivation for companies and nonprofit organizations around the world. He can be reached at 301-946-6636; e-mail: promocoach@aol.com; Web site: www.danmccomas.com.

When you are writing promotional literature, be aware of what I call "information-shaping." How a person presents information—what isn't said as much as what is—can make a big difference in the story slant. You can mold information to suit your own purposes. Statistics are often molded when taken out of context.

Classified Ads

Modest-sized classified ads have led to great fortunes. Did you know that Richard W. Sears put an ad in the *Chicago Daily News* for a watchmaker in 1887? It was answered by Alan C. Roebuck. These two later formed a corporate partnership that was to become one of the nation's premier retailers.

Yet thousands of other people have poured their classified ad money down a rat hole. I hope the tips in this chapter will ensure you don't fall into that category.

Every word costs money in classified ads—sometimes as much as $8 each for large-circulation magazines. For that reason, people frequently try to cut their ads to the bare bones. That's almost always deadly. Readers need enough meat to entice them to respond. The more you tell, the more you sell, so flesh out that skeleton. Be sure the ad expresses benefits. Let's face it, self-interest is the strongest force in human nature. Successful ads usually lead off by promising to do something for the reader.

There are two approaches in classified ads: You can either go direct for the action/order, or use a two-step method where you advertise for inquiries. Whether you can get orders or inquiries from a classified depends upon several factors. There is the proposition, the unit of sale, the publication you use, and if you can adequately describe your offer in the space.

Another important variable is which heading you will place the ad under. You may have to choose between "Business Services," "Personal," and "Jobs Wanted," for instance.

Be sure to track your results. The easiest way to code an ad is by affixing something extra to the address. Maybe it is P.O. Box 1500-R, or you might add a suite number after your address. If people are telephoning, ask during the conversation how they heard about you.

A single insertion of your ad is recommended to start. Don't respond to the urges from media salespeople to save money by committing to several consecutive ads. Sure you will save money per ad due to a "frequency discount." But what good is that if the ad isn't pulling? Best to wait until you have a proven ad and a proven publication before agreeing to multiple placements. One of the biggest ingredients in successful advertising is patience.

Another is repetition. There is a cross between a classified ad and a full-fledged display ad. I call it a "scatter ad." These are small—usually only one-twelfth or one-sixth of a page. Repetition is the key. Several of the same ads are scattered through a newspaper or magazine.

Scatter ads only work for certain things. If you can find one or two words to express the problem you solve, they may be ideal. Here are some examples: An acupuncturist might say "Headaches?" an attorney, "Bankrupt?" "Car trouble" might be the flag waved by an auto mechanic, whereas a doctor might declare "Hemorrhoids?" The ad continues with "Cured without surgery in 15 days, call XXX-XXXX." This kind of an ad campaign can have striking results when used carefully.

Display Ads

Larger display ads make sense for some organizations, although you can drop a bundle of money here in a hurry. Here you have more room to tell your story. You can forcefully appeal to your target audience's desire for quality, comfort, style, savings, convenience, fun, love, wealth, or status.

Display ads typically have four components: a headline, subhead, illustration, and body copy. The headline is your workhorse. If it doesn't do the job, they'll never get to the body of the ad. Don't be a copycat when it comes to headlines. Be original. Punchy. Provocative. Consider a lapel-yanking element of surprise or a ridiculously bold statement (that you can support). The whole purpose of the headline is to capture the reader's attention. Then craft a subhead that amplifies on the headline and transitions the reader into the rest of the ad.

The headline and illustration have to be complementary. They make up over 60 percent of the ad's effectiveness. In illustrations, if you are aiming at one sex, show a member of that sex in the graphic. Presenting people doing something rather than just sitting or standing is always more convincing. Although having your own graphic artist is the optimum in developing an illustration, it is only one option. You can buy clip art books at art supply stores or software for your computer. You may be talented enough and have the right equipment to do an original computer graphic. Another alternative is to wrangle help from a high school or college art class. Black and white photographs can also be used, but they reproduce better in magazines than on rough newsprint.

All of the elements must work together. Earlier we discussed how to write benefit copy. Now be sure your design and copy are coordinated. You can't put together a good ad by locking the designer and the copywriter in separate rooms, then slapping together the results.

As the ad size grows, copy can be expanded to include testimonials from satisfied clients/customers. This customer-selling-customer message is one of the most astoundingly successful techniques. Your satisfied clients can make bold claims that would sound ridiculous coming directly from you. This builds credibility and works wonders for getting prospects to contact you, pre-qualified and ready to buy.

Coupons usually increase response too. Perhaps a restaurant will include a two-dinners-for-one coupon, or a jeweler might offer a free ring cleaning with each coupon (hoping, of course, to find the prongs holding the stones loose and requiring repair, or to convince women they need a new piece of jewelry while in the store).

Always double-check your ad to be sure major points are present—and accurate. Make it easy for people to see your name and phone. Be sure to include the address and Web site. Should you add credit card logos? Hours? A guarantee?

If you are running more than one ad at a time, incorporate some way to track the results. One trick is to include a coupon for some inexpensive trinket. Then when they bring in the ad you know where the lead came from. When receiving phone calls, simply include a question about how they heard of you as part of the presentation. For radio, tell listeners to mention station XXXX when they come in to get their free trinket.

By the way, if you are aiming primarily at older people, there is a free booklet available called *How to Advertise to Maturity*. You can get a copy by contacting Modern Maturity, 420 Lexington Avenue, Fifth Floor, New York, NY 10170, 212-599-1880.

Another type of ad is the institutional advertisement. It isn't designed to evoke a direct response. It's purpose is to establish strong recognition within your industry. Such professionals as insurance agents, architects, and financial planners can use this very effectively. In the institutional ad the goal is to "humanize" the firm and build trust. A personal picture helps people feel they know you and tumbles barriers.

There are many tricks to make your ad stand out on the page. One is to use a *screen*, which means a lighter color of the ink will be used as a background. Screens are usually done in 20 percent so the lettering over them can be easily read. Another technique involves using a distinctive *border*. A border adds impact to even tiny ads and gives instant recognition. It could be a larger rule line than usual, or it might incorporate a symbol that ties in with your service or message. A string of hearts might encircle a florist's ad for Valentine's Day. Dollar signs could serve as the border for a loan company, a set of false teeth for dentists, flags for political advertisements, feet for the local shoe store.

Keep your ad simple: Don't use six different fonts and four pieces of clip art just because they're available. And resist the temptation to fill every inch of the ad. Studies have shown that those jam-packed with text and illustrations are not as effective as ones that use *white space* wisely. Many ads are too busy. Using a small amount of type and lots of white space helps make your ad stand out on the page.

Another technique to set you apart is called a *reverse*. With this approach, you have a black background with white lettering. Don't try this if you have a lot of copy, however. Words are harder to read when reversed; larger type works best.

Yellow Pages

Statistics show that people refer to various Yellow Pages 49,000,000 times on a typical day! Did you know 50 percent of these references result in a purchase? For many, this is the smartest place to put your advertising dollars. People don't let their fingers do the walking unless they are actively interested in buying something. Consequently, they literally prequalify themselves.

What kinds of establishments can most benefit from this medium? W. F. Wagner, in his excellent *Advertising in the Yellow Pages*, lists the most often looked up headings for residences. In order of inquiries, they are cleaners, physicians and surgeons, department stores, television dealers and service, taxicabs, beauty shops, and air-conditioning contractors and service.

Businesses also use Yellow Pages. In the top five of their most often looked-up categories are plumbing and electrical contractors and sign companies. You may want to consider business-to-business Yellow Pages. Chicago pioneered the first of these several years ago. Today more than 20 large metropolitan areas sport such editions. They go to business phone locations and carry headings of interest to—you guessed it—businesses. Rates for these directories are comparable or slightly higher than for the consumer directories.

Others apt to find this an especially viable advertising medium include tanning salons, video renting, computer system design and consulting, auto renting and leasing, carpet cleaners, florists, insurance agents, computer repair facilities, and temporary help agencies.

Many lawyers choose consumer Yellow Pages as competition increases and advertising in general has become a more accepted marketing

Yellow Page Ad Pointers

- Convenient location
- Credit cards accepted
- Awards you've won
- Extended hours (evenings/weekends)
- National brands you work on/carry
- Rush service available
- Free pickup and delivery
- One-stop/full-service establishment
- Free initial consultation
- Personalized service
- Custom work
- Special financing arrangements
- On-call 24 hours
- Free estimates
- Caring concern
- No muss/no fuss attitude
- On-site service
- Certified employees
- Mobile unit
- References furnished
- Satisfaction guaranteed
- Confidential help
- Preventative care
- Always on time
- Special rates for seniors/others

tool in their industry. The Yellow Pages are also a comfortable marketing strategy for dentists, chiropractors, and other health practitioners who make use of personal photographs, colored graphics, and slogans.

What should your Yellow Page ad include? Your name and phone number in large, bold letters, your logo, Web site, and your address. The idea is to establish trust. Citing years in business, size, family management, or association memberships helps confirm your reliability. Be sure to note special features or unique qualities that separate you from the herd. Of course, you will phrase these things as benefits, not features. Always remember you aren't selling you or your business—you are selling solutions to people's problems. The adjacent list of points will stimulate ideas applicable to your ad.

There are other considerations too. Ads appear in a given section according to their size. Thus, half-page ads precede quarter-page ads, which precede eighth-page ads, and so on. If you feel Yellow Page advertising is pivotal to your success, invest a large portion of your overall marketing budget here. It might be wise to consider cross-references under several headings as well. A secretarial service, for instance, could also list itself under "Word Processing" and "Data Processing." Some unusual businesses and professionals will want to run ads or listings in books for adjacent communities as well.

It may not be necessary to purchase a large display ad. Half-inch type-only ads, and even bold listings, help set you apart. If your budget allows, a way to really stand out on the page is to incorporate a second color into your ad. Studies done by Donnelley Directory indicate including red in an ad attracts the eye and gets faster recognition.

With the divestiture of AT&T, some communities now have as many different phone directories as they do churches. There are more than 6,000 of these directories sprinkled around the country. Many of these privately published books go to extreme lengths to look like "the real thing." Interestingly, some of them are actually better, because they contain a wealth of community service information. Find out which is the most popular book in your area, then go with it.

The RUB Formula

Once you've created a good ad, keep with it. Use the RUB formula. (RUB stands for Repetitive, Uniform, Basic.) To generate outstanding results you need to be seen over and over again. Repetition is what implants you firmly in the prospect's mind. (It has been said repetition is reputation.)

People seldom make a decision based on seeing one or two ads. It takes three, four, sometimes six months before you experience a notable outcome from ads. That's because most people who see your ad this week don't need you right now. You want to advertise often enough though, so when prospects do need help, they think of you instead of the competition.

Uniformity is the name of the game. If you do one kind of ad this week, another next week, and a completely different one the following week, you look as confused as a hillbilly in Manhattan. Previously we talked a lot about image. Your ads need an image—a steady, consistent presentation that people begin to recognize as you. Keep it uniform. And keep it basic. Cutesy, flippant ads are not the kind that endure. You want something clear, uncomplicated, and easy to understand.

Free-Standing Inserts

Most newspapers offer another kind of advertising option: It's called a free-standing insert. What that term refers to is a loose flyer inserted in the newspaper. Flyers are nice for several reasons. They stand out more than ads in the paper and are easier for prospects to set aside for future action. Another big plus is you can typically target specific zip codes. That way if you know your potential buyers are located in just one or two zip codes—or you feel only people in your immediate area will patronize your store—you can target just them. This is cheaper than trying to reach everyone. Of course, you also have more space to develop your message on an 8 ½-inch x 11-inch flyer.

Advertorials

An advertorial is a bit like the offspring from a horse and a donkey. It is neither an ad nor an editorial. It is space that is paid for, but it looks more like an article. The term "advertising" in tiny letters across the top is the only giveaway that this isn't a normal article.

Why bother with such subterfuge? Says ad magnate David Ogilvy, "Roughly six times as many people read the average article as the average advertisement." In the ad game that can mean dramatic results! These ads couched in the guise of editorial text and public service communications pieces definitely catch the eyes of the public.

Placement Ploys

One way to be distinctive is by seeing that your ad is placed in an advantageous location on the page. This is called a "preferred position." Most newspapers and magazines charge about a 10 percent premium for it. At least that's what their rate cards say. We know for a fact this is a negotiable point. If you are a new advertiser or a very good account, they often waive the extra fee. The best position is on an early right-hand page, above the half-way mark. That's what you want to request.

Talking about placement strategies, here's another idea. Suppose you want to advertise in the *Wall Street Journal*, *Time*, *McCalls*, or *Industry Week*. The costs for their full readership would be prohibitive for a small business. However, each of these publications, and several others, print regional editions. This is called a "split run" or "zone edition." You can advertise just in the western edition of the *Wall Street Journal*, for instance.

By the way, reprints of such ads make impressive handouts to clients or customers. They build your image and give you more credibility. One firm reproduces their ads from the *International Herald Tribune* and the *London Financial Times to* "get across awareness of our international capabilities," says a spokesperson. Sometimes reprints generate more long-term results than the ads themselves.

Then there was the clever entrepreneur who ran a tiny ad in a major national business magazine, then casually asked her clients, "Did you see our ad in *Newsweek?*"

Choosing the Media

Media selection will be different if you are dealing on an area basis around your hometown, rather than in a national or global arena. If your sphere of influence centers around one community or area, the print ad choices are less confusing. (I'll be talking about radio and TV shortly.) There is probably one major daily paper, plus several smaller neighborhood newspapers and a free shopper or two. In large metropolitan areas, there may also be an alternative newspaper that appeals to the more "hip" crowd, a New Age publication, a senior citizen paper, maybe even several ethnic publications. Often there is a regional magazine, such as *Arizona Living* magazine or *San Diego* magazine. If you plan to use print ads, these are your options.

Newspapers have an immediacy that can be a real advantage. Because of their short lead time, you can run an ad the beginning of the week and be getting business from it by the end of the week. This allows you to capitalize on timely events or situations. If your city has just been hit with a heat wave, advertising air-conditioning units could be a stroke of genius. (Better gear up to cope with the onslaught, though!) A locksmith might want to plug in some quick ads to counteract a local wave of burglaries. You could also synchronize your advertising with the payroll days of large local industries.

It may be best to avoid Wednesdays and Fridays. These are the "clutter" days when papers are chockful of grocery and entertainment ads. (Ignore this advice if you are in the grocery, amusement, or entertainment business.) Sunday is a good day as people spend more time perusing the paper. As with some magazines, a few big metropolitan dailies—such as the *Los Angeles Times* and the *Houston Chronicle*—publish zoned editions. Remember there is one distinct disadvantage with newspaper advertising: Tomorrow there is a new paper. The life span of your ad is very short.

One possible way around this is to consider supplements. These are special sections that newspapers run occasionally. They typically deal with targeted topics of interest to specific groups: seniors or job seekers, for instance. Or they cover a generic subject like health, landscaping, recreation, real estate, or automobiles. Since these stand alone, they are often pulled out and saved if the topic is of interest.

If you want to learn how to stretch your ad budget, here's an idea: Take a hard look at the small community periodicals. Advertising in coupon mailers is also a good low-cost option, especially if your target market includes coupon-clippers. And it's so easy to track if this is working when a patron or client presents a 10 percent off coupon.

Above all, don't forget who your audience is! Cable TV (which we'll address shortly) would be a lousy buy, for instance, for a health-conscious product, service, store, or restaurant because people concerned about their health aren't usually couch potatoes lolling in front of a TV.

Magazines are kept around for months, so your message keeps selling. There is also prestige value to having your ad next to that of some Fortune 500 company like Ford Motor Company or AT&T. Also ads simply look better in magazines; photographs reproduce well on the slick paper.

Obviously, price is going to be a prime consideration. But don't just take that at face value. A more expensive ad may be a far better value. Here's how to find out: For both magazines and newspapers, you need to determine the cost per 1,000 (CPM) formula. It tells you what it costs to have your ad seen by 1,000 people in each publication.

For newspapers, divide the cost of your potential ad by the paper's circulation in thousands. In magazines, the cost of a full black-and-white page is the standard. Divide it by the net paid circulation in thousands. Let's do a little math to make that more clear. Say ABC newspaper has a circulation of 40,000, and your ad would cost $400. The CPM would be 400 divided by 40—$10 per 1,000 subscribers. Now suppose you're considering an ad in XYZ magazine with a circulation of 100,000. But the price here is $800. That figures out to be $8 per 1,000 subscribers. Other things being equal, the magazine is a better deal even though it costs more. Before plunging into an advertising commitment, figure the CPM for each publication on your list to determine the best buy.

Of course, price is only one consideration. You may decide to pay a higher CPM because a particular publication is positioned ideally to reach your market. A funeral director or convalescent home may elect to advertise in a senior citizen newspaper. A reflexologist will fare better in a New Age or alternative newspaper than in the traditional press. An art gallery, day spa, or financial planner might choose a very different advertising medium: They would be wise to consider the print programs put out by a symphony orchestra, ballet, opera, or local theater groups, for instance. Here they can reach a captive upper-crust audience.

If your prospect territory is greater, perhaps a region of the United States or the whole nation, your challenges are elevated. Now you have national consumer magazines—some with zone editions—plus special-interest trade journals all vying for your advertising dollars. To learn about your options, consult *Standard Rate and Data Services*. It is broken into two main sections: "Consumer Magazines" and "Business Publications." Study the appropriate magazines, using the CPM formula plus your good common sense.

Understanding Psychographics

It used to be advertisers talked about "demographics": information about the age, income, and sex of prospects. Over the last decade, however, a more definitive way of measuring potential customers/clients has emerged. Called "psychographics," it further evaluates the lifestyles, interests, and behavior of people. This system classifies people according to what motivates them. Do they prefer the tried-and-true, or are they trendsetters?

A fascinating book, *The Clustering of America* by Michael J. Weiss, looks at our nation as 40 different types of neighborhoods or clusters. He ties these psychographics in with specific zip codes to determine what kinds of buyers live where. Each one has its own lifestyle and values. There are the Blue Blood Estates (Beverly Hills, California, and Scarsdale, New York), Shotguns & Pickups (Zanesville, Ohio, and Molalla, Oregon), and Money & Brains (Princeton, New Jersey, and Palo Alto, California). Then there is Gray Power (Sun City, Arizona, and Sarasota, Florida), Black Enterprise (Capital Heights, Maryland, and Auburn Park, Illinois), even the Bohemian Mix (Greenwich Village and Haight-Ashbury), to name a few.

Now this may sound like so much gobbledygook. Yet it has exciting implications. Let's say a PBS station is launching a fund-raising campaign. Clustering shows that Suburban Elite Business Buffs (SEBBs) are strong supporters of public television. By finding out which zip codes in their area are comprised of SEBBs they could practically hand deliver an invitation to support PBS via a direct-mail campaign.

Could not an inventive insurance agent make use of such information as well? With a little detective work, she could track down the area zip codes where affluent, forward-thinking young couples with new born babies live. Wouldn't a larger proportion of them than usual be receptive to taking out an insurance policy on the little one? Certainly health-care providers can use clustering information to target their efforts to the most likely potential patients. The possible connections are most intriguing.

Negotiation Tips

Another tactic to trim ad costs is to buy what is termed "remnant" space. As a piece of leftover cloth is called a remnant, so too is ad space that is unsold just before press time. This happens when another advertiser takes some, but not all, regions or when a magazine has had a bad month and hasn't sold its quota of ads. This space can often be bought for 25 to 50 percent below the rate card price. If you hope to cash in on this bonanza, have your ad already typeset and ready to go. Time is of the essence; you'll have to get them the ad overnight.

Some businesswomen have success in negotiating not only price but other benefits. By speaking to the magazine's salespeople (or directly with the publisher if it is a small, entrepreneurial operation), you may be able to arrange other considerations. Perhaps you can talk them into a two-color ad for the price of one color. Or maybe they will give you an additional ad at no extra cost. You might even ask for a complimentary list of their subscribers on labels or disk if the readership is directly targeted to your service. (Many magazines rent these lists, by the way.) Also remember to ask magazine ad reps about merchandising aids, such as easel-back cards, ad reprints, or decals with the name of the magazine. They can often be used as signs, display pieces, or in direct-mail programs.

If advertising plays a large role in your overall marketing mix, it may be worthwhile to establish what is called an "in-house" advertising agency. You simply set up another company name, address, and phone. In most cases, this will save you 15 percent for anything listed as "commissionable" on a rate card.

One last thought is "PI" or "PO" ads. PI ads mean per inquiry; PO, per order. Simply stated, you don't plunk down a cent for these ads. Instead you negotiate a deal with the magazine, newsletter, or newspaper where they get a portion of the profits on all activity. In effect, they gamble and provide the ad space free with the idea they will get anywhere from 25 to 50 percent of all business it generates.

Although this works better when there is a product involved, certain service businesses may be able to take advantage of the approach as well. It would work with a coupon when selling spa or athletic club memberships, for instance. A dry cleaner might be able to swing such a deal with an entrepreneurial-minded local magazine or newspaper publisher. Likewise, a hotel or motel owner might offer a kickback for each coupon they received from the publication.

Directories Help You Get Discovered

Besides the Yellow Pages, there are many other specialized and regional directories. Virtually every industry has one. They are typically divided into categories, arranged like dictionaries, and updated annually. If you don't know about these opportunities, look in *Directories in Print*. Some of these listings are free for the asking. What could they do for you?

Let's use my business as an example. As marketing and publishing consultants, listings in appropriate directories figure prominently in our marketing mix. A study by the Association of Industrial Advertisers found that when buyers look for sellers, 35 percent find them in business directories. This category leads all others (literature on hand, sales calls, periodicals and direct mail, recommendations, and Yellow Pages) by a significant margin.

Here are some tips for appearing in free directories: Use every bit of space the listing forms allocate. If they give you five lines to describe your services, use all five lines. This will make you appear stronger on the page. When a firm puts down only their name, address, and phone, their listing looks far less impressive. Choose your words carefully. Stress the benefits and your diversity of services. Code your listing by using a department number or some other address devise. Or use a different contact name to differentiate this listing.

When people use a directory, they are in a buying frame of mind. Rather than being lookie-loos, they intend to make a purchase. Your task is to influence them with your reputation and supply detailed information showing how you can meet their needs. You want to appear the dominant company on the page.

Free listings are becoming more scarce. Today smart directory publishers are going after paid appearances. There are three considerations when developing directory ads: which directory, what heading, what advertising level. Evaluate the headings to determine which ones are appropriate for you. It is better to place several small ads under each possible heading than a large umbrella one.

As to the advertising level, most directories have several alternatives. There is often a plain vanilla free listing, a chocolate variety where the information appears in bold, and a strawberry option that also includes your logo. The gourmet flavors offer various-size display ads.

The headline and copy for a directory ad differs from that of a magazine or newspaper. In this case, you aren't so concerned with grabbing their attention; they wouldn't be here if they weren't interested. Sell the inquiry. Your goal is to get them to contact you. Provide information. Draft a list of your sales points (refer to the list provided for the Yellow Pages), giving prospects many reasons to contact you. Then you have a better chance of hitting their particular "button."

As in all advertising, it is essential to track results. Many of your inquiries will come by phone, especially if a toll-free number is included. Source your leads. If you have a form on your Web site, be sure it asks, "How did you hear of us?"

Broadcast Media

Broadcast media—the world of radio and television—can lead to a huge influx of business. The power of the airwaves can be an effective advertising tool. The downside, of course, is that it's expensive. There is little point in buying a few commercials. In most cases, you have to commit to about three months before you can anticipate striking results.

Radio spots are a good solution for some businesses. They allow you to reach a small geographic area at an affordable price. Unlike TV, most stations don't tack on production costs.

To begin investigating radio, think about the format of your local stations. They will probably range all the way from country to classical, easy listening to heavy metal. Some service and retail businesses can be matched to the type of listener who tunes in different stations. A golf course would do best advertising on the classical or easy listening station, a bowling alley on the country station.

Contact the station and ask to have the advertising sales *manager* call on you. That individual can help educate you. Turnover in these types of jobs is notoriously high, which means many sales reps are new to the job and still unfamiliar with the particulars of radio advertising. Although they'll be happy to write up a contract, they won't be able to offer much helpful advice.

Radio spots can be purchased in one of two ways. Either as run of station (ROS) or for specified times. ROS is cheaper because they can plug you in to undesirable times, such as late at night. Ideally, you want morning drive time (6:00 A.M. to 9:00 A.M.) or afternoon drive time (3:00 P.M. to 6:00 P.M.). People listen to their radios as they commute to and from work. This is a prime advertising period. Of course, if you're trying to reach teenagers, it's a different story. Then you want early evening and Saturdays. Spots are usually 15, 30, 45, or 60 seconds long. We usually advise clients to get 30-second spots. We've found them to be the most sensible over the years.

Now let's talk about what will be said during the commercial. This is a place where professional copyrighting can be very cost-effective. There is an art to writing strong radio copy. It isn't something you master overnight. If you insist on being a do-it-yourselfer, here are a few tips: As I've preached before, write from a *benefit* rather than a feature perspective. Include your company name and phone number three times. Don't tell people to look you up in the Yellow Pages. Why direct them to where your competitors advertise? Instead suggest they check the *white* pages!

The script should be typed double-spaced in all capitals. For unusual names or words, spell them out phonetically. Indicate where any sound effects should be used. By the way, the station will have various sounds you can add for special effects. Consider using background music to accompany your commercial. Remember psychographics. If you are appealing to Young Urban Self-Help Buyers, for instance, they are jazz fans—so let that be your accompaniment.

It pays to tune in to the psychographics of your targeted audience. Merrill Lynch discovered that a few years ago. You may recall they used to show a herd of bulls galloping to financial success on their TV commercials. They learned, however, that the herd concept was a turnoff to the achievement-oriented people they sought to attract. Now they show a solitary bull that is a "breed apart."

Often an announcer simply reads your radio script. If the announcer articulates well, reads coherently, and has a dynamic, variable delivery style, you're in luck. If not, you're better off taking a different approach. Pay a few hundred bucks for talent, go to the studio, and "direct" the commercial until it is right. That way you end up with a proven product and have quality control.

Television may not be out of your reach, especially if you sidestep the network affiliates for cable TV. Here a prime 30-second spot that reaches perhaps 60,000 households may cost less than $200. One of the reasons you pay less is you reach a smaller area, which is desirable for an advertiser wanting to pinpoint only a 20-mile radius. Cable also allows you to target your audience. The upscale viewers of Cable News Network (CNN), for instance, are perfectly suited to businesses aiming for intelligent, affluent consumers. Cable networks dealing exclusively with sports and music offer other opportunities.

Gerald LaFrance, a cleaner in Florence, Massachusetts, decided to use cable TV after he purchased a new machine to press shirts. He bought 150 spots for $7 a piece (less than radio would have cost) and spread them over a three-month period. When asked how his shirt business fared, LaFrance reported, "I ended up tripling the volume in three months!" He had to stop advertising, because he couldn't handle any more business.

It used to be higher-priced items couldn't be sold successfully via TV. Today, however, the barriers have been crossed, and products and services worth several hundred dollars are being merchandised this way. TV is especially viable for things that can be visually demonstrated. An insurance company might show a house burning down, then being rebuilt for the happy policyholder. A burglar alarm firm could enact a scene where a potential intruder is scared away when the alarm goes off. A river-rafting company might show footage of an especially exciting trip. Some attorneys who have adopted TV as a primary advertising medium cite 50 to 75 new cases each month attributed to television commercials. Doctors are also turning to electronic advertising as never before.

Sometimes good values can be had at unusual times on regular TV. Years ago I promoted a vocational school specializing in welding. We used to run very successful 30-second spots on a late-night wrestling program.

Don't overlook the fact you will be charged for production. Prices vary widely: from $400 to $3,000. Of course, if you hire nationally known talent and directors, costs will skyrocket.

Speaking of prices, the published rates are not cast in bronze on either radio or TV. Naturally, stations are not going to discount rates just before Christmas, during prime times, or for especially popular shows. They are often open, however, to negotiation with savvy advertisers. You have nothing to lose by asking.

Your local movie theater is another possibility. On-screen advertising lets you contact area consumers. Companies using this medium typically reach 5,000 to 30,000 people in one weekend at a single theater complex. Costs range from $100 to about $1,000 per week, based on the previous year's attendance.

Imaginative Signage

Most businesses require signs of one sort or another. The most obvious is the one identifying a store or office. A day-care center might opt for something big and bright, whereas an attorney wants a sign that is professional and dignified. If your business is easily recognized by a symbol or emblem, you may want a sign cut in this shape. A bicycle shop could do this nicely, or mount an actual bicycle.

Think about the character of your enterprise and the image you want to portray. A dude ranch would use rustic wood, with bold, routed lettering. On the other hand, an upscale hair dresser might use calligraphy (swooping letters that look like handwriting) on a gold background.

Signs can do wonderful things. I'm reminded of the little store that was located in the middle of a rundown mini-mall. The adjacent businesses were remodeling and wanted to buy the owner out, but she held steadfast. As all the others revamped their facilities, they tried even harder to squeeze her out—all to no avail. Then opening day arrived. Over the door to her store hung a banner that read "Main Entrance."

Signs do indeed have far-reaching possibilities. What about removable magnetized ones for you and key associates to put on your vehicles? Speaking of which, personalized license plates are another way of advertising. So are bumper stickers. I saw a provocative one recently while traveling in Washington, DC. It read, "If Con is the opposite of Pro, what's the opposite of Progress?"

Harvey Mackay, best-selling author and CEO of Mackay Envelope Corporation, says the "easiest, least expensive and most neglected form of advertising is painting *on top* of your truck." Then all those people who work in tall office buildings and look out from time to time will see only *your* advertising. Mackay Envelopes has been doing it for 25 years and swears by this technique.

An Ohio man who operates a gas station asks customers to let him put bumper stickers on their cars and trucks. Everyone who agrees gets a free gallon of gas then and with each refill of 10 gallons or more. The bumper stickers read "I buy my gas from Jim Breeson—5th and Marlowe." So far, more than 1,000 people are driving around advertising for Jim.

Some merchants have been known to promote their ventures via sandwich boards, signs on the sides of buildings, in airports, and on ATM machines. Of course, tee shirts, caps, and coffee mugs are popular advertising vehicles. An amusement park might use inscribed balloons; an association, decals; a theater company, posters. Maps and restaurant menus are another location for placing advertising. If you believe in doing things in a "big way," what about skywriting, blimps, or banners towed by an airplane?

For retail outlets, display windows are natural advertising vehicles. Consider using something imaginative as a display centerpiece. Joyce Moore, owner of City Lights Bookstore, borrowed an old cook stove from a customer. It anchored a number of interesting approaches. One week cookbooks tempted readers from every conceivable surface. Other times signage highlighted different types of books proclaiming "A Hot Pick," "Your Cup of Tea," and "Savory Selections."

A big budget doesn't necessarily equate to great windows. They often work better if they're creative, somewhat hokey, and not too slick. Thrift shops are fantastic and inexpensive resources for props. One women's clothing store wrote Oscar Wilde quotes in a rough way on the windows, then featured garments inside with good lighting. People would stand around at night and read all the sayings…not to mention notice the clothes. It caused quite a local stir. Is an adjacent storefront empty? You could pay the owner a few dollars a month to put a small sign and display in the window. This is a cheap way to promote a timely special or event.

For restaurants, golf courses, swimming pools, etc., street or highway signage may also be a consideration. Each city, county, and state has different regulations, so be sure to check with the proper authorities before commissioning a sign to be built or erected. In some instances, public funds may be available for state tourism signs. Talk with your state senator about this.

Outdoor advertising can be very eye catching for some businesses. This includes ads at bus stops, in sports stadiums, and messages on the sides of buses and tops of taxicabs—not to mention billboards. As commuter traffic increasingly grinds to a halt, all eyes are upon billboards. Now they even have "talking' billboards where commuters are directed to tune in to a specific frequency on their radio dials to hear a commercial message.

Trade Show Exhibiting

Trade shows, exhibits, and trade fairs provide a viable opportunity for certain businesses. This booming $10 billion industry is seeing a profusion of smaller business-to-business events that cater to narrower, more vertical audiences.

According to an American Express/National Association of Women Business Owners (www.nawbo.org) New York City survey, women-owned businesses truly understand the value of trade shows as a marketing and sales vehicle. Although only 15 percent of men-owned companies used this venue, 26 percent of women-owned businesses took advantage of trade shows as a way to increase their revenues. This is one of the few effective ways a small business can compete on a level playing field with larger firms.

To be properly exploited, however, there are tricks of the trade show. First you need to know why you're there. Seems like a silly statement, doesn't it? But many businesspeople fail to recognize their prime objective is to generate leads and make sales! Whereas developing a better image, reinforcing customer contact, meeting potential partners, finding suppliers, networking, being there because the competition is, or getting a feel for the market are all nice, they simply don't justify the costs involved.

Now let's differentiate between a local or regional trade fair—where area businesses ply their products and services to local consumers—and a full-fledged national or international trade show. We'll discuss the local event first. It may more likely apply to your needs and budget.

Taking part in local shows

These kinds of exhibits are often sponsored by chambers of commerce. There was one here in Buena Vista, Colorado, recently. There were such enterprises as photographers, travel agents, insurance brokers, banks, upholsterers, construction/remodeling firms, and hairdressers. Even nonprofit organizations and a hypnotherapist exhibited.

At such events, each entry is usually allocated booth space of about 10 feet by 10 feet, a table, and a couple of chairs. The rest is on you. One effective way to establish a versatile backdrop is to create a three-fold (or Z-shaped) screen out of corkboard (or pegboard) with a lightweight wood frame. On this you can affix photos, signs, or lightweight objects. Additionally, it will fit in the back of a pickup, SUV, or van.

How do you inexpensively make your display stand out from the others? One way is color. Bright, fluorescent posterboard, balloons, or streamers attract attention and dress things up in a hurry. Another tip is to include motion. Perhaps something could be hooked up to a small motor so it revolves or sways back and forth.

Of course, people always take heed of freebies. If there are no restrictions, some unusual finger food (Can you be more creative than cookies?) will have people rallying 'round. There are hundreds of small novelty advertising items that can be given away. Try to be more original than an imprinted key chain. Ideally, select something useful that ties in with your product, service, or store.

Many companies have a free drawing for what they do. A cleaner offers a complimentary dress or suit cleaning. A restaurant, lunch for two. A chiropractor could provide an adjustment; a music teacher, a complimentary lesson; a Web designer, a free half-hour consultation. This has an added advantage besides attracting show attendees. You also get a mailing list from the entry forms or business cards collected.

Is there something you can do in your booth to focus attention? Maybe you could give a demonstration of some sort. We noticed a hairdresser was giving manicures. Charlotte is a clever businesswoman. Being new in a small community with more than its share of beauty salons, she sought a way to get acquainted with people. By giving manicures, she literally held women captive while getting acquainted and subtly promoting her services. Similarly, a massage therapist could give free five-minute massages.

Participating in major national events

Perhaps your sights are set higher than local events. If so, choose carefully. Major trade shows involve travel expenses, accommodations and meals, plus a commitment of several days away from your business. We haven't even begun to talk about booth rental, designing and furnishing your exhibit, shipping costs, plus drayage charges for union movement of freight and setup fees. Nothing is free here. (If allowed, one alternative to cutting costs would be to team up with a colleague in a similar or complementary business and exhibit jointly.)

The fastest way to research which of the over 4,000 annual North American shows might be right for you is to go online. The following sites let you glean the dates and locations of events in your industry and get an idea if you might fit in: www.tsnn.com, www.tscentral.com, and www.expoguide.com/shows/shows.htm.

Do your homework. Gather solid advance information about an event you're considering. Is it the biggest and best in your industry? Where is it being held? Party towns like New Orleans and Las Vegas, for instance, water down the amount of business you can expect to do. Are there any restrictions that would limit what you'd like to do?

Ask the show sponsors for a prospectus and a list of last year's exhibitors; call and talk with a few. Was it worth their time and money? Also consult with attendees if possible. Their feedback can be very revealing. If you are one who really plans ahead, consider attending this year's show as a spectator so you can make a truly informed decision about participating as an exhibitor in the future. (See the adjacent trade show checklist.)

Sometimes booth location is determined on a first-come-first-served basis; other times there is a formula that gives long-time and larger exhibitors preference. If possible, select a corner booth. Then you can anticipate traffic from two directions. When you get a corner booth, take down the pipe and drape on the aisle side to create a more open, inviting atmosphere.

Furnishing your bare 10-foot by 10-foot space can be an expensive proposition. I'd suggest you rent a portable or pop-up display first to test the waters. Although the trade show will typically have a vendor they recommend, you might want to investigate the following companies before renting or buying a setup:

- Skyline Displays & Services: 800-328-2725; www.skylinedisplays.com
- Downing Displays: 800-883-1800, www.downingdisplays.com
- Featherlite Exhibits: 800-229-5533, www.featherlite.com

Much of your success is determined before you ever leave home. Contact potential customers/clients a couple of weeks ahead. Tell them your booth number and try to pin down an appointment with them. Often mailing lists of conference registrants can be rented so you can approach them with a letter, postcard, invitation, announce a contest, etc. Statistics show that 33 percent of people who visit an exhibit are influenced by pre-show mailings. They prime the pump.

It's the event organizer's responsibility to attract attendees. Once in the hall, it's your job to entice them to your booth. Check with the show management to see if free admission tickets are available that you can pass along to prime prospects.

Be sure to give your travel wardrobe careful consideration. Take comfortable shoes. Trade shows have been dubbed "the agony of de feet." Plan to dress in layers. Then if the air conditioning gets overtaxed or the heat is skimpy, you won't be miserable. Always wear something with pockets so business cards can be easily handled. I always keep my own cards in the right pocket; calling cards I gather from others go into the left. Some people keep cards in their name badge.

Today most trade show attendees are serious shoppers. They are time-deprived and don't have hours to leisurely browse. Respect that need and be prepared to acknowledge people immediately and answer questions promptly. You might even want to develop a one-page sell sheet rather than depending on your more detailed brochure. Put these materials in two different locations in your booth so if you get captured by a prospect, others can pick up literature and be on their way. Try to find out what other decision-makers are involved; 60 percent of visitors share information with at least two other key players in their company after the show. Get these other names for follow-up.

For more guidance on how to design exhibits that sell, discover trade show trends, capitalize on your investment, and generally exhibit successfully, go to www.tradeshowresearch.com.

Although generating leads and sales is your primary task, trade shows afford other opportunities. They are supreme networking arenas. Here you are shoulder to shoulder with everybody who is anybody in your industry. We've been successful in personally approaching important people who are normally protected by gatekeepers on their own organizational turf. You'll meet colleagues here you won't bump into for the rest of the year. Perhaps you can explore a way to partner for mutual benefit.

Trade shows are also fertile ground for detecting what the competition is up to. Many shows sponsor educational sessions for the attendees. By monitoring some of these yourself you can also get a better grasp of your prospects' mind-set and needs.

There is that old saying about all work and no play and what it does to Jack. Never fear, Jills. Every trade show has a social whirl surrounding it. Some of the parties and cocktail receptions will be sponsored and open; others are invitation-only gatherings. If you remembered to pack some relaxing cassette tapes and lotion for sore feet, you may also find pleasure in retreating to your hotel room. If time allows, why not enjoy the sights of the city you are visiting? Just remember that exhibiting takes enormous stamina. You must constantly be "on" and "up." Don't get so sidetracked with the social aspects that you're ineffective when it's time to do business.

Most shows have some opportunity to meet the press. Big events often have a pressroom where you can leave a media kit; others allow you to prepare information that they dole out to the press. Because editors and reporters need to know what's new, they attend trade shows in droves. This may afford you an outstanding opportunity to be mentioned in a news or product story.

That's what happened to Annie Hurlbut's Peruvian Connection catalog. What began as a small wholesale business mushroomed into a prosperous mail-order business virtually overnight when a writer from *The New York Times* met Annie at an apparel show. The story hit the front page of the *NYT* Style section and generated more than 5,000 catalog requests. Today Peruvian Connection mails 6 million catalogs a year domestically and about 4 million internationally.

Renting a booth at a good show is akin to leasing space in a shopping mall. At a carefully targeted trade show, you can accomplish more in two, three, or four days than you could in six months of selling on the road. A recent study by the Laboratory of Advertising Performance/McGraw-Hill Research estimates each sales call costs approximately $230. A qualified trade show lead costs $107. Of course, it's paramount these *leads be worked* promptly after the show. You may also want to rent a machine to swipe attendees' badges to capture the lead on an imprinter or handheld computer system.

Although the subject can't possibly be covered fully here, do establish written goals. Is your objective to write $50,000 worth of business? How many new customers or clients do you intend to secure? With

Trade Show Checklist

- 10-foot by 10-foot booth
- Electricity/Internet access for lights, computer, business card reader, etc.
- Tables, chairs, display board (or actual booth set-up)
- Computer: CPU, monitor, keyboard (or laptop), and printer
- Carpet
- Product
- Posters, samples, etc.
- Promotional materials: business cards, catalogs, flyers, price sheets, giveaways, etc.
- Miscellaneous: wastebasket, paper towels, office supplies
- Drinking water, refreshments
- Copies of booth rental agreement, furnishing order, electricity order, etc.
- Plane reservations
- Hotel reservations

careful planning, definite goal-setting, and diligent follow-up, trade shows or regional fairs may open lucrative new doors for you.

Telemarketing: Yes, Nice Girls *Do*

There is no doubt about it: You can ring up extra results with telemarketing. Now don't tune me out until you hear me out. Telemarketing is much more than the obnoxious salesperson who calls during dinner to hawk something you don't want. The fact is, it can enhance your profits in six different ways.

First, it is a cost-effective way to follow-up leads. (Perhaps the ones you got from exhibiting at a regional or national trade show.) Over the phone you can quickly qualify prospects to determine who's hot and who's not.

Second, the telephone allows you to stay in contact with existing customers/clients. You can use it to herald the arrival of an innovative service you know they might like, introduce a new product line, or canvas active accounts on behalf of a special offer.

Third, it provides a quick way to activate old or forgotten accounts. Because it is far cheaper to do more business with an existing account than it is to find a new one, this is a key point. One phone call may reveal a simple problem you can quickly resolve, thus bringing the person or company back into the fold.

Fourth, how about using your telephone as a goodwill tool? In today's busy high-tech world, few firms ever call and thank a patron for their business. Nor do they tactfully suggest the individual might want to mention their positive experience to a friend, relative, or colleague. Because word-of-mouth is a top motivator, such referrals can quickly boost the bottom line.

Fifth, the phone can be used for prospecting. At its worst, cold-calling is done indiscriminately by low-paid individuals who work in "boiler rooms." At its best, it is handled by skilled professionals who actively *help* targeted prospects procure things they need.

Using your telephone in lieu of personal sales calls often makes perfect sense. It's important to stay in touch with many accounts. The telephone is a reasonable substitute for face-to-face appointments. And some companies use the phone to supplement personal contact. They check back monthly to make sure all is well and to service their customers.

Because the banking industry has been freed of the restricting government binds that tie, Citicorp has employed telemarketing very successfully. They decided to introduce The Home Equity second-mortgage loan in the Baltimore area. The problem was they were not well-recognized beyond their home base of New York. Using a detailed script, bank representatives were able to launch the new product triumphantly.

Having a script as a guideline is helpful. Parroting it like a dummy is disastrous. Find a happy medium between something that sounds phony and memorized, and completely freewheeling it. Train your associates by using excerpts of actual phone conversations that require their reactions. List possible objections and develop ways to overcome them. If you call only three people a day, at the end of a year you will have contacted over 1,000 new prospects! Should you plan an extensive calling campaign you may want to buy a headset that allows you to talk hands-free.

Sixth, treat inbound calls as telemarketing possibilities. When someone has phoned you, they are in a receptive mood. Yet we usually conclude the call with no effort at suggestive selling. This is an ideal time to trade up. Train yourself, your telephone receptionist, customer service people, technical specialists, every associate who comes in contact with a phone to suggest more expensive options or complementary services. And actual selling can be as simple as, "Mr. Jones, we have a special offer this week just for our phone customers…" Every inquiry is an opportunity.

Telesales in its various forms can work well for many organizations and professionals. Another plus is its speed. While your competition is trying out various ads and direct-mail approaches, you can be reeling in their customers. It may well prove a major component of your marketing mix. Remember to "reach out and sell someone."

Novelty Items and Giveaways

You've collected dozens of these over the years. They are the pens, thermometers, litter bags, matchbooks, combs, bottle openers, and key chains various merchants pass out. These advertising specialties can be both goodwill builders and useful sales tools. The intent of such gifts is that they generate a feeling of appreciation and favorable remembrance of the giver.

What are the requirements of such novelties? They should be inexpensive, such as $2 a dozen, $3.50 per 144, $55 for 1000. They must be useful—in the office, home, car—or for fun. They represent reminder advertising, such as the calendar mailed at year-end by banks, insurance agents, and real estate offices. They should tie in with the giver, either symbolically or because they're imprinted with the firm's name, logo, and Web site.

Over the years I've observed astute companies use novelties in conjunction with direct mail. One temporary help service sent a mailing each month to other businesses. Each was different and contained an inexpensive gift cleverly matched with the copy in the letter. One I recall was a jar opener. The letter talked about how they could "open" our employee horizons by providing qualified temporary personnel. I remember. And yet I received this letter over two decades ago. Add to that the fact I'm on more mailing lists than Campbell has soups. But this campaign still sticks in my mind. By adding a novelty item and doing repeated monthly mailings, Kelly Services made their communication memorable. You might use this same technique.

Let's allow our imagination's to run wild. A toy company has "goo goo eyes" for $1.10 a dozen. What fun an inventive optometrist could have with these! A coin eraser is a natural for banks or mortgage companies that want to help patrons erase their money/loan blues. A dentist might purchase a quantity of "goofy teeth." There are assorted badges you could include with a mailing or pin on a youngster who has been a good patient.

Thirteen-inch back scratchers are available by the dozen. If you depend on referral business, this is a natural. Send one with a note saying, "Thanks for scratching my back. Now I want to return the favor." (You could even wrap a $5 or $20 bill around the handle, depending on how valuable the referral was.)

Your advertising choices are as varied as wildflowers in spring. It might be a classified ad, full-blown display spread, an advertorial, trade show participation, telemarketing, or specialty items, but keep one thing in mind: there is an old expression that says "out of sight, out of mind." Don't depend on advertising to solve all your marketing problems. It won't. Do let it play a supporting role in the drama of your business. Use it, monitor it, revise it. Now let's move on to meet another of the important marketing cast of characters: irreverent publicity ploys.

Web Sites, *Wisdom,* and Whimsey

Need a fresh way to plan your PR or ad campaign? Try storyboarding. Walt Disney used storyboards to plan all his movies. Ad agencies also employ this technique to plan commercials. Get a 4-foot by 8-foot piece of foam board from an art store and several sizes of Post-it Notes in various colors. Across the top of the board, use the largest notes for major parts of your marketing plan. Below each, use smaller and smaller Post-its for each progressively lower-level idea, contact, or whatever. Use just a few keywords to capture the concept. Because Post-it Notes are easy to move around, you have complete flexibility and your whole project is available at a glance.

●●●●●●●●

Did you know…
That Lillian Vernon, the queen of catalogs, started out with a $495 ad in the September 1951 issue of Seventeen magazine? Her gimmick was that the items could be monogrammed with two initials. She received $32,000 in orders. Now that's results! "In those early days," says Vernon, "I didn't think much about being a female entrepreneur. Starting my own company was something I did because I had to: There was virtually no other way for a woman to earn a living wage in the jobs open to them 49 years ago." Her advice for today's female business owners includes: Believe in yourself, believe in your dreams, say no to naysayers, and go for it!

●●●●●●●●

Some restaurants are masters of captive advertising. Ever noticed the little information tents on the tables at some eating establishments? When my husband and I had dinner before the holidays at a local upscale restaurant, we observed a table tent that read: "Antero Grill Gift Certificates. Thank valued employees, loyal clients, and service people. The perfect stocking stuffer for friends and family." How's that for suggestive selling? And when we stopped for lunch at a Country Kitchen while traveling, the place mat was a colorful display titled "Sugar and Spice" that depicted a tempting array of desserts.

●●●●●●●

Talk about communications skills! A husband, determined to prove to his wife that women talk more than men, showed her a study indicating men use on the average only 15,000 words a day—whereas women use 30,000 words a day. She thought about this for a minute then replied, "Women use twice as many words as men because they have to repeat everything they say."
His reply: "What?"

●●●●●●●

Have a grammar question as you're writing that ad? Short queries about writing, correct usage, and syntax can be directed to various universities and community colleges. Simply go to www.tc.cc.va.us/vabeach/writcent/wchome.html. (Well, that isn't so simple after all, is it?) They are listed alphabetically by state and also include days and hours of operation. If you would like a copy, send a #10 SASE to Grammar Hotline Directory, Tidewater Community College Writing Center, Bayside Building B-205, 1700 College Crescent, Virginia Beach, VA 23456, or visit their Web site at www.tc.cc.va.us/writcent/gh/hotlinol.htm.

Extravagant site helps those traveling the roadway to success. The Women's Business Center (http://onlinewbc.org/) has terrific information on learning about business, running your company, information exchanges, and resources. This site is the realization of a vision created by SBA's Office of Women Business Ownership that is shared by the North Texas Women's Business Development Center and Women's Business Centers across America. These partners saw the value of bringing together the public and private sectors to further the empowerment of women everywhere. They do an excellent job. In their Marketing Mall there are 16 different categories, each overflowing with meaty articles. Read 'em and reap!

●●●●●●●

Comment from boss to his assistant: "This project is so important that we can't let things that are more important interfere with it." (How's that for sound logic?)

●●●●●●●

Independent local merchant beats the chain competition. When LensCrafters and Pearle Vision started moving into the Pittsburgh area in 1989, Norman Childs' eyeglass enterprise, Eyetique, was threatened by the deep pockets of the chains. His solution was to go upscale…way upscale…to such fashion labels as Oliver Peoples, Lunor, and Matsuda. And to develop an unusual marketing strategy, Childs decided to feature local celebrities in his ad campaign. A player for the Pittsburgh Steelers (the son-in-law of his photographer) was the first. Since then the ads have featured the fashion editor of *Pittsburgh* magazine, other journalists, local musicians, plus radio, TV, and sports personalities. It became a local status symbol to appear in an Eyetique ad. What did it do for the business? It has gone from five to 25 employees and from $500,000 to about $2.5 million.

Display your display ads! To get more mileage out of a major ad, clip it, add a nice mat and frame, then hang it in a place that gets lots of foot traffic, such as by the elevator or near the restrooms. All these extra impressions are free. If you're a retailer, you could also blow it up and put it in your store window.

●●●●●●●

Why do men like smart women?
Because opposites attract.

●●●●●●●

Woman builds $3 million business using flyers. When Andrea Arena launched 2 Places At 1 Time, Inc., she had only $5,000 and a dream. Today her concierge service has sites in 60 locations in the U.S. and Canada. The humble flyer started her on the way to fame and fortune. Andrea rented computer time and printed advertising flyers at Kinko's. Then she set about putting them under windshield wipers in church parking lots on Sundays and in uptown corporate parking lots during the week. It worked so well she counts Motorola and Arthur Anderson Consulting as clients.

Meet Scoop Cybersleuth—Your Internet guide. Scoop Cybersleuth is the Internet's ace reporter. He'll help you find some great sites such as those for the U.S. government and politics, state and local governments, reference and demographics, journalism tools, academic experts, and on and on. Tune in to him at http://www.courierpress.com/courier//scoop/.

●●●●●●●

A woman's place is anywhere she wants it to be.

●●●●●●●

Part II

Illuminating Publicity Techniques for Femme Fatales and Grande Dames

CHAPTER 4

To Get Famous, Be Shameless: Irreverent Publicity Ploys

Many businesspeople think advertising is the answer to their prayers. Those who subscribe to this theory miss the most viable business-generating medium of all. Remember the phenomenal success of the pet rock years ago? Not a penny was spent to advertise this product; it was all accomplished through publicity. Today, it's publicize or perish! This is all about going from media zero to media hero—how to get good at getting PR.

The Power of Print

An article in *Business Marketing* points out editorial coverage is typically at least twice as credible as advertising. Yet, the public relations cost of placing the story is a mere fraction of equivalent advertising. Yes, for entrepreneurs with budgets as tight as shrink-to-fit jeans, the answer is publicity.

Women and men in professional practice are also recognizing this is the way to bring home the bacon. Once viewed as a questionable activity by many CPA firms, public relations has—according to the firms themselves—evolved into a necessary function in today's competitive business environment. Law firms are exchanging country club selling for more creative forms of business development. Those who market nonprofits are also sensitive to public relations' (PR's) merits. The beauty is anyone who knowledgeably and methodically goes after media attention can share in the windfall.

In this chapter I provide the know-how; you have to consciously apply it. I can't teach you to charm the lard off a hog, but I can give you the skills to competently publicize even a humble sow's ear and put the profits in your silk purse. You'll be given tips on how to master the art of creating effective news releases and press conferences. Articles, columns, letters to the editor, and op-ed essays also give you instant visibility and credibility. Discover here how to work this facet of PR. And how to use a *book* as one of the most awesome prospecting tools imaginable.

We'll look at a variety of PR techniques. These are free or inexpensive ways to get your organization noticed. A good PR practitioner approaches her task like a good plumber. You've gotta use the right tools for the job. One time a plunger might do it; the next it takes a snake or even an air jetter. But one way or another, the blockage is eliminated and the flow reestablished. That's the purpose of public relations: to accomplish a constant flow of exposure for you. It's not a sprint though; it's a marathon—something you want to do perpetually.

Does it work? When Sandra Beckwith created The Do(o)little Report, a newsletter for women designed to explain male behavior in a lighthearted way, she sent a press release to a national media list of about 400. *USA Today* ran an item in its "Lifeline" column a week after her mailing went out. Two weeks later, it hit the *Wall Street Journal*. A couple of months later, *USA Today* picked it up a second time for a large feature. She also appeared on *Eye to Eye with Connie Chung*, *The Vicki Show*, and in various syndicated newspaper articles. "The publicity I generated in the first year, spending less than $5,000 for printing and postage, yielded more than $4.5 million in media exposure," Sandy reports. (The $4.5 million is what she would have had to spend for equivalent ad space and air time.)

But the story doesn't end there. The publicity generated a book contract from a major publisher (*Why Can't a Man Be More Like a Woman?*) plus professional speaking requests and corporate offers to serve as a spokesperson. In addition, she won a national public relations award, The Silver Anvil, from the Public Relations Society of America. Sandy goes on to say, "Such a simple and inexpensive publicity plan positioned me as an expert on gender dynamics with the press—a role I continue to enjoy and embrace today."

News Releases That Add Pizzazz Without Puff

Editors readily admit the majority of what you read in newspapers and magazines is the result of information provided by outside sources. They depend on "news releases" (also called press releases) to keep them abreast of industry happenings. It's estimated 70 percent of all news is *planted!* Releases can also lead to articles, a subject treated shortly.

The first ingredient of a news release is news. Although this sounds like a simplistic statement, it pinpoints the reason most never get into print. When information is old, it isn't news. It's history. When a piece is too self-serving, it also isn't news. It's puffery.

What are some newsworthy topics? Openings, expansions, moves, new products, services added, community activities, contests sponsored, awards received—even election to regional or national office of one of the principals. Company milestones—such as a 10th, 25th, or 50th anniversary—are appropriate for stories. If you, as the CEO, give a speech, this can often be parlayed into news. Another angle for coverage is studies or surveys conducted and trend forecasts.

When writing releases, there are several things to consider. You never know how much of what you submit will be used. For that reason, it is important to get the primary details at the beginning. The five "W's"—who, what, when, where, and why—should be contained in the first paragraph or two. When editors are short on space, they cut releases from the bottom up. Although some editors rewrite releases, many are too harried to do so. A good release will be printed virtually as is; a bad one hits the round file.

This medium demands short, snappy copy. If you can state a problem or concern with which the editor and readers can identify—and how you can *solve* it—your chances for acceptance are better. Begin with an intriguing statement, startling statistic, or provocative question. Add supportive information in a descending order. The goal is to get your message across no matter how much is sliced off the bottom.

One workable way to give your release fresh pizzazz is to use quotes. To make a release sound like promotional copy is to announce its death. However, stating a major point in a succinct conversational quotation lends variety and believability. Be wary of using jargon or riddling it with acronyms, however. And remember if they snooze, you loose. Recipients quickly doze off when your release reads more like VCR instructions.

Topics for News Releases

- The opening of your store, firm, or office
- Announcement of new management
- An anniversary
- The hiring or promotion of a key staff member
- Being awarded a new contract
- Business expansion or remodeling
- Adding a new type of service
- The owner receiving an award, accreditation, or other honor
- Timely tie-ins with national holidays
- Demonstrations, open houses
- Owner's appointment or election to a board of directors
- Financial news—your annual report is released
- Having an article or book published
- Special event or contest announcement
- Trend evaluations
- Surveys conducted
- Controversial rebuttals
- Joint partnership with another local firm
- Bringing in a guest speaker, expert, or artist
- Involvement/support for a charitable cause

Carefully hone a headline that commands attention. Try doing your headline at the end because after you've written the whole release, it will be easier to come up with a punchy one. You might say something like "Exclusive report...," "Revealed:," "7 Secrets for...," "5 Untold tips...." Put it in bold or capital letters. Some say enclosing it in quotation marks adds impact.

Presentation is important. Photocopy your release on letterhead, or have it printed on stationery. News releases, by the way, should not exceed two double-spaced pages; one-pagers often are better. (You can cheat and use 1½ line spacing to keep them that length.)

There are things you can include to increase your chances of being selected for publication. One is an appropriate photograph. (More about that in a minute.) Another is a clip sheet or computer disk with reproducible artwork. This might include your logo, an illustration, a chart, or other art.

It is easy to customize releases for different media. Doing a versioned news release only entails altering the headline and first paragraph in your computer. Then you have a message specifically tailored for each recipient.

To whom do you send this package? That depends. If you offer business services, the business editor of the closest major daily newspaper would be appropriate. A boutique or window-washing business would do better contacting the lifestyle editor. If in doubt, go to the managing editor. Spend time updating your mailing list before embarking on a campaign. The most carefully developed release is useless unless it is delivered into the hands of the proper person.

Using electronic mail to send news releases can save you time and money. Just one click and your news release can be on its way to dozens of people! (But remember that one click of the mouse is all it takes for that person to delete your release—often without even opening your e-mail.) So how do you give your e-mail news releases a better chance of being read? Here are some tips:

- Avoid dull subject lines. Don't put "For Immediate Release" in the subject line. Use something brief, relevant, and intriguing.

- Don't include a "CC" (carbon copy) list in your e-mail that's a mile long. Learn how to use the blind copy function of your program.

- Avoid using repeated dollar signs, all capitals, and exclamation marks in your subject line or your news release will look like the latest get-rich-quick scam.

- Never send your press release as an attachment. That's a sure way to get your release into the recipient's recycle bin. Not only does it take longer to read an attachment (the recipient has to save it to disk, switch over to a word processing program, hunt for the directory file it was saved in), but attachments can sometimes carry viruses. Many people won't even open them.

Our technological age has now made possible video news releases (VNRs). This allows you to spread the word visually. Because of costs, these are beyond the reach of many businesses. They can run as little as $10,000 or as much as $80,000 to produce and distribute to TV stations. But be sure your product or service hooks into a hot public policy issue or larger story. Otherwise your video will look like a commercial.

By the way, some companies are now using videos as sales tools. In just 11 or 12 minutes you can provide prospects with more information than if you filled volumes with print. It's an exciting and underused medium.

If you decide to consider this alternative, before choosing a producer, look at demos that relate to your industry, service, or objective. Finding one individual who can write, direct, and produce a VNR is the perfect combination. It is also helpful if she has a background in broadcast news. There is no point in creating a spectacular VNR if it never airs. It must be designed not only to inform but also to promote, influence, and motivate.

A Picture Says a Thousand Words

Photographs are prime tools in a clever PR effort. Let's look at photo releases, which are closely related to the typical print news release. They consist of an attention-grabbing photo combined with a tightly written caption.

There are tough editorial standards here. Editors want quality pictures that project clarity, simplicity, and creativity. They prefer action and human interest shots. In some cases using a visual element to establish size and scale will win their favor. Suggest the photographer add new interest by changing his or her point of view. Shoot down from a ladder or up from floor level. This adds a fresh perspective to your presentation.

Some shrewd people arrange to be photographed in the presence of someone important. This is a reverse twist of "guilt by association." The idea is people will perceive them as important because they are in the same photograph with a dignitary or celebrity. Famed California publicist Irwin Zukor was at a party on a movie lot recently when he met radio talk show host/therapist and best-selling author, Dr. Laura Schlessinger. He immediately asked her to autograph a book…using his back as a prop while he grinned over his shoulder for the camera. He carries his camera everywhere and loves being caught on candid camera with a celebrity or two. He simply asks, "Would you mind if I took a photo with you?" Irwin says he's never been turned down.

Although requirements used to be strictly black and white, today a stunning color shot might capture a magazine cover position or the front page of a newspaper section. These are coveted. One editor estimates the cover photo subject typically outpulls the average interior black-and-white photo subject four to one.

It is wise not to use people in your pictures until they have signed a model release. Your attorney can easily provide one. This even goes for photos that show a customer or client.

Once the photo has fueled the reader's interest, it is the caption's job to leverage that interest into an inquiry or an order. Use an economy of words. Choose colorful, arresting ones. Be sure your company name is included in the caption. Always affix a label to the back of your photo that states what the picture is of, so if it is separated from your other materials they can be reunited.

If you're shooting for an ad or brochure, pay particular attention to the composition of your picture and the written copy that goes with it. One ad for an electronics catalog that was stressing "technical support to fit your needs" and touting its well-trained support staff, pictured a technician on the phone *reading* to a customer from a computer manual. It didn't exactly portray their knowledgeable staff.

If you can't afford an expensive photo shoot, take a leaf out of Alexandra Volkmann's book. The CEO of Heavy Duty Skin Products, she needed art for her branding campaign. Her grandiose vision was a picture of a woman working as a mechanic on a vintage Cadillac. Acting on her dream, Alexandra convinced a dealer to lend her a car for an afternoon. Next she struck a creative deal with a professional photographer: He would do the shoot for free. In exchange, he could use images of her legs (as long as good taste prevailed) in a shoe campaign he was doing. Way to go, girl!

Creating a Memorable Media Kit

A media kit—also called a "press kit"—is to a PR person what the black bag was to the old-time doctor. It is an organized collection of all the materials that may interest a member of the media. Information is typically inserted into colored presentation folders with two pockets. Although some firms have customized folders printed, a label affixed to the front will work to identify your company. Attach your business card in the slots provided in the inner pocket.

Flexible in nature, press kit contents vary with the occasion. The backbone is your brochure. There are several other pieces of promotional literature that can complement this. In some industries, a corporate or organization profile is called for. Such background information is useful to editors in fleshing out their stories. This essentially gives a history of how the firm originated and what its primary focus is. It may also hint at future plans.

A personal biography of the CEO, senior partners, or owner may also be appropriate. Pertinent photos are appreciated by editors. This is a good place to make use of any previous publicity you've garnered. Include copies of articles by or about you. Such third-party endorsements always carry extra clout.

Good news bears repeating: "Reprints have been a wonderful marketing tool for us," says Kirk Perron, the owner of a San Luis Obispo, California, chain of blended-to-order smoothie shops called the Juice Club.

When putting together your media kit, don't overlook pieces authored by others—even if they don't mention you. If they make a good case in support of your cause, they can be useful in winning attention. Of course, a news release highlighting the main reason for the event is a necessity.

But you often don't need a fancy media kit when seeking exposure. Consider providing an entire feature about yourself. This makes the reporter's job so easy! Pack it with juicy quotes and include black-and-white glossies. It's best to center such stories around a timeless topic. This is called an "evergreen" piece.

A simple, one-page Fact Sheet can also be useful. Include a description of your service, information about the primary spokesperson, and how to reach you. This is ideal because it can be faxed to peak a media person's interest. Fax is still as essential to business today as the telephone was at the turn of the 20th century.

Getting "in Decent" Exposure
With a Press Conference

Hosting a press conference sounds glamorous and important. In reality, it's a lot of work and could be the wrong move. Before talking about how to pull off such a feat, let's discuss why you might *not* want to. Editors are deluged with invitations to these events. Many of them are dog-and-pony shows—just plain bor-ring! You don't want to get such a reputation with the media. So unless you have something truly newsworthy, stick with a news release or photo release.

For those who deem their news of significant value to warrant a press conference, here are some clues: Pay particular attention to when you schedule your event. Check out pending local activities to avoid going head-to-head with something—or someone—else of note. (No one will come to your press conference if the Pope is arriving or a well-liked area legislator is announcing his or her intention to run for governor.) Call the Associated Press and United Press International area bureau closest to you and check their "day book" for conflicts. You can get their local numbers in the telephone directory. Drive the main route to your site yourself to be sure there are no traffic hangups during the time slot you've planned.

The choice of location will also influence participation. Rather than the usual hotel conference room, consider something different. What about a historical mansion, museum, or yacht setting? Don't book a meeting place sight unseen, however. Mirrored walls will play havoc with TV lighting. Pillars are hard to work around. Also consider noise problems. An air conditioner that sounds like a jet engine will drown out your carefully prepared remarks.

Notify the media two to three weeks ahead of time. Include enough detail in your invitation so editors can intelligently determine whether your news affects their readers. Also include an SASE for their response.

On the day of the event, have plenty of staff available. While a couple of gracious secretaries can sign people in, company officials are needed to mingle and motivate. Friendships cultivated at such gatherings between editors and executives often result in future expert quotes or feature articles.

Editors will want to ask questions, challenge claims, and clarify points. In addition to a short verbal presentation, followed by a question and answer period, provide them with a media kit. Some sort of a souvenir of the occasion also goes over well if this commemorates a special event.

Perhaps you should consider an intermediate visual strategy. That's what Pamela Kostmayer, a Washington, DC, PR pro did. She represented a group of California apparel makers and importers who opposed a bill designed to restrict textile imports. Kostmayer dressed a delivery person in a panda suit and delivered teddy bears to every lawmaker on Capitol Hill. The bears carried current price tags—and higher ones that would have to go into effect if the proposed legislation were enacted. This was followed up with socks cautioning the bill would "sock it to America." Lastly, neckerchiefs warned the legislation would "choke the American farmer." The visual gimmicks attracted attention and paved the way for lobbyists working against the bill to present their story.

Letters to the Editor

Writing letters to the editor provides a less demanding method for attracting attention. Rather than being bound to a schedule, you simply submit a short letter in response to timely local issues or events in the news. Using the written word in this way can assure you of more windfall visibility. These are well-read platforms for getting your message, and your name, into the public's consciousness.

Done on a fairly regular basis, this helps establish you as a mover and shaker in the community. Be sure not only to end the letters with your personal name but also include your business name. Not all papers will publish this but some may.

Many people think because letters to the editor are short, they are easy. Nothing could be further from the truth. It is much harder to distill your message into 150 words than it is to strew it over three or four pages. Every word serves a purpose in letters to the editor. It's an outstanding training ground for developing a forceful, pithy writing style.

Another editorial showcase possibility is electronic media. We've all heard the general manager of a TV or radio station spout the station's position on a certain issue. Perhaps you've never tuned in to the comment that follows: "This station welcomes opposing views from responsible spokespersons." Does this give you any ideas? If what they said piques your professional interest—and makes you bristle—this could be a wonderful opportunity to get thousands of dollars worth of free air time. Those with a genuine concern and a desire for higher visibility should write the station and request an airing.

Newspaper Op-Ed Essays Build Visibility

The newspaper "op-ed" (short for opposite editorial) page refers to a physical location rather than an analytical or political position. It doesn't mean that pieces necessarily oppose the editorial point of view of the paper, rather it literally denotes where these pieces are found: opposite the editorial page.

This is a forum for opinion and observation that has come into its own over the last couple of decades as a wonderful vehicle for bringing attention to issues, individuals, and companies. These brief essays have been deemed by publicists as an effective and overlooked means of gaining visibility. It's a place where grassroots go-getters mingle with political pundits, where many people have their "public say." It's not just a place to rebut, settle accounts, serve notice, or exact revenge.

Pat Eisemann, vice president and director of publicity at Scribner, definitely believes in them. Broadcast media, such as *The Today Show*, reads the op-eds for possible guests—and not just those in *The New York Times*. Eisemann said *USA Today* creates a big stir for Scribner.

Op-ed page editors need fresh voices with new thoughts, classy writing, mind-bending revelations. "I like to think of the op-ed page as the people's page," says Diane Clark of *The San Diego Union Tribune*. It's where an informed outsider is granted a forum.

Businesswomen will find here a venue ideal for addressing their passions. And since op-ed pieces carry a bio line, you and your business are plugged as you sound off about topics close to your heart. A citation in the editorial pages can yield dramatic results.

Because of the immediacy of newspapers, one no longer has to submit a query or an article, then wait months to learn if an editor is interested. Newspapers make decisions in hours or days not months.

Present your credentials in a strong cover letter. Most op-ed pieces are the purview of guest experts with proven knowledge on important issues of the day. If you've got the background to write about a topic, flaunt it! And include both a day and evening phone number so you're easily reached.

Be pro-active rather than reactive. A forward-thinking PR practitioner anticipates. For instance, is Congress voting on a bill relevant to what you do? Then have a "reaction" piece already in the hands of a key op-ed editor *before* the vote.

I'm in the process of updating my one-of-a-kind *National Directory of Newspaper Op-Ed Page Editors*. It will soon be available in both a hard copy version and an easy-to-use database format. So if this venue appeals to you, drop me an e-mail to Marilyn@About-Books.com or send a note requesting info on the op-ed to Marilyn Ross, POB 1500, Buena Vista, CO 81211. I'll alert you as soon as it's available.

Contributing Articles and Columns

A large California CPA firm indicated they had received "tangible referrals on new clients from articles in the press." Speakers and seminar givers credit published articles as opening new avenues for speaking engagements. Consultants successfully prospect for new clients by contributing articles to targeted publications. So do other professionals and retail store owners with various "how-to" pieces.

You are an *expert* in your field. Why not capitalize on your specialized knowledge by publishing articles about this subject you know so well? It will give you visibility, credibility, and profitability.

There are several types of possible articles. How-to's are one of the easiest. You simply provide step-by-step instruction on how to accomplish something. Some people fear if they do this, they will lose business instead of gaining it because they are revealing their trade secrets. Quite the contrary. Most people recognize there is specialized expertise involved and you are a bona fide authority. Thus, you position yourself as a leader in the industry—someone they want working for them.

I found this to be the case time after time. Providing complimentary articles is an important facet of our publicity program. Never have we been short-circuited when openly sharing our specialized knowledge. In fact, our largest client came to us as a result of a how-to article.

Another popular article format is the case history. It explains how your product or service was used by a customer or client to solve a problem. It traces the path of an actual satisfied user. (Be sure to get their permission to write about them, however.)

Round-up articles are another common approach. This is a collection of several similar situations. It might offer an industry overview featuring input from you and two or three colleagues. Or it could be about several of your clients/customers and their different applications of your service. It may address the same subject but from far-flung geographical locations—how mental health practices differ in the United States, Canada, and England, for instance.

Still a different approach is the personality profile. Many airline magazines, trade journals, and general business publications run stories about colorful CEOs and entrepreneurs. This is a great way to generate publicity.

Lists are another great angle: seven ways to easier and faster cleaning (by a maid service), 10 things your children will love to do this summer (by a preschool), five ways to stretch your wardrobe (by a retail store).

A further recommendation is to contact likely magazines and ask for a copy of their annual editorial calendar. This pinpoints the major topics they will be discussing in future editions. When you see a subject that correlates with what you do, think about article slants. Then contact the managing editor with your idea.

Finally, seek ways to align your organization with a "hot" issue already in the news. Then you can piggyback on the attention it incites. A fast-thinking real estate agent did just that when Wall Street took a dive on "Black Monday." She told the media how her phone was constantly ringing with people who were bailing out of the stock market and looking into real estate investments.

Although articles can be offered for sale, it usually works best to donate them. Of course, you're not providing your article without getting something in return. Strike a deal that they will list information about how to reach you at the end of the piece. Some aggressive types ask for more. They try for a free display ad to run in the same edition as well.

Before writing a complete piece, you may want to send a *query letter*. This is a one-page sales letter explaining the scope of your proposed article, your credentials for writing it, and why it will appeal to the publication's readership.

When a respected publication prints information about a company, it is as if the editor is endorsing the company. This effectively sells prospects on the firm's or store's reputation, quality, reliability, and expertise. It sets your company apart from its competitors and creates instant credibility.

Although a story in *Forbes* or *Fortune* is understandably craved by business entities, "little things can mean a lot." The big client we previously spoke of came to us, not as a result of a powerhouse publication, but from something placed in a carefully targeted newsletter with a circulation of less than 5,000!

Writing a regular newspaper column is another excellent way to focus attention on what you have to offer. This is especially viable for health practitioners, financial experts, and consultants who want to expand their practices. It can also apply to owners of businesses who could provide consumer information—cleaning tips or automobile maintenance, for instance. Do be aware, however, that a column means repetitive work. As opposed to a feature article, column material must be churned out every week and by a strict deadline. Be sure you have enough to say and the time to say it before you commit to 52 columns a year!

Recycle, Repeat, Reuse

Want more than 15 minutes of fame? The old axiom, "Success breeds success" is so true. The media likes to climb on a moving bandwagon. Consequently the more exposure you get, the more exposure you'll get. And you can see to it that this happens by recycling your publicity. Reprints allow you to impress. Inform. Motivate. Educate. Persuade.

Recycle any print coverage that appears. It doesn't matter that the original publication's circulation base was smaller than your neighborhood. What counts is what *you* do with it! Although an amateur will be satisfied with what she gets, a pro will milk it for all it's worth to stay in the limelight. She'll get double and triple the bang for her publicity buck.

But how? "Do a mailing right away," advise home-based business gurus Paul and Sarah Edwards. "Use a copy of the article as the lead for your mailing. Accompany it with a letter or announcement that proclaims 'Look what we're up to.'" They remind us that publicity is as much about opening doors to future possibilities as it is about obtaining immediate sales.

We have a specific strategy for recycling our publicity. Because we belong to many associations that publish newsletters that include "Member News," we have all those newsletter editors on a database. When something happens, we write a short generic news release—and customize the beginning to match their format. Then mail, fax, or e-mail it immediately. Publicity is sort of like a boomerang: You have to throw it before it can come back. Also consider being incestuous: Do a press release about your press release!

Get copies of everything written or broadcast about your company. It's important to keep track of your clips. If you're doing a local campaign, you can probably track down any articles with an observant eye, a few phone calls, and perhaps a Web search. For a broader press campaign, use a clipping service to capture what is said about you.

Newspaper and magazine articles are often missed the first time around. Yet articles make people think your company is important and unique because the publication chose to write about you. Obtaining reprints provides a way for you to make sure existing and potential clients, customers, suppliers, bankers, stockholders, etc. get a look.

Most magazines offer a reprinting service for somewhere between 75 cents and $1 apiece for a four-color reprint. Have them add your logo, address, phone number, and Web site for added impact. Also consider matting and framing a copy to hang in your reception area, restaurant, or shop. If you own a retail establishment, put copies on the counter with a "Take One" sign. By doing so, you turn unbiased editorial material into a marketing piece that delivers real impact.

These print pieces solidify your credibility. They provide an ideal, low-key reason to get in front of prospects and should be used as a mailing for anyone you're trying to woo. Send copies to current clients or customers as well. Use them as enclosures in virtually everything you mail. Use quotes from the piece in your marketing and sales materials. Mention any articles in your company newsletter. Send a copy to your alumni magazine. Obtain permission to put them up on your Web site. And when soliciting additional publicity, include what has already been done. This helps establish your newsworthiness.

Another innovative way to use reprints is to make audio recordings of them. Put a customized introduction in front of the article and a call to action at the end with contact information. Then distribute these tapes at sales presentations, trade shows, in direct mail packages—

112

you name it. Not everyone has time to read newspapers or trade magazines, but virtually everybody travels to and from work and can use that time to listen to your message.

Producing a Newsletter

An external company newsletter has two purposes: to stay in touch with current prospects and to generate new leads in a cost-effective way. Although many people toss direct-mail packages in the wastebasket without so much as a guilty twinge, they hesitate to do so with a newsletter. Therein lies your power.

There are numerous decisions once you've made the commitment to produce an external newsletter. How often will you publish? It is a good idea to begin conservatively; you can always increase the frequency later. Quarterly is a good starting point. Regularity spurs your momentum, so avoid the temptation to discontinue mailings in the summer or winter. Will you send this communication via bulk mail or first class?

Think about the format. What size will it be? Many begin with a normal two-sided 8½-inch by 11-inch piece of paper, folded into thirds. Are two or three columns preferable? Should it be a self-mailer? Design a sharp-looking masthead. For an attractive appearance, have a year's supply of the masthead printed in a contrasting color. Then slip it into your printer for each issue—or have it printed professionally if you're doing a large quantity.

What will you call your newsletter? Don't be so cute you'll be embarrassed to claim the publication a year from now. (Reread the section called "What's in a Name" in Chapter 2.) Get a copy of *The Newsletter Sourcebook* by Mark Beach and Elaine Floyd, and Floyd's *Marketing with Newsletters*.

A newsletter provides news—something useful to the recipient. Although commercial clients are interested in business improvement ideas, residential customers appreciate household tips. Decide which is your market. You can provide either by subscribing to periodicals in your readers' area of interest, then culling interesting items and rewriting them. News releases from suppliers also provide story material. Will you want regular features, such as a profile of an outstanding customer or a standard column about Web resources?

Some professions, such as medicine, dentistry, and banking, are the target of national companies that produce "canned" generic newsletters for various industries. These are designed so the individual firm is mentioned on the front, but the information inside is all uniform.

Whether you create your newsletter "from scratch" or use a generic version, having such a communications tool establishes customer confidence and loyalty. Because it puts you in a position of authority, it can also lead to added profits. (See Chapter 7 for information on creating your own e-mail newsletter.)

Writing a Book Garners Goodwill and New Business

Suppose you've followed the above advice. What's to be gained by taking that a step further and putting your expertise between book covers? Plenty! Books offer unprecedented opportunities. Having one enhances your reputation, gives you a new promotional tool, and provides a fresh profit center.

You can use a book to position yourself and create new opportunities. Print has permanency. Books can lead to fame and fortune. The general public perceives authors as experts. When you've written a book, you are considered *the authority*. This gives you more clout in the minds of your prospects.

One of our past clients was a very successful management consultant before he retired. Joe Black was generous with copies of his books. He sent copies to CEOs, meeting planners, or key executives he had targeted as prospects. Amazingly, these virtually always got past the gatekeeper. Why? Because he *personally autographed them* to the individual he wanted to impress. Not only does having a book lay the groundwork for securing more work, it may allow you to command higher fees. Joe attributes a minimum of $200,000 in extra billings to his books.

Many consultants and speakers use a book as their calling card instead of a brochure. Brochures are tossed. Media kits hit the round file. Books, on the other hand, have genuine perceived value and aren't thrown away. Instead they are placed on bookshelves where they may be readily retrieved whenever a need arises. Meanwhile, they serve as impressive reminders of who you are and your area of expertise.

Prestige, however, is only part of the payback. Your book is a wonderful passive income generator. Once it's done and properly promoted, it earns money for you month after month and year after year—while you're busy doing your thing. During tough times, this residual income can mean the difference between profit and loss, survival or extinction.

A further advantage to having a book is that it is a time saver. When a client calls to discuss your area of expertise, instead of taking the time on the phone to explain every nuance of what you do, simply promise to send the prospect a complimentary book. This creates a powerful impression as well as providing a wealth of information.

And if you've self-published and handled the publishing arrangements astutely, you can sell large quantities of your books to corporate clients or when you speak. Organizations that have hired you are already "sold." Convincing them to purchase your book for internal training reinforcement—as goodwill gifts to give to their customers—or to use as a prospecting tool to attract new business—are all possibilities.

To give your book direction, create a mission statement for it just as you did when starting your business. It needn't be lengthy. The more condensed, the better.

Now create an outline or a table of contents. Group likely topics together and put them in the most logical order. If you have two or three main headings with many sub-headings, perhaps a Part I, Part II, Part III, etc. format would make it easier for readers to grasp your message.

Don't become preoccupied with trying to start writing from the beginning. Commence with whatever is easiest and most interesting to you. This gets you into the flow and releases your creative juices. Then after you're more comfortable with the written word, come back and create a dynamite beginning to hook readers.

It's a good idea to write the Introduction early since this sets the stage for the whole book. An Introduction tells the scope of the work and shows how people will benefit from reading it. It also keeps you focused. As in visiting the dentist, so in writing—brief is better than lengthy. Lean sentences are the most inviting to read. So are concise paragraphs. And short, pithy words. This isn't the time to parade your scholarly vocabulary. It's a place to communicate. Easily. Swiftly. Effectively. Spice your pages with case histories, anecdotes, stories, jokes, similes or metaphors, checklists, samples, examples of what works...and what doesn't. Such flavoring gives your message zest.

One approach some of our clients use is to dictate their thoughts, have the tape transcribed, then partially clean up the manuscript pages before sending it to us at About Books, Inc., for editing. This doesn't require a large time commitment nor the ability to be an experienced word crafter. Weaving a compelling book is no easy task. If you hire someone to write your book, be sure he or she has the skill to leave your mental fingerprints. The book should be written in *your* voice; it must be an extension of your personality and mannerisms.

But perhaps you already have the guts of a book. Have you written several articles or a column? Often these can be reorganized, linked together, and repackaged into an anthology. Collect similar topics under group headings and write transitions to bridge from one piece to the next. If you don't have such a foundation already laid, maybe now's the time to begin.

The company- or association-sponsored book holds much promise. It often takes the form of a corporate history or a biography of the founder or CEO. (It worked so well for Iacocca, people actually went into Chrysler showrooms clutching his book and saying, "I want to buy a car from the guy who wrote this book.")

Some other examples of this type of publicity include *The Safeco Story* (insurance), *The Only Way to Fly: The Story of Western Airlines, America's Senior Air Carrier*; *Marriott*; *The Story of Western International Hotels*, and *Firstbank: The Story of Seattle-First National Bank.*

Like the genealogy of a family, these stories document the life of a business. Whether for a corporate giant—or a small, family-owned business—such biographies capture forever the people, the frustrations, and the triumphs of commerce.

These corporate profiles are especially appropriate for 25-, 50-, or 100-year anniversaries. Not only are they ideal stockholder gifts, they heighten company pride when given to employees and create customer/client goodwill when presented to constituents. They may also do well in traditional bookstores.

Books are used by some firms as a prospecting tool. Usually these are created as how-to booklets or guides designed to help or educate clients/customers. This is a tried and true way to separate prospects from suspects.

AT&T advertises free copies of their *The Moving Book*, which is designed as a personal guide to a more organized move. Interlaced among the moving tips are subtle plugs for you- know-who. A smart moving and storage company could produce a similar "Moving Checklist." Those who request it are prime leads as they wouldn't be asking for one unless they anticipated a move. Why not have a salesperson offer to deliver the checklist in person?

These company-sponsored premium books are offered as "bait" to encourage prospects to raise their hands and identify themselves. The leads are then followed up by mail, by telephone, or in person. "Books are a wonderful vehicle for a message," says Ray Benjamin of The Benjamin Company. "It is a medium which is so effective that almost any sensible company in America or abroad should consider it."

Of course, writing and producing a book can seem like a herculean task to most people. Our flagship company, About Books, Inc., specializes in helping entrepreneurs and professionals with such projects. For more information, e-mail Marilyn@About-Books.com, call 719-395-2459, or visit our Web site at http://www.About-Books.com.

Years ago, we did a book for the owner of a dating service. When *How to Single Out Your Mate: A Guide for Twogetherness* came out, the author's business receipts jumped substantially. Yes, "bound messages" are often sound investments.

The two primary ways to get into print are turning to a trade publisher—such as Simon and Schuster, Prentice Hall, and HarperCollins—or doing it yourself (self-publishing). These days, big trade publishers accept few newcomers.

This may be just as well because we're entrepreneurial souls. We like to be *in charge*, to control our own destinies. We like to make things happen (not wait for a year and a half while a trade publisher gets our book in print). And we're businesswomen; we look at the bottom line. If we can see we'll make more money doing things ourselves, that's the approach we take.

Here's the reality of going with a trade publisher: Unless you're the likes of Stephen Covey, Barbara De Angelis, or Tom Peters, your book won't get much promotional support. But since you've signed over all rights to the publisher you no longer have the power to influence its destiny. Even if you pour your own money into an author tour to publicize your new baby, there's no guarantee the publisher will even have books in the bookstores!

Now let's talk money. The typical first-time nonfiction author, if she can get accepted at all, can anticipate an advance of somewhere between $3,000 and $7,000. Understand this is an advance *against* royalties. That means unless your book earns out the advance, this initial advance payment is *all* you will ever see for your work. According to Joni Evans, the former executive vice president and publisher of Random House, "Only 10 percent of the books published by any house earn out their advances." That's a 90 percent failure rate!

It is for these reasons many are choosing to publish their own books today. For them, self-publishing is indeed the "write" way to success. With this method, you invest in your own book and reap all the rewards. You keep control and turn out a product in mere months. For those who don't have the time or inclination to actually do everything personally, turnkey consultants such as ourselves are available to handle all the details. For complete information to clarify and de-mystify the process, get *The Complete Guide to Self-Publishing* by Tom and Marilyn Ross, http://www.spannet.org/cc/.

A book equals more jobs, more revenue, more exposure. It gives you a reason to be "news"—to gain notice not only for your writing, but also for your other accomplishments. By packaging your knowledge between covers, you'll have greater visibility, credibility, and profitability.

Getting in Broadcast News

Something not to be underestimated is the power of a short TV news spot. Today there are more outlets for broadcast news than ever before. News falls into two types: "hard," which covers matters of local, national, and international consequence; and "soft," which is the kind of human-interest feature people find fascinating.

You are more likely to capture the latter. You can also piggyback and "use news to make news" by packaging your subject matter with a current hot topic. Perhaps you can create news. Did you do a survey or study on a subject of timely interest? Are you a featured speaker at a convention or trade show? Have you received, or given, an award? All of these things can be catapulted into soft stories for the media.

News time is precious time. Learn to zero in quickly on the essence of your story. You may only have 75 to 90 seconds in which to pack your punch. Think of all the 30- and 60-second commercials that sell millions of dollars worth of products and services each year. (The sponsors have to pay for those!)

Soft news stories can actually be quite effective. A few years ago I was taped by a popular television station in Phoenix. The interview centered around a book I had just written. Imagine my surprise when I walked into my hotel room, flipped on the 6 o'clock news, and heard the anchorman say they would be talking about *Creative Loafing* later. Then a full-screen shot of the book appeared. I was glued to the set, afraid to blink for fear I would miss the anticipated few-seconds spot.

What transpired left me a little breathless. A 30-second clip from the prerecorded 15-minute interview had me introduce the subject and the book. Then for five minutes film clips from the station's files showed people participating in many of the activities suggested as pastimes in the book. These were interspersed with narrated closeups of the front

118

cover. Another 30 seconds of my prerecorded interview closed the segment.

Six minutes of prime TV time, including a long plug by a local news celebrity. Who could have guessed such a gem would be aired on the news program of the most popular network TV station in town? The great equalizer goddess struck! She can strike for you too.

The point, of course, is that a minute or two of prime-time news coverage can have greater impact than a half-hour midmorning talk show. Because TV is so prestigious, competition for available time is fierce—especially with all the celebrities out stumping. With imagination, a creative approach, and tenacity, however, you can probably land some shows.

As you work with prime media in the large markets, another dimension may be added. You could be asked for an exclusive. That means you will appear on that television show, that radio station, or in that paper *only* (or at least first). Don't take exclusivity lightly. Be sure what you're getting is worth the concession. Look at such things as audience size or circulation, prime-time exposure, the prestige of the program or publication, and the enthusiasm of the people involved. Then be grateful they feel you are important enough to warrant such a request.

Midget Moves for Mighty Results

Create a sell statement. Define your product or service in 25 words or less. Mention who your customers/clients are and quantify what benefit they will receive. There's no business that isn't show business, so don't be modest. You'll use this statement over and over in a myriad of different situations. It's a wonderful introduction when you do follow-up calls to the media and must be brief. You can use it when explaining your business to others.

Develop a list of key contacts. It is vital to identify your most important customers, prospects, and media people. The list may run several hundred names. These people hold your future in the palm of their hands. You want to favorably impress them—over and over and over again. By honing in on the most important, you can establish *personal* contact with them. Use any excuse to get in front of them…not "in their face" but tactfully. Of course, as your business develops, this list will evolve.

Use postcards. I'm a great believer in the often undervalued postcard. They can help you build your sales because people *read* them in this cluttered mail world. They are also fast, easy, and cheap. No envelop to print, stuff, and seal—and they're only 20¢ to mail if you stay under the 4¼-inch by 6-inch size. (Some people believe in oversizing them. But the larger 5 ½-inch by 7-inch or giant 6-inch by 9-inch size require 33¢ to mail.) They've been used to promote everything from vacation hot spots to long-distance phone companies to Elvis Presley. Put a photograph of your product, store, or yourself on one side; a brief sales plug, and PR/contact information on the other. (Be sure to leave enough room to write your message.) Or do them blank on the back, write customized messages on your computer, and run them through a printer or copier with the appropriate feeder.

Once upon a time we sent out a very expensive media kit promoting our book *Country Bound!* It got dismal results. So we sent out a follow-up postcard mailing asking, "Did you receive the media kit we sent?" The phones went berserk. So we got an idea. Now we send postcards *first*. They say, "Did you get our mailing?" (Of course they didn't because we haven't sent it!) They call and say, "No, and we want it." Bingo—you have qualified your leads and can now afford to send the expensive, full-blown media kit. Plus you've made a person-to-person contact, so working with them is more congenial in the future.

Because postcards are so cheap you can also use them for multiple mailings. Send your target audience one every week for a month and see what happens. A very affordable source is Modern Postcard. Call 800-959-8365 or go online to www.modernpostcard.com.

Understand and use wire services. One of the best-kept secrets is the enormous power of the national news wire services. Capturing publicity here gives you coast-to-coast coverage that often appears in literally hundreds of papers. Every daily and most weeklies subscribe to at least one wire service. Of perhaps even more significance, these wires are monitored by TV and national magazines, so your story could be catapulted to even greater acclaim. The Associated Press reaches more than 1,550 newspapers.

Interestingly, many wire service stories actually originate with a feature in a daily newspaper. Give you any ideas? If you get a good story in a daily, complete with contact information, you could approach it one of two ways: 1) When thanking the writer, suggest she or he submit it to a wire service. This gets their byline broadcast across the country and nets you more inquiries or orders. Or 2) *you* contact the bureau in the city where the article appeared with something like "Today's XYZ paper carries a story of great interest about us on page X. I thought you might want to pick it up."

Area news wire reporters can be found several ways. Either look up the news wire service in the phone book, or call the editor of your local paper and ask where the regional reporter for XYZ news wire is stationed. Then call information for the number.

Customize to win ink in national magazines. Study publications for the right editorial spin. Knowing the editorial focus of a magazine gives you a distinct advantage when pitching a story. Once you've determined a half dozen major magazines you want to penetrate, call the *advertising* department and request a media kit, including the three most recent issues. When you get the kit you'll be sitting on a profusion of fascinating facts. You'll know the demographics of their subscribers: age, income, education, interests, etc. This helps you pinpoint who their readers are. Included will also be an editorial statement and other literature telling how they view themselves. Tune in!

Now read those three magazines cover to cover. Delve into the editorial director's statement that appears early. *Family Circle's* Managing Editor Susan Ungaro typically praises her editors in her column. In other instances, the editorial director or editor-in-chief will show a passion for a specific subject or leaning.

Next study the masthead, which also appears early. It tells who is who. Often job titles are listed or columnists are specifically named. You can also determine the pecking order by examining the hierarchy of name listings.

The most practical inroad is to approach a columnist. Find a column that fits your business, then dissect it. What is the length and flavor of the headline? Is the style breezy? Serious? Intellectual? How long does the column run? Now write a short "exclusive" for that magazine. (That doesn't mean you won't submit similar pieces to noncompeting publications; simultaneous submissions are a proven way to establish momentum.) Naturally, you'll slip in information about your product or service, but the piece must focus on solving readers' problems. Also include a news release to help solidify your credentials.

Once you've graduated from short columns to articles, be prepared to present a full and holistic package. Make it easy for the editor to say "yes." Besides a headline, you'll include a blurb they can use in a call-out box. Additionally, you'll suggest lines to appear on the cover announcing the article inside. (You've really studied those three magazine issues. Right?) Is there a sidebar of related information? What about photos? Now be sure you send it to the right editor, and your chances of success are greatly improved.

Every month you can research more and more publications via cyberspace. Are you taking advantage of the Web in this way? Thousands of magazines, newsletters, and broadcast agencies are now online. By using Yahoo or one of the other search engines you can find their address, visit their site, and study their material. What a perfect way to get the pulse of their editorial direction—and learn how best you can fit in.

Have photos ready. We live in a visually stimulating world. Pictures in print publications increase the readership of an article by 35 to 40 percent, according to content analysis studies. Newspapers and magazines have to compete with TV and the Internet. They can do that more effectively with photographs. And you can compete for space more effectively by offering them a selection of quality professional photographs. When you hire a professional photographer, examine her portfolio ahead of time and look for imaginative settings, good composition, and sharp contrast.

Shoot in both black-and-white and color. The demand for color publicity photos is growing. Newspapers prefer CDs over transparencies or slides. It saves them the money it would cost to make color separations and the time it takes to return transparencies. And you can purchase single-write CDs for about a buck apiece. To be graphically appealing, don't rely on just head shots. Get creative with the setting and props. Have your pictures tell a story. Papers often put color shots on the covers of sections. You might want to send 5-inch by 7-inch black and whites initially, but tell them color shots are available. (And don't limit yourself to photos. Consider providing charts, graphs, or illustrations that would enrich the visual appeal of a story.)

Finally, be sure you include a caption. It should contain something enlightening about your business. Many people only read photo captions, so also make it easy for them to determine how to reach you.

Don't overlook little media. Sometimes it pays to be a big fish in a little pond…and to make a big splash. Early in his career, best-selling author Wayne Dyer was interviewed by a little obscure radio station. A producer from the old Johnny Carson Show happened to hear him. It led to Dyer being on Carson's show some 20 times! The biggies like David Letterman, *The Tonight Show, The Today Show, National Enquirer,* and *USA Today* have staff members who constantly scour small town newspapers, radio, TV, and specialty magazines for interesting story leads. If you are lucky enough to be selected by major media, rejoice! There is no way you could afford to buy 10 minutes with Jay Leno.

You can also make a killing in small community "giveaway" newspapers. Throughout North America, about 3,000 such papers are distributed free of charge to a community base. Although some of these publications only serve 5,000 people, others produce more than 5 million copies weekly. Fully 50 percent of them carry hard news and all are run by small, overworked staffs. They welcome interesting stories and photographs. Many of these papers belong to the Association of Free Community Papers, which maintains a site at http://www.afcp.org/. Once there, do an online search for those in your area, or reach much broader and access the entire AFCP member listings. The detailed format includes not only the address, phone, and fax, but many more particulars. Because they are overlooked and undervalued by most PR agencies and big companies, this is an excellent source for placing stories across town—or across the land.

Recycle your media contacts. Do you maintain a database or have some method of keeping track of editors, reporters, and freelancers who have written about you before? Have you a list of producers and hosts from past radio appearances? If not, start one today! Send them news releases about new developments, copies of your newsletter, new product information, reprints of your publicity, etc.

When sales get sluggish, one of the smartest and most economical things you can do is put out a mailing or launch a calling campaign to these contacts. Assuming you did well initially, they're already sold on you.

And these folks have a challenging job: They're constantly trying to come up with new ideas, fascinating concepts, interesting experts. It's wise to stay in touch with a postcard or note about every three months. Keep feeding them. When they have a page to fill or a guest drops out at the last minute, you'll be there to save the day.

Remember that persistence pays off. Those who expect to send a news release and be overwhelmed with interest, have lost touch with reality. If you are not diligent, your efforts will sink like a stone. It takes ongoing contact to get results.

With today's voice mail, you'll probably need to leave several messages before you connect with a live human being. Be perpetually upbeat; letting your frustration show in your voice is the sign of an amateur.

Follow-up needn't be confined to phone calls, however. Mail a postcard. Use e-mail. Fax. Tenacity is an incredible quality. So don't give up too early.

Capitalize on free local and regional opportunities. By beginning on a local level, you can generate a ripple effect that will carry you regionally, then nationally. You can accomplish real saturation with a regional campaign. Greater New York, for instance, has some 600 newspapers. You'll generate much more thorough coverage by going after more than just the four large dailies. Additionally, people are impressed when your products are written up in their hometown paper. You can often start developing a mailing list by inquiring at the chamber of commerce or visitor and convention bureau for their local media resources list.

Publicity and promotion are almost like Siamese twins. What you haven't learned here, you'll discover in the next chapter. Onward!

Web Sites, *Wisdom,* and Whimsey

Marketing wizardry for the asking. This is a gateway for lots of useful advice. You can join their e-mail list for a regular free supply of handy business tips and information, find links to helpful sites, even learn "how a single dot can help to promote your Web site." Curious? Go visit http://www.tka.co.uk/magic. In the Archive Area there are dozens of articles to boost your learning curve; you can even approach them about submitting your own tips and pieces to generate publicity!

Want to pitch your idea into the arms of America's fastest-growing age group? Look no further than your own backyard. The City and Regional Magazine Association reports the majority of its members publications' readers fall into the 40-55 age range. According to CRMA, "They buy more personal care and beauty products than any other age group and have a huge appetite for fine dining, fashion, home furnishing, electronics, entertainment, and travel." If your company provides anything in these areas—pursue, pursue. The 76 regional member magazines boast an aggregate total of more than 2 million readers. For more information, contact CRMA by calling 323-937-5514 or e-mailing jdowden@prodigy.net, or go to their Web site at www.citymag.org.

●●●●●●●

Everyone has a photographic memory.
Some of us just don't have any film.

●●●●●●●

Stay in touch with prospects! Mary Ellen Lipinski covers all her bases when she sends out a PR packet to a prospect. She also sends a fax to keep the interest level up. Her fax contains a sketched photo, her e-mail address, recent news flash, and her Web site URL. This gives recipients an opportunity to view and review her capabilities more closely if they choose. She usually gets a follow-up response saying they looked her up on the Internet. We take a similar approach to stay in close touch when sending out proposals to potential clients, only we use e-mail as many of them initially learned of us on the Web.

Bargain book for finding syndicated columnists. To get the most up-to-date information on where to mail information to syndicated columnists in 53 categories, get a copy of the *2000 Syndicated Directory*. It's a steal at $8.50 and can be put on your credit card by calling 888-612-7095, ext. 4. The subjects covered include everything from travel to food, hobbies to business, entertainment to outdoors, and oodles in between. If a columnist decides to write about your venture, chances are the column will appear in dozens, often hundreds, of newspapers nationwide. Scoring here is definitely major league.

●●●●●●●

Scientists have discovered a new phobia. It's called
regret-aphobia, which is the fear of thinking up a
much better headline just after you've sent out all
your news releases.

●●●●●●●

PR coach extraordinaire awaits you online. I'm very impressed with the content at http://www.netrageous.com/pr/. Surfers are welcome at "The NETrageous publicity resource center" and it's just that. The free publicity advice here is based on successful, proven experience—not theory.

By the time you finish exploring their Web site, you'll know exactly why their experts have received over $6 million of free publicity and how you can do the same. Be sure to check out the following: Paul's "Brooklyn Bridge" story, how you can write a killer press release, sample press release, and how to distribute your press release. Then just keep clicking for information and links to other interesting publicity sites.

●●●●●●●●

It's been said that women who seek to be
equal with men lack ambition.

●●●●●●●●

Personalized Post-it Notes give you individuality. Want to appear as though you personally handwrote a note on your press kit? Write out your brief message, reproduce it as a self-inking rubber stamp, then stamp your message on a Post-it Note. Bingo…you've given it the individual touch.

Strategies for penetrating newspapers. Did you know there are 1,489 daily newspapers with a total circulation of 56 million? Not to mention some 8,500 weeklies with 70 million readers, most of whom live in the wealthy suburbs? They also get considerable "pass-along" readership—on average 2.2 readers for each copy sold. Have any interest in infiltrating this institution? Your best ammunition lies in the following strategies: 1) Don't just go to departmental editors, who are already swamped. Seek out feature and Sunday editors who are often hungry for material. 2) Send what they want: releases on diskettes. New information reveals that most top 500 dailies and nearly 9,500 other dailies and weeklies are using more diskette releases and fewer paper manuscript releases. 3) Go with color. Nearly all newspapers now print in full color. They give color huge space: often full pages and half pages in weekend sections—sometimes even page one of special sections or inside front positioning. To get what *you* want, give them what *they* want!

●●●●●●●●

The patient's family gathered to hear what the spe-
cialist had to say. "Things don't look good. The only
chance is a brain transplant. This is an experimen-
tal procedure. Brains are very expensive and your
insurance won't cover it," the doctor explained.

"So just how much does a brain cost?" asked one of
the relatives.

126

"For a male brain it's $500,000. A female brain is $200,000."

Some of the younger men tried to look shocked, but all the men nodded in understanding. A few actually smirked.

Then the patient's daughter inquired, "Why the difference in price between male brains and female brains?"

"It's a standard pricing practice," replied the doctor. "Women's brains have to be marked down because they are used."

●●●●●●●

And speaking of brains, did you hear that researchers have learned how to transplant brains into the feet of dogs? I don't know about you, but it sure gives me paws for thought.

●●●●●●●

New angle for getting into *USA Today*. Although you might feel like Cinderella before the ball trying to interest reporters in doing a feature article about your business for this widely circulated national newspaper, there's another way in the door that is seldom explored. Ever notice the "Voices" column on the editorial page? They seek people to offer opinions on major news items. To toss your hat in the ring, simply send your name, address, occupation, and age—plus a day and evening phone number and your photo—to *USA Today*, Voices Submissions, 1000 Wilson Boulevard, Arlington, VA 22229. Once your opinion appears, you can add to your written PR material: "As featured (or quoted) in *USA Today*."

●●●●●●●

Lack of listening ability of game show host:
Tell me a bit about yourself. What do you do?
Contestant: *Well, I'm a widow...*
Host: *Oh, great, that's great!*

●●●●●●●

Free databases await you online at http://www.gebbieinc.com/. Gebbie Press, publishers of the useful *All-in-One Directory*, provide TV and weekly newspaper databases for free. Included are some 3,284 e-mail addresses for radio and TV stations. Lots of value at this site.

Is publicity really "free"? People occasionally take me to task when I mention that publicity is free. After all, they say, you have to pay for mailing costs, faxes, and phone calls. Do you really? Why not use e-mail; no cost there. And some phone companies give you free calling on Fridays. I know one woman who regularly sends long-distance faxes every Friday, then reaps the rewards the rest of the week.

●●●●●●●

Early to bed, early to rise,
work like mad and publicize.

●●●●●●●

Newsletters to keep you on the PR cutting edge. If you're serious about securing publicity, consider subscribing to the following:
   Bulldog Reporter 800-959-1059 (expensive and sophisticated)
   Phillips PR News 888-707-5814 (expensive and sophisticated)
   The Publicity Hound 262-284-7451 (affordable and motivating)
   PartyLine 212-755-3487 (succinct and current)

CHAPTER 5

Provocative Promotional Ideas for Getting Known and Getting Ahead

Women who understand the power of promotional activities don't wait for their ships to come in—they swim out to meet them. There are dozens of things you can do to boost your business to greater profits.

In this chapter I'll give you the keys to unlock dozens of promotional doors and windows. Some of them lead to elaborate activities; others are simple. Together we will explore the topics of consumer education, community involvement, and event creation. And in addition to discovering how valuable directory listings can be, you'll learn about contests, serving on boards of directors, and be treated to an array of miscellaneous and mischievous promotional tactics.

Consumer Education

Canny leaders all across America are finding ways to inform, entertain, or assist the public while maximizing their own exposure. They lead seminars, symposiums, and workshops; give talks; sponsor clinics; provide in-store or in-office demonstrations; even hold open houses or receptions. All of these functions are designed to bring together prospective clients or customers, patients or patrons. And they're phenomenal goodwill builders.

Sheehy Ford sponsors a learning situation far afield from a Harvard University class. Rather than wearing tweed and having tenure, the instructor dons a shop coat and speaks from practical experience. His students are all female. Although they fully realize a distributor cap is not the latest in fashionable headgear, their knowledge about their cars is limited. The aim of this Philadelphia dealership's Auto Clinic for Women Only is to educate the area female population about their vehicles. Naturally the dealership anticipates picking up new service customers in the process, not to mention future new car purchasers.

The AMI Denver Broncos Sports Medical Center offers a free sports injury evaluation. They implore athletes to "Give us your tired ankles, your poor knees, your tennis elbows…"

One health professional who had spent $150,000 on an ad campaign that netted no known results switched to seminars. Eighty new patients were tracked to this activity!

Based in Massachusetts, the InVision Institute—a nonprofit organization—sponsors "Eyes on the Road," a 45-foot traveling van. It houses an educational facility that promotes eye care and vision correction with interactive displays. With a tour agenda that includes 80 U.S. cities, the van appears at high-traffic locations like science museums, trade shows, and outdoor events. The institute was formed by Bausch & Lomb to heighten the public's knowledge of eye care.

The other day an invitation came in the mail from AT&T to attend a complimentary seminar on "Telemarketing for Small Businesses." The content covers how to creatively improve sales support, order processing, account management, and customer service. Of course, it is also aimed at improving AT&T's bottom line. The more small businesses understand the power of telemarketing, the larger their phone bills will be!

These are just a few examples of consumer education projects. You can do similar things. Many businesses lend themselves to in-office or in-store clinics. A travel agent could give a demonstration on how to pack a suitcase. A landscape architect would find an eager audience for a workshop on easy-care plantings—especially if it were offered to recent home buyers in a new subdivision. A financial planner or accounting firm might sponsor a Personal Finance Fair—a consumer show providing pertinent seminars, speakers, and attractions.

A nutritionist, ad agency, plant-watching service, employment counselor, Internet service provider, tax consultant, modeling agency, or caterer might sponsor a free public seminar to generate exposure and patronage. Chiropractors could put together a mini-program about the spine; veterinarians a short presentation on how to keep your dog or cat healthy. A child-care facility might sponsor a nursery school art show; a boutique a fashion show. The possibilities abound for individuals using imagination to discover topics of general interest that also correlate with their business.

Such activities can often be held right in your place of business. If this isn't practical, consider renting a local hotel banquet room or a private dining room in your favorite restaurant. Other possible options are schools, community centers, banks or savings and loans, perhaps even the conference room of a business associate. To let people know about your activity, use the techniques you learned in the previous chapters.

Hospitality Happenings Mix Business With Pleasure

Conventional wisdom says business and pleasure don't mix: They're as contradictory as silk and burlap. A more unorthodox view weaves them skillfully to increase a company's visibility and build sales. Let's explore the latter attitude.

Corporate entertaining can help differentiate your firm. Parties give you a chance to talk with prospective clients as well as thank current customers. Many executives and saleswomen recognize this form of hospitality saves them countless hours of individual breakfasts, lunches, and dinners. Mass corporate entertaining allows you to reach many people at once. It's cheaper than one-on-one entertaining and much more effective time-wise. When employees are included, business socializing often enhances the company in associates' eyes, forging a deeper bond of loyalty.

Whatever kind of gala function you have in mind, planning is fundamental to having a successful get-together. First consider timing. People prefer these events be tacked on to the normal business day rather than scheduled on a weekend. Don't conflict with important trade conventions for your industry. Also avoid both secular and religious holidays.

Compile the guest list with input from key staff members. Invitations will, of course, go to prime prospects and current clients. What about including major suppliers, such as your attorney, accountant, banker, and landlord? Perhaps local government officials or area association executives should be on the guest list. Invite more than you hope will attend; not everyone can or will come. It is more personal if invitations are hand-addressed and carry regular stamps.

A flower arrangement or two is nice for such occasions. Have you ever thought of turning your office into an art gallery? Many local artists and artists' societies welcome a chance to hang their work on consignment. You can then have a "showing" complete with refreshments and a small printed catalog.

Always assign one person responsibility for coordinating corporate entertainment functions. She makes sure executives review the guest list the day of the event, mingles with the attendees, monitors how things are going, and troubleshoots.

Some firms find this such a good policy that they schedule event-driven marketing activities about every three months. In the summer it might be attending a sports activity or a picnic. Because selling has to do with relationships, many find it makes dollars and sense to socialize with prospects.

Networking to Establish Synergy and Momentum

Networking is not a destination; it's a journey, a way-of-life for the savvy entrepreneur. Not only does it yield fantastic business contacts, it also can lead to enriching personal relationships. Networking provides ideas, leads, advice, and support. The next best thing to knowing something is knowing where and how to find it. The results of your networking—the contacts, colleagues, and ability to make something happen with one phone call—can dramatically enhance your business. And it's not just who you know. It's who knows you!

Networking is *not* taking advantage of other people! Good networking is reciprocal. It's important you approach it with the attitude that you want do everything you can to assist others in their goals.

According to the Business Women's Network's *Wow! Facts* book, the five top reasons for women to network are:

1. It builds sales profitability.

2. It is a cost-effective way to market a business.

3. It is free advertising in its purest form: word of mouth.

4. It is a catalyst for introducing and linking people to those in need of their services, who may later return the favor.

5. Everyone is a potential customer or a lead to a potential customer.

Networking is forming a human chain. No doubt you've heard of the six degrees of separation that says you can connect with anyone in the world, no matter how powerful or important they are, by going through just six people. It's not just who you know, it's who *they* know, and so on.

You've been using this technique all your life without even realizing it, I'll bet. Remember when you asked a friend to refer you to a good cleaning person or alteration lady—and she checked with her friends to find just the right person? You got what you wanted by going through a contact. There was nothing "usury" about it. You weren't rude or aggressive or pushy. When one person leads to another everybody wins because we all enjoy the feeling of helping someone else.

So if you want to succeed in business, expose yourself! Well, not literally, of course. What I'm suggesting is to take off the wraps and pursue new alliances. Developing fresh relationships—and rekindling old ones—is not only enjoyable but profitable.

How do you begin? First collect current contacts' names, addresses, and phone numbers from various databases, Rolodex files, address books, holiday card lists, business card holders, etc. Compile them into one master list. A computer database is ideal for this purpose. (Also include fax numbers and e-mails. You never know when you'll want to quickly send something to a colleague.) Now prioritize these names as "A," "B," or "C."

Initially work only the As. Build a file on each of these people. Include such things as spouse name, number of children, hobbies, pet peeves, food/drink preferences, community involvement, causes they support, birthday, etc. As you have future meetings with these folks, embellish their file.

Of course, many people you'd like to network with are not yet in your sphere of influence. Start watching for information about specific people (or individuals in key fields) you've been wanting to meet. Assemble individual files on them from newspaper and magazine feature stories, ads, radio shows, TV programs, Web sites, even conversations with mutual acquaintances. A graphic designer I know who moved to a new town and had to build a client base got a part-time job in an industry that put her in touch with dozens of potential clients. When she left the job after just four months, she had more business than she could handle.

Have your assistant look up potential key contacts in who's who directories. (Perhaps you can meet them by joining a club, group, or

17 Ways to Outdistance the Herd

1. Price point: Are you expensive, moderately priced, or cheap?

2. Size: Small may be beautiful; so might large or odd-sized.

3. Ease of purchasing: Do you accept all credit cards? Offer layaway?

4. Convenience: Can people find what they need easily?

5. Have a gimmick: What makes you better or different from the competition?

6. Delivery: Do you offer overnight pick up and delivery?

7. Guarantee: Have you a money-back policy?

8. Packaging: Could you use innovative, reusable, or fun packaging?

9. Giveaways: Do you offer small free gifts to potential customers or purchasers?

10. Piggybacking: Can you combine two or more products to create a kit or gift basket?

11. Samples: Could you offer little teasers to entice buyers?

12. Seminars or demonstrations: Should your product or service be showcased in this way?

(continued on next page)

cause with which they are affiliated or by attending a charity affair where they will be present.) Also check membership rosters of organizations to which you both belong. Additionally, collect data on new people you hear of who impress you.

One way to draw these people into your personal circle is to acknowledge them. (Don't limit this to strangers, however. It is seldom done and will be much appreciated by those you already know.) When people are elected to an office or selected to serve on a board of directors, send a note of congratulations. If they volunteer their time to a worthy cause, earn an award, or write a provocative letter to the editor, seize these opportunities to get in touch. A local bank laminates newspaper articles or photos and mails them to the featured subjects to broaden their reach into the community.

Just a few words to introduce yourself and send your personal congratulations is all that's needed. This is a prime example of "it's the thought that counts." Of course, use your letterhead, and slip in a business card. You may get no immediate results, but the long-term benefits can be impressive. Also watch your mail for items that could prove useful to your colleagues. Just this week we received a sample copy of a printing trade journal we are passing on to the editor of our local paper.

As a matter of course, I duplicate and mail copies of articles that will appeal to friends, clients, or business associates. We'd love to start a trend where business and professional people regularly remember each other with appropriate articles and information. That way you have the eyes of all you know watching out for *your* best interest. Such a practice, however, necessitates action in return. Be sure to always thank people who do kind things for you. This can take the form of a brief note or a phone call.

Speaking of thank yous, have you ever thought of printing a public thank-you in the daily paper? Although you will have to pay for it, it isn't perceived as an advertisement but rather as a show of appreciation. This allows you to keep a low-key professional image. You would state

> **17 WAYS TO OUTDISTANCE THE HERD (continued)**
>
> 13. Contests: Would some form of competition focus attention on you?
> 14. Can you conduct a survey to generate publicity?
> 15. Audience segmentation: Should you slant toward teens? Adults? Retirees? Gays? Hispanics?
> 16. Service: Do you offer extraordinary assistance to your customers?
> 17. Technological edge: Do you have a compelling Web site? Secure online ordering? An e-mail address for fast, free correspondence?

something like "(name of firm, address, and phone) wishes to thank its 235 clients for allowing us to serve your needs over the last year. May this coming year be even more profitable for you than the one just passed." Signing your name is a nice touch. An appropriate time to run such an ad would be at Thanksgiving.

Becoming a "joiner" is a proven way to meet new people. Linda Gulgowski, a marketing professional from Milwaukee, suggests that attending nonbusiness-related events is an excellent way to network. "I worked with the fire department on one of their fund-raisers and now I know restaurant owners, golf course managers, elected officials, members of the hotel/travel industry, and sports figures. I would never have otherwise had an opportunity to meet such a diverse group of people if I hadn't gotten involved with the fire department."

Chambers of commerce also often provide fertile meeting grounds. Bigger metropolitan areas have city, county, and state chambers—even ethnic chambers for blacks, Hispanics, and Jews. Jaycees are sometimes the most dynamic bunch around town. Made up of young business owners, professionals, and executives on the way up, this organization typically attracts accomplished, high-energy people. You'll get the most out of chamber membership by working in the organization, not just paying your dues. Volunteering to chair a committee with high visibility will help the chamber and is a good personal strategy. Attend their monthly mixers.

But how do you work a room without breaking into a sweat? Realize that feeling a bit shy and uncomfortable is natural. Mingling maven Susan RoAne suggests you start with small talk about subjects you have in common, then graduate to more meaningful conversation. Having three to five topics ready will ease you into most conversations. They can range from national news to industry gossip to something great you and a friend did recently. Read the newspaper or check big events on the Web that day and scan your industry trade journal before leaving home. Then you'll be prepared to chat without getting too self-conscious—or flagrantly self-promotional.

Smile and make eye contact. A big part of successful schmoozing is acting more like a host than a guest. When you concentrate on making others feel at ease, you automatically forget about yourself. Always wear your name badge on your right side so when you shake hands with others it's in their line of sight.

Once you've been introduced to a new person, you want to say something to help bond with that individual. If you've met before, refer to it. Other bonding ideas include mentioning mutual acquaintances or giving a genuine compliment. Face-to-face connections establish rapport like no other form of communication. When you meet someone you want to further cultivate, send an attractive handwritten note the next day. It needn't be long: "Dear Pat, It was a pleasure meeting you at...If I can ever refer business your way, I certainly will." This reinforces you in their mind and lets them know you have their best interests and needs in mind.

Of course, every town has civic organizations like Rotary, Kiwanis, Optimists, and Lions. Most cities have groups comprised of high-powered women executives. Join. "Leads" clubs where only one representative per industry is admitted to membership is another option. The sole thrust of these groups is referring business back and forth. Another networking front is charity groups. Seminars, workshops, and classes also provide an arena in which to become acquainted with like-minded people.

Political involvement certainly nets some useful contacts. Participating as a volunteer in local, regional, or national campaigns can quickly get you on the inside track. It makes sense to cultivate your legislators and other appointed officials. It's only human nature to go more out of our way for someone we know. If you need a zoning vari-

136

ance, want guidance through a maze of bureaucratic red tape, or seek to get a statement into the Congressional Record, these contacts pay off.

Networking can also come to the rescue during especially slow periods. One entrepreneur doubles up on her social contacts during tough times. She hits with gusto every meeting and cocktail party she can find. And when asked "How's business?," her reply is always "Great!" even if things are shaky. "I want to program my subconscious to expect wonderful results, not feed it negative tripe," is her rationale.

You can speak volumes—while keeping your mouth shut. When Marcia Yudkin, a consultant and the author of *Six Steps to Free Publicity* attends a networking event, she informs people who she is without ever saying a word. Instead of wearing the usual name badge, Marcia sports a 3-inch by 4-inch laminated color photocopy of her latest book. Even though she isn't the official center of attention, she typically sells four books at each meeting.

An unlikely place some businesswomen are making good connections is in the bed and breakfasts where they stay. Says Bernice Chesler, who has written about B&Bs for many years, "I can't count the number of times I've seen salespeople having breakfast with other travelers and they walk away with fresh leads."

"We need to seek out potentially 'bankable' places to network," believes speaker and consultant Andrea Nierenberg. Her first client can be traced back to a conversation on a train ride. "She was sitting across from me and pulled out a book I had just read. We began a conversation and before we knew it, two other people had joined in." When it was time to leave the woman said, "I'm looking for someone to design a customer service program, so send me your material." Nierenberg did better than that. She hand delivered the material the next day and left it with the receptionist. The prospect called her the following afternoon and they've been working together ever since.

Andrea finds opportunities to network e-v-e-r-y-w-h-e-r-e. She bought an outfit from a salesperson with whom she decided to stay in touch. After the first purchase, she stopped in to say "hi" and referred other shoppers. The saleswoman ultimately returned the favor by suggesting that Nierenberg contact the new management team. As it turned out they were looking to provide corporate training for the whole chain. The rest, as they say, is history.

"It's like walking through a farmland and throwing out seeds," philosophizes Andrea. "You know they all may not bear fruit. However, if you don't start with the seeds, there will be nothing to water, nurture, and eventually harvest."

The computer can also serve as a masterful networking partner. It's faster than a speeding handshake and more powerful than a "Hello, My Name is…" tag. By harnessing the superpowers of online networking, not even kryptonite can stand in your way! Wired entrepreneurs are discovering that online discussion groups present many of the same types of opportunities as attending real-world networking events. Except on the Web you can schmooze day or night and wear your PJs instead of a business suit.

Today there are an estimated 300,000 e-mail lists out there, though most people don't have a clue about using them to develop business. Not so Sharon Tucci, owner of ListHost.net. "The customers we have came through our participation in and visibility on discussion lists," she says. "In fact, only a few clients have come about through more typical marketing methods." Tucci estimates that at least a half million dollars of her company's sales can be directly attributed to her participation in online discussion groups. (This is covered in depth in Chapter 7.)

Connecting—that's the bottom line of what this whole book is about. Now let's move on to more ways to promote yourself and your business.

Creating a Special Event

For those who shun outright business/personal hobnobbing, many other kinds of events can be staged. Although breweries and tobacco companies lead the way in sponsoring big-league wingdings, special grass-roots activities and offbeat events are thriving.

One that especially impressed me was sponsored by Sheree Clark of Sayles Graphic Design. For the last few years this small business owner has been traveling between Chicago and the company's main location in Des Moines, Iowa. "I often meet women in our field [communications] with common interests who I'd like to introduce to each other. Finally I decided to do something about it—and threw one hell of a party," Clark reminisces. "I called the event Birds of a Feather and—to excerpt from the party invitation—our guests were a 'flock of Chicago's classiest chicks' who 'spread their wings for an evening of fun.'" She sent a Save the Date letter several weeks before the actual invitations were mailed, then followed up with a thank-you letter after the event.

The "invitation" this creative woman designed was something else: a box measuring 7-inches by 4½-inches by 3-inches tall and covered with feather-printed paper. Inside reposed a bird's nest and a plastic egg, complete with an invitation to "stick together" and a promise of hors d'oeuvres and cocktails at one of Chicago's finest hotels.

The guest list consisted of current and prospective clients, vendors, and a few personal friends. As she mingled during the party, to her surprise and pleasure she discovered everything from reunited college sorority sisters to a current client "selling" her firm to several prospects. The idea was so successful, she's already thrown the second Birds of a Feather party.

In Yuba City, California, an event of a very different tone took place at The Grain Mill, a natural foods store. They staged a "Half-Ton Bake-Off" with proceeds going to the American Heart Association. Using a Bosch bread maker, on one Sunday between 6:00 A.M. and 2:00 P.M., they, along with many volunteers, baked half a ton of bread— approximately 1,025 loaves! They enlisted the Veterans Memorial Community Building kitchen and were allowed to sell the baked loaves of bread outside local markets and other establishments. Newspaper ads told people, "We 'Knead' You!" and "Help us make a mountain of 'dough' for the American Heart Association." It was ingenious and done on a very low budget. (A well-bread effort, wouldn't you say?)

Teaming up with a nonprofit organization helps both entities. Instead of sponsoring existing events, why not pioneer something new? Work with the nonprofit to mold a newsworthy event, a solid fundraiser for the charity, and an investment that yields you measurable mileage. Negotiate for visible recognition, such as banners posted around arenas, public address system announcements, mention in event advertisements, acknowledgment on the Web site, and an ad in the souvenir program. See if you can entice a radio station to do a "remote." This is a live radio broadcast emanating from the actual location of the event.

A mother/daughter function sometimes works well. You might get likely candidate names by working with Job's Daughters, Rainbow Girls, YWCA, or Scouts. When sponsoring similar events, have flyers printed and distributed at key points in the community. You could leave some with bookstores, restaurants, laundromats, beauty and barber shops, libraries, and other public places.

Sports marketing is becoming as popular as e-mail. Such sponsorships allow corporations to reach a finely targeted market in a nonintrusive way. Joe Barrow, president of Louis Barrow Limited in Denver, produces and manages a series of walking events called the

Grand Walk Series. Barrow feels that special events should do more than just be a public affairs tool. He works to convert participants into prospects, then into customers.

It is important to find a sport that matches the sponsor's service or company image. Each sport and its participants have their own cultures. Possibilities range from fly-fishing to bowl games, tractor pulls to marathons.

United Bank of Denver used to sponsor the Tennis Classic. When they had a major portfolio with agriculture and farming groups, United worked with various rodeo associations. (Talk about aligning your events with the markets you aim to serve.) More recently they affiliated with the International Film Festival and the Denver Botanic Gardens outdoor concert series.

Vicki Morgan of San Francisco's Foghorn Press got attention in spades for the first book she published: *Forty Niners: Looking Back* by Joseph Hession. To launch it, Foghorn teamed up with the Pro Football Hall of Fame to stage a media event that would tie in with the 49ers' fortieth year. It also coincided with the book's arrival. The gala evening was held at no less than the prestigious Mark Hopkins International Hotel on Nob Hill. (Women really know how do to these things, don't we?) It featured former and current members of the San Francisco 49ers, hosted cocktails and hors d'oeuvres, door prizes, NFL films, music, entertainment, and—of course—a copy of the book. Tickets sold for a hefty $65. Three hundred people attended.

Although Morgan wanted the party to draw fans, her main priority was to capture media attention. Thirty-one members of the media showed up, including all three major local TV networks. A radio station carried the party live. The result? *Forty Niners* sold 8,000 copies the first month it was out! And Foghorn now is recognized as a real force in the publishing community, not to mention having valuable contacts with sportswriters and editors throughout the Bay Area.

When embarking on a major event, try to locate the promotions manager in a nonrelated industry who will candidly share her experience with you. Ask things like how much did you spend? How did you plan for the occasion? Did it work as well as you anticipated? The first year is a learning process. It takes a minimum of three years to establish an event and reap maximum benefits. Immediate payoffs may not be overwhelming, but downstream the impact of a good event is solidly felt.

Community Involvement

There are many socially conscious steps your business can take to help individuals or groups in your community. Initiating such actions not only aids others but assists in promoting you.

During a major recession, a commercial printer offered 25 copies of a resume free to unemployed people, plus a booklet on successful interviewing tips. A paper supplier even donated a case of paper. Four newspapers and two radio stations picked up the news item. This gave the printer a couple thousand dollars worth of free advertising and helped countless out-of-work individuals.

There are also other creative ways to contribute. Could some worthy cause use your support? A word processor or secretarial service, for instance, might advertise that 1 percent of their total receipts will go to buy computers for a local school or library. Add a company nameplate to the gift and get a photographer and reporter from the paper to cover the donation ceremony.

Many retail companies are doing well by doing good. Cause-related marketing can boost business and provide other intrinsic benefits. A supermarket in California sponsors an ongoing "Food for Families" program that gives food to the needy in regions served by the stores. Another grocery prints photos of missing children on the back of consumers' register receipts. A retail chain with strong feelings about animal and human rights cosponsored an Amnesty International concert where customers were encouraged to demonstrate support by leaving their thumb prints on in-store petitions.

Although you do cause-related marketing because you want to—it's part of your company's culture and core values—it usually has favorable results for you as well. When employees get involved, they feel enormous pride. This helps to motivate staff and curb turnover. Cause-related marketing benefits both the community and your store. It lets a company add the dimension of community service to the purchase of their product or service. Because women are the primary shopping force in U.S. retailing, and we appreciate companies that perform kind deeds, this helps differentiate a store and keeps them in our minds.

Especially appropriate for professional firms such as attorneys, certified public accountants, or engineers is to sponsor a scholarship. You might also talk with suppliers to see if they would cooperate with you in such a program.

In what other ways might you serve your community? Do you have a conference room or meeting space going to waste? By offering a free meeting room to charities, civic, or youth organizations you build your image and help them. These groups often only need a room for a couple of hours a month, but are extremely thankful when one is provided.

One chiropractor held a Community Appreciation Day. He offered his services at a greatly reduced fee and all the proceeds from the event were given to the local volunteer fire department. This was a clever way to supplement his normal advertising program and create goodwill.

A manners and etiquette expert conceived of a plan to teach inner city kids the right way to use their utensils at posh restaurants—and butter her own bread in the process. Dana May Casperson got local restaurants to volunteer their services and food for the sake of educating disadvantaged kids. The *Chicago Tribune* wrote about Casperson's project, and local TV news picked up the story as well. Some children said they had always felt like society outsiders. Now, with manners, they were more self-confident. Others were excited to share their newfound skills with moms and dads.

Donating and Volunteering

Doing good is indeed good for business. Volunteering your time to a worthy cause can pay big dividends. An attorney might do pro bono work one day a month. If you're an artist, have you thought of creating an eye-catching poster to help publicize a nonprofit organization's special event? A graphic designer we know of provides reproductions of drawings he has done of sports figures. Auctioned at fund-raising events, they bring in tidy sums—especially when signed by the celebrity.

Linda Dial, the founder of World Hope Creations, makes Special Angel Dolls. The company's mission is to "give hope" to disadvantaged, sick, or abused children. In addition to selling the dolls, she donates them to hospitals and law enforcement agencies, which give them to abused children to hold during the terrifying interview process. She also gives them to seriously or terminally ill children. Just one year after she started her business, Dial sold $5 million worth of dolls. Obviously, presenting free dolls to worthy recipients has brought her heaven-sent success.

Many smart businesspeople believe in making their donations count double: once for the worthy cause and once for themselves. Laura Wyraz, co-owner of Barry Bagels, has a no-cash donation policy. "Yet people are amazed at how much we return to the community," says Wyraz. Her company recently gave 250 *dozen* bagels to runners and workers at a big local fund-raising race. In exchange, the race organizers distributed money-off coupons she devised and posted a big sign thanking them. Thus Barry Bagels not only received lots of local recognition, but also used this as an opportunity to expand their customer base when the coupons were redeemed.

Mary Nack Childs, president of the Relocation Counseling Center headquartered in McLean, Virginia, donates hundreds of hours each year to her community. "Truly believe in the organizations you choose to affiliate with," is her advice. Because she feels society needs to support the arts, she joined the Fairfax Symphony. At cocktail parties before the concerts, she socializes with many trendsetters and high-level corporate executives. However, Childs cautions, "Don't talk business there, simply make contacts. If you care about your community and develop a level of personal trust, people will automatically want to do business with you." She builds coalitions with constituents while serving the needs of the community.

Before long she was involved with the symphony's fund-raising. This not only tapped into her own contacts to benefit the nonprofit organization, but allowed her to access important area CEOs as she prospected for symphony support. Consequently, Childs developed a unique entree to top management in many local companies. She can now either call the president directly and ask who in the organization to talk with regarding her business-to-business services, or talk with decision makers farther down the corporate ladder and tell them she has spoken with their president.

What about donating your services? This can be done individually or in tandem with others. For instance, chambers of commerce, TV stations, and other entities hold annual fund-raising auctions. Those who contribute receive a plug. Not to mention that helping others can "plug" dwindling cash flow holes and infuse your business with new vitality.

A B&B owner in Madison, Wisconsin, offers fellow innkeepers a free night's stay in her Canterbury Inn. Her hope is they will refer customers to her when there's no room at their inns.

Holding Contests, Giving Awards

While mass marketers often run games and contests on a nationwide scale, small business can't afford this kind of promotion. But what we lack in money, we can make up for in moxie.

Texas is the birthplace of a lot of big ideas. The first Living Legends Classic, an annual bodybuilding competition, was held in Warton, Texas. What an ideal contest for a gym to sponsor. And you might know a Texas bank, TransFirst, came up with a sweepstakes idea to encourage customers to use its Moneymaker automatic teller machines (ATMs). A joint promotion with a local radio station and 7-Eleven stores, where the machines were placed, made the costs affordable. Sweepstake numbers appeared on each Moneymaker ATM transaction slip. A whopping 2.5 million entries resulted.

On a more realistic scale, one Halloween a market placed a giant pumpkin in its window and offered cash prizes to the person who guessed closest to the number of seeds inside the pumpkin. The contest drew thousands of entries—and sold an unprecedented number of pumpkins. Experimenters counted the seeds, seeking clues to aid in the guesstimating. Could you mold this concept to fit your operation in some way?

Any business with a lot of foot traffic and a window can draw additional customers into the store. Try to use your contest to do double duty: In addition to getting the contestant's name and address, ask for information that will help you better serve your customers and market your products. Analyzing this information is definitely market research on the cheap.

Restaurants are famous for the fishbowl inviting customers to leave a business card for a drawing on a free meal. In return the restaurant gets a mailing list of their customers and a ready database to solicit for parties and meetings.

Do be aware contests could dump you into legal hot water. Most states have laws regulating contests and declaring lotteries illegal unless they are sponsored by the government or a charity. The Federal Trade Commission also monitors some contests, as does the Federal Communications Commission and the U.S. Postal Service. You may want to check with an attorney before embarking on a journey into this highly regulated jungle.

Contests are limited primarily by our imagination. What can you do to delight someone else and get free promotion for yourself? Just be sure your contest is relevant to your business. A beauty shop might give a free shampoo and style to the woman with the longest hair, a church could award their longest-standing member a token gift. An insurance agent could honor the driver with the longest safe-driving/no-ticket record. How about a travel agent giving the customer who has logged

144   www.BrazenHussiesNetwork.com

the most miles in a year a free trip to somewhere or a catered breakfast in bed *at home*. A weight control center might make the woman who lost the most pounds Queen for a Day.

In a promotion aimed at bookstores, Bard Books, Inc.,—publishers of an offbeat corporate biography titled *NUTS! Southwest Airlines' Crazy Recipe for Business and Personal Success*—doled out 10 free round-trip tickets to anywhere Southwest flies. To qualify for the contest, store managers had to "Go NUTS!" creating a window display that portrayed the zany style and maverick spirit of the airline.

Want free radio exposure? Call a talk show host or disk jockey on a popular morning drive-time show in your area and suggest an idea for a call-in contest that ties in with your business. Donate a dozen prizes and be sure to ask the host to mention where listeners who don't win can purchase a prize. Ask them to announce your phone number or address.

Awards are another intriguing promotional tactic. If no one in your area is doing so, why not institute a Good Citizen award? Have your assistant scan papers watching for stories of people who have performed a kind deed or helped significantly in the community. Each month select a winner, then send him or her a certificate and a letter explaining the program. Also be sure the media gets a copy of the letter and the name of that month's award recipient. Cap it with an annual award drawn from the monthly winners—and a big media splash.

A New York–based consultancy, The Communication Workshop, annually presents the Percy Awards. They are presented for the business world's most fuzzy, laughable, and misworded communications. Although copies of the winners are available, company names are not released "to protect the guilty."

Award programs work both ways. Perhaps there is a local, state, or national award opportunity *you* could be entering. Even if you don't win, you and your work will be exposed to important people in your industry. Those selected as judges are usually movers and shakers. And just because a project doesn't win one time doesn't mean it won't another. Juries change. People have better days. Your acumen increases. Resubmit eligible projects even if they were previously rejected.

Here are a few hints on award-winning strategies: 1) Submit actual examples of material. The real thing is always better than a photograph. 2) Make it easy to read and follow. Use tabs or some consistent graphic element to separate sections. Adding subheads in your written copy to delineate different components will also be appreciated. Type all paperwork. Judges don't have time to plow through unreadable hand-writing. 3) Sell yourself succinctly. Long-winded dissertations make judges' eyes cross. Remember they are evaluating dozens, often hundreds, sometimes thousands of other entries too. Write snappy and to the point. 4) Package your materials well. To protect your entry, be sure it goes out in a sturdy box or container and is insured.

Some accolades honoring businesswomen include *Working Woman's* Entrepreneurial Excellence Awards and Avon Products, Inc.'s Annual Women of Enterprise Awards. Additionally, many city and regional business magazines compile lists of Top Entrepreneurs in the area.

Do awards constitute a genuine demonstration of peer respect—or do they simply cater to the vanity within us all for winning things and coming in first? Does winning an award really carry much clout? You bet! In fact, you don't even have to capture the number one spot. Being a runner-up, receiving honorable mention, or a citation of excellence can also lead to perks. That is, if *you* take advantage of the honor and publicize it!

Find out what publicity the awards sponsors are doing themselves, but never leave it to them alone. Immediately get out a news release. (And don't just headline it "XYX company wins award." Instead start it with a provocative or informative quote, which then indicates you are the "winner of the ABC award.") Pursue radio interviews. Alert your company associates, sales reps, distributors, and major accounts. Update your collateral materials. Display your award. Milk it for all its worth. Receiving a prestigious award often opens the door to new business.

And don't overlook awards for your Web site. Capturing one or more will lead to recognition, credibility, and additional traffic. There are over 800 award sites around the world. To help you apply and track your activities go to wysiwyg://2/http://websiteawards.net/. You'll find specific usable suggestions on how to prepare your site, then how to apply for awards. An index of articles written by leading authorities in the field of awards offers valuable insights.

Sassy Lassies Conduct Surveys

Besides a huge jump in the number of politically oriented commercials, what else accompanies a national election? Yep, political polls abound. You don't have to wait for an election to focus attention on industry issues, however. You can conduct a poll—complete with percentages and statistics—any time. Surveys display your knowledge and specialty. They establish you as the expert and inevitably lead to new business.

According to *PRink*, the best topics for surveys are those that make for stimulating conversation: health, leisure time, hobbies and interests, sports, retirement/life cycle issues, quality of life, education, the arts, and people's feelings about entrepreneurial behavior.

Author Lisa Kanarek (*Everything's Organized*) contacted 600 women who responded about how much time they spend each day looking for lost items. The study was given generous coverage in *Entrepreneur* magazine.

A study commissioned by the Girl Scouts turns out interesting findings that support "smart cookies" join this organization. Girl Scout alumnae end up with a lot more than merit badges. The study found that 61 percent of the 1,339 women queried credit their professional success, particularly in terms of self-confidence and teamwork, to their scouting experience. That should make for good recruitment material!

If you have the bucks, you can hire survey help. A public relations firm typically spends anywhere from $18,000 to $45,000 to complete a survey. For most, that's out of the question. But some research firms do what are called "omnibus polls." These polls are organized by the research firms to cover a broad range of topics. You can buy in for around $1,000 a question. For those on more restricted budgets, smaller polling samples, and less sophisticated methods are the order of the day. Word survey questionnaires objectively, get as large a sample as possible, and double-check all mathematical calculations.

Your survey can be an informal analysis done among your customers/clients. A health spa, for instance, might shape questions to explore attitudes about exercise, weight loss, and the importance of a careful diet. Another approach is to explore your company files. You may be sitting on proprietary information that could be molded into a fascinating survey. Be sensitive to gathering information that will involve your prospects. Human interest stuff is always appreciated. For instance, the public "gobbled up" Nabisco Brands, Inc.'s study on how people eat their Oreo cookies.

Once the poll is complete, write up your conclusions and offer them both locally and to the wire services. Recycle this information in other ways. How about a direct-mail piece, slated for prospects, summarizing your findings? Conducting a research study, then circulating the results, is a low-budget, high-impact way to promote yourself.

Become an Industry Leader

Why should a prospective client choose your firm over the competition? Why would a potential customer shop at your store or a patient make an appointment with your office? One reason might be because you've established yourself as a leader in your industry, someone they can trust and respect.

There's an adage that says you have to give to get. Nowhere is this more true than in business. If you aspire to more publicity, elevated success, and greater affluence—it's time to get involved.

One way is by becoming a nationally recognized leader in your industry. This doesn't happen overnight; such prominence takes years to cultivate. You'll have to join the right groups, spend time serving on panels and committees, maintain contact with the media, and "know your stuff." But it pays big dividends.

When you become a source the media can depend on—and they need the big picture about trends and issues that impact your industry—*you* are the person they will turn to. Most smaller companies couldn't possibly afford to buy such coverage. It gives you a significant competitive edge. Such credibility pays an enormous return on your investment of time and energy. You'll be a resource. Resources are people with a *presence* in their field. They are the experts. Reporters for both print and electronic sources seek them out.

Dr. Robert R. Butterworth of Contemporary Psychology Associates, Inc., in Los Angeles is a master media player. "To make comments, you have to know what's going on. Do your homework," he counsels. "I read three newspapers and use my computer to access the wire services."

This psychologist is an authority on teens and youngsters. Butterworth has been noted and quoted about teen drug abuse, letting kids view the disastrous shuttle *Discovery* launch, the ramifications of punk rock, how teens worry about nuclear war, etc. He began by sending out two- or three-page evergreen features—stories that are timeless.

While he started small with local newspapers and radio stations, he soon graduated to larger media, such as the *Los Angeles Times* and TV. Dr. Butterworth's comments and observations have appeared in most of the major newspapers in the U.S. and Europe. Additionally, he's been interviewed on the news by all three networks and frequently appears on CNN and various other talk shows.

"Identify your expertise and let people know about it," Butterworth advises. "This makes reporters' jobs easier." Once they recognize you have knowledge in a specialized field, they'll contact you when an appropriate news story breaks.

When the San Francisco earthquake hit, Dr. Butterworth's phone didn't stop ringing for three days. Understanding—and coping with—the quake's lingering effects on children was a hot topic. In a nonintrusive way, he offered help. Of course, this resulted in more people learning about this clinical psychologist who specializes in children at his offices in Downey, West Los Angeles, and Sherman Oaks.

Every industry has one or more trade associations that cater to the needs and interests of their specific profession. Join. Get active. Run for an office. Affiliating has many benefits. In addition to magazines or newsletters chockful of useful information, most associations sponsor educational workshops and conventions.

Women are much more likely than men to seek out assistance from other business owners and use trade associations to make contacts. Although 28 percent of women-owned businesses surveyed by American Express and NAWBO of New York City indicated they used trade associations to build their revenues, just 15 percent of men-owned companies utilized this resource. The business relationships fostered through trade and professional associations can have major benefits for small businesses. Networking is more than just passing out business cards. It's really getting to know your peers, those who can help you—and whom you can help in return. Association participation allows you to create a pool of people and information you can call upon to assist with your business.

Association membership affords an ideal opportunity to rub shoulders with the giants in your industry. The way to make such contacts is to leave the fringes for the inner circle. This is where the movers and shakers of any industry congregate. When you're planning strategy at committee sessions or hammering out decisions at board meetings, people really get to know one another. And the typical opportunities for breaking bread or sharing a drink that accompany such work sessions further set the stage for fruitful professional and personal relationships.

Another way to solidify your industry leadership position is to offer your services on a complimentary basis. Provide free help or information. You can lend your professional expertise to nonprofit groups. Sue Collier, a publication designer, volunteers her services in designing a monthly newsletter for a nonprofit woman's organization in her town. In exchange for her design services, she gets an advertisement in the newsletter—not to mention a free lunch at the monthly meetings. The exposure she's received has turned into many a paying client.

A corporate business development firm works with local economic development groups, supplying them with valuable free statistical information. In turn, the firm either receives verbal credit, their corporate name appears on the data, or the groups give them direct referrals.

And you can capitalize on this goodwill by making the media aware of it!

Boardroom Bound

Serving on a board of directors is time-consuming. Eye-opening. Professionally enriching. These plums are doled out to women who are already successful. If we're talking the big time, the 1999 Catalyst Board Report shows women made few gains in the Fortune 500s. They hold only 11.2 percent of the seats at the 500 largest publicly traded U.S. companies, a total of 685 director chairs. And Fortune 1000s ranked even more poorly. Firms in this second tier were more than twice as likely to have *no* female board members.

I guess that shouldn't be too surprising. For eons boardrooms have been strictly men's clubs with directors being buddies of the company's CEO or chairman. While we're a long way from parity, we are starting to make some inroads. Catalyst's president Sheila Wellington asserts, "We plan to shine our spotlight on them until we see growth." (Visit their Web site at www.catalystwomen.org.)

Judy Haberkorn, president of consumer sales and service for Bell Atlantic and chairwoman of the prestigious Committee of 200, finds the boardroom her favorite classroom. "To sit with CEOs from 10 different companies in 10 different industries who are at the top of their game and listen to the questions they ask and the way they approach problems…I have never left a board meeting without having some kernel of a new idea for my business," she reports.

If you aspire to a director's seat, there are several things you can do to get board-ready. You must develop the right set of skills and expertise, communicate those traits to the proper people, and build a network of peers who can help in your quest.

Start by volunteering for nonprofit boards. They provide a platform from which one can be seen and evaluated. And you can also use your hard-won business seasoning to advance a cause you really believe in. A good way to check them out before offering yourself for a board position is to volunteer; then you can see the group in action. Go so far as to sit in on a board meeting if you can to determine the tone and efficiency of the group and get a sense of who you would be working with. For a helping hand, contact the National Center for Nonprofit Boards at 800-883-6262 or visit their Web site at http://www.ncnb.org.

Large associations like the United Way and educational institutions are great training grounds. United Way even offers a six-month training program to prepare people to serve on nonprofit boards. Other possibilities for experience include arts and culture nonprofits, those offering human services, trade associations, and religious-related groups. In this arena you'll be more likely to discuss fund-raising than profit margins. Said one woman, "I got involved with boards because I was interested in helping kids. I didn't go in to help my business, but that was the icing on the cake."

Getting "line" experience that deals with profit and loss is invaluable. Instead of serving on the marketing, public relations, or membership committee, go for the finance or strategic planning committee. Besides nonprofits, consider small private companies that are on the rise. Then graduate to publicly held corporations.

Always ask "What's in it for me?" The head of a $20 million construction firm in Denver, Barbara Grogan credits her service on three boards: "I've been involved in mergers, acquisitions, divestitures, opening and closing plants, and hiring and firing. It has really helped me grow as a CEO."

What should you anticipate? The pay is typically lousy. You'll be expected to attend a minimum of four meetings a year, each of which requires 10 to 30 hours of preparation. Then there are committee meetings. And if the company hits a crisis, you'll be extremely involved. (Read the company's proxy statement to determine what existing directors are paid.) Large corporations are starting to toss stock options into the mix, tying director compensation directly to the company's performance on Wall Street.

Accepting a board seat may put you in a touchy legal position. Find out what type of liability insurance the company offers its directors and do your own due diligence. Because a board of directors has fiduciary responsibility to see that the group is fulfilling its mission, you can be held personally liable if the organization is sued.

When preparing for a meeting, highlight important sections in your packet. Then select two or three areas you feel qualified in and strongly about. Speak up so you're recognized as a contributor. And leave the ultra-short skirts and lacy blouses for another time. Conservative is the dress code here.

Seek Professional Listings

Publicizing your firm via professional directories is a tangible way to market an intangible. There are thousands of such directories, some admittedly more powerful than others. At About Books, Inc., we find it revealing that a sizable number of inquiries are generated from free listings in *Literary Market Place*. After several years of fine-tuning this source, we appear under so many different headings, we've coded the addresses to track which sections work best.

One of the especially appealing aspects of directory listings is that most are free of charge. Every industry has such directories. Yet few people know about them or bother to do the paperwork necessary to be included even when they are aware of such publications.

This is one of the first things we do for a new client. When a Houston management consulting and training firm hired us to come on-site for an individualized three-day PR conference, we tracked down the following potential listing sources: the *Consultants Directory, Business Consultants Directory, Management Consultants*, and the *Consultants and Consulting Organizations Directory*. To promote the CEO, we requested listing forms from *Who's Who in America, Who's Who in the World*, and *WHO Houston, Inc.*, where the company is based.

Additional personal listings were solicited in *Dictionary of International Biography, International Businessmen's Who's Who, Biographical Dictionary of American Business Leaders, Directory of Distinguished Americans*, and *Men of Achievement*. Because he is the author of three management books, we also went after *The International Authors and Writers Who's Who, Contemporary Authors*, and *Who's Who in the U.S. Writers, Editors, and Poets*. Whew!

Some directories are only published every other year, so you will have just missed a few deadlines. It sometimes takes up to three years for these listings to get into print. However, this shouldn't bother any forward-thinking company. If you want fast action, investigate directory listings online; a whole other bonanza awaits you there.

Miscellaneous Promotional Schemes

I've been collecting ideas for this book for several years. Because many don't fit into any overall section, they are gathered here under a "miscellaneous" umbrella with the hope one will spark your imagination.

■ Sponsoring a telephone hotline can lead to increased revenue. A Littleton, Colorado, law firm provides a recording of basic information on bankruptcies. A dozen potential clients leave messages at the end of the recording each week.

A freelance copywriter who specializes in direct-response advertising has an advertising hotline. Callers are treated to three- to five-minute taped messages on such subjects as "10 Ways to Stretch Your Advertising Budget" or "13 Questions to Ask before You Create Your Next Ad Campaign." Her mini-messages are changed every week. This gimmick could be used successfully by travel agents, gardeners, clothing stores, animal boarding kennels, insurance agents, health food stores, printers, and a host of others.

■ When Margaret McClain McEntrie started her business in her garage (while also home-schooling two children), little did she dream that 10 years later she would reign over a $40 million dollar enterprise with 410 franchise stores all over the U.S.! She came up with the idea to offer delicious chocolates and candies in colorful arrangements as an alternative to sending flowers. But not enough people knew about her in the beginning. So to promote her wares, Margaret began giving away "bouquets" in high traffic locations such as banks, popular restaurants, and cleaners. As a result, people started calling, some to place orders and others to learn how to make the attractive bouquets. That's how the Candy Bouquet franchise began. By giving, Margaret received in bounteous measure.

■ Can you use greeting cards to hitch your business to a special event or time? The average business letter takes 24 minutes to complete and send. The average business greeting card takes only three minutes. And the response rates from cards are significantly higher than from the average business letter. An accountant or tax planner might devise a humorous greeting card to send out before tax time. A dating service or therapist who specializes in relationships could capitalize on Valentine's Day. A boutique could send primary customers birthday wishes.

Speaking of greeting cards, always keep a supply at your desk. You will be perceived as a thoughtful person when you remember a key prospect's or client's birthday or anniversary. Sending congratulatory cards for a new job, baby, or home is also an appreciated touch. So is a get-well or thinking-of-you card when illness or tragedy has struck. Have you ever thought of sending a thank-you card after someone retains your services?

Do you realize each year around Easter a dramatic promotional opportunity occurs? Daylight savings time is welcomed by all. Have you ever thought about how you could use this annual occurrence to your advantage? Anyone who deals with growing things can play on it. Because people will be outdoors more, many recreational and sporting facilities will also find it a natural. Can you think of other ways to tie in your business?

■ Here is an idea for nonprofit organizations that need to produce more revenue. Why not create a special Committee of One Hundred? To be part of this committee, 100 people (or businesses) have to donate $100 apiece. (Large associations or groups could expand this to a Committee of One Thousand, thus potentially raising $100,000 instead of $10,000.)

Speaking of nonprofits reminds me of the story of Grace Memorial House of Prayer in Fort Lauderdale, Florida. To support their ministry, every Friday and Saturday afternoon they sell take-out barbecue alongside a busy thoroughfare. Pork ribs and chicken wings smothered in the Reverend Noble Harris' barbecue sauce have been sustaining the church for more than a decade. No rummage sales, bingo games, or bake sales here.

■ Jennifer Gilbert needed to find a bootstrap way to drum up business for her New York–based events planning company, Save the Date. In the beginning, she spent long days cold-calling local large corporations. "I had called one bank over and over and they never returned my calls," recounts Gilbert. So she decided to show up in the bank's lobby anyway, carrying 50 yellow balloons. Gilbert waited five hours with a sinking heart. But when the bank executives finally emerged, they took one look at her and cracked up. They have been clients ever since—and this lady with chutzpah made roughly $15 million in revenues last year.

■ Talking about doing gutsy things, how about seeking governmental recognition? For the lionhearted, it may be available in several forms. There are resolutions from the city council or the county board of supervisors. You might approach the mayor or governor to make a proclamation. Legislators have also been known to get statements entered into the Congressional Record. All of these, by the way, make impressive reprints.

■ Speaking of being impressive, let me tell you about Judie Sinclair, who is the marketing director for a health-care agency. Her responsibility was to come up with unique techniques to set their agency apart. So she sent an old shoe to a doctor she had been trying to get in to see for some time. The attached note read, "Now that I have one foot in the door…" The physician was so amused that she readily got an appointment and eventually a referral. Another out-of-the ordinary technique she uses when missing seeing a doctor or the office manager is to leave a bag of nuts with a note that reads: "Nuts, I missed you." Then the rest of the message. Any saleswoman can apply these clever tactics to her product or service.

But Judie doesn't quit there. "I can always pick up on the climate of an office by the response of the receptionist or nurses. When they seem overwhelmed, I arrange a 'Happy Party' at their office," she explains. She arrives wearing a tee shirt with a smiley face and toting yellow- iced cookies with smiley faces (which she orders from a local bakery), napkins and plates to match, a smiley face balloon bouquet, a CD player with "Don't Worry, Be Happy," and fun handouts for everyone in the office. Sometimes it's pencils, other times super balls or stickers—all with you-know-what faces. People are so taken aback with the ridiculous nature of her antics they all end up laughing and getting in a better mood. (What a great idea for *any* office. Want to be considered the boss from heaven? Throw a Happy Party!) Sinclair reports that offices actually sometimes request a Happy Day from her team.

■ One final promotional idea. Although it won't work for most businesses, it could succeed royally for a few. How about *starting* a national nonprofit trade association? Such action would definitely put you in the limelight. Associations typically offer educational services (workshops, seminars, conferences), publish a regular newsletter, provide discounted member benefits, and offer networking opportunities. Often they also serve as an information clearinghouse on the topic around which they are formed. What a way to position yourself as the official expert!

Be aware that launching such an organization requires a huge commitment—both in time and money. You would need an advisory board representing both a geographic and size mix in the industry. You must decide on a carefully honed mission statement encapsulating your purpose. Membership categories, such as charter members, regular, professional, and associate (vendor) members, must be determined. Most importantly, you'll need a strong marketing plan to sell people on your idea.

Some of these people followed the advice of "fake it, 'til you make it." Others employed provocative promotional ideas for visibility and success. Just remember, you are the sculptor not only of your today but also of your tomorrow. You have the chisel—in the form of a keen imagination—to create anything you want!

"Promotion" is creativity "in motion." With *all* these ideas you're sure to get known and get ahead faster. Let us now move on to exploring how radio can add air conditioning to your tongue—and profits to your bottom line.

Web Sites, Wisdom, and Whimsey

Finding your computer files for PR and promotion overwhelming? Here's a simple trick to pull the most important ones to the front of the line. Just rename them starting with the underline "_" character. That way those files will appear first in the list and be easy to find.

●●●●●●●

Why do so many men look sad?
Because they finally got it all together,
then they forgot where they put it.

●●●●●●●

Networking on the fly. Kathi Jones, a human resources and recruiting manager at Aventail Corporation in Seattle, always arrives at the airport early. Is she paranoid about missing her plane? Hardly. This shrewd lady cases other people's luggage for company tags featuring the names of her big-time competitors such as Cisco Systems and Raptor Systems. She also watches for people wearing tee shirts or baseball caps from her competitors. Then she creates an opportunity to chat up the owners of the luggage about business-related issues. You might be surprised what she learns and who she recruits.

Promotional Web wisdom and wonders await you at http://www.virtualpromote.com. This is an exceptional site for those already somewhat savvy about Internet promotion. Virtual Promote will lead you to the biggest places to list your site; take you on the high road to spiders, robots, and hits leading to higher traffic; and point you in the direction of search engine forums where Web gurus gather. You can also subscribe to *The Gazette*, one of the fastest growing weekly marketing newsletters on the Net. It's free and you can browse past issues to be sure you want it before subscribing.

●●●●●●●

A woman on the golf course said to her friend,
"I just got a new set of clubs for my husband."
"Good trade," replied the friend.

●●●●●●●

Take a tip from P. T. Barnum: This circus owner was one of the world's greatest showmen. His goal was to capture people's attention in whatever audacious way he could. At one point he had an elephant plowing his fields. (Yes, you read right.) Why an elephant, you wonder? Because that field was near the railroad tracks that carried passengers into New York City. And Barnum knew he would grab their attention and people would talk about this unforgettable publicity stunt. How can you use this principle to pique the curiosity of your prospects?

●●●●●●●

Sophia Loren says mistakes are the dues one pays
for a full life. I say if you're not making mistakes,
you're not doing anything!

●●●●●●●

Become part of the ongoing Brazen Hussies Network today! At our Web site we run a clearinghouse for forward-thinking female entrepreneurs. You can find over 100 links to powerful women's business and entrepreneurial sites. Business-related books to round out your professional reading, a free weekly e-mail tip to help boost your bottom line, money-making articles by industry leaders, a classified ad section where you can promote your business, plus much more. Those who join the Network also receive my monthly e-mail newsletter packed with the same kind of information I've been giving you here. And, because there's clout in numbers, I'm also negotiating wonderful cost-saving discounts on products and services Network members can use in their businesses. For full details, go to http://www.BrazenHussiesNetwork.com. I'd love to welcome you as a member!

CHAPTER 6

Radio Interviews:
How to Be Hip
and Shoot from the Lip

Talk is *hot*, whether it's on the radio, TV, or Internet. In 1983 there were only 53 radio stations with news/talk formats. *American Demographics* magazine recently reported there were more than 1,000 and they continue to escalate. News/talk is the most-listened-to radio format, capturing 16.8 percent of all listeners. It is most popular among those over 65, 41.1 percent of whom are tuned in. It's popularity goes down with age: 28.6 percent of listeners 55 to 64, 19.6 percent of those in the 45 to 54 bracket, 13.9 percent of 35 to 44-year-olds, and 9.3 percent of the 25 to 34 crowd.

This emergence of talk radio seems to serve the need for connection with others. Today we often don't know our neighbors; we don't visit over the backyard fence like we used to. Instead we have a virtual, electronic, sometimes global, media community…people with like minds and interests. Show topics often revolve around what you would talk about with your best friend over lunch: such things as relationships, saving money, dealing with an illness or a difficult boss—real-life subjects.

Since commutes to and from work are growing longer each year, Americans on the road are a captive audience for talk radio. Forty-two percent of radio listeners are in their cars, 37 percent listen at home, and 21 percent at work, often while engaged in other activities. According to *Talkers* magazine, the industry trade journal, the typical talk fan is between 35 and 64 years old, 66 percent are white, 47 percent are female, 32 percent have at least a college degree, and 58 percent of them make $50,000 or more a year. Impressive demographics.

Advertising agencies have realized that talk radio listeners tend to participate more directly in the actual listening process than music radio listeners. Talk show devotees use the medium as primary foreground entertainment. Not only are they educated, attentive, and affluent, they're also activists. These characteristics make them ideal targets for you.

With today's popular "talk radio" format, stations need lots of guests. Early morning and late afternoon drive times, when folks are traveling to and from work, are the first choice for those seeking to reach business commuters. Midday programs are good for companies targeting homemakers. Of course, a lot depends on the host. Some have vast listening audiences even during bad hours because they are talented, controversial, and dynamic.

Imagine for a moment what a 30-minute commercial would cost—not 30 seconds, 30 *minutes*. Do you realize if the host likes you and things go well, in essence you get that? It won't cost one red cent! The beauty of publicity demonstrated again.

Knowing the Ropes

Your mailings can go out as little as four weeks in advance of your being on the air. To solicit appearing as a guest, your material should be addressed to the producer of an individual show. If in doubt about which show would be best, call the station program director's *secretary*. This is an undervalued, yet highly knowledgeable person who can point you in the right direction. A couple of weeks after the mailing, follow-up by phone. Be politely persistent.

When an interview is scheduled, ask questions. Find out what they want to cover. Suggest areas you'd like to touch on during the show. You may get insights into the personality of the host or hostess and some hint about the slant needed to put yourself and your cause in the most favorable light.

Shows come in several types and hosts come in various degrees of preparedness. Some interviewers will not have bothered to bone up at all. Others pride themselves on being informed on their guest's subjects and will chat at length about specific aspects of your industry. One thing to remember when doing radio is that your voice must do all the work. A smile is important; it *does* carry over a microphone.

By having in mind a clearly defined agenda that you wish to explore, you'll cut through apprehension like a hot knife through butter. Make specific notes of the points you want to cover. Some people even prepare a list of questions to provide interviewers. Train yourself to expect the unexpected. Anticipate in advance the questions you're likely to get; don't dodge the difficult ones. Then you won't be surprised when you're thrown a "zinger." Remember, you're the expert. You already know your subject backward and forward. Rehearse your answers and comments to build your self-confidence. The key to successful interviewing is organization; it keeps you focused.

Be sure to speak in human terms; don't get mired in a bunch of statistics. Talk about how your service solves listeners' problems. Brief, precise answers are better than rambling replies. Mention the name of your store or company several times; don't just say "we." The whole point of your being on the air is to increase your image and prospect for business. Listeners must know who you represent.

Suppose you get a sticky question—one that requires you to pause and gather your thoughts? Don't panic. Tricks I've used to stall for think time include either repeating the question or saying, "That's a good question…"

One other aspect of radio that could be very meaningful is public service announcements, better known as PSAs. If you are a nonprofit organization (by official IRS structure, not happenstance), you are probably eligible for some of this air time. What a boon to churches, associations, and other not-for-profit groups who could benefit from unpaid commercials. This free time goes to those bold enough to seek it. If you qualify, get your share.

The Entrepreneur as Radio Guest

If you don't have time to trot from station to station all across the country, or you shudder at the thought of a microphone thrust in your face, many radio programs conduct interviews via phone—from the comfort of your office or home. Radio stations across the land will interview you long distance. These are called "phoners." If your business is national in scope, this can be a bonanza.

Syndicated and network shows often go to hundreds of stations. This is a superb way to get national exposure. Financial consultancies, law firms, Internet providers, or those with widespread locations should keep this in mind.

Statistics have shown results from radio promotion are often even more imposing than those from TV. First, you have more time to expand upon your subject. On television, the guest spots usually last less than five minutes—whereas with radio, some talk shows give you an hour. Besides discussing your particular area of expertise, you also interact with the audience, answer questions posed by listeners, and get into an extended conversation about the topic. With today's lower long-distance charges, radio talk shows are now able to team up with a variety of experts in subject areas from aardvarks to zoology. Chances are you can be one of these experts.

Prospecting for Appropriate Shows

There are radio stations all across the country that would welcome you telling your tale. You could do this virtually all day for months and still not have reached all of them. However, this isn't what I suggest. It doesn't make sense to repeatedly spend hours of your time talking to people in tiny places like Podunk, Idaho. Go for the numbers. And there's a practical way to do it. This is just one of the secrets I will reveal to you.

There are several different directories that list radio shows. Go to your library, or online, and research. If you want the greatest reach, look for "syndicated" or "network" shows. Some of these go to as many as 1,000 different radio stations around the country! That really makes your time count. Sure the competition is tough. But after you get some experience doing the little shows, it's time to graduate to the big time. New York and Los Angeles are where most syndicated and network shows originate.

Be sure you're using the most current information available. Media people seem to change jobs like most of us change underwear. Always call and verify who is the producer or guest booker (and the correct name spelling), plus the current address. With time and tenacity, you can find the big time yourself instead of paying thousands of dollars each month to a publicist.

There's nothing wrong with doing some smaller stations in out-of-the-way places for practice, to really get your act together and refine it. Start small and craft a thing of beauty: an interview that is really powerful. Then move on to the larger shows.

What's your approach? You're not promoting a product, service, or retail outlet; you're providing *a solution to people's problems*. Always keep that uppermost in your mind. Remember it when you're creating your news release, pitch letter, making follow-up phone calls, and appearing on the show.

Send them a personalized pitch letter and a news release. You may not want to send a full-blown media kits unless they request it. Follow-up with a phone call. Be prepared to make many phone calls for popular shows. Have ready a brief, provocative reason why their listeners would want to hear from you.

You are being considered because you're an "expert." (You might even pitch radio and newspapers by saying you've just completed research on XYZ [your particular topic], and if they need an expert in that area, you're available.) Promoting your business is secondary. You are filling a need, responding to a "hurt" listeners have.

Of course, if you work just locally, your thrust will be to the hometown shows. Find the stations in the phone book, then call for particulars.

Potent Radio Maneuvers

■ As soon as you pick up the phone, assume you're on the air. This won't usually be true as the producer typically comes on first, but you never know when your comments will be broadcast live.

■ Try to listen to the station and show ahead of time. If it's out of your area, one idea is to call the station and ask to be placed on hold: You'll hear the show airing!

■ Target your pitches for the season. Grace Housholder does Top 10 Funny Kid Christmas Stories, then Top 10 List of Funny Kid Stories Involving Love for Valentine's Day. Of course there's Mother's Day, Halloween, Easter—you name it. Can you give your message a seasonal twist and get on the air again and again?

■ If you're offering a demo tape, don't send it to another station in the same city. Nobody likes to be a runner-up. Producers prefer exclusives in big markets.

■ Stand and deliver. When you do a phone interview from a chair, you're slouched and your diaphragm is scrunched. Stand. Walk. Pace. You'll sound more dynamic. You may want a longer phone cord—maybe even to purchase a headset—to allow this flexibility.

■ Relate your service or product to current headlines. Maybe

(continued on next page)

POTENT RADIO MANEUVERS
(continued)

you have an alternative viewpoint. Attack the commonly held notion. Explode the myth.

■ You may want to "plant" friends or loved ones to get the call-in ball rolling. Coach them with a leading question.

■ Remember that radio producers and hosts talk to each other. There are sites on the Internet, such as Bit Board and Morning Mouth (closed to the general public), where they gab about outstanding guests. They also have conventions where they network. Be extraordinary and they will seek you out like butterflies quest after nectar.

■ Always be on your best vocal behavior. You are "auditioning" from the moment you open your mouth. Think a producer is calling just to check that detail? Nope. She or he wants to hear your voice inflection, how enthusiastic you sound, if you're quick on the mental uptake, etc. Same thing when you call them. Turn on the verbal charm.

Motto of the Successful Sister: "Be Prepared"

One of the biggest secrets is to be fully ready. Mark Twain once said it takes three weeks to prepare a good ad-lib speech. Perhaps the easiest way to prepare is to role-play with another individual, or use a cassette recorder to tape what you say. The point is you need to get used to talking about your subject in short, colorful phrases. These are called "sound bites." The idea is to train yourself to present your message in an abbreviated, punchy way. Use Velcro words and vivid statements that stick in listeners' minds. In today's fast-paced world the average sound bite has shrunk from 9.4 seconds to 4.3. It takes intense practice to put your meaning so succinctly.

Have two or three major points you want to make. What is your core message? You need to refine it, hone it, sharpen it until you've got 15 to 20 forceful words. Then literally memorize it—not so it becomes a rote announcement but rather a lively and precise declaration.

Practice aloud. We see things differently with our eyes than we hear with our ears. As you're role-playing, also get in the habit of presenting your main point right at the very beginning. Don't wander into an interview. Dive in! Say something stimulating. You must capture the imagination and the interest of the audience at the onset.

Get in the habit of making a short statement or giving a brief answer, then elaborating on it. That way if you are put in a position where time is limited, you've already said the most important thing. When you're on a more leisurely show you can then expound by telling a story

(Listeners love stories!), sharing a startling statistic, giving a case history, or in some way embellishing your initial statement.

Don't try to become too perfect. You don't want to sound like a suave politician. Be human. Strive to come across as someone who's deeply credible and involved in the subject. Be excited. Enthusiastic. Forthright. It's much more important on a longer radio show to be captivatingly conversational than perfectly polished.

If your subject lends itself, try to think of something that would be easy for the average listener to understand and relate to. For instance, a computer company spokeswoman explained, "Today we can put all the intelligence of a room-sized computer from the 1950s into a silicon chip the size of a cornflake." Not everyone relates to silicon chips, but everybody understands cornflakes. Look at your own subject. See what you can find that makes it easy for the average person to grasp.

Don't be afraid to let people get to know the real you. If you love gardening, why not use an analogy about roses or tomatoes? Or if you're a music buff, perhaps you want to use a comparison to an orchestra or a jazz band. Allow listeners to learn a little about you as a person.

Behind the Scenes Action

Now that we've talked about what you're going to do for your actual verbal presentation, let's discuss another kind of preparation. There are two items you should create before you ever go on the radio. First is a set of 3-inch by 5-inch cards, three for each interview. All should contain your name, the name of your company, the theme of the interview, plus full contact information. See the accompanying sample.

Media Reminder Card

Guest Marilyn Ross

author of

Shameless Marketing for Brazen Hussies™

Publisher: Communication Creativity

Call orders to:

1-800-331-8355
($19.95 plus $4 shipping)

Day/Date_____ Time_____

You're going to send these to prime people *before* you go on the air so they have them in their hot little hands when your interview occurs. These cards go to the following: the producer of the show, the host or hostess who will be interviewing you, and the station phone receptionist. For the telephone operator, put a little flag on the card noting when you're going to be interviewed. Also write a notation that this is for her or his convenience so if calls come in, the information is readily at hand. By doing this you've helped these folks help you. Make it easy for them to direct people to you.

The other item we're going to create is some sort of a giveaway, a "freebie" you can announce and make available as you're being interviewed. It doesn't have to be elaborate, just a one-pager will do. Americans love trivia. Why not create a trivia quiz from information about your industry? Or perhaps a list of tips would be helpful to people: 8 strategies for building Web site traffic by a Web design firm, for instance. Or 10 tips to break the debt cycle by a financial planner. Your giveaway should be a fun, intriguing gift or something of real value. Of course, you'll also include a company brochure or flyer. By offering a tip sheet or quiz, you encourage people to get in touch with you directly and pinpoint another prospect to add to your database.

The Curtain Rises

When you're on the air, it's important to be lively and animated. Put yourself in the audience's position: If a guest starts in a monotone, disinterested voice, you fail to become excited as well. Be dynamic in that first minute when you're welcomed by the host or hostess. Show passion for your message! Begin with something important. Remember, you are the authority; that's why you're being interviewed. It's essential you show that expertise in your explanations.

One of the biggest flaws in most interviews is the guest typically talks about "my company." Or "we" this and "we" that. Unfortunately, this doesn't help listeners interested in connecting with you. Slip the name of your business in several times. You can do this by saying, "At webdesign.com, we...," or you might say, "What people tell us they like most about the sites we create at webdesign.com is..." There are all kinds of ways to weave in the name of your firm. Think about it and have some ready.

Get the name of the person who will be interviewing you ahead of time; use his or her name as you talk. It gives the interview a more personal touch. Remember, however, that you're not talking to only that individual. You're addressing the entire audience. Frame your comments for all listeners, not just the host.

Don't overlook the opportunity to capitalize on controversy. If you can link your subject to a timely, current issue—or use it as a springboard to discuss something controversial in the news—by all means do so. Controversy presents an opportunity for wonderful interaction with your listeners. A talk show really hums when you get a lot of audience involvement. Of course, when you're dealing with controversy, there will be times you are asked difficult questions. Keep your cool. Some interviewers will deliberately attempt to provoke you.

Even in noncontroversial situations, the host may try to blind-side you with an offbeat or hostile question. You simply "bridge" to solid ground. A bridging technique is "I'm not an expert on XYZ, but I *can* tell you…" And you're back on track. As long as you know your subject well and stay calm, you're not likely to get into trouble.

What do you do when the host or hostess starts rambling and gets totally off the subject, focusing the show in a direction of no value to you? Take a lesson from Jacqueline Susann, who wrote *Valley of the Dolls*. She was a master at handling the media. If an interviewer tried to get her onto a topic she didn't like, she'd say something like, "You know, that's a fascinating subject. It reminds me of a chapter in my novel…" And she'd be right back on track with her book. Use that same strategy to help the host or hostess stay on the subject you're there to discuss.

I had just the opposite thing happen on one interview. It was set for an hour and once the host introduced me, he shut up! I talked for about five minutes, anticipating him to break in with another question any time. He never did. Except for commercials, it was virtually a one-hour monologue. I learned that day that silence, unlike the retriever, is *not* golden!

Most women need to be conscious of their voice level. Many of us tend to talk at too high a pitch. Practice lowering your voice. Variety is important for everyone. Project a tone both low and occasionally high. Consider your vocal pacing: Say some things rapidly, state important points slowly and emphatically.

When you're actually on the air, it's also useful to think about where this show is being aired. For instance, if you're talking to a Midwest audience, they're typically going to be turned off by casual attitudes toward sex and marriage. If you're addressing people in southern California, they have a much more relaxed and open attitude toward most subjects. If it's a nationally syndicated or network show airing many places around the country, play it safe. And if you're taping the show for later airing, don't mention anything time- or date-sensitive.

If conducting a telephone interview is nerve-racking for you, there are things you can do to make yourself more comfortable. One is to have handy some slightly warm water laced with a little lemon juice. It helps lubricate your throat. When doing a phone interview, always have something available to drink Another trick if you're very tense is to use a bit of petroleum jelly to moisten the inside of your lips. Talking for an hour can be a strain for anyone. Before beginning, take a couple of big deep breaths and exhale slowly to relax.

I mentioned a giveaway before. Now is the time to bring it into play. Toward the end of the interview, it's appropriate for you to comment, "By the way, John, I've created something I think many of our listeners would like to have." State you have a free gift you'd like to make available (naming whatever it is). Explain that to get a copy all they have to do is send a self-addressed, stamped envelope. Then give your address. Make it simple and as quick as a hot flash. Rather than saying "P. O. Box 3789," just say, "Box 3789." Don't take up a lot of time on the address. Ideally, you want to be able to repeat it, so make it as easy as possible. Instead of giving a long company name, say "free gift" or something similar.

After the Performance

An important follow-up to your interview, something often neglected, is a thank-you. Send a brief note to both the producer and the host. Surprisingly, this is seldom done. It's not only polite, but wise. If you have done well on a radio show, it's quite possible you'll be invited back in a few months. This has been the experience of many of our clients. And if you've used this way of staying in touch with people, they're going to be thinking more favorably toward you.

Another wise move is to have the interview taped. If you don't tape it on your end, you can always send a cassette to the radio station *ahead of time* and ask them to tape the interview. (If it's an especially important interview, send a better DAT tape for the highest quality sound.) Listen carefully to that interview. Critique it. What did you do well? Where were you particularly outstanding? What do you need to improve? You can learn much from listening to your interviews. You'll be better once you've evaluated strengths and weaknesses, and taken steps to improve them.

Of course, a good demo tape may be just the "open sesame" you need to corner an invitation on a major syndicated show.

Radio has been a preferred medium by Americans since it was first invented. It continues to play a role in most of our lives. A new kid on the block, the Internet, is what we'll be addressing next. Hold on to your bonnet; this is definitely the future!

Web Sites, *Wisdom,* and Whimsey

Want to target 150,000,000 Americans? That's how many of us listen to radio on an average day. These listeners, representing primarily homemakers and people commuting to and from work, are spread out over some 6,500 stations. If you reached only 1 percent of them—then sold just one-fourth of that audience—that would equal 37,500 customers/clients! Interested? Listen up. Many of these stations depend on the same basic news releases you're sending newspapers and magazines, only rewritten for radio. In that format, they're called a "script" and are read by "talent" that works at the station. They must run just under 30 or 60 seconds (note this time and the number of words in the top right-hand corner). Use a brief headline, make the body of the release in all *caps* and use one and a half line spacing. Try for a consumer tip angle and add your toll-free number once at the bottom. Read the script aloud to be sure it flows well, sounds punchy, and is conversational. Good luck—150,000,000 Americans. Wow!

National Public Radio (NPR) tips. Pitches that get air time on this bonanza are ones showing an impact on society or those that address change or trends. They aren't interested in product launches. Although the average length of a news spot is only 45 to 59 seconds, it's typically heard all over the country and makes nice copy when you can say thereafter "Featured on NPR." Your best bet is to e-mail the appropriate desk, whether it be national, cultural, science, or general. Don't blindly send pitches to a dozen contacts. Research whom to contact on their Web site at http://www.npr.org.

⬤⬤⬤⬤⬤⬤⬤

Have you noticed that women's problems often start with men? There's mental illness, menstrual cramps, and menopause. And then we have HYSterectomy!

⬤⬤⬤⬤⬤⬤⬤

Lock into radio stations. By surfing over to http://www.ontheair.com. you can link to 644 radio stations covering the total range of formats. There are listings for alternative, Christian, classical, classic rock, college, contemporary, country, dance/top 40, jazz, news/talk, netcasts, oldies, rock, sports, and urban. Whew—something for everyone! And if you're set up for it, you can also listen live so you know exactly what goes on whether the station is based in New Orleans, San Francisco, Baltimore, or wherever. Another good site to check is Radio and Records' Web page at www.rronline.com. Buried here is a wonderfully complete list of stations, also divided by format.

Give Me Talk! is a do-it-yourself Internet radio service that gives anyone the chance to do a talk show distributed worldwide. They have the largest library of independent audio programs on the Web and subjects are broken down into 15 categories: business, health, sports, etc. You can sign up and produce your own show, from five to 30 minutes worth, absolutely free. Just log on to their site at www.givemetalk.com and follow the directions.

Using radio to "massage" a publicity opportunity. Joan Stewart writes about her friend Dana Burke, who heard a disc jockey on a Milwaukee radio station complaining that he had hurt his neck that morning. Dana called him and offered him a free massage—courtesy of her client, Scott Mathison, a massage therapist. A few days later Scott was standing in the radio studio working the kinks out of Luke's neck while the disc jockey was on the air. Between songs—when Luke wasn't oohhhing and ahhhhing—he was giving out Scott's phone number. Dana was a hero. Luke felt better. Scott got free publicity and a gushing endorsement from a radio celebrity. Way to go!

●●●●●●●●

Have you failed lately? I hope so! The road to success is always under construction. As the economy develops a pothole or new competition obstructs our way, we have the opportunity to fail—then to rebuild our professional house with even stronger materials.

●●●●●●●●

Heard your company got a great plug on national TV but you haven't a clue where or what was said? National Aircheck can come to the rescue. This firm hunts down the news clip you need. They also audit radio, so they can cover these bases for you. There are two subscription op-

170

tions: a $285-per-year version and a more costly one. To get full details go to www.national-aircheck.com.

Wonder what America's talk shows are discussing—and how you might fit in? Then check out www.talkers.com where the industry trade magazine serving the talk radio industry, *Talkers*, is online. It can help you capture the mood of the public, not to mention glean ideas for tie-ins to current events. As the magazine continues to grow (it was started in 1990 and presently costs $50 a year for 10 issues), it adds more regular features. These now include the Washington Section, Sports Talk Radio, Tech Talk, Law Office, Programmer's Point, Hot Radio Guests (Who wouldn't want to be listed here?), Interviews, News & Gossip, Opinions, Entertainment Radio, plus letters and statistics. They also list the topics, events, and people most talked about for each week. During the Week in Review for August 17 to 21 the leading topics in descending order were: sex/scandal/politics, foreign affairs/terrorism, values/the media, the legal system, sports, the economy, gender relations, arts/entertainment, gossip/relations, and science/technical.

●●●●●●●

Q: *Why does it take 100 million sperm to fertilize an egg?*

A: *Because not one will stop and ask for directions.*

●●●●●●●

Want to come across like a pro on TV and radio? Brian Jud has created a product, *You're on the Air!*, that I'm very excited about. The centerpiece of this new marketing tool is a 90-minute video chockful of never-before-revealed tips from professionals at the top-rated shows. They tell you precisely what to do and say when you're on the air. You'll hear from representatives from *Larry King Live, Good Morning America, CBS This Morning, The Charlie Rose Show, Maury Povich,* and many others. Additionally, a media coach gives you insider secrets that will perfect your performance and show you how to really sell on the air. Along with this revealing videotape comes a 100-page companion book titled *It's Showtime* and a bonus book, *Perpetual Promotion,* which describes how to organize a promotional tour and locate the correct contact person at any media outlet. If you're serious about promoting yourself or your business, this is a must. The whole package sells for $99.95 plus $6 shipping and handling. Call 719-395-8659 to order *You're on the Air.*

Dynamite site for major radio contacts. Whether you're talking about computers, clothing, or interior decorating, whatever—head over to http:/

/www.radiospace.com/index-nj.html. Feast on the possibilities! Here you'll find links to sites regarding radio shows of all types in the United States and Canada...and the people behind them. Some of the stuff you can learn about the personalities, such as their hobbies and interests, may give you just the edge needed to become a guest. It will take some diligence, but this site can lead you to wonderful possibilities for syndicated talk shows, nationally distributed public radio shows, other nationally syndicated offerings, plus popular local personalities and programs. Have fun!

●●●●●●●

*They say women talk too much. Then why is it
the congressional filibuster was invented by men?*

●●●●●●●

Using radio to "massage" a publicity opportunity. Joan Steward writes about her friend Dana Burke, who heard a disc jockey on a Milwaukee radio station complaining that he had hurt his neck that morning. Dana called him and offered him a free massage—courtesy of her client, Scott Mathison, a massage therapist. A few days later Scott was standing in the radio studio working the kinks out of Luke's neck while the disc jockey was on the air. Between songs—when Luke wasn't oohhhing and ahhhhing—he was giving out Scott's phone number. Dana was a hero. Luke felt better instantly. Scott got free publicity and a gushing endorsement from a radio celebrity that was more effective than any paid commercial. Way to go!

Part III

"Out of the Box" Thinking— Nontraditional Marketing

CHAPTER 7

Enterprising Internet Strategies: Tech Max (No, It's Not Served With Salsa!)

E-commerce isn't he-commerce any more. In February 1999, 47 percent of the total online population was made up of women. By December, according to Nielsen/NetRatings, it had risen to 50 percent. Jupiter Communications reports that women will dominate the online population by 2002. And female entrepreneurs are the fastest growing segment of women online: There has been a 450 percent increase in the past four years!

What's more, businesswomen rely on technology more than their male counterparts according to the National Foundation of Women Business Owners, a nonprofit research organization that concentrates on women business owners and their firms internationally (http://www.nfwbo.org). Twenty-three percent of women business owners post Web pages, compared to only 16 percent of men. "The most important reason for adopting technology is to explore new strategies for growth," say 70 percent of female business owners. Only 10 percent of male business owners concur. It's obvious we've gone far beyond that old statement, "Her technical ability is such that she has no problem turning on a light switch."

So are you ready to really stake a claim on the wild, wild Web? The Internet has become one of the world's biggest industries, generating $301.4 billion in revenue in 1998. Just as some companies rent space in physical shopping malls, your Web site is a digital retail storefront with an infinite number of shelves, total customer convenience (you're open 24 hours a day, 365 days a year), and a global reach. You also have a vehicle to communicate with your customers via e-mail. Others may surf the Internet; this chapter will show you how to *harvest* it.

But perhaps you feel a bit like the woman who remarked, "There has been an alarming increase in the number of things I know absolutely nothing about! Don't send me updates," she quipped. "I need down dates!" Yes, high-tech marketing can certainly be mystifying. In the next few pages I'll pierce the secrecy, solve that riddle, and lay out a game plan to take advantage of this powerful opportunity. Of course, in this brief chapter we can't cover all the bases. I strongly recommend you study the many books available on creating a Web site and fully utilizing the Internet.

Online retail sales are soaring and so are many of these site owners' bank balances. The market research company GIGA Information Group projects by no more than three years from now a third of all business transactions will be influenced by the Internet. In the year 2002, merchandise and services worth a trillion dollars will be sold over the Web. Even sooner, moreover, 75 percent of companies' core functions—such as sales, marketing, and customer service—will be conducted online or at least electronically supported.

Some successful cyberpreneurs have both brick-and-mortar traditional stores and click-and-mortar virtual outlets. That is the approach Brooklyn clothing designer Stacy Johnson took. She wanted to reach more customers without the expense of opening a second store or printing and mailing a catalog. Her answer was the Internet. Now her New York store sells to customers as far away as Texas and California.

Today there is a new phenomenon in the marketplace: Instead of big businesses beating out small businesses, fast businesses are besting slow businesses. Small retailers can gain market share because the convenience of shopping from home any time day or night helps attract customers. Talk about fast: When Johnson got an order for a size 12 jacket, which she didn't have in her Brooklyn store, she was able to make and ship it in three days. Because Web commerce is automated, retailers can generate more revenue with fewer employees than a traditional store, thus saving on overhead.

The Web is also proving to be the salvation of some mom-and-pop establishments. Gallucci's, an 87-year-old Italian grocery in Cleveland, now takes 100 orders a week at tasteitaly.com. The Web has made them a merchant to the world. This means rather than choking in the superstores' grip, innovative small businesses can fight them on equal cyber-footing.

Artists and crafters have a whole new venue on the Net. Instead of relying on local fairs, farmers' markets, house parties, or gallery and boutique sales, these artisans can establish their own Web site for as little as $2,500. Techno-savvy twentysomethings and thirtysomethings can design an inviting site where customers can print or download pictures, descriptions, and prices of unique handcrafted jewelry, art, or fashion accessories. The whole world becomes their customer base and there are no middleman fees to be tacked onto the merchandise.

The Web allows entrepreneurs to find a little corner that the great predators have overlooked. That's what Brad and Gia Boyle did. They created Walkabouttravelgear.com, an electronic shopping site for hip, laid-back adventurers like themselves. The Boyles run their business out of their Fleetwood Pace Arrow rec vehicle, a "mobile command center" as they call it. They buy stock from suppliers around the globe and live comfortably on their commissions of $250,000 a year.

Getting Your Web Feet Wet

Web-generated revenues hit $18.6 billion in 1997. Forrester Research of Boston estimate an incredible $1.3 *trillion* in sales for 2003! The vast majority of that commerce will be business-to-business (B2B), which is projected to be 17 times the size of the consumer market.

So should you have a Web site? Absolutely. This is a learning process. Begin to prepare *now* for the fortune that lies waiting to be unearthed on the Web. You can reach a huge audience here. Well over 25 million Americans access the Internet. And it gives you global outreach to an upscale audience in both income and intellect. Who could have guessed that a mouse would one day rule the world?

It's only natural, once you have a site, for you to want to create a presence—make your new marketing medium pay off in reach and revenues. With an estimated 1 million new home pages appearing on the Web every month, the challenge to stand out from this cyberspace crowd of eye candy grows ever daunting.

Statistics now tell us that 41 percent of U.S. households own a PC. And Web TV now gives those without computers the ability to access the Internet through their television sets!

You're smart to be getting set now so you can work out any bugs and really be ready when Net use hits critical mass. Already, congestion is beginning to rear its monstrous head. A few years ago Yahoo, considered by many to be the best search engine, came out and found you. Now it takes as long as eight weeks to appear there…if they even agree to list your site. They don't include them all, as others do.

Many people still shun the Internet because it's too slow. They have no patience to sit and wait. But that's about to change. The problem is the bandwidth of transmission lines. As it increases, images will appear on the screen faster and the Internet will become a marketing tool unlike anything we've ever experienced! Whereas it sometimes feels like traveling in a covered wagon, tomorrow it will be like racing in a Ferrari. People are already finding it as essential as they do the telephone and the fax.

The question is often asked, "Is anyone making money on the Web?" The answer is a qualified "yes." Those who are making money offer the right products or services for this audience and have developed unique marketing habits. The majority of Americans still aren't online, so this naturally impacts sales. But the number of people who are connecting to the Internet is increasing on a daily basis.

Please don't think of your Web site as just another brochure. To be successful online, you need to make a commitment. You must take personal responsibility to allot the time to do what it takes…or assign that task to someone else. It requires patience. Frequent updating. Experimentation.

Be aware that online marketing simply offers another method for reaching prospective customers. It should be part of your marketing mix. Don't abandon your traditional publicity and sales efforts. They should all be used in tandem. In that way, you create a synergy where each effort reinforces the others. One of the interesting things about the World Wide Web (WWW) is that it has a ripple effect. If you are selling a product, people may learn about it online, then go to a store or elsewhere to purchase it. If you properly "work" your site, you'll not only get direct orders, but you'll also see an increase in traffic from those who carry your product. Media types will find you there as well. Last week I did two interviews with reporters who discovered me on the Web.

Each thing feeds the other. A survey conducted by NetSmart of New York City found that 27 percent of Internet users have already purchased items online, while 46 percent ended up buying products at traditional retail outlets after finding out about them on the WWW. A whopping 81 percent of them used the Net to research new products and services.

Smart students of the Web realize that generating direct orders from their site is only one way to use this medium. With a guest book, you can also build a database list of prospects for the future, increase consumer awareness of your company, gather information about customers' preferences to guide future product development, and test consumer responses to various products and services.

Now let's move ahead and investigate the specifics of how to untangle the Web. If you want to spin yourself a successful home, you'll use a rifle-shot strategy rather than shotgunning. We'll be discussing how to attract more people to your site, get greater exposure for yourself, practice electronic schmoozing, become an online celebrity, use e-mail to the maximum, and more.

Giving to Get: Adding Value

In the restaurant business, the old adage is "location, location, location." On the Web it's "content, content, content."

There is a Universal Law that says the more you give, the more you get. Nowhere is that truer than online. Savvy marketers enrich their sites with valuable information. Then people come to visit because they can find helpful or entertaining data there. This is considered "value added"—meaning you give something extra.

Your imagination is the only limit to what you might include. A restaurant could have copies of recipes. And perhaps a luscious photograph of the finished dish. The seller of classic cars might include photos of some of these beauties. Trivia quizzes work well. Perhaps you award a free goodie to the first person with all the correct answers. You might offer a downloadable coupon. These are very popular now. Streaming audio and video are favored by the Net savvy. If you make content available in an audio or video format and they have the right software, this opens up an entire new way to communicate online.

Providing surfers with one-stop shopping is always appealing. Perhaps you can become a clearinghouse of information on your topic. You want to develop what is called a "sticky" Web site where people will come frequently and stay a long time. That's what we've done at http://www.BrazenHussiesNetwork.com. We have an incredible array of links to other sites of value for women business owners. And we've set up affinity programs that allow users to easily connect with products or services they want right from our site. We also post weekly tips to keep visitors coming back frequently and are working at creating an unusual, cult-like community to exclusively serve the needs of female entrepreneurs.

Of course, the centerpiece is our content-rich online newsletter. If you want to continue getting a monthly motivational dose of the kind of money-making tips you've reaped so far in *Shameless Marketing for Brazen Hussies*™, you'll subscribe. Go to http://www.BrazenHussiesNetwork.com for details.

Search Engines Help Everyone Find You

A search engine, sometimes called a directory, is a Web site that helps you locate others and guides them to finding you. It's like an interactive index. You type in a keyword, such as "florists," and up pops a list of florists and florist-related sites. With search engines, "being well-connected" takes on a whole new meaning!

There are hundreds and hundreds of these. You've probably heard of several: Yahoo, Infoseek, Lycos, Alta Vista, HotBot, and Excite, for example. They identify your site by keywords.

Think carefully about the information you want to convey before you decide on these keywords. In what categories do you want to be included? Remember that the purpose is to *entice* people to your site, not describe everything that's there. You want to attract your target audience, titillate these prospects, then get them to visit out of need— or greed.

In addition to keywords, you'll need a short paragraph, about 25 words, of description. In registration, words are precious. While it used to be prudent to list the same words over and over, today search engines kick out such sites.

To enhance your search capabilities, descriptions are better. Some engines chop off the end of long descriptions. You might even submit 10-word strings at different times.

Using a divide-and-conquer approach is wise. List with so many each day or each week. Saturday and Sunday mornings are often the best times for the do-it-yourself registration process.

Some search engines, called "spiders," don't rely on receiving submitted information; they go out and automatically fetch your pages for indexing. Some of them follow links from the address they are given; others don't. Note those that don't follow all subsequent pages as they are the ones to which you'll need to submit underlying pages.

But don't think once you're done, you're done. It's a good idea to check every few months and re-register as this can get you closer to the top of the list. Be sure, as you add new pages or features to your site, to alert the search engines. Submitting to each individually takes a while. Keep in mind the "paste" function to trim your time investment. Of course, you already have that succinct, benefit-oriented statement about your business if you followed the earlier advice. Plug it in, plug it in: especially to the directories that require you to submit information to them.

One way to keep yourself organized is to start a notebook to track your online marketing activity. Have one section devoted to search engines, another to links, another to news groups. (More on these two shortly.) Keep track of when you submitted, the results, and create a tickler system for when to check back. Does all this effort pay off? The number of self-publishing clients we now serve has almost doubled since we put up our Web site (http://www.About-Books.com).

Links Level the Playing Field

People love to surf and lurk, cruise and peruse, browse and behold. Links from other sites to yours allow them to instantly jump to you. Depending on how assertively you cultivate them, you may get more hits from links than from being listed on search engines.

Your aim is to find other sites with similar or complementary information, products, or services. Let's say you raise herbs. You'd want to contact the Herb Importers Trade Association, the Herb Promotion Council, sites about healthy eating, natural health remedies, cooking, etc.

So where do you find this plethora of possibilities? Now it's *your turn* to use the search engines! Enter "herbs" in any search engine and you'll be busy for hours clicking on relevant home pages, evaluating their usefulness to you, and tracking down e-mail addresses of the owners or Web masters.

To make the actual contact, craft a brief message that compliments their site, explains who you are, what your URL is, and why a link would make sense. Sometimes your creative connections will be "reaching" with these links, so be sure to make your rationale clear to them.

Most will want a reciprocal link. That means they will require a link from your site back to theirs. Links are usually free.

Out of Site, Out of Mind: Advertising on the Net

First, let me say that advertising just on the Internet is probably unwise. Successful companies using the Net to advertise are doing it as part of a campaign that includes other media. U.S. Internet advertising is expected to increase from its current $2.8 billion to a mammoth $22 billion by 2004.

Should you want to spend a little money to test the waters, you can purchase classified ads on some sites. They are cheap because you get limited exposure. The other advantage is they're quick. Within literally hours you can begin to see results. And online classifieds provide a great test mechanism. Debating between two names for your product? See which gets the most inquiries.

"Banner ads" are another advertising possibility. They are just what they sound like: little rectangular billboards on someone else's site that announce your product, page, or site, with a connecting link. This can be cost-effective for certain products. For example, mattresses promoted on a site for sleep disorders, pet supplies announced on one devoted to choosing the right pet, or quilting supplies advertised on a site for quilters.

But you must mind your banners. They are best used when a company has a niche product, when the product or service is delivered online, or when your product can be explained in five words or less.

Banners typically cost about $35 CPM—meaning you'll pay $35 for every 1,000 impressions. If 10,000 people see it, you'll pay $350, and so on. Only 1 percent who view it will click on it and of 100 people who visit your site only one will buy. Concerns about the decreasing effectiveness of banner ads are very real, say some experts. Software programs for blocking ads are becoming popular and click-through rates have dropped significantly. People are becoming more adept at ignoring banner ads.

One way to recapture their attention is to make your banners flashier. This is done with so-called streaming media animations and also embedded voice, music, even video. The goal is to transform static banners into compelling, television-like zones in which viewers can play games, find out more about a product, and even buy it. You need tricks to bring up your clicks.

Should you decide to proceed, once you've found the right site or sites, you need to find the right message and present it in the right way. Go for pain or gain. Briefly state what problem your product or service will solve—or tell what fundamental desire it satisfies.

When designing your banner use bright colors and animation. Always add the words "click here." If you can, place your ad at the top of the page and repeat it at the bottom. As in all advertising, track results to ensure maximum return on your investment.

There is a site that contains basic concepts and how-to guidance. It ranges from making the banners or contracting them out, to how to choose a designer, what to expect, choosing a banner exchange or network, how they work, even pros and cons. Learn it all at http://www.emarketer.com/enews/011000_banners.html.

Another possibility is getting banners *free* in a two-for-one program developed by SmartClicks. You get the benefit of their unique targeting technology, which ensures your banners appear where they earn the best response. In return for each banner they place for you, two other members' banner ads appear on your site. For details go to http://www.smartage.com/promote

If moving and morphing is your style, another ripe online advertising venue is "sponsorships." These liaisons can take many forms and are very flexible. An advertiser and the content site might cooperate to create cobranded information. While it will include some commercial message, many feature a lot of helpful editorial. An example is the Crayola Activity Center that resides on the Women.com site and provides activities for women and their children. Sponsorships place a product or service in tandem with an appropriate site and use buttons, icons, banners, cobranded editorial content, and contextually integrated links to make the marriage work.

Nothing gives a small dot-com credibility faster than becoming a partner with big offline companies that can help it grow. That's what happened to WeddingChannel.com, a one-stop site for prospective brides and grooms launched by thirtysomethings Tim Gray and Raj Dhaka. They realized that the two biggest players in that industry were *Bride's* magazine and Federated Department Stores, a prime bride's registry location. Big established companies like these will only partner with someone who is going to be around, who is going to extend the brand, not tarnish it, however. The two entrepreneurs worked hard to build a really great product, establish trust, and foster a solid relationship. A trial relationship led to the inking of a deal that has given the fledgling site enormous clout and traffic. Do be aware, however, that traffic only provides eyeballs. The reality check is: are they buying?

It used to be that ad rates depended on a cost per thousand (CPM) impressions formula. Although that has been the dominant model for compensation for many years, it may give way to a more performance-based metric. When you negotiate good performance-based deals you get more for your money since all you're paying for is the action.

If you want knock-their-socks-off advice on how to market on the Internet, go to http://wilsonweb.com/articles. (Look at the Web Marketing Checklist: 26 Ways to Promote Your Site, for instance.) Dr. Ralph Wilson is an e-commerce consultant and extremely generous guru. He puts out a free monthly e-mail newsletter, Web Marketing Today, and he has links to literally thousands of terrific articles. If you intend to play hardball on the Web, I'd suggest you devote a big chunk of time to devouring this portal e-commerce site.

Electronic Schmoozing Equals Free Publicity

The Internet is a lot like direct marketing in that it allows you to specifically target your market. Because the online world is fragmented into thousands of different groups, you can find and reach your potential customers easily. They literally sort themselves out for you! Bird lovers hang out here, *Star Trek* fans there—physicians can be found somewhere else, computer geeks another place—and so on.

These gatherings of folks into Special Interests Groups (SIGs) are called by many names: news groups, forums, listservs, chat groups, etc. News groups are on the USENET. "Forums" is usually the term used for Web-based and online service (AOL) areas. "Listservs" are mail lists that operate by e-mail, while "chat groups" are typically online services. (See the sidebar on Finding Internet Discussion/Chat Communities.)

Thanks to the Internet, networking no longer means standing around in a roomful of strangers, cocktail weenie in hand. You can win exposure, credibility, and customers by becoming an active participant in appropriate discussion groups. Networking online is the next best thing to being there. Better sometimes. Instead of merely working a room, you can work the whole world! It's the perfect way to make contacts in special interest groups.

Jane Dvorak, a Denver public relations consultant, often hangs out in business chat rooms on America Online. By doing so, she recently hooked up with a Chicago manufacturer looking for advice on creating

184

a company brochure. "We became friends and established a trust level through e-mail, instant messages, and eventually talking on the phone," Dvorak explains. She nabbed him as a client to develop an identity campaign for his business.

A good first step when visiting a new group is to read their Frequently Asked Questions (FAQs). This general information will answer many of your queries and lay the groundwork for participating in the group.

There is an art to approaching folks online. Soft and subtle are the "open sesames" of news groups. Don't ask for the order; instead offer to send information to their e-mail address. If you come on with a strong sales pitch, you'll be "flamed," which means people will send you hostile electronic messages. Judith Broadhurst enjoys excellent word-of-mouth for her newsletter and writing classes by making herself a constant presence in writers' online forums.

You've got to be *customer*-centered, not self-centered. One of the best ways to introduce yourself to a new group is to ask for help. When you receive positive responses, thank them…and be sure your e-mail signature—which we'll discuss shortly—has a tag line about your business.

Another approach is to dole out free samples. Offer information that will entice a response. You could offer 7 tips on how to…10 myths about…a short mailing list, a report, newsletter article, contacts, etc. Mes-

Finding Internet Discussion/Chat Communities

Wonder how many news/chat groups and e-mail lists there are? Estimates place the figure at more than 300,000! The possibilities are e-n-d-l-e-s-s. At any given time there are 3.4 million individual chat line users on the Internet.

■ If you're a beginner in this electronic realm, check out http://web.presby.edu/computer/newsgroups for guidance. The range of issues covered is limitless and alluring. If you're a new user, hosted chats that feature defined topics and moderators might be a more comfortable place to start.

■ Another great beginning spot is Chat 101 at www.ker95.com/chat101. This site lays out the basics in simple terms and is perfect for beginners. Chatiquette gives helpful hints on the dos and don't. Then take your newfound knowledge to some starter sites (click on Etc., then Places to Chat), and you'll be chatting in no time.

■ For a site devoted exclusively to business networkers, visit www.industryinsite.com. It attracts a wide variety of surfers looking to dig up industry scuttlebutt and contacts. Upon filling out a profile, you can search their database for users from your alumni association, in-

(continued on next page)

dustry trade groups, or previous employers.

■ How do you locate the news useful to you? Here are several possible sites to delight your soul. They cover every imaginable topic and facilitate electronic "chatting" with others of relevant interests. When you subscribe, you'll typically receive subscription verification plus information about what to do if you wish to leave the list. Don't lose the latter as it's sometimes more difficult to get off a listserv than on!

■ By going to http://www. lsoft.com/lists/listref.html you'll find some 33,813 lists. And at http://www.liszt.com a whopping 90,095 lists await you, along with some intriguing free offers. At http://www.paml.alastra.com you will locate a conveniently alphabetized list that goes from "abuse" clear through "youth." And DejaNews has a news group search engine at http://www. dejanews.com/ that should also prove helpful.

■ Still another approach is to e-mail liszter@bluemarble.net. List keywords in the message portion. This is going to a computer, not a human, so only list words; don't make sentences. When the list is complete (it will probably take anywhere from 20 to 40 minutes), prepare to prospect for gold! Just remember the old divide-and-conquer advice. You

(continued on next page)

sages you post are identified by a one-line description. Make it short and catchy: Free Tax Planning Tips. When you e-mail them the promised item, be sure you insert a brief plug for yourself at the bottom and list your full URL.

Liberally posting free information also works well. Susanna Hutcheson is a direct mail specialist who spreads her wisdom around the Net. She posts an article each month to a dozen forum libraries on CompuServe and to three news groups. The results? An average week brings five faxes, five phone calls, and up to 20 e-mail inquiries from serious prospects.

Bulletin Board Systems: New Version of the Town Crier

A close cousin of SIGs are computer bulletin board systems (BBSs). These are electronic versions of the old-fashioned corkboards where notices are posted. They come in various sizes, colors, and styles. Some are run by commercial enterprises, others by local groups, SIGs, or hobbyists. According to *Boardwatch* magazine, there are more than 65,000 public bulletin boards and perhaps as many as 150,000 private ones nationwide. BBSs have three sections: message, file, and conference capabilities. All can be used successfully for PR.

Some operate on a broad scale, others locally. To find local ones, check the library, computer stores, or computer user groups. It's a good idea to participate in major local BBSs; they often have a ripple effect that goes far beyond area boundaries. Most BBSs have different forums, or sub-categories. Although a few charge for their services, many are free.

Here's how they work: A person chooses one of the forums—"Reviews," for instance—then types in a note people can read in the future. For example, a user might write, "I thought *Snow Crash* was a waste of time. I much preferred *Zodiac*, which was Stephenson's second book."

The next day another BBS user who read the notice might respond, "If you were disappointed by *Snow Crash* (I was too), maybe you should read Gibson's *Johnny Mnemonic*. Much more fun." By auditing this BBS an author could get honest reader feedback—and plug her own books.

Talk Shows in Cyberspace

Appearances on such shows as *Oprah, Sally, or Rosie*, are not the only way to attract attention. You can be the center of attraction at special online events where you make live appearances for an hour or two. At America Online's Center Stage, for instance, there are four cyberspace "auditoriums," each with a capacity of 5,000. So there is a good chance of getting on if you can angle your subject to hitchhike on something in today's headlines. Coordinator Amy Arnold is encouraging: "Even if a proposal is not appropriate for Center

FINDING INTERNET DISCUSSION /CHAT COMMUNITIES (continued)

can only investigate a few each time. You have nuggets here for lots of digging. Yes, it's slow and laborious work. But the potential is enormous.

■ The ever-expanding Go Network has an excellent selection of chat rooms categorized by age and interest. Reach it at www.go.com/Community/People?topic=chat. Talk City is designed for those who "celebrate intelligence, friendship, difference, and sameness." Talk citizens can even design their own chat rooms or join one of the existing ones. Find it all at www.talkcity.com.

■ Yahoo! Chat (http://chat.yahoo.com) has listing info and links to the day's top chat events around the Net. Featured rooms are at the top of the page. Click on Complete Room List to see the depth of offerings. Have fun and make great contacts!

■ To give and get advice on industry-specific message boards, or bombard experts with your burning questions during regularly scheduled chats, go to http://www.careerpath.com. Another excellent career site that has an active message board searchable by industry or keyword is http://www.vault.com.

■ A word of caution: Be sure to research a list before you join or here's what could happen: Let's take "pit bulls," for instance. This

(continued on next page)

FINDING INTERNET DISCUSSION /CHAT COMMUNITIES (continued)

could be a newsletter or discussion group of aggressive salespeople. Or it could be for owners of that species of dog—or it might consist of those who crusade *against* pit bulls. It might be a group of stockbrokers who meet for lunch on Mondays and call themselves the "Pit bulls." It could be ex-jocks from a team dubbed the "Pit bulls." Or even groupies who love a new rock band called "The Pit Bulls." See what I mean? These groups often have a strong sense of community and you don't want to barge into the wrong environment. Also be sure not to sign up for anything that doesn't give clear directions on how to get *off* the list in case it doesn't measure up to your expectations.

Stage, it might fit one of the other areas." Try contacting the service or forum administrator for details on how to appear: RJScottV@aol.com.

Most appearances typically draw crowds of about 300 participants. However, transcripts of these events might reach another 300 people, many of whom are journalists or freelancers looking for story angles.

Suggestions for being effective online don't vary greatly from what you would do for typical media: 1) Provide the host with an introductory script with details on how to buy your product or service; 2) alert people about where it can be purchased online and give a toll-free order number; 3) provide a list of sample questions to ask you; and 4) keep your answers short and remind people where they can find more information.

It's also a good idea to require they include ordering information for your product or service at the beginning and end of the transcript. And remember, unlike radio, this is a visual medium. Including an interesting graphic or photo with your initial materials will increase your success ratio.

Getting booked here is a real coup. "Sell us on your idea," advises a CompuServe spokesperson. "We have 2.8 million subscribers online, so it should have universal appeal." Even more targeted ideas, however, stand a chance with product managers in an appropriate specialty. For a proposal kit, e-mail Mary Sieler at msieler@cs.com.

Watch forums to see if a "thread" develops that fits your topic. A thread is a series of messages centered around a specific topic. When author Lisa Reid looked in on CompuServe's My Family Forum she decided this was a prime place for a guest appearance. The sysop (system operator) agreed and she did a stint on *Raising Kids with Just a Little Cash*. Lisa was prepared and had her uncle and dad standing by to pop in electronically and ask where they could get the book.

One agent we know of schedules his clients for electronic tours. He posts notices on appropriate bulletin boards that such and such will be available at a given time and place to answer questions about a certain topic. You can reach thousands of people in a short time with this approach.

Speaker Steve Miller set up his own forum to give him higher visibility and credibility. He did a series of seminars online by loading several 1,000- to 1,500-word articles on different trade show topics (his specialty) into the forum library. After reading them, subscribers could ask him questions based on the information. He responded to over 200 questions on the public forum and received another 50 or so private messages via e-mail. A spinoff was that an association asked him to upload his seminar lectures on their Internet bulletin board, then proposed they hire him to facilitate another online seminar.

Guest appearances online are an excellent way to promote your product or service. Be sure to get your share of this free publicity. Think of it as a media tour—on steroids!

E-Mail Lets You Outsmart Your Rivals

E-mail—used in tandem with Web site search engine registration, links, advertising, participation in SIGs, and guest appearances—forms a solid foundation for Internet success. According to a recent Forrester Research report, the number of users will zoom to 135 million by the year 2001. And that's just in the United States! E-mail lets you lob statements, information, and comments to prospects, customers, and online forums—not to mention influence individuals and reporters around the world.

E-mail (femail?) puts both you and the recipient in control. You can send it at your convenience, she or he can read it at theirs. It also allows you to send a single message to many individuals at once. Phone calls must be done one at a time. For busy professionals, parallel efforts beat serial efforts every time, especially when you're in business for yourself and delivering results, not punching a clock, is the goal. Just remember that e-mail is unforgiving and irreversible. Double-check everything before you send it.

It brings us together—and can push us apart. It's a fabulous tool...and a deal buster when used exclusively to replace phone conversations or personal contact. If you want to know the ins and outs of e-mail, go to http://www.everythingemail.net/index.html. Here you'll discover many tips that help alleviate confusion and make your e-mail more productive. There are links to e-mail programs, autoresponders, forwarding services, e-mail list search engines, etc. They also have an online bulletin board forum to discuss issues and questions on the topic.

Wally Bock, who authored *Cyberpower for Business*, and has a great site at http://bockinfo.com uses e-mail in a multitude of ways:

- As part of a regular contact strategy
- To set up mailing lists as a way to create virtual teams
- For surveys
- To send birthday greetings
- To forward articles that might interest a prospect
- As a follow-up device
- To deliver his newsletter
- For placing orders
- To acknowledge orders placed with him
- To get past gatekeepers who guard the telephone

The first and foremost way to use e-mail as a marketing tool is to develop a "signature." This refers to a small file of identifier lines automatically attached to every message or news group post you send. Properly thought out, it becomes a soft-sell commercial, yet is appropriate "netiquette" because it doesn't compromise traditional standards forbidding advertising.

Naturally, it will include your name, company name, phone, fax, snail-mail address, e-mail address, and URL. It should *also* include a line with a brief benefit statement about your company. This is like wearing an online name tag. The beauty is you create it once (or several different ones if you prefer) and plug it in indefinitely. Or you can revise and customize it daily if you prefer. A maximum of six lines is preferred. Always include the "http://". Most mail programs automatically create a link to your site then.

You can locate the e-mail addresses of prime journalists. Briefly e-mail them to identify yourself and give your area of expertise. Then when they're looking for a resource for a story, you're in their files! A new "Print Media in Cyberspace" survey showed that while only 17 percent of journalists searched online for story ideas in 1994, that number climbed to 48 percent in 1998 and escalated to 73 percent in 1999. The potential of e-publicity is growing exponentially.

Many who visit your site will not buy. But if you encourage them, they'll leave their e-mail address to receive future information. Treat

190

these online leads like any others. Don't settle for a brief e-mail reply and hope they'll decide to purchase. Add them to your newsletter list. Get their snail mail address so you can send them things through regular mail too. Follow-up again and again.

E-mail newsletters are an empowering marketing device. They are often delivered free as a business-builder. Frequently put out weekly, they're short and informative, offering value as well as a soft commercial. Since, with the right software there are no costs to you, this is an excellent means for staying visible to your prospects. There are no design, printing, or mailing costs. And the immediacy is great. You can decide one morning to launch a sales campaign for a new product…and have it accomplished with orders pouring in that afternoon!

We have several places on our About-Books.com site where visitors can opt-in (that's Internet lingo meaning "subscribe to") for our occasional newsletter. (I wasn't willing to be captive to doing one on a regular schedule.) It never fails to generate business when we send one out.

Here are a few tips on how to catch more flies with honey in the e-mail business: 1) Use a compelling headline in the "Subject" space. You are competing for the receivers' attention…deliver the goods! 2) We also add (Please forward to colleagues, friends) in the subject space to encourage them to help us spread the word. 3) What you say in the first five or six lines is decisive. Many e-mail programs only show that many lines at a time. Naturally, you'll personalize the greeting, then get off to a roaring start with a benefit statement. Also remind them they asked for this. Many folks forget they subscribed and might feel they're being spammed. 4) At the end, be sure to inform them how to UNsubscribe, should they want to, and include your full signature.

It's vital that you set your newsletter as "blind carbon copies" or BCCs. This omits the e-mail addresses from the header above the actual text. You know what I mean; you've received mass e-mail from people who reveal the whole list they're going to. We know of one man who forgot to do the BCC function and a list of his 1,100 customers were all exposed at the beginning. Twelve pages later the actual text began! Not only was this frustrating to recipients, it invaded their privacy and made the sender look like an idiot.

One speaker we know, Ron Kaufman, includes an "On the Business Side" with a quick rundown of his recent presentations and an "On the Personal Side" that tells what he and his family have done the past month. Ron reports he is amazed by the number of people who write and thank him for including the personal section.

Another version of the online newsletter is the e-zine. Although typically more elaborate, many of the same game plans apply. If you're thinking of starting an electronic magazine, go to http://e-zinez.com/. I was amazed at the volume and quality of free information available at this site. You can read an online tutorial, The Handbook of E-Zine Publishing, which covers market research, offers templates, discusses distribution, and addresses making a profit. And there's a FAQ list dubbed "Ask Dr. E-Zine" that answers a multitude of practical questions. Happy publishing!

Promote Your Site…and They Will Come

Newspaper, newsletter, and magazine editors are always looking for interesting sites to write about. Publicity about your Web site is a terrific way to generate traffic. Hold a zany online contest, become a unique information resource, or create an elaborate story within your site to pitch to these folks. Use the traditional press release, sent via e-mail or snail mail, to trumpet your message to those who can get the word out.

And don't overlook e-zines. There are thousands of online publications that might be interested in you or your business. The subjects they cover range from alternative lifestyles to cooking, health to politics, religion to sports.

Some people say their sites are most useful in reaching the media for publicity. Editors, columnists, and freelancers, as well as radio and TV producers, are using the Internet more and more to seek story ideas and interview subjects. Keep visible and they'll come to you!

Industry heavyweight PRWeek revealed the success of the micro-budget horror film The Blair Witch Project was largely due to the company's savvy use of the Internet as a marketing tool. Much of the work was done in advance by the film-makers, who were creating Web sites even before they had written the script! Artisan Entertainment took something small and made it huge. Five first-time film-makers with a budget of $60,000 are predicted to hit $100 million, which would make Blair Witch one of the most profitable films of all time. They built a buzz, averaging $56,002 per screening on its opening weekend—as compared to Eyes Wide Shut with an average of $9,003 per screening and two top stars.

Although you want to integrate your URL into all your materials, don't be intimidated into thinking you must try to match this wizardry.

Few ever will. You simply need to take prudent advantage of what the Web offers. One proven way to promote your site is to offer sweepstakes prizes. Research from Jupiter Communications shows that 76 percent of those surveyed liked sweepstakes-style prize giveaways. These don't have to consist of fancy cars, elaborate trips, or big cash prizes. Make it relevant. They need to appeal to the precise mind-set of the audience you're trying to reach. A chiropractor who sells ergonomic chairs and other comforting items for those with spinal injuries, for example, sponsors a drawing for a free travel pillow.

A final caution: Although you want your URL to be very evident, don't rush out and print all new literature to include it. One approach is to have it printed on a quantity of see-though labels, which you then affix in strategic places until you're ready to reprint your literature, or have a rubber stamp made. Put it everywhere! We even found a URL on a wine cork recently. Here are a few more traditional places to list it:

business cards	catalog sell sheets
letterhead	advertisements
envelopes	invoices/statements
shipping labels	articles about you
flyers	articles/columns by you
brochures	newsletters
catalogs	on phone answering/voice mail messages
postcards	announce during radio/TV interviews
order forms	on product labels

The Web has unlimited potential. None of us even has the slightest clue of what this tool will mean to us in another decade. Sure, it provides a new way of conducting worldwide e-commerce. Yes, it links you with more media than you've ever imagined. Although much of the outcome is in the hands of technology—and people's acceptance of it—you can still have a huge impact on the results. Be proactive. Get involved. Make this a magical part of your marketing mix. It may be just the thing to give your competition their dot.comeuppance.

Now let's explore one of the most powerful ways to grow your business: forming strategic alliances. In the next chapter I show uppity women how to unite!

Web Sites, *Wisdom,* and Whimsey

Visit (and get listed with) Nerd World. No, you don't have to be a computer geek to appreciate this site. It gets a whopping 2,000,000 hits each month and has 260,441 links, so we're talking about the big time here. The site features 23 leisure and knowledge categories with scads of subcategories. For instance, I pulled up "health" and found the following sub-topics: beauty therapy, books on health and fitness, e-zines on health, family health, first aid, fitness, health news, and information, health reports, living, marketplace, health and fitness, medicine, mental health, nutrition, self-improvement, skin care, support groups and programs, and weight loss. Whew! This is an incredible place for any health professional, manufacturer of health products, etc. Go to http://www.nerdworld.com/ and go for it!

●●●●●●●●

Latest computer best-sellers:
Gates of Wrath
A Tale of Two CDs
Gone with the Windows
War and PC
Moby Disk

●●●●●●●●

Let HerAssistant.com be yours. Here you'll find the latest tools, articles, hot tips, and up-to-date info for your business growth and success as women help each other learn the ropes. Go to http://HerAssistant.com and see for yourself.

Web Marketing Forum a bonanza! Now you can easily access articles about general strategies for Internet marketing via http://www.marketing.com/HyperNews/get/forum/strategy.html. For instance, here you'll find, "Using contests and giveaways to promote business," "Going global with your business," "Creating links to celebrity home pages," and "Analyzing your Web site traffic." Although some of these and other articles may be self-serving and used as vehicles to sell Web services or hosting, many offer valid information. Under the section on "Promotion," there are links, tips, and incredible strategies for increasing traffic to your site. And a click on "Trends" lets you find out in what direction the winds are blowing.

Hanker to know more about e-commerce? Then go to http://ecommerce.internet.com/. Here you'll find a comprehensive resource for news about electronic commerce. This is also a gateway to hundreds of sites and resources on the WWW devoted to the evolving electronic commerce industry. You'll love their links. There is also a library with an extensive compilation of articles and reading lists. Their resources section offers details about online commerce regulations, research groups, consortium, news groups, industry standards, and more.

●●●●●●●●

Computer cuties:
Ram: a male sheep
Rom: a ram after a sex change operation

●●●●●●●●

Use the grocery store to improve your Web site! (No, I haven't lost it. Honest.) In fact, we've discovered there are many common denominators between supermarkets and good Web sites. Why not learn how to entice customers to buy more from the research and strategies used in the fiercely competitive grocery industry? Two important factors were revealed in the most recent Point-of-Purchase Advertising Institute's "Consumer Buying Habits Study": 1) 70 percent of purchasing decisions are actually made in the store, most of which are unplanned, and 2) shoppers are more likely to purchase a product that is highlighted via an in-store display. So how do we translate this information into Web sales? Help those who come to your site by highlighting certain items like the grocery store end-of-the-aisle displays that draw shoppers' attention to products. Feature your biggest seller, however, not a "dog." Push your strengths. Notice the razors, cigarette lighters, playing cards, glue sticks, etc., to tempt one at the checkout stand? Mimic that merchandising tactic. Choose high-profit items and feature them prominently at the end of your order form (the equivalent of a checkout stand). By tempting those who are already ordering with an additional impulse item you can definitely build your sales. So "check out" what they do the next time you go to the grocery store. This kind of market research can yield big dividends.

Learn about everything from anarchy (5,768 listings) to zebras (259 listings) here. This site gives you access to the conversational forums on the Internet. Many Usenet groups are archived for a month to a year on Dejanews. You can search by keywords and find virtually anything. This will save you countless hours rummaging through Usenet news groups. In fact, rather than reading all the postings every day, you could just enter the subject you want to know about and see what comes up. Although you lose the aspect of active participation, it's a wonderful time-saving technique. Reach them at http://www.dejanews.com.

●●●●●●●

*Definition of a keyboard: a device used
to enter errors into a computer.*

●●●●●●●

Need a reminder for important follow-up dates, birthdays, or prioritized "to-do" lists? Then you'll be delighted to learn about eOrganizer, your free personal online electronic organizer. Simply customize it for your needs and this nifty site will nudge you via e-mail on the morning of any must-dos. In addition to providing space for tasks, appointments, and special days, eOrganizer lets you enter names and addresses of key contacts. So if you need access to these people when away from home or office, just bring it up on your laptop and presto! Everything is at your fingertips. Find it at http://www.eorganizer.com.

●●●●●●●

*A bus station is where a bus stops.
A train station is where a train stops.
On my desk I have a work station.*

●●●●●●●

Great links await you at Media Central. This is a site overflowing with useful and unusual places for media and marketing folks. Within Media Links you'll find electronic paths not only to newspapers and magazines but also television and radio. Under Critical Links there are URLs you can't live without…well, maybe that's a *slight* exaggeration. Seriously, a conglomeration of intriguing resources live here. The *Internet Advertising Resource Guide* will lead you to sites containing advertising, should you be so inclined. Looking for software freebies? www.Shareware.com overflows with stuff you probably want to download. Under their Agency Links you can find ad agencies on the Web and perhaps connect with one that has a client who would like to purchase quantities of your product. There is also a Zine and Noted E-Zine Resource Guide for finding your way around cyberspace publications. A whole new way of publicizing awaits you here! All this resides at http://www.mediacentral.com/.

Exciting search engine makes your research easy. There's an embarrassment of riches on the Internet. But where do you find them? In Yahoo!? Alta Vista? Lycos? Or one of the other countless sources? Now you can do one-stop shopping! Go to http://www.search.com and you can access more than 250 Web and Usenet search engines from a central Web page! Instead of searching each engine individually, Search.com's "slave driver" engine organizes engines both by category and alphabetically and eliminates duplicates. What a tremendous time saver. Furthermore, you can locate people's residential phone numbers and addresses here via Switchboard. It's a big, diversified, fascinating site. And they update it constantly. One week I found seven new search tools.

●●●●●●●

Change is inevitable...except from
a vending machine.

●●●●●●●

Three tips to increase your traffic: 1) Be sure to use an imbedded link in your e-mail. This means you type in your full Web address (including the http://) so readers can click on it and go directly and effortlessly to your site. That way you can post a brief message like "Hello, Sherri: Thanks for your inquiry. I'd love for you to consider our products. 2) Another suggestion is not to simply state in your advertising or electronic signature "Check our Web site at..." Give them a reason to go there. A more inviting approach would be to say "Free articles and resources to help you (make more money, save time, lose weight, etc.) are available at..." 3) Make your Web URL and e-mail address easier to read by using capitals. The rule is up to the .com, .net, .edu, or .org, you can use capitals to help Internet users understand. Notice how much easier to read this is http://www.SallySamuelsDesigns.com versus: http://www.sallysamuelsdesigns.com.

It's a marketer's dream. On http://www.advancingwomen.com, DigitalWorks Send Direct E-mail service allows you to deliver your own message to people who actually want to hear about it. And since each recipient has chosen to receive the e-mail, no one can complain about spam. All you do is choose the category you want to target from their extensive list, enter your message in the template, and they'll send the e-mail for you. AdvancingWomen.com is also full of information for women, from workshops and financial info, to book reviews and articles.

●●●●●●●

Do you know what "WWW" stands for
on the Internet? Wait. Wait. Wait.

●●●●●●●●

One-stop resource for marketing and managing your site. You'll find useful checklists, explicit how-to articles, and advice from guest experts at www.workz.com. Business plans, domain names, banner ads, even inventory management are covered. And be sure to investigate the Tools & Utilities area to check your site's performance, including a function that looks for dead links, another that examines load time, and one the analyzes browser compatibility.

CHAPTER 8

LinkThink: Strategic Alliances to Ignite Your Sales

There are innumerable ways you can partner with other businesses or organizations to sell more product; introduce your service, store, or restaurant; and sweeten your margins. I call this LinkThink. You may have heard it referred to as affinity marketing, forming strategic alliances, joint venturing, or fusion marketing. It's sort of like braiding hair: You take a handful of unruly strands, weave them together, and create unity.

When President Lincoln was chided by northern congressmen for befriending the Southerners, he replied, "Am I not destroying my enemies by making them my friends?" I'm not suggesting you destroy the competition, but rather make them a marketing partner. There is definitely strength in numbers. The pair-ups we'll explore here allow you to operate independently, yet compete collectively.

Why Partnerships and Collaborations Yield Big Bucks and Bold Results

Larraine Segil, author of *Intelligent Business Alliances*, projects 30 percent of the annual revenues of most U.S. companies will come from alliances. Fast joint ventures will overtake old structures. They will last a shorter time and change within that framework. Dot-coms will contribute to this trend as companies reinvent themselves. She also forecasts that small-business-to-large-business collaborations will become the norm. As big companies struggle to meet the need for speed and responsiveness, they will team with smaller, more fleet-footed firms.

Even the small business owner can create "glitz by association." It isn't brain surgery. It takes vision. Creativity. Resourcefulness. Imagine it's Christmas Eve and you are presented with an unassembled toy and no instructions. How do you put it together? Trial and error. Fitting this to that. Trying one thing with another. That's what LinkThink is all about: finding the matches. Who already reaches your customer base? Ponder this for a while and you're sure to come upon an idea that seizes your soul.

We did this for a previous book, *Country Bound! Trade Your Business Suit Blues for Blue Jean Dreams*. This is a guide to escaping the big city rat race, choosing the right relocation spot, and earning a good living in Small Town, USA. We reasoned that United National Real Estate, which has some 300 offices around the country specializing in *rural* real estate, would be a good partner. They also produce a catalog twice a year. We met with President Lou Francis in Kansas City, Missouri, and put together a win/win proposition.

We provided him with a half-page ad that he would run in his nationally distributed catalog at no charge to us. In return he gets $5 for every book sold. We've merchandised over $15,000 worth of books this way so far and also get purchasers' names and addresses for our database. Of prime interest to him, this book shows people who want to leave the corporate culture—but need a livelihood—how to prosper in paradise. Thus, it helps his potential customers realize their dream.

Fitzroy Hilaire, director of supplier development for Avon Products, Inc., suggests women business owners form strategic alliances with other female entrepreneurs before bidding on major contracts. "For a long time this has been a male-only game. Times have changed and corporate America has changed," he says. Avon and others are reducing the number of outside suppliers they deal with, so competition for contracts is fierce. Consequently, we women must unite!

Examples of Successful Alliances

Carolee Jewelry teamed up with Estee Lauder cosmetics a few years ago to create a new and exciting way to wear makeup and jewelry. An in-store promotion called Custom Color Consultations gave women complimentary makeovers. The beauty consultant determined whether the customer had "warm" or "cool" skin undertones, then the Carolee representative coordinated a pearl ensemble to go with the customer's new cosmetic shades.

General Electric refrigerators teamed up with Culligan Water. When people went to their G.E. fridge's ice maker to get a drink of water or for ice cubes, it was compliments of the Culligan man. Starbucks is on a caffeine high. They have partnered with United Airlines, which serves Starbucks coffee.

Calvin Klein cosmetics can now be found in music stores. Yep. The new fragrance, cK, is targeted to both men and women and is available in 85 Tower Records stores. A Klein spokesperson said it's selling the fragrance next to CDs because of the "synergy between music and fashion." (Okay…but it seems to me a little like opening a clothing store in a nudist camp.)

Binney & Smith was concerned their flagship product, Crayola Crayons, was too low-tech by today's standards. So they forged an alliance with a software development company called Micrografx, which developed digital crayons and a software drawing program for kids that can be used on home computers. It was a marriage made in heaven.

Small dot-coms paired with giant Internet sites enjoy tremendous exposure. After Cara Zanoff France launched her site in November 1998, she secured about a dozen partnerships with some of the biggest names on the Net, including Yahoo and amazon.com. Pretty heady stuff for a lady who sells handcrafted gifts. By hooking up with these two behemoths, she leveraged herself into high visibility. Most deals require her Artisangifts.com site to share a percentage of revenues with the partners, which she is happy to do.

Another Internet cooperative venture was spearheaded by Dee Power, a management consultant from Fountain Hill, Arizona. At her urging, the Cooperative Business Bookstore offers not just books, booklets, and newsletters—but also software and seminars from almost two dozen consultants and authors who figure that many experts can build more traffic than any one of them singularly.

In a more traditional pair-up, Troll Communications books and Advantage Learning Systems software have been bundled together. The two companies jointly market their products and take advantage of distribution systems each has developed.

Also consider banding together with a nonprofit organization. You can contribute the resources it needs while piggybacking on its cred-

Special Dates to Piggyback On

Why not capitalize on the calendar to build sales? All kinds of holidays—Valentine's Day, Labor Day, Halloween, Thanksgiving, even the changing seasons—are great opportunities to get in touch with customers or prospects with greeting cards. Set yourself apart by sending a card to acknowledge less traditional holidays. You'll make a huge impact when your greeting comes out of the blue. To get a catalog of many creative cards, contact IntroKnocks at 800-753-0550.

If you're looking for media PR tie-ins to special days/weeks/months, get a copy of the reference book, *Chases's Calendar of Events*. (For a free trial version, go to www.chases.com.) It provides literally thousands of LinkThink possible publicity hooks to give your business a fresh perspective.

Another ideal resource is a searchable dates archive that resides at http://dailyglobe.com/day2day.html. It is set up as a table for each day of the year and divided into the twelve months. You can either browse by month or look up a specific date. In addition, there is information about each month at the beginning of that month's listing, as well as data about moveable dates (holidays celebrated on a different

(continued on next page)

ibility. That's what Raczal Corporation of Wayland, Massachusetts, did. Wanting to gain acceptance in the teen market for its fruity soda, they teamed with Mothers Against Drunk Driving. On behalf of MADD (and itself), Raczal contacted 4,000 high schools in New England about an anti-drinking poster contest. It worked wonders. In areas with high participation in the contest, soda sales doubled or even tripled.

Cross-Promoting With Area Businesses

If your enterprise is local in nature, other ways to connect for profit abound.

You've noticed the fishbowls or large brandy snifters full of business cards in some restaurants. Using this concept, you can team up with another business to get yourself before the public and develop more leads. Offer something for free—such as an hour of consulting, a lube and oil change, a lesson, or free admittance for two. Print a little sign to explain the prize and attach it to a transparent container in which people can deposit their business cards for the drawing.

All that remains is to make arrangements with a receptive merchant. This is a win/win/win proposition. The proprietor gets the benefit of providing a free bonus to his or her customers, you gain exposure before hundreds of prospects. The lucky winner gets a freebie. Alliances can be set up with beauty shops, drug stores, boutiques, bookstores, florists, music stores, etc.

There is another way businesses in a small town, or those located in a neighborhood of a larger city, can band together for mutual gain. How about printing a discount coupon book? This has proven to be a wonderful sales stimulator in several places.

When my husband and I gave a seminar in Steamboat Springs, Colorado, a few years ago, we picked up such a book at the chamber of commerce office. It contained coupons for reduced rates or special bonuses from hotels, motels, and resort accommodations—plus recreational activities like balloon trips, river-rafting, hydro-tubing, bicycle rentals, golfing, and a kayak school. Other participants included restaurants, a picture framing shop, service stations, a landscaping firm, gift shop, and a video camera rental shop.

When doing such a promotion, be sure to protect yourself. Print an expiration date on the coupon, limit one coupon to customer, and don't honor it in conjunction with any other discount. One of the advantages of this type of program is, simply by keeping the coupons, you can clearly track the results. Discount booklets can be mailed to area residents, made available on the counters of participating businesses, and dispensed at the chamber of commerce, town hall, library, etc.

SPECIAL DATES TO PIGGYBACK ON (continued)

day each year such as Easter and Mother's Day).

Here is a year's worth of possible money-making monthly marketing maneuvers:

■ *January promotional ideas.* After the holidays, it seems like everybody's thoughts turn to diets, fitness, and New Year's resolutions. And therein lie wonderful angles for PR. In fact, January is National Diet Month. Maybe you can inject a motivational, inspirational, or health-related business with fresh pizzazz by giving it a "new beginnings" twist to tie in with all those resolutions everyone makes.

■ *PR tie-ins for February.* Of course, with Valentine's Day and President's Day falling this month, there is much grist for the creative publicist's mill. But you needn't stop there. It is also Vegetarian Month, American History Month, Black History Month, and Celebration of Chocolate Month (yummy!). Additionally, there is Pay Your Bills Week (yuk!). And every four years, we all get another option: February 29th. Cypress Gardens in Florida used this as an angle to offer free millennium weddings on leap year day. Each happy couple received free park admission, a complimentary wedding photo, and a mini-reception. Wedding guests were offered special discounted ad-

(continued on next page)

mission. (Just be glad your birthday doesn't fall on February 29th...or maybe that would be good!)

■ *March promotional opportunities roar like a lion.* In this time period we have National Procrastination Week (but if you practice that, you won't make profitable pairings!). Procrastination could prove an intriguing linchpin, however, for businesses or professional practices that need to encourage people to "Act now!" Additionally, it's National Empowerment Month, National Craft Month, and National Talk to Your Teen About Sex Month. Glenn Miller has a birthday on March 1, Jerry Lewis on March 15, and Edgar Cayce on March 18. What great fodder for a music store, a stand-up comic, and a psychic. World Day of Prayer occurs in March, as does St. Patrick's Day—not to mention National Organize Your Home Office Day. Have fun!

■ *PR suggestions for April.* This month is replete with things that connote new hope: Easter, Daylight Savings Time, plus the birth of spring and all things green and growing. Can you hitch your product or service to that theme? In April we have Professional Secretaries Day and Take Our Daughters to Work Day. This is also Pets Are Wonderful Month (I agree!) and International Twit Award Month.

(continued on next page)

Another way to fight the high cost of advertising and share printing costs is to go together on a jumbo postcard. Ask noncompetitive business to join your pursuit. If six of you—perhaps a realtor, plumber, pizza parlor, dry cleaner, computer consultant, and chiropractor—share the printing and postage, no one invests very much, yet everyone gets exposure.

Group promotions can yield nice benefits. By taking a "strength in numbers" approach a neighborhood or mall can get extra bang for its buck. Cross-promoting strategically aligns businesses that target the same market but don't directly compete. For example, a group of local businesses banded together to put on a Valentine's Day promotion. The group included a massage practice, bookstore, women's medical clinic, florist, health food store, shopper newspaper, and a beauty salon. The bookstore hosted a series of demonstrations and seminars on the theme of "Beauty Inside Out." Each was led by a manager of one of the participating businesses. The presenters all distributed a handout with a joint offer of services from the other businesses. They also each wrote an article based on their presentation for the shopper newspaper.

Taking this a step further, one retail store might display a sign for you if you exhibit one for them. Or a beauty shop, which usually has display windows going to waste, may be glad for a few extra dollars each month in exchange for a colorful display.

Barbara Brabec, who wrote the wonderful *Handmade for Profit!*, tells of a toy maker who offered health clinics free toys for their waiting rooms…on the condition they posted a list stating who made each toy and how it could be ordered. Two clinics initially agreed. It was a win/win proposition: The waiting children had a diversion and the crafters had orders pouring in.

For a different take on this general subject, mall developers are racing to improve their layouts and maps. In an effort to compete with the allure of online shopping, malls are departing from conventional retail wisdom and clustering competing stores together to make it easier for customers. Shoppers report enjoying finding all similar resources in one wing, instead of having to trudge from one mall end to the other.

"Happy Holidays from the Hyatt Downtown and Tattered Cover" read the $59 gift coupon. The Hyatt Regency in downtown Denver combined with the Tattered Cover bookstore to offer an evening's stay in the hotel and a $10 gift certificate for a book. What a nice and imaginative holiday treat.

In a move toward friendly rivalry, three Dallas–Fort Worth RV park owners are proof that aligning *with* the competition works. Traders Village RV Park, Treetops RV Village, and Cowtown RV Park refer business to each other and even share the price

■ **May equals money-making publicity ideas.** Promotional opportunities abound this month. Mother's Day, Armed Forces Day, and Memorial Day, for starters. May is also National New Friends, Old Friends Week, National Sleep Month, Flower Month, Mental Health Month, National Barbecue Month, National Senior Travel Month, and National Photo Month. Of course there are many weekly designations as well. The second week of May includes Golf Week, National Hospital Week, Be Kind to Animals Week, National Tourism Week, etc. It doesn't take a genius to see the many connections available.

■ **Taking advantage of June opportunities.** Do something connected with fishing? Or antique cars? Or other mainly mens' hobbies? Are you pitching your wares to the media for Father's Day? Helen Keller's birthday—June 27—is ideal for anything connected with vision. Of course, June is a natural for graduation gifts. And many brides and grooms tie the knot this month. Think about your product, service, or store and how you can target specific timely events to promote it.

■ **July dates on which you can capitalize.** Don't overlook Independence Day as a hook. Your message needn't be strictly patriotic. One can declare

(continued on next page)

"independence" from spousal abuse, overeating, cleaning their own house, being financially naive—any number of things. These would be fitting angles for a therapist, diet center, maid service, or financial planner, respectively. Get creative.

■ **Think back-to-school for August.** Do you have a product or service that would appeal to busy college students, elementary school youngsters, or young people in middle school and high school? Now is the time to roll out the publicity campaign big time. There are also a lot of birthdays in August around which you could plan a PR campaign: Yves Saint Laurent (1st), Betty Boop (9th), and Margaret Mitchell (16th).

■ **Promotional ideas for September.** One of the more obscure holidays, National Grandparents Day, falls on the first Saturday after Labor Day. Many mature folks have lots of discretionary income. Get imaginative and funnel some of it into your bank account! Since both Rosh Hashanah and Yom Kippur typically occur this month, the possibilities for Jewish-themed promotions are ripe. Strip off the blinders and look ahead for special days, weeks, months, or people for a fresh publicity angle.

■ **October harvesting possibilities abound.** October is National AIDS Awareness Month and Breast Cancer Awareness

(continued on next page)

of an ad that features all three. By splitting the costs, they are able to afford an impressive advertisement that commands more attention than any of them could individually. "Whichever one of us is full, the first place we'll try to send them is to the others," reports Allan Hughes. Their excellent working relationship and reciprocation proves that it's wise to make friends with your foes.

John Nale owns the Evergreen Café in Buena Vista, Colorado. He opens only for breakfast and lunch. But it was a waste for the place to sit idle every night, so he and a friend got creative a few years ago. They put together a deal where Mary Lou Morgan used his facilities and equipment to operate her own business.

During the day the Evergreen served health-conscious breakfasts and lunches. At night it morphed into Italian cuisine that even included nine tempting vegetarian dishes. At 5:00 P.M. there was a total transition with candles, place mats, cloth napkins, and fancier dishware. Operatic music serenaded diners.

"There were many details to work out," reminisces Nale. Are there challenges in running two different restaurants out of one facility? Decidedly. Storage space was one. Mary Lou bought her own freezer, two-door cooler, and salad prep table. Orders come in on separate invoices. John explains how he handled the utilities: "I contacted the gas and electric company and got the monthly totals for the last three years, then came up with an average for each month. She reimbursed me for any additional costs over that average."

The Evergreen became a popular evening dining spot with locals and tourists alike. John received a percentage of Mary Lou's receipts, while she had little overhead. Both scored a knockout with this ingenious approach. Of course, a dinner house seeking to make better use of its facility could reverse this idea.

Without a doubt, it can pay big dividends to go in cahoots with other companies. So get on a train that's already going in your direction and watch your profits soar.

The Magic of Mentoring

I debated about writing this section from the perspective of the new entrepreneur receiving guidance—or from the position of the more seasoned business owner offering help. My conclusion was that since *both* tend to benefit, I would explore the best of all worlds. It seems that in mentoring, "what goes around, comes around."

Although the term historically was used to describe a teacher-student relationship, todayit's indicative of something that occurs when a well versed professional (the mentor) gives significant career assistance to a less-experienced person (the protégé). Mentoring engenders feelings of great satisfaction, improved productivity, and documented bottom-line results.

SPECIAL DATES TO
PIGGYBACK ON (continued)

Month. Perhaps you can tie in a promotion and donate a portion of the proceeds to benefit research into one of these diseases. Of course, there is Columbus Day (or Discovery Day as it is sometimes called) and United Nations Day. And don't forget Halloween, which screams in on October 31st along with a plethora of opportunities.

■ *November dates for possible PR pitches.* Two wonderful humorists were born in November: Will Rogers on the 4th and Samuel Clemens (Mark Twain) on the 30th. Can you use their wit and wisdom to apply to what you do? Additionally, Election Day falls this month, as does Veteran's Day and Thanksgiving. These three events furnish excuses for any number of ingenious twists.

■ *December dates on which to hang your hat.* Whether you wear a baseball cap, fedora, tam, cowboy hat, beret, or helmet, there is an appropriate date in December on which to capitalize. The Christmas/Hanukkah/New Year's Day cycle is the biggest buying season of them all. Many famous people also have birthdays that fall this month. One of them may give you a PR hook. How about Walt Disney on the 5th, Nostradamus on the 14th, Ty Cobb on the 18th, Kit Carson on the 24th, or Rudyard Kipling on the 30th? Go for it!

In corporations it is also often responsible for employee retention when experienced managers share their knowledge and contacts with women coming up the ranks.

Results of the 1998 Avon "Mentoring Matters Survey" prove that mentoring makes a decided difference in career advancement and business success of women. Revealing that 68 percent of women 18 to 29 had mentors, the survey indicates that mentorship is on the rise. Among mentored women owning small businesses, an overwhelming 94 percent say the experience was "Crucial/Very Helpful" to their success.

Mentoring is a vital training tool in the small business arena, believes Catalyst President Sheila Wellington. "Established women business owners who share their knowledge and expertise with the next generation of women entrepreneurs are providing them real-world experience that simply cannot be taught in the classroom or a textbook," she says. There needs to be a "fit" or synergy between the participants. When that occurs, the mentor becomes a wise and trusted confidant—and the possibilities are endless: nuts-and-bolts technical advice, market access, endorsements, potential partnering on procurement, motivation to grow, etc.

There are several myths about this process: One is that the protégé benefits more than the mentor. (Never have I taught without personally learning.) Another is that a person can't have several mentors at the same time. Still another is that the relationship must last a long time; some mentoring experiences are a brief, one-shot thing. People who help people can be any age, any race, either sex. In fact, don't ever discourage a male mentor. In my early career, one of my bosses taught me many truths about myself and the world of business that I still rely on heavily today.

Ask women of color to cite the biggest obstacle to starting a business and the answer is consistently lack of a mentor. Bernadette Williams—a young African-American female who heads i-strategy.com Inc., in Culver City, California, which does $1.5 million in annual revenues—is out to provide minority women with experienced guides to the tech business. Her Women's New Media Alliance makes matches all over the world using instant messaging or e-mail. Participants are asked to commit to a six-month relationship. To learn more go to http://www.wnma.org.

Bernadette also recognizes that mentoring needn't always take traditional paths. She realized how much people working in other industries could teach her. "When I would read articles or biographies about successful businesspeople," she relates, "I'd call or e-mail or fax them and ask for 15 minutes of their time. All they could do is say no. If they agreed to meet me for coffee, I would bring five or 10 questions and then I'd listen."

The San Jose Mercury News recently reported that Latina-owned businesses are the fastest-growing business category in the United States. Their mushrooming growth is partly attributed to greater availability of mentoring groups and professional organizations for Latinas. In addition to opening business in traditionally female industries, Hispanic women are breaking ground in male-dominated areas such as construction, agriculture, and wholesale trade.

The SBA's Office of Women's Business Ownership sponsors a program called WNET, which is short for the Women's Network for Entrepreneurial Training mentoring program. It puts together mentors (or in this case, "woman-tors") with protégés in a year long, one-on-one program. If you want to participate on either side of this excellent project, contact a Women's Business Center or the Women's Business Ownership Representative in the SBA district office in your area. To reach the substantial SBA site online go to http://www.sba.gov.

As we continue to build a support system linking newer female entrepreneurs with experienced business owners, our momentum will grow. That energy will strengthen women's overall position in America's economy—thus opening the door to meaningful change!

So whether it's forming relationships with other businesswomen, partnering with national companies, or doing a joint venture with the store down the street—join the surge to merge!

Let's journey forward now and enter the far-reaching world of catalog sales.

Web Sites, *Wisdom,* *and Whimsey*

Step-by-step guidance from a woman who did it. When Ruth Owades set out to establish a catalog operation that sells flowers and plants, she had no idea she would end up cultivating a hotbed of strategic alliances with companies all over. In this revealing article from *Inc.* magazine, she shows us the 28 steps she took to fashion those vital partnerships. Read it at http://www.inc.com/incmagazine/archives/0493096I.html.

How can you get noticed if you're a nobody? By applying LinkThink and teaming up with a somebody! That's what the ad agency of a gun manufacturer did to draw traffic to their client's trade show booth. The unknown company got celeb cachet by hiring football Hall of Famer Larry Csonka as a celebrity endorser. "Every male in his forties and fifties idolizes this guy, and that was our target market," explained an agency spokesperson. The booth was mobbed. Something so dull it could give you a dry mouth one day, can be so dynamic it could light road flares the next.

●●●●●●●

A wife called her husband on his cell phone to warn him of a radio alert. "Some nut is driving down the freeway the wrong way!" she cautioned.

"Goodness, honey," he replied, "there're hundreds of 'em."

●●●●●●●

Incredible site for any entrepreneur! Now you can find what you need without wasting time looking for it. EntreWorld.org searches every corner of the Web and delivers the best resources so you can devote your attention to business. They filter through the Internet's sprawling entrepreneurial information, streamlining the best of the best into their highly useful site. Then they organize it into three main departments: Starting Your Business, Growing Your Business, and Supporting Entrepreneurship. There is also a useful glossary of business terms if someone throws an unusual word at you. What really impressed me, however, was their search engine. Since I was looking for ways to promote *Shameless Marketing for Brazen Hussies™*, I was curious what a search for "women" would bring up. Wow—would you believe 472 meaty entries complete with links? What a marketing bonanza! It led me to 196 off-site resources, two women's bookstore resources, 238 calendar events, seven discussion threads, 12 EntreWorld articles, 14 experts—and a partridge in a pear tree. Find it all for yourself at http://entreworld.org.

Think "link" by franchising or licensing your business. Franchising as a growth strategy offers advantages if you are short of expansion capital and have a concept that can be packaged and taught to people who want to invest in a business. If full-blown franchising doesn't fit your operation, perhaps you can license your idea to other folks. Although the legal aspects of both can be burdensome, with a good product, service, or idea, your business can become many times more profitable.

●●●●●●●

Quote from James Thurber: "I hate women because they always know where things are."

●●●●●●●

Imagine cooperation, not competition, advises Jay Conrad Levinson, author of the *Guerrilla Marketing* series of books. He explains fusion marketing as "making not only the competition but also every business around you a marketing partner. Help them in return for helping you." Maybe it's a shared mailing. Perhaps a referral program. Our friend Joe Black coined a wonderful word for turning competition into cooperation. He calls it "coopetition."

A great site for female entrepreneurs resides at www.womanowned. com. Dedicated to women in business, it provides you networking opportunities and business resources galore. Starting Up is for those just launching their company and needing funding or assistance from the state government. CEO Central is targeted to women whose businesses have been around a few years and who face the challenges of employees, government red tape, and raising growth capital.

●●●●●●●

Did you hear about the man who was so stupid he thought magna cum laude was a cloud formation?

●●●●●●●

Would you like to form alliances with other women business owners? Check out Women in Business Cyberspace Field of Dreams at http://www.fodreams.com for a unique amalgam of listings. Whether you're looking for information on advertising and promotion, computers, event planning, or women promoting women, you'll find a directory listing here.

Stop throwing pity parties! Have you ever noticed when you throw yourself a pity party, nobody comes? Not every brilliant idea you hatch will jell. Some people (dense idiots that they are) simply won't see the value in partnering with you. When that happens, accept "no" graciously. It's important you don't shoot yourself in the foot...then admire your marksmanship. Just because you had a set back is no excuse to kick back. The next person you approach may be enthralled with your proposal. Be persistent and apply LinkThink!

CHAPTER 9

Broaden Your Success
With Catalog Sales

Catalog sales: Easy? Profitable? Ongoing? Yes and no. Well actually, no, yes, and yes. There are more than 14,000 print catalogs in existence. Thousands more wait to tempt surfers on the Internet. Getting your product in them isn't easy. You're not going to be as lucky as the guy who accidentally installed the deer whistles on his car backwards—and everywhere he went he was chased by a herd of deer. Catalogers won't chase you. It works the other way around. Smart entrepreneurs are in hot pursuit of them.

Catalogs Mean Cash

Selling merchandise via catalogs is the road less traveled. Many manufacturers overlook this bonanza. Although almost any product can find a home in a catalog if you are inventive and persistent enough, certain types flourish in this marketplace more than others. This is an ever-expanding opportunity. The industry experiences growth in sales of 6 percent per year. According to Simmons Market Research Bureau, 56.6 percent of all adults bought from a catalog in the last 12 months. What are these purchasers like? Overall, demographic statistics show that buyers tend to be married, female, and between 35 and 54. Cata-

logs typically pay promptly and can become one of your largest accounts.

What Fits? Everything From A to Z

Catalogs come in as many varieties as Ben & Jerry's flavors. They
cater to an enormously wide variety of whims. Here are just a few examples of consumer ones: There are sports catalogs like Gold Day, Bike
Nashbar, and American Tennis Mart. For crafters there's Stitcher's
Sourcebook, Keepsake Quilting, and Woodworkers' Store. Have a game
or novelty to sell? How about Spy Headquarters, Magic Masters, or the
Gamblers Emporium? Those seeking better health turn to The Vitamin Shoppe, Allergy Resources, and Healthy Living, for instance.

Businesses depend on inspiration from Successories. Businesspeople
also browse in-flight catalogs on various airplanes, and buy many computer and other high-tech products via mail order offerings and the
Internet.

These business-to-business catalogs are flourishing even more than
ones directed to general consumers. This is evident when looking at
Catalog Age's fifth annual ranking of the top 100 catalog companies.
Here's the line-up of the top 10: Dell Computer Corp., Gateway 2000,
J.C. Penney, Digital Equipment, Micro Warehouse, Spiegel, Fingerhut,
Viking Office Products, Land's End, and CDW.

Of course, not all catalogs are specialized. No doubt you're familiar
with the offerings of Lillian Vernon, Walter Drake, and Hanover House.
Perhaps you also receive the Wireless or Signals catalogs of more upscale gift offerings. And for those who really like to shop expensively
by mail, there is Bloomingdale's and Neiman Marcus, not to mention
the Metropolitan Museum of Art's catalog.

How and Where to Find Appropriate Catalogs

You probably receive possible candidates in your mail on a weekly
basis. Yes, it's what you used to consider "junk mail." Now it may be
grist for your sales mill.

There are many directories that list catalogs, which are typically
grouped according to subject matter. Most are quite expensive; you probably want to look at them in a public or university library before
considering a purchase. Here are some to investigate: *The Directory of
Mail Order Catalogs* (lists over 7,000 general catalogs), *Directory of Business to Business Catalogs* (contains 6,000 business catalogs), *Mail Order
Business Directory* (lists 10,000 catalogs and mail order firms), *The Di-*

rectory of Overseas Catalogs (contains information on over 1,300 mail order catalog companies from around the world), and the *National Directory of Catalogs* (9,000 mail order catalogs).

To reach folks living in our neighboring country to the north, research in the *Catalogue of Canadian Catalogues*, which has about 1,000 entries. Then there's the *Kid's Catalog Collection* with over 500 catalogs featuring books, toys, and clothing for children. And the Direct Mail Association publishes the *Great Catalog Guide*.

Our favorite is a very affordable directory ($25.95 versus the several hundred dollars for most of the others) called *The Catalog of Catalogs*. Although it is designed with consumers in mind, you can use it to handily track down possibilities in some 900 categories. To give you an idea of how obscure some of these topics are, here's a list of their newest categories: astrology, block printing, bulletin and chalkboards, calculators, gingerbread houses, pagers, safes, scooters, thermometers, and wines.

In a resource the size of a hefty phone book, they cover more than 14,000 catalogs. This is a superb place for market research. You can order it by calling 800-331-8355. We're impressed by the detail of this reference's organization. Let's say you have a pasta you'd like to sell via mail order. If you look under "Foods," there are no less than 22 different categories ranging from ethnic to health and natural, from meats to sugar-free and dietetic. Ditto for gardening. If your vocation involves bonsai, herbs, orchids, rock gardens, vegetables, wildflowers, or a dozen other sub-subjects, you'll have a field day. (Pun intended.) Of course, each of the above categories has several catalogs so the opportunities are multiplied.

Trade shows are another hot place to find catalog matches. Most big conferences hold an accompanying trade exhibit. Look in the *Encyclopedia of Associations* at a major library to target major organizations in your field. Determine where and when their next convention is. Go armed with samples and promotional materials and walk the aisles. Talk

Catalog Possibilities Online

A plethora awaits you on the Net and it's easy to order the catalogs as you identify likely ones. You can take a general approach: Visit various search engines and plug in the word "catalog" plus the subject of your product and see what comes up. Or you can go directly to the following sites and do searches for topic-specific catalogs:

- Catalog City (www.CatalogCity.com)
- Catalog Link (http://cataloglink.com)
- Catalog Site, The (http://www.catalogsite.com)

with vendors. Seek out those with related products. Many of the firms exhibiting produce catalogs you might never see otherwise. If you have a "gifty" item, gift shows are another fine place to meet potential bulk buyers.

What about the magazines published in your field? A careful read of their display and classified ads is likely to reveal catalogs aimed at your audience. Don't think just of consumer magazines. Also peruse trade journals.

The Way It All Works

Most catalogers will want to do a test first. This usually involves a purchase of a few score items to as many as 1,000 for a huge catalog. If your product passes their test, the rollout order can mean a few hundred copies—or as many as 50,000. Subsequent orders for major catalogs may end up being your biggest revenue producer.

Timing can be important. For holiday catalogs, you must catch them very early in the year. By April their selections will likely already be made. Generally, most companies tend to purchase in two seasons: Fall negotiations are completed by the end of July for delivery the beginning of September. Spring buys are finished by December 1 for delivery February 1.

Not all follow this schedule. Some publish as frequently as quarterly, bimonthly, even monthly. The average is seven to eight times a year, so they're always looking for new products. And if you miss one window of opportunity, don't fret. Stay in touch as they may consider you at a later date.

Most entrepreneurs give catalogs a 50 percent discount. This works fine until you start dealing with the big boys. Larger catalogers will send you a product submission packet and *their* contract with required discounts and terms. Don't be surprised if they want 80 percent off the retail price. If you've priced your product properly, you can give them that on orders of several thousand and still make a profit. Remember you have no expenses or financial risk: They produce and mail the catalogs.

It's important, once you've negotiated a catalog sale, you be able to supply product. Sounds simple doesn't it? Not so. This stocking issue can get as sticky as flypaper. You need to have a good channel of communication with the buyer so you have adequate stock, yet aren't sitting on inventory they won't eventually want. And if your product really takes off, you must be prepared to deliver inventory within four to five weeks.

If you're really serious about making a commitment to this marketing strategy, it's wise to read the trade journal of the industry, *Catalog Age*. If it's not available in your library, you can get subscription information by calling 800-775-3777 or check them out online at http://www.catalogagemag/com. You can access selected stories from the current issue, check their archives, or do a keyword search.

A new kid on the block, *Catalog Success*, offers in-depth and sophisticated articles on all aspects of catalog development, fulfillment, customer service, etc. Visit them on the Web at www.catalogsuccess.com or call 215-238-5300. Other good publications for those interested in this area are *Target Marketing*, *DM News*, and *Direct Marketing*.

Success Secrets for Securing Sales

Do your targeted catalogs carry similar products? Great. If not, you have a bigger challenge. They just don't carry your type product *yet*. Often you'll notice their other products are more expensive than yours. So how can you build your ticket to get it into the range of their other merchandise?

Think packaging. Can you combine it with another complementary item from a different manufacturer? Or maybe you can develop a "mini-kit" with a couple of other things that relate to your topic. One catalog I researched included The Feng Shui Kit. It consisted of a 112-page instruction book, compass, mirror, and sheets of stickers.

Make it *easy* for them to want you. Develop a one-page sell sheet that is reproduced on your letterhead and contains all the vital information. Here are some guidelines on the actual process:

- Pinpoint likely catalogs using the strategies outlined above.

- Call and request a copy (most have toll-free numbers and will gladly provide a free copy).

- Study it. Consume it. Think about it. Relate it to your product(s).

- If it looks promising, call again. This time you want the buyer's name (get the spelling too), address, direct phone number, fax, and e-mail. Request any available submission forms or guidelines.

- Complete their form, if applicable; write a benefit-oriented sales letter that emphasizes why their customers need your product and cites specific examples of their current offerings that relate to it.

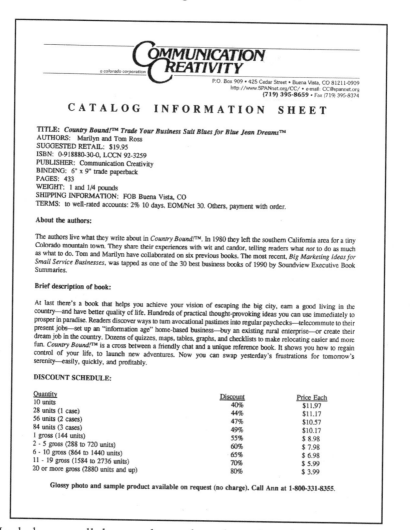

COMMUNICATION CREATIVITY

a colorado corporation

P.O. Box 909 • 425 Cedar Street • Buena Vista, CO 81211-0909
http://www.SPANnet.org/CC/ • e-mail: CC@spannet.org
(719) 395-8659 • Fax (719) 395-8374

CATALOG INFORMATION SHEET

TITLE: *Country Bound!™ Trade Your Business Suit Blues for Blue Jean Dreams*™
AUTHORS: Marilyn and Tom Ross
SUGGESTED RETAIL: $19.95
ISBN: 0-918880-30-0, LCCN 92-3259
PUBLISHER: Communication Creativity
BINDING: 6" x 9" trade paperback
PAGES: 433
WEIGHT: 1 and 1/4 pounds
SHIPPING INFORMATION: FOB Buena Vista, CO
TERMS: to well-rated accounts: 2% 10 days, EOM/Net 30. Others, payment with order.

About the authors:

The authors live what they write about in *Country Bound!*™. In 1980 they left the southern California area for a tiny Colorado mountain town. They share their experiences with wit and candor, telling readers what *not* to do as much as what to do. Tom and Marilyn have collaborated on six previous books. The most recent, *Big Marketing Ideas for Small Service Businesses*, was tapped as one of the 30 best business books of 1990 by Soundview Executive Book Summaries.

Brief description of book:

At last there's a book that helps you achieve your vision of escaping the big city, earn a good living in the country—and have better quality of life. Hundreds of practical thought-provoking ideas you can use immediately to prosper in paradise. Readers discover ways to turn avocational pastimes into regular paychecks—telecommute to their present jobs—set up an "information age" home-based business—buy an existing rural enterprise—or create their dream job in the country. Dozens of quizzes, maps, tables, graphs, and checklists to make relocating easier and more fun. *Country Bound!*™ is a cross between a friendly chat and a unique reference book. It shows you how to regain control of your life, to launch new adventures. Now you can swap yesterday's frustrations for tomorrow's serenity—easily, quickly, and profitably.

DISCOUNT SCHEDULE:

Quantity	Discount	Price Each
10 units	40%	$11.97
28 units (1 case)	44%	$11.17
56 units (2 cases)	47%	$10.57
84 units (3 cases)	49%	$10.17
1 gross (144 units)	55%	$ 8.98
2 - 5 gross (288 to 720 units)	60%	$ 7.98
6 - 10 gross (864 to 1440 units)	65%	$ 6.98
11 - 19 gross (1584 to 2736 units)	70%	$ 5.99
20 or more gross (2880 units and up)	80%	$ 3.99

Glossy photo and sample product available on request (no charge). Call Ann at 1-800-331-8355.

Include your sell sheet and a product photo. It is also wise for *you* to write a catalog blurb in their style. Bingo—you've just made their job that much easier. Most agree it's better *not* to send the product at this stage.

- Follow-up two weeks later with a phone call. Find out when their decision-making committee will meet. Offer to send a sample.

- At the designated time send the sample (along with copies of all the previous PR materials).

- Follow-up two weeks after the committee was to meet if you haven't heard anything. (If the answer is "no," try to find out their objection so you can overcome it at the next round of meetings.)

■ Don't get discouraged. Be tenacious. When we published *Country Bound!* a few years back, we were sure it was a natural for *Mother Earth News*, which had a self-contained catalog in their magazine. But we could never get to "yes," let alone catch the decision maker. Finally, on my *fifth* call, I reached the woman, gave her my pitch— and was promptly put on hold. She came back a couple of minutes later saying, "You know, you're right. I just pulled your book off the bookshelf and it's perfect for our readers." Then she gave me a purchase order for several cases. We sold to *MEN* month after month, year after year thereafter.

When you've had initial correspondence and they come back with a Vendor Information Sheet, they're serious. At this point you probably want to ask them some questions:

1. What do you need from me?
2. What are your projections: How many do you expect to sell over what period of time?
3. Will my catalog blurb copy work or may I see yours?
4. When will the catalog drop (mail)?

On a fling and a prayer, Dayna Steele decided to start *her own catalog*. For five years she kept thinking someone would start a catalog dedicated to selling space-related gear. But it never happened. So this Houstonite, who is married to a NASA test pilot, launched an online catalog. The Space Store carries over 400 different space items including NASA flight suits for adults and kids, space food, real astronaut mission patches, space toys, and more.

Also at www.thespacestore.com surfers can find out about the latest space shuttle mission, find educational links for kids, and even download an actual astronaut application. "The best thing about this whole new career," says Steels, "is that I can stop whenever I like and hang out with my kids."

Annie Hurlbut, whom you met in an earlier chapter, is collecting money big time from her Peruvian Connection catalog of elegant knitwear. Not only does she produce a four-color 48-page U.S. version with photographs of models shot on location in Peru, she also does a German version. It contains German-language copy and pricing is in deutsche marks. Additionally she has a separate edition for the United Kingdom with prices noted in pounds sterling.

If you're an inventor or manufacturer of a product, don't overlook this sales venue. Catalogs, once won over, pay promptly and provide a long-term income stream. Or you just may decide to start one of your own.

Want to make outlandish profits? Then let's move on to another way to super charge your balance sheet: selling your merchandise as premiums.

Web Sites, Wisdom, and Whimsey

Selling to the various Williams-Sonoma catalogs. This catalog giant offers multiple opportunities as they publish the flagship *Williams-Sonoma* catalog (foods, cookbooks, etc.) the *Pottery Barn* (casual home furnishings), *Hold Everything* (storage solutions), and *Chambers* (linens and accessories for the bed and bath). To do a bit of research, check out their Web site at www.williams-sonomainc.com. For more details call 415-421-7900 and ask for the "Product Submission Information Line." You'll be requested to send a cover letter, photo, and pricing sheet and told the name of the appropriate buyer. (Be patient. It can take eight to 10 weeks for a reply.) Good luck!

●●●●●●●

Q: *Why do most middle-aged women pay more attention to improving their appearance than to expanding their minds?*

A: *Because most middle-aged men aren't too bright...but only a few of them are blind.*

●●●●●●●

Reach 3,500 mail order catalogs in 55 categories! If you aspire to place your product in catalogs, this site is like finding a pool of cool water in the middle of the Sahara. I pulled up catalogs for travel, craft supplies, sex/erotica (all in the name of work, you understand), office supplies/equipment, plus cooking/food prep. This is a bonanza of places to sell your products. To access them go to http://www.buyersindex.com. You can then either connect directly to a catalog's individual Web site or find general contact information.

●●●●●●●

Why isn't phonetic spelled the way it sounds?

●●●●●●●

References galore all in one spot. For easy surfing, we suggest you bookmark http://www.refdesk.com/. Here you'll quickly access over 290 links to reference and research information, 260 search engines covering 19 categories, a virtual encyclopedia covering 45 subjects, and loads more. You can read *USA Today* and other worldwide newspapers, plus find head-lines and summaries for the following topics: top stories, business, technology, world, sports, entertainment, politics, health, weather (five-day forecasts), human interest (including crime), and community (including a Latino link). Looking for a publicity news peg? What a time- saver this will be as you scan for breaking news stories on any of the above subjects. Another intriguing link goes to "My Homework Helper." Though the title sounds sophomoric, the material is broad in depth. You can find out about architecture, astronomy, aviation, birds, building, the census, chemistry, dentistry, diamonds, drug abuse, gravity, guitars, health, leadership, magic, Mars, nutrition, oceanography, physics, plumbing, and much more. What a great place to research!

"Never give up" is a worthy motto. We approached the Real Goods catalog back in 1992 when *Country Bound!* first came out. They refused us flat. We tried again a couple of years later and weren't welcomed any more graciously. The book, however, debuted in the 1998 holiday catalog and is still advertised there today. It only took six years!

●●●●●●●

Quote from Laurel Thatcher Ulrich:
"Well-behaved women rarely make history."

●●●●●●●

Astute missies visit this Web site. Considered the world's leading application service provider for small businesses, www.smartonline.com even has a Smart Entrepreneur self-assessment quiz. And if you've already decided self-employment is for you, they have sections on how to start your business, finance growth, market, incorporate, protect your legal rights, build your team, plus expand globally. There's even a currency converter and global clock for those thinking internationally. And for $5 each, you can access nearly 4,000 forms and documents to help you solve financial, legal, human relations, and sales problems. They also have 17 affordable Web-based tools to automate your overhead.

Sales and marketing advice bonanza. I'm impressed by the wealth of resources for small business owners, professionals, and home-office entrepreneurs available at http://www.bizproweb.com. Awaiting you here are 1,500 pages of business links, information, and articles. Their section on Sales & Marketing overflows with meaty articles from some of the best in the business.

CHAPTER 10

Premiums and Incentives Supercharge Your Balance Sheet

Selling thousands of units of your product to one company, organization, or association is a phenomenal money maker. These are called premium or incentive sales. Besides giving a gigantic boost to your bottom line, the beauty of these deals is they don't compete with your other marketing efforts. Plus you are paid when the product ships, and the sale itself is great PR.

Further good news is you don't need the magic of David Copperfield to pull it off. Premium sales usually consist of about 60 percent inspiration and 40 percent perspiration. Now I'll guide you to cultivate and close these colossal deals.

Think big, really BIG. Quantities range anywhere from 500 to 100,000 units. There have even been a few sales into the millions. The majority fall between 5,000 and 20,000 units—certainly worth the effort of any self-respecting entrepreneurial lassie.

Is this really doable? You bet! Kim Gosselin of JayJo Books, L.L.C., received a check for more than $330,000 for the sale of 110,000 of two of her books: *Taking Asthma to School* and *Taking Asthma to Camp*. Nice going, Kim! And Diane Pfeifer of Strawberry Patch pocketed $68,100 for selling 15,000 copies of her *Gone with the Grits* book to Quaker Oats.

What's Hot

If you decide to pursue this avenue, be aware premium customers swarm around certain areas as bees do around honeycombs.

Some industries are more likely than others to participate in premiums and incentives. Food and beverage companies are heavy users, as are appliance makers. Then there's the automotive field, especially for tires, batteries, and accessories. Pharmaceuticals are another huge possibility. And, of course, banks and savings and loan institutions often present gifts to their customers. General corporate tie-ins run a wide gamut: gifts to VIP customers, stockholders, board of director members and prospects; incentives for members of the sales force; training tools for various departments.

Applying Creativity

There are no limitations. You're bound only by your own imagination. In fact, small businesses can get away with a lot more than big corporations. Take advantage of your size to think provocatively. Go for whimsey, character, fun.

How do you dream up premium matches for your books? Roger Von Oech says in *A Whack on the Side of the Head*, "Discovery consists of looking at the same thing as everyone else and thinking something different." Let us embark on such a journey of discovery. To succeed at premium sales, we must get out of our normal marketing rut: expand concepts, open ourselves to new paths, practice creative thinking. Here are some guidelines to help you accomplish just that:

1. Look for links, similarities, and connections between your product and other companies, other products, slogans, even associations and nonprofit organizations.

2. Don't be judgmental. Let the ideas flow.

3. Ask "What's the fit?"

4. Play the "what-if" game. Follow it with some contrary-to-normal condition or idea.

5. Probe the possible, the impossible, the ridiculous.

6. Challenge the rules. Ignore "we've always done it this way" thinking.

7. Seek the second right answer. It may be an offbeat, but more innovative, solution.

The Mechanics of How It Works

The one drawback to this merchandising strategy is that nothing
happens fast. Sometimes it seems like premium and incentive deals
take about as long to mature as trees do to grow. Sales take months,
sometimes years, to develop. But they are worth waiting for!

Diane Pfeifer of Strawberry Patch tells of working on one deal for
four years! It's not that it was so difficult; it's just that the Quaker Oats
contact people kept changing. She would no sooner develop rapport
and gain their interest, than that person would be replaced.

Your customer may want to buy a couple hundred units for initial
testing purposes before committing to a large quantity. Be flexible. Some
premium purchasers will want to customize the item to include their
name or logo. They may want to make slight modifications or add something to make it more appealing to their customers.

And now to the $64,000 question: What do you charge? Whatever
the traffic will bear. On amounts up to 5,000 units, 50 to 70 percent off
the retail price is typical. In large volume, experienced buyers will expect to pay manufacturing costs plus 10 percent.

Be sure to get a written purchase order or agreement that spells out
all details, such as who pays the freight. If there is any question about
the integrity or financial status of the company with which you're dealing, insist on at least half payment before you manufacture or establish
an escrow account to hold the money. In some cases, companies get
lines of credit from banks based on the purchase order. Go for the balance being due on delivery.

When I discuss this topic in seminars, attendees often ask if they
can sell to more than one company. The answer is a qualified "yes."
Your customers have the right to demand exclusivity—either within
their industry or their geographical locale. You don't sell to Pepsi, for
instance, then go to Coke and try to strike a deal. Did you connect
with a regional savings and loan? Don't muddy the waters by contacting their competition in the area.

Finding the Golden Needles in the Premium Haystack

As you might expect, there is a directory for this industry. Finding
it is like discovering manna from heaven. Go to the reference or business section of a major library and request the *Directory of Premium,*

Incentive & Travel Buyers. Your best business contacts are right there: 12,000 corporations plus 19,000 premium and incentive buyers by name, title, address, phone, and fax. Additionally, you can find prospects by city or state, company name, or type of product or service they sell. (If your coffers are flush, you can purchase a copy for $259.95 by calling 800-223-1797.)

This secondary research, however, is but the tip of the iceberg. What about checking trade shows and exhibitions yourself to locate suitable matches? The library has reference directories that list such shows all around the country. There are also trade show/exhibition sites on the Web. Perhaps a show will be held nearby so you can do hands-on primary research.

Just as we all have industry-specific trade shows, the premium/incentive industry does likewise. The granddaddy is The Motivation Show, held in the fall at McCormick Center in Chicago. This event has been going on for over 65 years and attracts some 25,000 people. Decision makers who attend seek premiums and incentives to increase sales and foster attitudes of loyalty. Many also have internal company agendas such as strengthening productivity, reducing absenteeism and employee turnover, or improving work habits and leadership skills. For more information on the show, call 630-434-7779. There are also regional shows in New York, California, Texas, Ohio, and New England. If you're considering exhibiting, reread the section on "Trade Show Exhibiting" in Chapter 3.

Go where manufacturers of related products will be. Position yourself with others interested in your market. Think about who else reaches your potential market and how your product can serve their needs. Maybe you've identified cereal companies as a target (they're ideal for kids' toys). Perhaps it's garden equipment manufacturers or the maker of a well-known beverage.

Sometimes an ad agency will come to you. Eileen Johnson, formerly of Dearborn Financial Publishing, Inc., tells of being contacted by ad personnel who saw one of their books in a bookstore. The client, U.S. West Direct, was looking for a book on customer service to mail as an appreciation gift to their Yellow Page advertisers. They chose Dearborn's *Talking with Your Customers*, buying 2,000 at a 60 percent discount.

So while the first step is identifying likely industries, perhaps the larger challenge is finding out how to reach the players in these industries who might be interested in purchasing your book in bulk. Get online and hold onto your hat! The *Thomas Register of American Manufacturers* awaits you in cyberspace. This is a massive directory of virtually every company that manufactures virtually every thing in the United States. It currently lists 156,914 companies, 135,415 brand names, plus 63,669 products and services.

The beauty is you can do keyword searches that pull the information immediately to your fingertips. Got a cooking utensil you want to sell to a food company or appliance manufacturer? Bingo. Have a gizmo for travelers? You could approach RV manufacturers (58 companies listed); trailers and travel (61); or RV parts, accessories, and supplies (129). The list goes on and on.

Once you've accessed the appropriate product heading, you can either use their internal hyperlink to go directly to the manufacturer's site or contact them via fax if they are not on the Web. The other good news is membership to access this information is free and takes all of about 30 seconds. Tune in at http://www.thomasregister.com. Of course, if you're not on the Web, you can use the paper version of *Thomas Register of American Manufacturers* in the business or reference section of a major library.

Another vital tile in the mosaic of your research is *Hoover's Handbook of American Businesses*. Called "The Reigning King of Corporate Profiles" by *Fortune* magazine, it has 14,000 free

Courting Local Premium Sales

There may be a wealth of opportunities waiting in your backyard. Here are some strategies to woo local business.

■ Get a mailing list of corporations and associations in your community from the local chamber of commerce.

■ Contact the corporate librarians at large companies in your area. They can tell you who buys what for their organization.

■ Call the administrative assistant of key decision makers for research help.

■ Learn as much as you can about their business and needs so you can make suitable suggestions.

■ Begin a dialogue with the key decision maker.

■ When you receive a small order—perhaps an individual manager buying for her or his staff—use this as an entry to reach further. You might be able to sell products to the director of human resources. Position yourself as a premium resource. Set up a program that helps area companies understand how to reward employees with premiums or use them to build goodwill and prospect for new customers. Use suggestive selling.

company capsules. These one-page overviews of major companies come complete with a hyperlink to their site, contact information, a synopsis of the firm's products or services, number of outlets, earnings, top management's names, and a list of key competitors—which could lead you on to many other marketing possibilities. Find them on the Internet at http://www.hoovers.com or in your main library. I found their database immensely helpful when researching companies to approach for purchasing bulk copies of this book. (Once you've entered a company name and gotten the Search Results page, click on "Capsule" for the best results.) To secure more in-depth information, you can also pay to subscribe to their Company Profiles service.

When capturing information, always include the name of a primary contact person. Titles vary from company to company. You really want the VP of Promotion, or the Promotion Director, or Promotion Manager. But you may have to go to the VP of Sales or Marketing to locate the above person. If you're going after a food manufacturer, "find the *brand manager* of that particular product. It cuts hours off your research," Diane Pfeifer advises.

Do your homework. Know the company you're targeting. Look them up on the Web. Peruse that site thoroughly so you become familiar with their internal attitude and workings. Get a copy of their annual report by calling their office and speaking to the public relations office or, if the company is local, check in the library. Call the librarian at their major local newspaper or search the Web. An article may have run about them lately that gives you new insights.

Using Premium Reps to Peddle Your Wares

These sales reps usually have substantial corporate training in sales and marketing and were often former premium managers themselves. They are sharp individuals with incredible contacts who specialize in forging the right marriages between premiums and product offers.

If you are fortunate enough to attract a member of this ready-made sales force, expect to pay a commission of 5 to 10 percent. Of course you don't pay salary, pension plan, health insurance, expense account, etc., as you would to a salaried employee.

Most premium reps belong to the Incentive Manufactures Representative Association, Inc., (IMRA). You can reach this organization at 703-610-9021, 8201 Greensboro Drive, Suite 300, McLean, VA 22102.

Of course, membership in IMRA would put you in immediate contact with about 150 reps as you hobnob at their annual Marketing Conference. This four-day working meeting is devoted to the analysis of industry trends, problem solving, and knowledge sharing between reps and manufacturers like you.

IMRA also publishes *The IMRA Handbook*. Although the hefty price of $225 will dissuade some, those serious about pursuing this avenue will find practical, proven ideas here for organizing and managing an incentive department, interviewing reps, plus developing appropriate sales support materials. You'll discover why intermediaries can be more important than end users. Along with the *Handbook* you get other goodies such as a model contract, membership list, and a set of rep member labels. This makes it easy to solicit their interest.

Tips From the Sage of Premium Sales

Before premiums can take you to the promised land, you need someone who knows the way. Kim Gosselin of JayJo Books is the supreme guide. Kim has racked up a total of over $1.5 million in premium revenue working out of her home and by herself, so she knows! This lady could sell sand to a sheik. She also does hourly consulting. Call 636-861-1331 for details.

Here are some of her secrets: Once you've identified the right contact person and done your homework, call and make a short pitch. If there is interest, send a package and proposal. This will not be your normal mailing. To catch the potential buyer's attention for one of her titles, Kim enclosed the book manuscript in a clear plastic backpack—complete with custom imprinted pencils carrying their company name, bookmarks, and a full-color cover.

Another time she hired a specialty ad company to do a prototype of a big clear aspirin bottle with the prospect's logo on it, then placed her book inside. Other times she makes up a fancy gift basket. Be creative. Don't just send a proposal in a manila envelope. "That first impression may be your last. Make it look the best it can be," Kim counsels. "Send it FedEx or UPS overnight."

Call two weeks later and try to set an appointment for a presentation. "If they give you an appointment, they're halfway sold," she says. During that presentation, show your passion for the project. Passion sells! Explain to them how you're creating a win/win situation, how it's going to increase their sales. Have your discount policy ready. Her prices range from 50 to 80 percent off the retail price with payment due in 30 days. "Ask for the order," she instructs: "Why don't we test market 10,000 and see how it goes?" Always have something dramatic you can leave behind.

You may run into objections:

1. "We have no money left in the budget," they tell you. Counter it with a suggestion that they write it into next year's budget.

2. "We can't afford it." Could they comarket it with another compatible company?

3. "Our lawyers will have to take a look." Fine.

4. "We want our name on it, a message from the CEO, commercial plugs…yada, yada, yada." Wonderful. Give them anything they want—and are willing to pay for.

Kim is a great believer in servicing the sale before, during, and after. If you constantly please the customer, they may be interested in buying more products. What size cartons do they want? Do the cartons need to be labeled specifically for them? How many on a pallet? She calls their warehouse to alert personnel when to expect the shipment. It's called customer service.

After the merchandise is delivered, she sends personal thank-you notes to the marketing director, production supervisor, secretary, anyone who was part of the deal. And she remembers them at Christmas with gifts. But it doesn't stop there.

Kim sends a Customer Satisfaction Form. Are the books okay? Is there anything you'd like to change for future runs? How's the book doing? Has it increased your sales? "Go for the gold," she encourages. She has sold one company 10,000 to 15,000 copies of one title every year for five years. "Repeat business is the key. Create a club or a series to keep them coming back."

No question, there are BIG bucks to be made in premium sales. I wish you much success! Now let's address how to make prospects hot for you by creating a dazzling, daring, dramatic brochure.

Web Sites, Wisdom, and Whimsey

Primary trade journals of the industry can help expose your product to potential buyers and further educate you. The biggest is *Potentials in Marketing* (50 South Ninth Street, Minneapolis, MN 55402; 612-333-0471; www.potentialsmag.com). They run free "new product" color photos and blurbs. Needless to say, the competition is ferocious. If they pick your merchandise, they refer interested people to a reader's service "bingo" card, which is a postcard where premium buyers are invited to circle appropriate numbers for more information. The magazine then sends you a computer printout of the names of information requesters.

You could get hundreds of requests for more information. Statistics show about one in 10 will typically jell when promptly followed up. If your budget is flush and your item an especially likely premium candidate, you may even want to run a display ad in this publication. Another magazines that goes to potential customers is *Incentive* (355 Park Avenue South, New York, NY 10010; 212-592-6400; www.incentivemag.com). You can get a free one-year subscription from their Web site. Also *Promo* (11 Riverbend Drive South, Stamford, CT 06907; 203-358-9900; www.promomagazine.com) focuses on product sampling, contests, sweepstakes, events, and interactive promotions.

●●●●●●●

The early bird gets the worm,
but the second mouse gets the cheese.

●●●●●●●

Ad agencies can be death to premium sales. If you approach a large corporation and they talk about getting their agency involved, say pleasantly but firmly that you only work directly with the company. Otherwise, the agency is likely to feel jealous that *they* didn't come up with the idea and nix the whole project.

Interested in a specific industry throughout the U.S.? Check out the Top 25 lists printed in many weekly business-to-business newspapers and magazines. These publications frequently compile a list of local companies in a particular industry such as manufacturing, hospitals, insurance, etc. Usually included are such key facts as number of employees, annual revenue, and contact information. A good place to start your search is at the American City Business Journals Web site at http://ww.bizjournals.com. Newspapers in each city also frequently put together a special Top 25 book representing lists from all 52 weeks. The book, usually about $25, will be available at the corresponding main library or from the chamber of commerce.

An incredible how-to resource for small business resides at http://www.smartbiz.com. This site has literally thousands of free resources geared specifically to help you run your business or department smarter. You can browse over 60 categories, quickly search for the information you need, or spend hours (actually days) foraging for delectables here. You'll definitely want to bookmark their Smart Business Supersite.

●●●●●●●

Overlooking selling your merchandise as a premium makes about as much sense as nuns getting together to write a treatise on sex.

●●●●●●●

Another Web site to help with your homework: Dun and Bradstreet's Companies Online (http://www.companiesonline.com) offers info on most public and many private businesses.

Seize every opportunity. Susan Carter, who wrote *How to Make Your Business Run Without You*, discovered she could make extra sales during the holidays by selling her book to small business consultants. They gave them away to their clients instead of more traditional holiday gifts. To sweeten the offer, she gave a nice quantity discount and supplied each consultant with personally autographed copies. Give you any ideas?

●●●●●●●

Don't tie yourself up in "nots." Attitude surpasses skills every time. A go-getter will run rings around the person with adequate abilities but no passion. Remember: American ends with "I can."

●●●●●●●

Learn more to earn more. Learning shouldn't wait until you attend a professional conference, enroll in a course, or read a new book. It should be a daily experience. We're constantly provided with exciting opportunities to increase our knowledge and sense of things. Every project, if you approach it openly and enthusiastically, can yield knowledge and sharpened skills. Look for that new nugget of wisdom in each day.

Diversity's many faces affect you. Diversity runs across both genders, all races, every age group. Did you know that in the next six years, white male representation in the U.S. labor force will decline from 53.4 percent to 44.3 percent? Meanwhile African-American female representation will grow from 4.6 percent to 6.2 percent. While Caucasian women make 73¢ for every dollar earned by white men, African-American women make just 63¢, and Latinas earn only 53¢ on the dollar. More than 17 percent of woman aged 65 to 69 are still working. Lesbians, even though they have similar jobs and educations, make 14 percent less than their heterosexual female peers.

●●●●●●●

The trouble with the guy who talks too fast is that he often says something he hasn't thought of yet.

●●●●●●●

Extraordinary Web site awaits women business owners. Their slogan is "women with their modems running" and Digital Women is indeed a site for fast-paced female entrepreneurs looking online for a place to gather resources, free business and sales tips, home business ideas, and a place to network with like-minded women. Their How To section and Biz Help Desk overflow with hundreds of helpful articles that can serve as a library to launch and grow your business. Just surf over to http://www.digital-women.com

Part IV

Mission Possible—
Unstoppable
Direct Marketing

CHAPTER 11

Your Brochure:
The Bridge to Burgeoning Profits

Every product or service needs promotional literature. Your brochure is the marketing engine that drives sales. It convinces potential buyers of your merits. You'll use this piece of literature in a multitude of ways: It's fast and effective when responding to daily inquiries from potential buyers. You can hand it to prospective customers you meet in person. It makes an ideal direct mail piece to use when prospecting for sales. You can use it as a "bounce back" that routinely gets stuffed in packages and letters you mail. And it can be placed on tables at trade shows and networking events.

Your brochure has an additional function: A well-crafted one also serves a peripheral PR purpose. Attach a copy of it to other paperwork when talking to your banker, accountant, and lawyer. These professionals are in a position to refer you business...*if* they understand what you do.

Initial Planning Decisions

Don't fall into the trap of thinking once you've produced a killer brochure, your marketing is done. Although an important component in your overall arsenal, it is only part of the marketing mix—one of some 15 key weapons.

A good plan is not a substitute for skill, but a tool to increase success. Think about how you'll use your brochure. Will it be to promote your product, service, organization, or store? To announce something new? Who is your target audience? What are their likes and dislikes? Is there an advantage to coding or folding some differently than others? Of course, it never hurts to study the competition when you feel like you're up to your ass in alligators. Take up a collection. Learn from what other promotional pieces do well—and note things to avoid.

In the most simple form, a basic brochure does the following:

■ Explains what you are promoting

■ Shows why it is of interest or use

■ Describes the people and/or organization behind what you are offering

■ Tells how to find out more

Although you want a brochure that stands out from the pack—one with snap, crackle, and pop—we're not talking thousands of dollars here. While four-color photographs reproduced on glossy paper and cut into unusual shapes make for an impressive piece, this isn't necessary. There is a happy medium between that extreme and black ink on white paper.

It is important that you project a quality image. Your brochure is your salesperson in print. Think of an 8½-inch by 11-inch or 8½-inch by 14-inch (legal size) piece of paper, printed on both sides and folded to fit into a normal #10 business envelope. This is an ideal size as it easily slips into a woman's handbag or a man's pocket. Depending on the size of the paper used, folding creates six or eight surfaces, or panels. Now that we've determined the size, it's time to consider what it will contain.

Including the Right Components

Just as a loaf of bread needs flour, liquid, yeast, and other ingredients, a successful brochure needs standard elements. Form follows function. Conclude what the contents should be first, then think about design. If you try it the other way around, you'll feel like you've been caught in a thunderstorm with a leaky umbrella. The design should grow logically out of the subject matter. We'll be talking more about design specifics later.

First grab the potential buyer's attention. This is usually done with a headline and an eye-catching graphic on the front panel. Its sole purpose is to lure the reader into the brochure.

Unlike ads, which tell your story on one flat surface, a brochure allows the reader to see only the front panel initially. Your headline must seize attention. Be succinct. Benefit-oriented. Generate interest. Don't put your company name on the front! Who cares? Instead ask a targeted provocative question—or state a startling statistic. The adjacent photo or graphic should actively support and correlate with the headline. Together they make a forceful statement to woo readers inside. Next have introductory copy that addresses the specific needs or problems of your prospects, then explains how your product or service will meet those needs or solve those problems.

Impartial third-party accolades are another key element. Testimonials give clout to your overall message. Try to get a diversity of comments. Think about your target audience and include quotes that will appeal to different niches of potential buyers. Don't sign them with just initials; this looks phoney. Use full names and/or company identifiers.

Include a money-back guarantee, if possible. Give your prospective customers every reason to trust you. Guarantees are sales stimulators. If you're offering a quality product, returns will be a tiny fraction of sales.

Ask for the order. Just as a good speech has an introduction, body, and conclusion, so does a brochure. You must close the sale. Tell readers what you want them to do: Call your toll-free number, go to your Web site, make an appointment, send in the order coupon, etc. You can create a sense of urgency by encouraging them to act "today," "now," or "immediately."

Don't overlook a reply device; tests prove coupons multiply responses. It can be attached or done as a separate form. It's also a good idea to include ordering information in small print somewhere else on the brochure. That way when the coupon is detached from the main part, people can still find you. And if your brochure is designed as a self-mailer, the back outer panel must be devoted to the address section. Include your toll-free number plus your e-mail and Web site addresses.

Sales Sizzle: Emphasize Benefits Over Features

There are a few individuals on this earth who could sell refrigerators in the North Pole, but most of us have to work at being strong

Features Versus Benefits

First make a list of the features that make your book unique or better than the competition. To guide you in this process, we've done a features/benefit comparison for a custom-made, wooden lawn chair.

Features:

1. Hand-crafted
2. Made of teak and brass
3. Curved back
4. Adjustable back angle
5. Natural teak finish

Now determine the benefit of each of these. Translate the lawn chair features (and those of your book) into benefits—things that meet your *customers*' needs:

Benefits:

1. Heirloom quality
2. Strong, durable, maintenance-free, naturally resistant to weather
3. Excellent back support
4. Comfortable, perfect for a nap in the afternoon sun
5. More in harmony with the natural landscape than a plastic or aluminum chair

salespeople. You'll seduce prospects much faster with a "you" or "your" approach rather than "me," "we," "our," or "I." When you emphasize benefits instead of features, you tell the customer what he or she will get out of the deal—you give tangible reasons to buy.

Let's look at an example of how to write benefit copy: Suppose you have a property improvement business. Tell prospective customers that your services can increase property value quickly, conveniently, and cost-effectively. If you are a hypnotist who emphasizes how hypnosis can improve memory, point out that these techniques will have them astounding their friends and impressing their business associates. And they'll never need to be embarrassed again because they've forgotten someone's name.

Got a software program on inventory control? Don't preach about how you'll set up and monitor their inventory control system. Instead tell them inventory shortages and surpluses will be a thing of the past. Maybe your thing is physical fitness. People don't want to hear about diet and exercise. Instead romance them by explaining how they—and their friends—will see a marked improvement in their appearance and stamina. Emphasize the *result* people want. As Elmer Wheeler wisely said, "Sell the sizzle, not the steak."

To arouse a potential buyer, use punchy verbs and adjectives. Yet don't totally unleash your imagination. Terms like "miraculous," "magic," or "spectacular" sound exaggerated and unconvincing. On the other hand, words with honest pizzazz produce the greatest positive mood change. Cut through the communications chatter with clear, memo-

240

rable copy that offers prospects viable solutions to nagging problems. Marketing is hype only when the product or service doesn't deliver.

The Cast of Brochure Readers

There are three types of brochure readers. The *casual reader* spends a few seconds scanning the headline on the front panel. The *interested reader* opens your brochure and reads the headlines, subheads, and photo captions—but nothing more. The *serious reader* devours everything. Your aim is to convert casual readers to interested readers, then to serious readers. This tells us we'd better concentrate some mighty creative effort on headlines and subheads. They are the carrots dangling before prospective buyers.

Be aware of what I call "information shaping." How one presents information—what isn't said as much as what is—can prove a creative way to present your story. The media constantly molds information to suit their own purposes. Take, for instance, two teams that played against each other. It is easy enough for the winner to say, "We won!" But a clever loser might comment, "We came in second." Statistics are *shaped* when they are taken out of context.

One last thought about writing copy: Avoid terminology or information that "dates" your brochure. If you must include information that will soon change, consider putting it on a separate sheet that will fit into the regular brochure. It will be much cheaper to produce than redoing the whole brochure. And watch photographs so they don't show faddish clothes or other tipoffs that will rapidly make your brochure obsolete.

We've explored how to plan your brochure, include the right components, and add sales sizzle by emphasizing benefits over features. Now we move ahead to the visual aspect of this important sales piece.

Designing for "Aye" Appeal

Graphic design is the body language of a brochure. It's a "de-sign of the times" that attention to the nurturing of visual appeal has a seat at the big table today. Companies can rise and fall based upon their ability to design for a customer base.

As you grapple with this issue, there are several questions to answer. What tone will you set? Friendly? Elegant? Humorous? Professional? Avant garde? Decide on the feeling you want to convey. (This goes back to image and branding, which we discussed in Chapter

2.) Of course, this is not exclusively the domain of design. Copy must work with graphics to establish a harmonious whole.

One trick for giving your brochure variety and focusing attention on key points is to use "call-out" boxes. These are frequently employed in magazine articles where they extract a sentence or two from the text and run it in larger type. This gives you another shot at interested readers. If the headline doesn't catch their fancy, perhaps your call-out box will.

For visual diversity there are other options besides photographs. Illustrations can be tailored to your needs and add zest to an otherwise dull brochure. If you can't afford an artist, there's always clip art. Today a wonderful array is available in software programs or sometimes even free online.

When you're planning how the various elements fit together, give special consideration to the order coupon. Put it on an end panel facing out for writing convenience. Then it's easily clipped and doesn't destroy the rest of the brochure when removed. This also gives you greater flexibility. Need a brochure for more institutional purposes—such as a mailing to wholesalers? Simply cut off the order coupon, add a sheet explaining your terms and conditions, and you have it! If you're using a self-mailer approach, plan your address panel back-to-back with the order coupon—especially if you do a lot of direct mail campaigns. That way when people return the coupon you have the coding from their address label on the back and can track which mailing list is pulling best.

Also consider what you want on the address panel if you're heavily into direct mail. Including a few words of "teaser copy" here increases the odds of tempting recipients inside. Do you need a bulk mail permit number? Should you be printing accepted postal terminology to get the piece forwarded and the new address sent to you for list cleaning? Check with the post office to make sure what you're planning satisfies all postal regulations.

Let's talk a moment about type. Typefaces have different personalities. Some are casual, some formal, some sophisticated, some just plain fun. Unless you're going for a specific effect, stick to standard typefaces. And don't mix too many different styles. One face for the text and another for headlines typically works well. A reminder when using your logo: Work from an original rather than taking one off a business card or letterhead. This sacrifices sharpness.

Did you know that words in all capitals are difficult to read, not to mention less visually pleasing? In fact, lowercase text is read 13.4 percent faster than copy set in all caps. So be wary of putting headlines in all caps. Large blocks of text set in italics are also tiring on the eye. You can have the right-hand margins justified (meaning all the same length) or kept ragged right. The latter gives an open feeling as there is more white space.

Cost-Effective Production Pointers

Perhaps the best advice I can give you is to proofread carefully. Then do it again. And again! Nothing is more aggravating—and costly—than getting 5,000 brochures from the printer only to discover a glaring error in a headline or a wrong digit in a phone number. Errors at this point are as unwelcome as ants at a picnic. In addition to diligently proofing regular text copy, carefully examine addresses, phone numbers, fax numbers, e-mail addresses, and URLs. Watch the spelling of names, all headlines and subheads, and any photo captions. These elements are easily overlooked and computer spell checkers can sabotage you. Double-check every detail. Get two or three other people to inspect things too; one person can repeatedly overlook the same error.

Two colors of ink are preferred, but even one color used creatively will do the trick if you must be very budget conscious. Going to a color only adds about $15 and will energize your literature. Look at Pantone Matching System (PMS) color swatches at an art supply store, graphic designer/typesetter, or your printer. There's no need to settle for the standard blue, red, green, etc. Black and one PMS color are also attractive and cost-effective. By the way, studies show younger people prefer bright hues, while more mature folks respond to soft colors.

To get more mileage out of ink, think about using screens of 10, 20, or 30 percent. This lays down a lighter shade of the color over which you can print text in the full strength ink. For additional variety, consider making the front panel 100 percent of the color and reversing the headline in white.

While we're discussing color, there's another option: How about using a colored paper stock? Just be sure to take into consideration what will happen when you add the ink color. Research from the Panatone Color Institute, which conducts studies on color's impact on us, found that yellow paper with black ink scores the highest in memory retention and legibility. (Move over big blue—the Monarch butterfly, caution lights, and fire hydrants have taken your place.) Yellow is the first color the human eye notices in a crowd of colors.

Nowadays paper is a large part of the expense of any printing job. Consult with your printer to see if they stock a paper in quantity that will work for you. Glossy coated stocks will cost more but add an elegant look. They come in various weights. Beware of one too flimsy as its lack of substance will downgrade the feel of your brochure. Another tip is to inquire if they have any paper left over from another job. Sometimes you can pick up these remnants really cheap.

Get a written price quotation (not an estimate) from several printers. You may be surprised at the wide variance in charges. Think through your project first and determine what the bid should include. What quantity? Most people print at least a year's projected supply. How many folds? Are halftones needed for photographs? Any trims? Bleeds? What is their turnaround time? If they say 21 days they probably mean more than four *working weeks*, not three calendar weeks. Encourage printers to suggest cost-cutting measures. And when the job is done we recommend you get the camera-ready art back. Then there's no question about who has it if you need to make changes before going back to press next time.

A compelling brochure is a sure-fire way to cultivate consumer purchases, get more traffic into your establishment, or cultivate prospects. Without one you're like a turtle in a horse race. These tips will enable you to get swiftly out of the starting gate and create winning sales literature. Now let's focus our attention on direct mail. It can turn your business into a "contact sport" and boost you into the big leagues in a hurry.

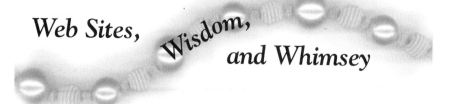

Web Sites, Wisdom, and Whimsey

Let your sales materials catch a free ride. Do you automatically stuff promotional literature in merchandise you ship and monthly bills you send? Why not sail your offers into consumers' or trade accounts' hands? All it costs is the paper it is printed on. These "buck slips," as they're called in direct marketing lingo, can round out your marketing mix and add a few more dollars to your coffers.

Need answers to English questions as you craft your brochure? It's all waiting for you at the Purdue University's On-Line Writing Lab at http://owl.english.purdue.edu. They can deal with your grammar quandaries and troubleshoot other writing problems. And you'll find the indispensable *Elements of Style* online here. They can also link you to other writing labs on the Internet and additional resources of interest.

●●●●●●●

Speaking of brochure headlines...
A daily column titled "News in a Minute" misplaced
a blank space, creating a much more eye-catching
headline: "New Sin a Minute."

Small details can yield big results. Have you any idea what power decimal points, commas, and zeros pack? When writing promotional materials pay attention to how you express numbers. When you want to minimize prices, write "Only $20." On the other hand, to maximize savings say "Save $20.00." The rule of thumb is if you're giving something *add* zeros. And pay attention to whether you write $1,634 or $1634. The latter is perceived as less. These tiny tweaks can have a subtle, but important, impact on your results.

How to "guarantee" more business. Want to increase sales? Looking for a vehicle to increase your direct marketing results? Guarantees may well be your answer. Offering one relieves apprehension on the part of potential purchasers. It lets them know that if they are dissatisfied, they have recourse. Interestingly enough, if you've created a sound product, very few people will take advantage of your guarantee. There are many kinds of guarantees: all the way from seven days to a lifetime. Statistics show that the longer the guarantee, the *less* likely you are to have returns. Consumers somehow figure there is no urgency in returning the merchandise and keep putting it off. Ultimately they forget. Even though it may sound ludicrous, a lifetime guarantee is often more effective than a seven-day guarantee. As well as guaranteeing the product itself, you may want to reassure purchasers in other ways. For instance, guaranteeing delivery within 48 hours. Or in the case of audiotapes, guarantee the replacement of a defective tape.

●●●●●●●

I recently read a brochure so dull the writer's school colors must have been "clear" and "transparent."

●●●●●●●

A cool graphic design site can be found at http://www.ideabook.com. Extremely attractive and rich in content, it's the brainchild of Logic Arts Corporation's Chuck Green, who specializes in graphic design and desktop publishing. (It loads slowly but is worth the wait.) There are 24 intriguing boxes that lead to such things as creating a clip art logo, design ideas, type as art, templates for Adobe PageMaker, even an idea jolt! to get you thinking about the magic of mail. If you're the curious type, you can click on a magnifying glass on each screen to see the thinking that went into the design and development of individual pages. Much food for thought here.

Give your brochure the "fax test." Inevitably you'll occasionally find the need to fax your material to a prospect. That could be disastrous if your type is so small it becomes illegible, graphics have poor contrast and look muddy, or text is so close to the edges it's cut off. To add insight to injury, fax your brochure—and other important documents—to yourself and see how they fare.

●●●●●●●

Q: What do most men think Roe vs. Wade is?
A: Two possible ways to cross a river.

●●●●●●●

An unorthodox brochure approach is used by Dillanos Coffee Roasters LLC in Summer, Washington. Since potential customers can't always come to the roasting facility to check it out, and Dillanos believes in being different, the owner brings the facility to customers via a lively sales video. The 15-minute video showcases smiling employees and company-sponsored coffee seminars. "It's worked tremendously," reports the owner.

CHAPTER 12

Lightning-Charged Results from Direct Mail

Someone once observed a successful direct marketer must have a hog's nose, a deer's legs, and a mule's back. It's a tough medium. Yet carefully conceived and executed, direct marketing to consumers—or from one business to another—can be a powerful and lucrative merchandising tool for selling any product or service.

It masquerades under a variety of names: mail order, direct response, direct marketing, and direct mail. Some people even have the audacity to refer to it as "junk mail." Mastery of this medium depends on imagination, persistence, and following established rules. If you want to be a mogul-in-the-making, study them well.

Planning for Profits

Prior to embarking on a direct mail program, spend time planning—especially your budget. Not everything warrants using direct marketing. Consider your price point. Is your product expensive enough to make this approach worthwhile? Today, you'll need a retail price of $25 before the numbers make sense. If your product falls below that, consider partnering with someone to raise the stakes and lower the investment.

Clients frequently ask me what results to expect. If you're selling a high-ticket item like a Mercedes Benz, 0.5 percent would be acceptable. On the other hand, 2 percent is normally considered a good return.

I favor a different formula, however. You need to make at least 2.2 times the money you spend for the mailing. Include the costs of copywriting and design if you hire them done, plus printing, list rental, postage, and mail processing if you use an outside firm.

No doubt you're wondering about the response timing on direct mail (DM). Once the mailing is out, how does the response come in and when is it finished? Third-class bulk mail is typically delivered in two to three weeks. Your response will be 75 percent finished within four to six weeks. You'll see a few additional orders for a couple more weeks. By eight weeks most mailers consider the response final.

Seldom will a one-shot effort shake lose the desired results. You need a concerted, ongoing plan. Since the amount of third-class bulk mail has escalated dramatically over the last few years, to effectively penetrate the market you must often do repeated mailings. And remember that one form of advertising reinforces another. Use a mix of marketing approaches. Launching a well-thought-out direct marketing campaign can create an ever-widening ripple of sales.

Components of a Successful Campaign

A good direct mail package is like the couple who captures first place in a dance contest. It's lithe, limber, and all the body parts work in rhythm. It may be as lively as a rhumba or as smooth as a waltz, but it does the job: It gets response!

Your direct mail campaign needs to "work" in several areas. First, it must present the right offer. Next, the copywriting has to be strong. Finally, the mailing list needs to be good. Let's dissect these components.

Your offer is the stimulus that creates the decision to buy. Price often plays an important role. One company tried selling their product all the way from $24.95 to $79.95. Ultimately, they found it moved best at $39.95. Other aspects that affect offers have to do with whether you provide a discount, offer a money-back guarantee, include a gift (often called a premium enhancement), or suggest a deluxe alternative.

Injecting humor into your program can also be rewarding. That was the approach taken by KSK Communications Ltd. for their client, Wolverine Software Corporation. The objective was to increase sales

248   www.BrazenHussiesNetwork.com

of Wolverine's teaching and simulation software among college engineering professors. Using a humorous caption and a whimsical cartoon of a wolverine, they developed a well-targeted self-mailer that pulled more than a 2 percent response.

Package Contents

The traditional direct mail package consists of an outer envelope, a letter, a brochure, an order form, and a business reply envelope (BRE). More elaborate packages include additional pieces.

Outer envelope

If you hope to hit the Yellow Brick Road to DM success, you'd better pay a lot of attention to this element. If you fail here, it doesn't matter what's inside. But many businesswomen feel a little like Dorothy at the gates to the Emerald City.

Just how does one go about baiting the hook? How do you get from the "to oblivion" pile and into the "to open" stack? There are three schools of thought. One says, "If you've got it, flaunt it"; another goes for elegant simplicity. The third advocates being a sneaky Pete. Here's how they work:

Some envelopes shout for attention. Most of these sport a "teaser message." Clever copy can do an excellent job of provoking the inquisitiveness of recipients and pulling them in. (A word of caution here: Don't give away the punch line. If you reveal the entire sales pitch on the envelope, people have no incentive to go inside.) Another approach is to use a colored envelope. They get noticed and opened more frequently.

Many business-to-business mailers must get through a secretary to obtain a response. That's tough. In this case you need elegant simplicity. Competent secretaries are shrewd gatekeepers. They screen for executives in nearly 87 percent of cases. To win their approval, be so sharp looking, so distinctive, so legitimate, so professional that they can't resist.

With sneaky Pete, the objective is anonymity, to camouflage any resemblance to junk mail. Rather than a return address of Brookside Enterprises International you might use BEI or a person's name and street address in the return. With this approach you need to handwrite the recipient's address rather than using computer-generated labels, which immediately give you away. These envelopes carry a postage stamp instead of being metered mail. Whereas obviously this tactic isn't practical for large mailings, it can be fruitful in small doses. An envelope that's anonymous has a better than 50/50 chance of getting opened out of sheer curiosity.

Sales letter

The letter is your salesperson. It accounts for 65 to 75 percent of the orders you get. The brochure is responsible for 15 to 25 percent; the order form for 5 to 25 percent. Fail at the letter stage and your mailing is doomed. (See the adjacent checklist.)

Direct Marketing Sales Letter Checklist

✓ Does the headline attract attention by promising an important benefit?

✓ Is interest built quickly by enlarging on the promise?

✓ Have you appealed to the emotions to arouse a desire to possess?

✓ Have you emphasized the unique features of your product or service, but stated them in benefit terms?

✓ Is one central idea emphasized so strongly it avoids confusion?

✓ Have you included believable testimonials (either here or in the brochure)?

✓ Do you offer a guarantee?

✓ Is your letter organized and designed to be inviting and easy to read?

✓ Have you closed with a clear call for action?

✓ Is a postscript included?

This is one place where more is usually better. A two-page out-pulls a one-page format; four pages is often stronger. Some DM experts advocate eight pages. You're asking people to part with their money. This takes information and persuasion. It isn't done with a brief message.

The secret to success here is saying what the prospect wants to hear, *not* what you want to say. Forget features. Savvy marketers write from a benefit standpoint. Emphasize how you will solve readers' problems: make them healthier, wealthier, wiser, sexier, or whatever. Start with a powerful headline. Write in easy words. Short sentences. Brief paragraphs. You want simple language the average person can understand. The goal is to keep them reading, not re-reading! Keep the format open and airy. Use underlining and CAPITALS for emphasis. Include a punchy, intriguing P.S. And be sure to ask for the order several times. Use a colored ink for your signature line.

For minimal expense, a direct marketing campaign can be targeted to many different audiences by simply customizing the sales letter. You can use the same brochure but slant to the needs of different constituencies by what you say in the letter.

Brochure

While many direct mail packages sport huge, elaborate, four-color brochures, this isn't necessary for most products. An 8 ½-inch by 11-inch or 8 ½-inch by 14-inch sheet, printed on both sides, and folded into panels that fit a #10 business envelope works well. Put your selling message on the front; it works like a headline. Incorporating testimonials lends clout and dilutes apprehension. Again, ask for the order. Tell the reader specifically what to do.

Pretend you're writing to one person. Envision what that individual is like. What age? Sex? Income level? Education? Interests? Hot buttons? Keep it friendly and personal in tone. Talk in specifics. Rather than saying this is "an inexpensive investment," you might tell prospects it "costs less than you spend for a daily paper." Usually the brochure picks up where the letter left off, going into more detail about the benefits customers will gain.

It often makes sense to ensure customer satisfaction by offering a money-back guarantee. This reassures people. The stronger and longer the guarantee, the fewer returns you'll receive.

When we write promotional literature for a full-blown direct mail campaign, we usually put the guarantee in a fancy box and add a personal signature, thus focusing attention on this important aspect of the offer. So when you are looking for another way to increase business, remember that guarantees alleviate buyer concerns. By advertising that you back your merchandise, you invite those who might be hesitant to make a positive buying decision. (For more details on creating a Wow! brochure, see Chapter 11.

Order form

Order forms are frequently treated like Cinderella…ignored and unadorned, they stay home while the rest of the package goes to the ball. As in Cinderella's case, this can be a grave mistake. Busy people may scan your letter and, if the proposition interests them, go directly to the order form. Never stop selling. Use a benefit-laden headline on the order form—one that encompasses your offer.

Put opportunities before obligations, rewards before restrictions. Encourage people to "act now," "respond today," or "call immediately." Order forms should be cleanly engineered to make it *easy* for people to respond. Provide specific instructions and lots of contact point options and payment mechanisms. Include a toll-free phone number, fax number, and e-mail address for credit card purchasers. Explain that you take checks or money orders and where to send them. To be sure your order form is user-friendly, fill one out yourself.

Business reply envelope (BRE)

Some mailers use a business reply envelope. Once again, the idea is to make it easy for the prospect to respond. Although most feel these postage-paid envelopes increase results, this adds considerably to your costs. If you don't supply postage, be sure to print a box with the words "place stamp here" in the upper right-hand corner of the envelope.

Other Alternatives

Self-mailers

Full-fledged direct marketing packages are not an inexpensive way to sell products. Yet a modified version of this dynamic merchandising method can be viable for virtually every business. Companies with budgets as tight as banjo strings can wrap all these elements into one. This typically takes the form of a brochure designed as a self-mailer.

Statement stuffers

Some firms praise statement stuffers. These are typically flyers inserted in monthly bills. Another form of direct marketing is catalogs. And you might consider developing a co-op mailing with a complementary company. By combining your in-house lists and sharing the costs, you literally divide to multiply.

Card packs

Card packs are another intriguing possibility. Stan Feingold, president of Visual Horizons in Rochester, New York, feels they are an "excellent additional marketing tool to supplement traditional ways of doing business. I can't buy mailing lists or do a solo mailing at a profit," he explains. "The only thing I can do profitably is to go prospecting in a deck. And there are a lot of companies like us. We're niche marketers."

Because your card is often in a deck with those from Fortune 500 companies, this provides positive "guilt by association" positioning. Says Feingold, "You look just as good as General Motors." Card packs are best used for products or services with a price point of $50 or more. Watch your mail for samples and contact the card pack publisher/owner.

Unmasking Mail List Culprits

To be successful in DM, it takes the right offer and a package with pizzazz. But stopping there would be like trying to sit on a three-legged stool...with one leg missing. Many feel the most vital ingredient is the mailing list. These databases of prospect names are the carrier pigeons of today's commerce.

Lists, and the strategies surrounding them, can be confusing. Yet knowing how this facet of direct marketing works is critical to your success. So let's unmask the mail list culprit.

There is a major misconception: You don't buy lists, you *rent* them for one-time use only. If you want to use that list again, another rental fee is due. (Don't cheat; lists are seeded with decoy names so the owner knows if it is being used without authority.)

Once someone has responded directly to your mailing, however, you can legitimately add their name to your own in-house database. Lists rent anywhere from $50 to $170 per thousand names. But don't just look at dollars, look at results.

When you rent several lists, there is often name duplication. This can be eliminated by requesting a "merge-purge." This is a computer program that merges lists together and tosses out duplicate names. You don't want the expense of sending several pieces to the same person...or the unprofessional impression such a mailing leaves with the recipient. A good merge-purge program will also typically identify undeliverable names, such as those with incomplete zip codes, so you don't have to pay for sending them.

Using Brokers

List brokers connect those who want to do a mailing with available lists. They earn their living like a yenta: matchmaking. These women and men are specialists who make all the arrangements for one company to use the lists of another.

Your broker is a consultant in many ways. She or he is responsible for knowing about the more than 40,000 lists available, doing any research necessary for you, then recommending the best possible lists for your offer. As you get more involved, your broker may be able to negotiate prices for you, help evaluate results, and give you advice on many aspects of your direct mail plans. Used wisely, a good list broker can be a valuable member of your sales team. She or he can guide you to expand or reduce your potential universe through geography, selects, functions, and title addressing.

Direct Marketing "Freebies"

Here are free sales aids, publications, and services that can help you generate better results from your direct marketing campaigns:

■ A valuable freebie is *How to Compile and Maintain a Mailing List.* It goes into such topics as database construction; where to find the data for your customer list; how to locate inquiry, prospect, and suspect names; ways to keep your list clean and efficient; and how to physically store and work it. Get a copy by contacting Quill Corporation at 100 South Schelter Road, Lincolnshire, IL 60069; 800-789-1331.

■ Two dynamite specialized publications are available on a complimentary basis to companies serious about DM. Request them on company letterhead. They are *Target Marketing,* 401 North Broad Street, Philadelphia, PA 19108, www.targetonline.com and *DM News* at 100 Avenue of the Americas, New York, NY 10013, www.dmnews.com. Not only do they carry how-to articles and columns but also revealing case histories of what works—and what doesn't.

■ The U.S. Postal Service puts out several things you may find useful. Their *Direct Mail Delivers Kit*™ is impressive. It contains a three-ring binder of case studies and advice, a 96-page book titled *The Business Guide to Advertising With Direct Mail,* and a free hardcover guide from Random House titled *Being Direct:*

(continued on next page)

But don't put all your confidence in someone else. Having gotten this far in *Shameless Marketing for Brazen Hussies*™, your own creative juices should be surging. DM guru Dan Kennedy suggests looking for creative matches. If you've invented a new device to reduce back pain, for instance, you should be renting the lists of buyers from the BackSaver catalog.

And what about clubs? Dan reminds us there are "beer clubs, wine clubs, coffee tasters clubs, chocolate clubs, travel clubs,…" Not to mention various fan clubs. You can get breakouts by state, zips, gender, etc. If you're selling a regional guidebook on the beer pubs of Colorado, for instance, this could be one of your best marketing ploys.

Jo Ann Martin, co-owner (with Vickie Hutchins) of Gooseberry Patch in Delaware, Ohio, tells of developing a list on her own through the Yellow Pages—and not receiving one single response. Now she works with a consultant. "Get someone with experience in list management and brokering," she counsels. "You need someone who knows what they're doing." Apparently her consultant does. From a starting point of distributing 7,000 catalogs in 1985 for a gross of $27,000, Gooseberry Patch sends out over 4 million catalogs today.

Sue and Bob Prenner traded careers as successful lawyers to launch the Ben Silver Corporation, which manufactures blazer buttons stamped with insignias in cloisonne enamel or gold. Sue heartily recommends getting professional help. She also observes, "No list broker has your inherent sense for your customer demographics. You need to use your intuition to get a good sense of where your market is." She believes a broker can direct you into less obvious areas and is especially useful in analyzing returns and seeing what works.

This expert help doesn't cost *you* anything. List brokers are typically paid a 20 percent commission by whoever owns the list. Because they must survive on these commissions, they're interested in working with companies that contemplate doing volume mailings now, or will be good long-range customers.

To find quick professional help, let your fingers do the walking. Brokers are cataloged in the Yellow Pages under "Mailing Lists." The largest assembly of lists is contained in *Standard Rate and Data's Direct Mail List Rates and Data*. This whopper volume resides in your main public library. Here you'll discover detailed information on who rents what, plus firms and individuals who serve as list brokers.

Be careful list brokers don't oversell you. Quality is more important than quantity. You might ask which customers repeatedly rent the lists your broker recommends, then check with that firm's DM manager to determine results. Brokers aren't interested in talking with you, however, until you're ready to rent at least

BRAINSTORMING GUIDELINES
(continued)

Making Advertising Pay. Order it by calling 1-800-THE-USPS (843-8777, ext. 2085), www.usps.gov.

■ *Memo to Mailers* is a free monthly newsletter. To subscribe, write National Customer Support Center, U.S. Postal Service, 6060 Primacy Parkway, Suite 101, Memphis, TN 38188-0001.

■ Additionally, Uncle Sam provides a complimentary service to help direct marketers correct undeliverable addresses. It's called Operation Mail. This program puts addresses in standardized form and assigns the correct nine-digit zip code to each. A random sample is actually forwarded to individual local post offices where the deliverability of each is scrutinized. Ultimately, you receive reports of addresses and the new standardized form, plus an explanation of those addresses that could not be matched. This can save a lot of wasted postage dollars! Talk to your local postmaster for more details.

■ The U.S. Postal Service also offers Making Direct Mail Easy seminars that can provide you with the information you need to create a successful direct marketing program. Direct mail professionals will take you through the process of designing a campaign, including using the Internet to make your direct mail piece a success. Seminars are held in cities throughout the country. Visit the U.S. Postal Service Web site at http://usps.com for more information.

5,000 test names. Therefore, let's look at how you can begin generating lists on your own.

Self-Prospecting for Effective Lists

There are many enterprising ways you can personally obtain obscure yet productive lists. Some of these ideas are plain vanilla flavor; others are like pistachio ripple.

An excellent place to secure intriguing lists is through associations. The *Encyclopedia of Associations* indexes organization names and keywords in Part 3 of their three-volume set. There is an association for absolutely every interest, from the American Kite Fliers Association to the National Council of Savings Institutions, the Railway Historical Society to the Center for Environmental Research.

Often you can rent their membership lists quite inexpensively. If they don't rent them, but publish a directory, there are a couple of other alternatives: You can either buy the directory or join the organization, then compile your own list.

Directory of Directories is also a productive place to prospect. More than 6,000 reference works are logged in this volume. They run the gamut from sports to acting, medicine to gardening, ecology to business. Obtaining obscure directories isn't always easy. Seek unusual ones through special interlibrary loan arrangements or see if they might be available on the Net. Don't work with anything outdated.

If you're dependent on very localized traffic, consider local mailings. Talk with your postmaster about SCF (Sectional Center Facility) carrier routes. These are the paths area carriers walk or drive. By coordinating an area map with the carrier routes, you can determine the number of carriers and get delivery counts. This is very affordable advertising for a neighborhood restaurant, cleaners, dentist, etc.

The post office has written instructions on how to sort your third-class (bulk) mail to be cost-effective for you and efficient for them. Or you can find a mailing service in the Yellow Pages to handle all the actual details.

Understanding the Kinds of Lists Available

There are several kinds of lists. Some are extremely effective; others aren't worth the labels they're printed on. To help you better grasp the differences, here are your choices:

Compiled lists are derived from phone books, reference manuals, and other directories. Therefore, they are generic rather than targeted. In most cases, compiled lists don't perform very well.

Publisher R. Marilyn Schmidt of Barnegat Light Press is the exception to that rule. She told us of getting up to a 15 percent response to lists she compiles. This press publishes books on seafood. To get names she looks in organization directories for fishing clubs, and even found a directory of seafood markets. Her distribution is both wholesale and retail and extends from coast to coast and into Canada.

Occupant lists include every household in a given geographic area. This works ideally for boutiques, dog groomers, service and repair facilities, and others catering to a neighborhood clientele.

Response lists pull better than the first two types because they're made up of people who have already bought related products or services. These individuals have a proven propensity to purchase by mail.

Hotline lists contain names and addresses of people who have bought within the last three to six months. Because they are more current, they're also more expensive—and more productive.

Your in-house list is the best there is! These people have already bought from you. They trust you; they're far more likely to buy from you again.

If you see direct marketing playing a large role in your marketing mix, contact the Direct Marketing Association, Inc., 1120 Avenue of the Americas, New York, NY 10036, 212-768-7277; http://www.the-dma.org. These folks are the true experts in the DM field.

Equipped with all these approaches for taming the mail list beast, you're sure to make better use of your mail list dollars—and reap more profits in return.

Mailing Smarter

With postage hikes announced on a regular basis, you need to be more savvy than ever. Forget mass mailings. Shrewd marketers are targeting their mailings to the most refined marketplace they can uncover.

In this business it's important to test, test, test. Be sure to do this before you roll out with big numbers. When generating your own lists, you could start testing with as few as 200 names, although 1,000 will give you a more realistic response. After all, 2 percent of 200 would only be four orders. When playing with the big boys, you have to rent a minimum of 5,000 names for a test.

Request an "nth" name selection for a good random cross-section of the file. (Perhaps every tenth name.) This avoids the problem of having every contact be from California—or New York—when buying habits for the two areas differ significantly.

Once you find a list that works, roll out big time and keep mailing to it (seasonal offers excepted) until it peters out. When you get going in DM you may rent several lists to go out at the same time. How do you track which one is working best? You can "key code" your labels. Instruct your list broker to put "XXX," for instance, on one list to differentiate it from the other. Of course, you must make sure the customer knows to include the key on order forms—perhaps they peel off the label and affix it to the order form or write in the code. On phone orders your telephone staff needs to be trained to ask for it. Otherwise the coding will be useless.

So how are these names supplied? The methods vary, depending on what you're doing. You can apply pressure sensitive labels yourself. Cheshire labels require a letter shop to apply them. You may want to outsource this job to a service bureau or letter shop, which you can find in the Yellow Pages. (It takes a lot of time to put out a 5,000-piece bulk mailing.) If you plan to merge-purge several lists, you'll need them on disk. Many letter shops also require disks, so be sure to find out their requirements if you plan to outsource your mailing.

Escalating postage costs mean list cleaning is getting higher priority. Accuracy is vital; you can't afford to waste postage on dirty, undeliverable pieces of mail, which are called "nixies." Ask your broker about a list's nixie rate. Also inquire if the list owner guarantees that a certain percentage of the names are deliverable. There's no point in paying to put out mail that never reaches its destination.

A final bit of counsel is to watch when you drop your mailing. If you're sending first-class mail locally, Monday is the best day since most pieces will reach their destination on Tuesday, which is the lightest day of the week. When mailing across the country, however, you might want to drop it on Friday, with the hope it will arrive on the desks of your prospects by Tuesday or Wednesday.

Developing Your Own Database

Your own customer mailing list can become one of your company's most valuable assets. These are people who have already bought from you. Assuming you do right by them, they will buy from you time after time. Jo Ann Martin increases her list by encouraging customers to send in referrals for their friends. "These are very valuable names," she comments. "We track all customers to know what they spend and when."

They have surveyed their buyers as to age, sex, whether they have children or own a house, the amount of money they spend on mail order purchases, where they live, even what magazines they read! This educates Martin. Using her present customer demographics, she knows precisely what kinds of outside lists to rent.

After you've amassed 5,000 or so names, you can also go into the list rental business yourself by contacting companies listed in *SRDS*. Or you can barter your list for other ones. This plays an important role in the strategy for Ben Silver Corporation. "We exchange lists a great deal," says Sue Prenner. "About half of the time we use our own list. The other half we exchange it for another good list. This reduces our mailing costs dramatically." Because she sells unique merchandise, Prenner finds her in-house list is in demand and isn't concerned about competitors.

Whether you rent your names or use them exclusively yourself, good list management is essential. Databases should be updated, cleaned, and evaluated on a regular basis.

It's been said that successful people have a strong will—and lazy people have a strong won't. If you want to strengthen your predilection for prosperity, consider public speaking as a venue for developing new business. To learn how, simply keep reading!

Web Sites, Wisdom, and Whimsey

Want association mailing lists? MGI Lists calls itself the "Association List Company." Among others, they have lists covering healthcare, education, science, and youth at risk. Call them at **800-899-4420**, www.mgilists.com.

How much direct mail is too much direct mail? Let's say you put out a mailing and get a 3 percent response, which is considered very good.

Should you go to that same list again? If you mail a follow-up offer within six months to those same prospects, expect to get half your original response. Armed with this statistic, you can easily compute if it will be profitable to hit that list again. By the way, prices for using the same list are often cheaper the second or third time around. Ask your mailing list broker about this or negotiate with the list owner if you rent directly.

●●●●●●●

A woman's place is in the House—
the Senate—and the Oval Office.

●●●●●●●

Frustrated by returned mail when you try to reach customers in your database? Have I got a nifty solution for you. Switchboard is a directory of people, businesses, Web sites, and e-mail addresses. The next time the post office returns mail and it looks like a dead end, go to http:// www.switchboard.com and enter the person's old address. This can help you retrieve a large percentage of former good customers who slipped through the cracks.

Want sophisticated help with direct mail? You'll find it at http:// www.horah.com. If you are into serious DM, this site is worth checking out. Their postage chart will help you determine the price of direct mailing and what discounts are available. They can also calculate the weight and thickness for you before the paper pieces are even off the printer. And there are articles and checklists on cutting costs, etc.

●●●●●●●

Father to son: I'm writing this slow
'cause I know you can't read fast.

●●●●●●●

ZIP + 4 means extra savings for direct mailings. Coding Accuracy Support System (CASS) certification refers to the extra four digits after normal ZIP codes. If you rent mailing lists from others, look for this feature. If their lists are not prepared this way, try requesting a discount as you will be deprived of lower mailing fees. The post office is trying to get away from hand sorting mail. They decided that giving a business discount for the ZIP + 4 is a practical way to get businesses behind the movement.

News and resources for printing, graphic arts, and direct marketing await you. I found several goodies at the North American Publishing Company site. Clicking on *Target Marketing* magazine led me on a merry trail to articles in present and past issues. If you're into direct marketing, this is a site you should bookmark. Find it at http://www.napco.com/. And if your company qualifies, you can also get a free subscription to *Target Marketing* here.

●●●●●●●

How do you tell when you're out of invisible ink?

●●●●●●●

More DM goodies live at http://www.mailingstuff.com/. Find vendor lists, printing and lettershop information, and much data relating to direct marketing here.

Want the look of colorful hand-affixed stamps and the savings of machine imprinting? You can use the U.S. Postal Service's "precancelled stamps" bulk mail program. You still pay for the permit, and sort, bundle, and process the letters like any other bulk mailing. But instead of the ugly postage imprint, you affix a colorful precancelled stamp worth 10 cents, then pay the difference at the post office.

If you're in insurance or financial services, listen up! The Direct Marketing Association commissioned a study to measure the return on investment (ROI) of direct-response marketing by insurance and financial services firms. The study reported each dollar invested in direct marketing in 1997 yielded a whopping $8.01 in revenue. That's a phenomenal 700 percent ROI! It just goes to prove sending a compelling package to a targeted list can generate wagonloads of business.

Want a cheap way to test your mailing list to buyers and media types? Before sending an expensive mailing, try e-mailing the same list first. This gives you a sneak preview of who has left their employment. When e-mails are bounced back, you have an effective way to cull the dead wood from your list. Otherwise, you could mail forever to people who are long gone from the company.

●●●●●●●

"God gave women intuition and femininity. Used properly, the combination easily jumbles the brain of any man I've ever met."

—*Farrah Fawcett*

●●●●●●●

Help from copywriting guru Bob Bly is available at http://www.bly.com. Here you'll find samples of direct mail packages, sales letters, brochures, etc. And he offers a library of downloadable how-to articles that could make a grown woman drool.

Want to get attention on the cheap? While we discussed the value of using postcards earlier, I want to remind you here what a blessing they can be...especially if you get a little creative. You can design them in-house and produce them four-up on your laser printer using a *colored* card stock! These dazzling cards call attention by making recipients stop, look, and read. They are also memorable. Simply mention "the _____ colored postcard" when you place follow-up calls, and you'll usually hear, "Oh, yes..."

CHAPTER 13

Speaking and Teaching: Impressive Ways to Prospect for New Business

Speak and ye shall sell. Tapping into the presentation market—which includes seminars, workshops, lectures, classes, and demonstrations—can open lucrative doors for many entrepreneurs and professionals. It's a way to cash in on your intellectual capital.

Just as oregano gives added zest to spaghetti sauce, you can give your business new zip by exploring this avenue. Lectures or seminars work well for financial types, chiropractors, therapists, consultants, etc.; demonstrations are excellent for travel agents (how to pack) or restaurants (how to shop, prepare foods, or entertain). Classes are a natural for Web design firms, marketing counselors, interior decorators, etc. You have a captive audience who, when properly primed, are eager to partake of your services.

Additionally, this gives you an edge with the media. Speakers are often considered newsmakers. Put out a news release to local newspapers. And if it's a big event, invite media reporters to attend. You just might find yourself on the evening news.

Why the Gift of Gab Works So Well

As a speaker, you're considered the *expert*. This positions you ahead of the competition. In the public's mind, you are the master, the authority, the guru. It also gives you a platform to demonstrate your knowledge and give a gentle commercial.

In 1998, after running an investment management firm for several years, San Franciscan Liz Davidson began offering women's investment seminars. These two-hour presentations provided practical, easy-to-follow tips on how to become financially secure and independent. The response was fantastic. Women sent thank-you notes saying the seminar had changed their lives. That seminar changed Liz's life too. It served as a model for her Financial Finesse, a national company dedicated to providing women with high-quality financial information through seminars, products, and services. This membership-based business provides members with personalized ongoing support to make smart investment decisions.

This venue works in all kinds of situations. Puppet maker Margie Ann Stanko does free demonstrations at schools, bookstores, and craft shops. "Each and every one of my free workshops has led to at least one order or reservation for a paid workshop," she relates. Her premise is that free leads the way to fee.

Ariel Gore, who founded *Hip Mama* magazine in 1993, says, "Hip means aware and informed." Not only has the magazine spawned mothering groups up and down the West Coast, but Gore's up-front attitude has made her a hot commodity. She is called to speak in bookstores, for community groups, and at colleges like Stanford and the University of Washington. Naturally, *Hip Mama* plays a central role—and gathers new subscribers—wherever she goes.

Working Through Established Adult Educational Facilities

Extended studies or adult education facilities sponsor seminars and classes on a wide range of subjects. There are learning centers all across the United States and Canada that specialize in quenching the thirst of adults who crave continued learning. Some are noncredit courses sponsored by community colleges or universities. Others are called the Learning Annex, (headquarters in San Francisco), Colorado Free University (Denver), Open U (Minneapolis), Leisure Learning Unlimited (Houston), and the Learning Connection. Look on the Web or in a local phone book to find contact information for cities where you wish to propose a class.

Editor and publication designer Sue Collier teaches a four-week evening class four times a year through the school district in Fort Collins, Colorado. The class, which covers how to research, write, and edit a book or publication through design and printing, usually nets several clients from each session who hire Sue's company, Lead Dog Communications, to do all or some aspect of their book or publication.

The Learning Annex contacted us to do courses in their four outlets. The classes typically run three hours on weekend nights and are often held at a hotel. They run $29 to $39 and instructors get about 15 percent of the receipts. Classes are set and work on their catalogs begins three to four months in advance, so you have to plan ahead.

Some of these centers have huge mailing lists. In many cases, hundreds of thousands of people who don't attend are still exposed to your name, company, and bio. Julian Block, noted tax attorney, always asks schools that offer his adult education courses to mention his book, *Julian Block's Year-Round Tax Strategies*, in any instructor bio. Though people may not attend his class, they become aware of him and the book as a resource.

At the Learning Annex, product sales are permitted and you keep 100 percent. Estimates are that 40 to 80 percent of the students will purchase something. You may want to create a book or workbook to capitalize on this captive audience.

Launching Your Own Public Seminar Program

The real goal here is to sign up business from the people you meet at your seminar. This can work—or it can be a tall order. Should you decide to launch a seminar program where attendees buy their own tickets (or you give a free presentation as a prospecting tool), be prepared to work hard and spend money. This approach plays best in a big city where you have a million or more people to draw from. Advertising and promotion are crucial. How will you attract attendees? Will you buy newspaper space advertising? Use a direct mail campaign? Develop a referral fee arrangement? Hope news releases will fill some seats?

How much must you charge? The intent here is to cover your expenses, not make a profit. Where will the seminars be held? You can probably rent a hotel room for under $500, or perhaps find a meeting room in a restaurant for very little because management hopes to get more business from exposure. How will prospects sign up? Who will handle registration? Overseeing all the details can be an arduous task. (Take it from folks who have done it both ways; it's a heck of a lot easier to just walk in and do your shtick.)

Besides a lot of work, self-sponsored seminars can be expensive. Your major cost will be advertising. The idea is to collect enough money to cover your advertising nut. Some people even find it acceptable to incur a small loss doing the seminar in anticipation of landing several clients.

Suppose you plan on a mailing to 5,000 people. Have any idea what that will run? You'd better! To rent the list you'll probably pay around $500. Prices to print a direct marketing package vary greatly. You might get by with about $1,000; more likely you'll spend double that. (And we're assuming here you write the promotional copy yourself. Many people elect to hire a seasoned professional for this crucial step.)

Then there are the costs of a fulfillment house to physically do the mailing. This tacks a few more cents onto every piece. Bulk mail for this size list will typically be about 19 cents a piece. It doesn't take a mathematical genius to deduce that you'd better have a lot of people at a reasonable price—or a few people at a high price—to make any money. Or you'd better convert a large percentage of attendees to clients or customers.

Honing Your Presentation

Know your audience. What will be the gender mix? Educational level? Primary age group? Typical occupation? Have they any other common dominator you should be aware of? Without information about your audience, you're a blindfolded fool with a dart. You can shoot, but the chances of hitting the target are slim to none. The fact is, without audience demographics, you don't even know which wall to face. Once you understand the makeup of those who will hear you, you're in a much stronger position to hit the bull's eye by giving them real, customized value.

Your actual presentation style has a lot of bearing on how much business you generate. If you're a dynamic, animated speaker, people are much more likely to want to do business with you. Friendliness and a smile go a long way in winning over an audience. Make people feel welcome and comfortable, and they'll be on your side.

A recent study revealed 55 percent of the audience responds to your body language and facial expression, while 37 percent react to your voice—including pacing, pitch, inflections, and overall delivery.

Only 8 percent react to the actual content of your message! Based on these findings, it's the show that makes it go.

There are little tricks for making your presentation successful. Audiences love stories, so come up with anecdotes to illustrate your wisdom. People will remember your main points better. They also adore humor. You don't have to be a funny person to interject levity into your presentation. Simply find a joke that fits the situation. (And don't introduce it as "a joke." If it falls flat, then you aren't embarrassed.) If you pick a few receptive-looking people around the room and talk directly to them, your eye contact will be good and everyone will feel included. Do remember, however, to come from an ethical position. You are there to speak, not give constant commercials.

Be sure to take along customer brochures. Put them at each attendee's place during the break. By then they'll be more open and interested. Also have business cards available.

Remedies for Laryngitis

Losing your voice just before a speech can be almost as terrifying as running into a grizzly with only a switch to defend yourself. Here are some tips to ease the situation:

1. Keep quiet. Speak off the platform only when absolutely necessary to give your vocal cords a rest. Don't whisper either; that also strains your voice.

2. Avoid coffee and soda. Caffeine dries out vocal cords.

3. Sip lukewarm water with a little lemon juice.

4. Get some Ricola cough drops. They contain healing sage instead of drying menthol.

5. Use a humidifier at night.

6. Go to a health food store and get some sesame tahini. (It looks a lot like peanut butter.) Put a spoonful on the back of your throat.

Tips for Becoming a Paid Presenter

It never hurts to query an organization about whether they have a budget for speakers. Most often, the answer will be "no." But sometimes they will offer you an "honorarium," which can range anywhere from $25 to several hundred dollars. Frequently, they will help with expenses. This typically includes transportation, hotel, and sometimes meals.

If you discover they do have a budget for speakers, try to find out what it is *before* you volunteer financial information. If they can afford $2,000, for instance, and you tell them your fee is $1,000, guess what you will be paid? You might want to have a lesser fee structure when speaking to nonprofits, as I do.

Require a deposit to hold the speaking date. We learned the hard way how important this detail can be. A few years ago we were hired to speak to a national organization. Since they were picking up the travel tab and paying us a nice fee, we decided to build book signings and PR around the speaking engagement. Two weeks before we were to give the seminar, they canceled. Our ethics dictated we do the trip as we had made commitments. It was an expensive lesson. Now I require half down when booking a date. That gives my client more motivation to make the engagement work, and it gives me a pad if they do cancel. The balance of the fee is due the day I speak.

Other things I cover in a letter of agreement are how long the presentation will be, its title, and exactly what expenses the client is picking up. I also get in writing that I have the right to sell not only our own books but also other related titles the audience would find helpful. *I* provide the sales copy for their brochure, flyer, and/or newsletter.

Professional speakers coach the person who introduces them. Most provide a typed, double-spaced "canned" introduction. That way, there is no temptation for the introducer to say something like, "Maria really needs no introduction." Every presenter needs and deserves a well-rounded introduction to establish her or his credentials and set the stage properly.

Associations have annual conferences and more frequent workshops at which they offer their members a bevy of topics. Check out which ones might be a match for you in the *Encyclopedia of Associations*. They begin thinking about next year's meeting about a month after this year's event. Ask questions: When does the planning start for the next meeting? What is the theme? Who books the speakers? Think like the decision maker and relate why your message will be helpful to their attendees.

Another idea is to get a corporation or organization to "sponsor" your talk. Laurie Beth Jones of Encinitas, California, reports that "groups which want to sponsor me to speak have often enlisted the support of corporate co-sponsors that help foot all or some of the bill. Among the most enterprising were students at George Fox University in Portland, Oregon. They got the Marriott to pick up my entire fee, as well as the cost of live goldfish in little bowls in front of each of the participants." (The meeting theme was "Launching Into Unknown Seas.") Jones also had a similar experience with a church. They wanted her so badly they went to their board and raised the fee in 45 minutes. Who could you tap to ease your financial burden?

Wellspring for More Exposure and Information

If you feel like you need a female version of Viagra so you can "stand and deliver," here's another option: Toastmasters International has more than 8,800 clubs in 68 countries where people gather in their communities to get comfortable speaking in front of an audience and practice honing their public speaking skills. It is a wonderful nurturing training ground to help overcome shyness and conquer the fear of public speaking. And once you're comfortable speaking to an audiences, one-on-one presentations become a piece of cake. For more information, phone 949-858-8255; fax 949-858-1207, or visit their Web site at www.toastmasters.org. I was a communications major in college and I contend that while it didn't specifically train me for *anything*, it prepared me for *everything*!

A couple of other suggestions include Dale Carnegie Training. Reach them at 800-231-5800 or online at www.dalecarnegie.com. And if you're feeling especially tongue-tied, log onto www.fsb.com/fortunesb/ for more information about finding a speechmaking group near you. Additionally, for a stellar tutorial on how to write and give a great speech, zip over to www.augsburg.edu/depts/infotech/present.

For more sophisticated learning, I recommend the National Speakers Association. (Members of NSA are listed in a directory, receive a monthly magazine and audiotape of insider tips, can gain tremendous insights at the annual convention and regional workshops, and have the option of joining area chapters for networking, support, and promotion within their area.) My fellow colleagues in NSA are a uniquely caring group of folks. For information, phone 480-968-2552, fax 480-968-0911, or go online to www.nsaspeaker.org.

Dottie Walters, CSP, can be a budding speaker's best friend. She and her daughter, Lilly Walters, authored *Speak and Grow Rich*, which overflows with techniques and shortcuts used by today's top professional speakers. Dottie also edits and publishes a newsmagazine called *Sharing Ideas*. For subscription and workshop information, call 626-335-8069 or fax 626-335-6127.

For certain professionals and entrepreneurs, speaking is a superior way to target potential business. Perhaps you should be capitalizing on having a captive audience.

Now let us move into Part V where you'll learn to further maximize your strengths…and reap the benefits of some truly gutsy strategies, starting with stellar saleswomanship.

Web Sites, Wisdom, and Whimsey

Trying to locate trade shows, conferences, or exhibits that parallel your expertise? Have I got a beaut of a site for you! Go to http://www.expoguide.com/shows/shows.htm. This is both a fast and smart site. I did a general search by concept for the word "environment." It not only brought up events that are obviously environmentally oriented, it also showed ones that dealt with forestry, chemicals, paper, etc. Furthermore, they are labeled "highly relevant," "probably relevant," or "possibly relevant" so you don't waste time on marginal research.

●●●●●●●●

I heard that the definition of a dynamic presentation is a good beginning and a good end…with both sides as close together as possible.

●●●●●●●●

Suffer from stage fright? One entrepreneur's husband suggested she tell herself that only one person is watching the show: a sweet little lady in Kansas City who has the TV set on in the background as she irons. Then challenge yourself to be so interesting that the lady will put aside her ironing and start watching in earnest.

Taking an electronic bite of the Big Apple. Most of us don't live within easy visiting distance of the New York Public Library. But that's no problem because an incredible collection of information awaits us at http://www.nypl.org/index.html. I had a ball hopping among What's New, Resource Guides, Catalogs & Indexes, and Publications. I knew there used to be something like *Gebbie's House Organs*. But although my regional librarian went online to find out what it is now called and if it is still being published, she came up empty-handed. By entering the old name into the CATNAP search engine at the New York Public Library site, I discovered it has been assimilated into another publication and was quickly on my way to mining the information I needed. They also have staff-compiled resource guides on a variety of subjects here. Browse to your heart's content. I defy you not to find something valuable.

●●●●●●●

Speaker to audience: "My function as I understand it is to talk to you. Yours is to listen. If you get finished first, just raise your hand."

●●●●●●●

Consider teleclasses as a marketing device. Meeting with several people at once via telephone is becoming a popular way to generate clients—and cash. These are called teleclasses or teleconferences and they offer many advantages. They allow people to experience your power and help you build relationships right from your home or office. Besides being convenient and foregoing time-consuming travel, they are cost-effective. Your investment will usually be about $16 per hour including your bridge line and long distance call. Each participant pays a fee, just as she or he would to attend a seminar. Teleclasses are ideal for professionals who can use them as a link to selling more sophisticated and customized help.

Unorthodox way to get audience feedback: Wondering what people *really* thought of your presentation? Hang out in the ladies room! You can get candid reactions while sitting in a cubicle in the restroom during breaks and listening to what people say about your speech. Just be sure you're ready for such frankness.

●●●●●●●

Some people think the world is made of atoms...but it's really made of Eves.

●●●●●●●

Read speeches by famous women. If you would like to read the full text versions of speeches by dozens of notable women leaders, surf over to http://gos.sbc.edu. This site is supported by Sweet Briar College.

Phenomenal site for women's resources. You'll feel like you've been on the most exciting Easter egg hunt imaginable when you enter the section on Bizgrowth.com called The Business Woman's Internet Directory. To assist in your online research they've assembled a remarkable collection of women-oriented resources. It includes brief definitions and hot links to search engines, online databases, international sites, newspapers and magazines, women's business, health resources, publishing specifically geared to women, women of color business resources, and much more. Find it all at http://www.bizgrowth.com/bizdirectory.html.

Part V

Maximize Your Strengths—More Gutsy Strategies for Wonder Women

CHAPTER 14

How to Capture More Sales With Less Effort

Sales is perhaps the noblest profession. The higher art of selling is service. When we are truly serving others, we are selling in the purest form. Capitalizing on our feminine persuasion, we can overcome stereotypes and restrictive taboos to become the true masters (mistresses?) of the art of the sale. Women have an inborn ability to be motherly, warm, and attentive to others. That charm can turn lions into lambs.

Be aware, however, that selling is not about making appointments, being drop-dead gorgeous, running ads, having promotions, or winning awards. It's about selling the most stuff and collecting the most money—making consumers hot for you and what you do. Sales must translate into financial victory for you in the roaring 2000s.

In this chapter we'll look at prospecting and effective lead handling, then investigate strategies for suggestive selling. Retail establishments will be coached on how to attract and satisfy more customers. I'll tell you how to expand your market; diversify to multiply your profits; and generate those golden testimonials, endorsements, and referrals. Finally, we'll examine whether you should "go mobile, young woman, go mobile."

Effective Lead Handling

Prospecting precludes persuading someone to purchase your wares or contract for your help. Experts are in agreement that a person must hear about you at least *five* times before he or she will make a buying decision. Of course, those five contact points can take a variety of forms: phone calls, personal contact, ads, publicity, postcards, promotions, letters, e-mail messages, faxes, signage, word-of-mouth—you name it.

What does not vary is that you must never stop! Realize you are not "selling" people. Rather you're *building relationships* and telling folks about something to make their lives better. Prospecting needn't be an arduous task, once we get over our own wimpiness, stop complaining that roses have thorns, and rejoice that thorns have roses. Just think, if you made only three calls a day, in a year's time you would have made 1,000 contacts. Spend at least one hour a day prospecting. (Of course if you're a professional saleswoman, your entire efforts will be focused here.) And don't think you can quit when business is good. That's foolhardy. When business bottoms out six months later, you won't have anything in the pipeline. So let's ramp up and take the initiative to make things happen! The only goal you can't accomplish is the one you don't pursue.

After you've generated enough interest to get a person or business to contact you, how that lead is handled spells the difference between success or defeat. It is paramount that people be treated well. Just being responsive can yield amazing results. A few months ago we received a letter that began, "Thanks for your prompt response to my inquiry. I've received zero feedback from my two other leads and so have decided to sign your contract." The letter was accompanied by a check for $24,523.97. Another prospect wrote, "Thank you for your continuous support, calls, letters, and e-mails. There were times when I became very frustrated with the politics involved with this case and writing the book. But your continuous support is very much appreciated."

It angers me that some businesses are so lackadaisical they don't even reply to leads. Such enterprises deserve to fail. I've found this to be especially pervasive with e-mail. In this new electronic medium, often professional courtesy is abandoned.

When working with prospects, use their names. This makes people feel special; it also sets you apart. Few business people bother to employ this simple approach. How do you get their names? That depends on your individual operation. In professional circles, it is natural to introduce ourselves. If they are paying for repairing their vacuum or for alterations on a suit, you have a natural vehicle to discover who they are. Their name will be on their claim check, personal check, or credit card. If all else fails, ask.

In some instances, a show-and-tell technique will help you score sales. A carpet cleaner could have samples demonstrating before-and-after cleaning; a picture framer might display the same painting or portrait with and without proper matting and framing. Of course, remodeling contractors need a portfolio showing interiors and exteriors before and after their handiwork. Ditto for plastic surgeons. Such visual statements say a great deal.

Nothing takes the place of knowledge. When we speak with potential clients they can sense immediately whether we know what we're talking about. People also know when you are bluffing. No matter whether you deal in such divergent things as real estate or engineering services, educate yourself so you can guide those you wish to influence.

As Earl Nightingale told us in many of his dynamic motivational presentations, if you study your profession just one hour per day…in only five years you will be the country's foremost expert. Read trade journals, listen to tapes, attend seminars, watch videos—become that expert!

Betsy Komjathy, a partner in the communications skills company Rogen International—which counts among its blue-chip clients Merrill Lynch, Nabisco, Citigroup, and Proctor & Gamble—is adamant about being client-focused. "The pitch is often won prior to the presentation," she says. Komjathy believes in detailed preparation. Those who walk out with the business are usually the ones who walk in saying, "Here's what we understand you need to achieve, here are our insights into what's going on in the marketplace, and by the way, here's the evidence to demonstrate how we can help you." She recommends calling the prospect a couple of days before the initial meeting and saying you'd like to ask a few questions so your upcoming presentation can zero in on what's particularly important to them. Decisions aren't necessarily based on credentials and experience. "It's about intimacy, chemistry, and rapport between the client and individuals on the team. Small guys [gals] can pull that off, too," comments Komjathy.

Be prepared to counter objections. When I was the director of marketing for the West Coast's largest vocational school, I trained the salespeople to overcome resistance. How? First, you determine what the standard objections are. In every business you'll have three to six reasons people feel they can't buy. Then you think about ways to surmount them. This kind of preparation allows you to be one step ahead of your prospect. I literally scripted each objection with a written description on how to handle it. This resulted in a 25 percent increase in business.

One vitally important aspect of handling leads is to *ask for the sale*. Does this seem like a stupid bit of advice? It is surprising how often this crucial selling step is overlooked or bungled. Naturally, you don't want to be crass about it.

There are several graceful ways to ask for the sale. One approach is to give the prospect two alternatives—either of which is acceptable to you. For instance, don't ask if they want to make a purchase. Instead say, "Would you prefer to handle this by check or credit card?" or "Which would be more convenient for our service representative to come out, Tuesday or Friday?" For institutions or firms where contracts must be signed, some people favor asking the person to "write your name here" rather than saying "sign here." Be careful you don't go too far and talk a prospect *out* of a sale. Once they indicate the answer is yes, stop selling! Practicing your pauses can be like Santa Clauses.

Before deciding to move our company to Buena Vista, Colorado, we contacted several chambers of commerce in potential locales. We were impressed when a letter arrived from the bank president of Moffat County State Bank in tiny Craig, Colorado. The letter invited us to make them our financial institution. That's asking for the order in spades. Had we moved to Craig, that bank would have had our accounts.

Another sales strategy is to make it *easy* for the person to buy or participate. Credit cards facilitate sales. So do toll-free phone numbers. If applicable, a free trial period will also reassure people; so will a money-back guarantee. Postage-paid business reply cards increase results. If you're writing people asking them to do you a favor, including a self-addressed, stamped envelope (SASE) will bolster results.

Follow-up. These two little words will have a big impact on your success. If you promise to do something, do it. If you expect someone to do something for you in a certain time frame and they don't, get back in touch. If you feel you have a hot lead and nothing comes of it, recontact the person. Try to get them talking and discover what the obstacle is. The person with good follow-through techniques doesn't let business slip through a crack.

On this subject, should you borrow a follow-up tactic used by dentists? Remember the friendly reminder to get your teeth cleaned about every six months? This same strategy can be applied by veterinarians (It's time for Rover's shots), physicians (Your last physical was…) and optometrists (You haven't had your eyes checked since…). It would also work for plant nurseries (We just got in our annuals for this year, or it's pruning time), beauty shops (Time for a permanent), and chimney sweeps (Avoid fire hazards).

Joan Welsh, who owns a floatation tank business in Fort Collins, Colorado, sends out postcards to customers reminding them of when their last float was, along with an offer of 8 dollars off their next float or a gift certificate to a friend. Carefully worded, timely reminders stimulate business and give you a perfect excuse to follow up.

Speaking of postcards, I'm compelled to give these midget marketers with mighty mastery another plug. A marketing fella I'm aware of sends them frequently to announce new clients to his whole database of prospects. He uses postcards because they're cheap (inexpensive to print and only 20¢ for first class mail service) and they're read by almost 100 percent of recipients. All you're asking for is 20 to 30 seconds of a person's undivided attention. The impressions he hopes for include: 1) Wow, another new client. This guy must be really good. 2) Such a variety of clients (automotive, computer, health care, trade associations, etc.). He could probably help my company too, and 3) If I need outside professional advice, I want to remember this guy. He's generated a lot of new clients this way.

Another thought about postcards: Don't send all of them at once. If you have a database of say, 500 people and you mail to everyone simultaneously, you could be deluged. (Nice problem, eh?) Much better to send 167 of them out each month for three months, then start over again. That way your responses will be more evenly spread and you can service the business properly.

Of course, tracking leads is paramount. You must know where your business is coming from so you can replicate what works and drop what doesn't. Track results as if your life depends on it…your business life does. Code ads and mailing lists. Ask callers how they heard of you. Inquire of people who walk into your establishment what prompted them to visit. You should be able to identify the source of at least 85 percent of your transactions.

One of my speaker friends tells of developing an elaborate system for tracking every inquiry by source, topic, and sales volume. The results? She discovered her firm was spending time and money generating plenty of inquiries—but they were the wrong kind. They resulted in unprofitable sales. So you not only want to know where your leads come from, but which ones generate actual sales, the cost per new customer/client, and if that business is lucrative. It may be time to rethink your entire prospecting strategy.

Speaking of tracking results, here's a true retail story that relates: During a three-day promotion, a clever discount merchandiser gave away "all the free peanuts you can eat while shopping at our store." By the end of the promotion, the merchant had distinctive litter trails that provided information on the traffic patterns within the store. Trampled peanut hulls littered the most heavily traveled aisles and heaped up in front of merchandise displays of special interest to customers. With this ingenious trick, the merchant compiled a graphic picture of what most attracted customer attention. How's that for literally "tracking results"?

It isn't necessary, however, to constantly recruit new business. Your current customer is your best customer. I'll bet if you allocated more time to increasing repeat business from your existing customers, your profits would shoot straight up the chart. This is often referred to as "working the back end." These follow-up sales to customers who initially purchased from you can end up becoming your greatest source of revenue. They usually have a lower development cost than the initial item, yet are related in some way. When you market to present customers, you fully leverage the credibility you've established with them. Once people know you'll deliver what you promised, it's incredibly easy to sell to them again. And again. And again.

Suggestive Selling

Try to think of ways to entice your customers, clients, or patients to buy more. Suggestive selling can turn a marginal operation into a profitable one. This is done all the time in better clothing stores. When you purchase a dress or suit, the salesperson brings over accessories to complete the "look." Good restaurant servers are also brilliant at building their dinner tickets by suggesting tasty-sounding appetizers, then coffee, an after-dinner drink, or a scrumptiously described dessert to top off the meal.

Why not make suggestive selling part of your strategy? An answering service might trade up a client to include coverage on weekends and evenings. A dentist could push add-ons by suggesting special fluoride treatments with teeth cleaning. An upholsterer might reap extra business by suggesting a footstool or matching pillows.

How to Capture More Sales With Less Effort

Some firms offer employees perks to inspire them to help with suggestive selling. They give a bonus when workers write add-on business. A carpet cleaner, for instance, might pay the folks who go into homes and businesses an extra reward when they sell the customer on cleaning drapes or waxing floors. It's wise to coach associates so they can take advantage of the one-to-one moment with a customer.

Service people are often in ideal positions to build greater sales numbers. By listening to customer comments, they are tipped off to new needs. The person who repairs air-conditioning and refrigeration, for instance, should be trained to recognize the potential when a customer says, "Our house is often uncomfortable." This may well be an invitation to upgrade registers, duct work, or air-conditioning units.

Also look for ways to sell upgrades. This is a better version of the same product or service. I'll bet you experienced this if you've ever purchased a new car. First you get the base- price vehicle. Then there's air conditioning, power seats, antilock brakes, a CD stereo player, special undercoating, extra warranties, etc., etc., etc. Same thing on televisions. Do you want the bare-bones TV—or would you also like a remote control, small picture of other channels in the corner, perhaps a VCR included? When you drive into the carwash do you settle for plain vanilla—or perhaps succumb to that irresistible hot-wax treatment, undercarriage wash, or leather cleaning? By making such upgrades available, many consumers choose to move up to the next level. How can you apply this to your business?

Jay Abraham, in his new *Getting Everything You Can Out of All You've Got*, says add-ons, which are a close cousin to upgrades, are a no-brainer. He has his cars hand-washed every week at his house. When the carwash man came out, instead of offering to do one car for $10, he presented a better plan to include Jay's second car, and an even more attractive deal to do all three vehicles. And he made the triple sale. Jay also tells of a lawncare business that sells a season of full yard maintenance instead of a one-shot summer mowing job. How many of your clients could benefit from receiving a continuous supply of your service—or a larger quantity of your product?

We were tickled by another form of "suggestive selling" that came to our attention. The owner of a document-shredding service on the East Coast developed a real knack for attracting customers. He roots through trash bags collected from the local dump by two young helpers. When he finds sensitive pieces of correspondence, he sends them to the place of origin with a note saying, "Should I be reading this material? If not, why did your company make it public by throwing it away in one piece?" It typically takes less than 24 hours for a response.

Expand Your Market

Many companies miss lucrative opportunities for capitalizing on what they already have. Yet there is a proven method for expanding your market. With this technique you look for ways to get individuals or businesses to use more of what you offer. Kodak, for instance, switched from advertising film to promoting photography.

If you own a window cleaning business, is there a way to create a higher demand for this service? How about encouraging businesses to paint their windows for various holidays? Then after Christmas, Easter, and Halloween, you have a world of glass that requires cleaning. A bicycle repair shop might mount a local campaign to encourage using bikes as a cheap, nonpolluting form of transportation. An upscale gallery might spur interest in cultural activities.

Look for ways to bundle your product. Marcus Allen (www.markusallen.com) tells of a toothpaste company that was plagued by sluggish sales. So they bundled their toothpaste with a brush, dental floss, and mouthwash, then merchandised it as a travel kit. Their sales skyrocketed. Computer companies do this all the time. When you buy a computer, you also get a free keyboard, a mouse, a modem, and oodles of software. McDonald's Extra Value Meal is another prime example. You get a sandwich, fries, and a drink all for one low price.

Retail stores can expand their market by applying some simple principles. Paco Underhill, the author of *Why We Buy: The Science of Shopping*, points out some interesting facts about gender differences. Men rarely ask for the department or item they want in a store. They'd rather wander around lost and leave if they can't find it. (Universal truth: Men hate to ask for directions!) While 86 percent of women shoppers look at price tags, only 72 percent of men do. And when it comes to trying on clothes, 65 percent of men purchase what they try on. Only 25 percent of women do.

According to Underhill, apparel retailers should provide women a comfortable place to "park" their husbands. It's not an amenity; it's a marketing tool. If a woman's husband is comfortable, she becomes an infinitely more effective shopper. He also advises keeping the dressing room area clean and picked up. (While that certainly isn't rocket science, it never ceases to amaze me how many messy fitting rooms I find in stores these days.)

The actual facility itself needs to have a personality and project a good image. Since the amount of time a shopper spends in a store (assuming it's not waiting in line) determines how much she or he will buy, make it visually stimulating. Seventy percent of buying decisions are made *after* a customer enters a store, according to *Chain Store Age Executive* magazine. Keep it bright and cheery. A skylight and spotlights featuring certain merchandise will lighten the environment. Greet people with some comment relevant to the merchandise they're near or a question that requires more than a yes or no answer. The tired old "May I help you?" inevitably gets a "No" and the conversation comes to a dead halt. Since most people turn to the right when they enter, consider that in your positioning of goods. Let shoppers feel the merchandise. The Gap is a master at making it easy to touch, stroke, unfold, and examine at close range everything on the selling floor. So if visions of happy customers dance in your head, create a welcoming atmosphere that will have them buying today and excited to return to your store again soon.

Diversify to Multiply

When you stick your big toe into multiple streams of income you diversify your business and multiply your dollars. It's a result of synergy: the combined effect of two or more things working together. Have you thought of expanding your business with sidelines to create additional income sources? That's what Luce Press Clippings did.

They offer a new option to their clients, most of which are public relations (PR) firms. The new wrinkle is dubbed Comparative Ad Costs. It provides comparable advertising figures for clippings Luce cuts from magazines and newspapers. This way PR agencies can show their clients how much they *would* have spent for the exposure, had it been placed as a paid advertisement. With little extra expense or effort, Luce added a whole new spectrum to their services.

Let's examine fresh approaches for any organization that wishes to develop a new revenue source. You can set a course for a significantly improved bottom line by spinning off peripheral revenue centers. Offering complementary services or coming up with other creative combinations adds excitement and diversity to your business. More importantly, it augments your income stream.

Inventor Marilyn Searcy of Fremont, California, found it difficult to attract sales reps for her "It's a Keeper," an attachment that slides over the top of most ladders and holds a paint bucket, tools, etc. So to be more appealing to the network of sales reps she needed, Searcy began production on a faux painting stencil tray, a painter's pallet, a fruit-picking bag, and a scaffolding adapter. By having more of a product line, she gains clout in the marketplace.

Sometimes diversifying to multiply is what keeps you ahead of your competitors. When Linda Torres-Winters realized others noticed she had a good thing going with her Linditas Salsa Mix, she decided to wrap up packets of her hot and mild salsa spices with a can of diced tomatoes and a 6-inch serving bowl. This product expansion moved her to a new level.

Another reason to apply this strategy is to combat seasonal slowdowns and economic fluctuations. That's what motivated Laurie Swift and her husband Bruce to expand their dry cleaning, laundry, carpet and upholstery cleaning business in Clarksville, Tennessee. "People cut down on dry cleaning during economic downturns and few wanted their carpet and upholstery done in the winter," Laurie reports. Yet people contacted them after fires or floods damaged their homes. So the Swifts expanded into fire and flood restoration, adding specialty equipment and products to attack the soot and smoke odor. They also boosted their presence in the Yellow Pages, where most people turn after such emergencies. The result has been a 15 percent increase in their revenues. And since they do such jobs during the slower times of the week, it balances out the work for their 26 full-time employees.

An additional bonus is that many times doing something different is an outstanding traffic builder for your flagship business. It pulls in prospects you wouldn't normally attract. Gary Beals, CEO of Beals Advertising & Public Relations Agency, is a perfect example. One reason his San Diego–based agency prospers is because he also developed a product called *Finderbinder*. Besides being a freestanding revenue source, this news media directory positions him as THE expert on area media.

"It's the large tail that wags our dog," says Beals. "It pulls attention back to our company." Conceived as a worthwhile diversification when reinforcing the company image of being the power agency of communications services, Beals confides it's "an excellent tool for finding and landing new business. Its value is as much for the visibility as for the income," he remarks. His directory builds company identity and prestige.

Beals is an ideal example of how adding a new spin to your business can turn into increased publicity. Such activity gives area newspapers,

TV, and radio a reason to focus attention on your enterprise. You're suddenly "news." This clever businessman doesn't stop there. He has franchised the concept and now has *Finderbinders* in some 20 other cities. And he has diversified further, both to publicize his agency and create a new income stream. Gary is a speaker who specializes in doing 60- to 90-minute breakout sessions for national conventions. He has given over 500 talks. New business is a natural fallout from these speaking engagements.

When a carpenter and builder offered to teach Faye Cook the remodeling business back in 1962, he had no idea he was coaching a woman who would ultimately build one of the nation's top 50 remodeling businesses in the nation, according to *Remodeling* magazine. "I got out in the field with the men and that's how I learned the business—from the ground up," recalls Cook. What's her blueprint for success? Faye attributes the longevity and strength of her business to an expanded array of services. Over the years she has added new capabilities, growing her firm into a full-service operation. In addition to remodeling and new construction, she also builds all types of room additions and offers free interior and exterior decorating. But it doesn't stop there. This astute entrepreneur also handles landscaping, water features, sprinkling systems, decks, arbors, even outside lighting. "People want a lot of different things and I never want to give them a reason to go somewhere else," Cook says.

Multifunction is a key to the future. In her book about trends, *The Popcorn Report*, Faith Popcorn wrote that multifunction was important in the streamlined 1990s. It is even more so in the dynamic 2000s. This means products or services that accomplish two or three things at once or allow you to get more than one job done at a time. "The biggest idea is *cluster marketing*," Popcorn says. "Why should we have to make one drop at the dry cleaners, another at the tailor, a third at the shoe repair, and so on?"

Innovative merchants can subcontract some of these functions. Let's say you own the dry cleaners. Why not team up with a shoe repair person and a tailor...both of whom could work out of their homes using your facility as a pickup and delivery point? Everybody wins.

In our ever more demanding life, time is a most precious commodity. To conserve it and avoid unnecessary stress, consumers will patronize establishments that help them combine shopping and errands. Marketers who capitalize on this need will thrive.

Spinoff Business Ideas

■ Real estate office that also has a corporate relocation department and a property management division

■ Childcare facility that offers elder care

■ Childcare providers that furnish creative day-care programs for the children of parents who are attending seminars, conventions, or participating in adult vacation activities

■ Beauty shop that includes a tanning salon and carries cosmetics and jewelry

■ Gardener who also sells fertilizer, plants, etc., plus offers window washing, gutter cleaning, and hauls large items to the dump

■ Small ranch or farm that turns a pond on the property into a fish-for-fee establishment or encourages "do-it-yourself" picking of fruits and veggies

■ Hotel or motel that puts together entertaining tourist packages

■ Campground and riding stable combination that offers trail rides, hayrides, guided horseback hunting trips, moonlight rides and steak dinners, etc.

■ Laundromats that team up with a bar, restaurant, tanning room, video rental, exercise

(continued on next page)

Without incurring any expense for facility development or additional startup costs, other businesses can benefit by thinking through how to use their existing structure more effectively. A beauty school, for instance, could embellish its traditional curriculum. A refresher course—including updating of new styles, cuts, and techniques—might be of interest to operators and salon owners. This type of instruction holds special appeal to those who haven't worked for a while and want to get back their manual dexterity.

Or what about a salon management course that teaches the business side of hairdressing: purchasing, accounting, marketing, plus personnel selection and supervision? Cosmetic merchandising might be another subject to offer. This is a natural as more shops become boutiques with hair product lines, cosmetics, jewelry, and other accessories for sale. Shopping malls have even tuned into this *diversify to multiply* concept. Many now sport driver's license renewal booths.

Going global is, of course, a fantastic way to capitalize on this concept. Small business that export typically grow faster and are more stable than their nonexporting cousins. Although it's logical to look at your immediate geographic markets as the primary area for expansion, no company is too small to sell overseas. Women embrace this strategy more than men. In an American Express and NAWBO New York City study,

286

they found that 17 percent of women-owned businesses surveyed plan to expand into international markets in the future, while only 10 percent of men-owned firms were thinking globally.

There is tons of help available on this subject. The U.S. Department of Commerce has a toll-free number (800-USA-TRADEO) you can use to order reports, learn about markets, and speak with trade specialists. Several branches of the government pulled together to produce a Web site to assist entrepreneurs doing business overseas. TradeNet Export Advisor offers tutorials, trade leads, and country data at www.tradenet.gov. And by going to http://home3.americanexpress.com/smallbusiness/resources/expanding/global/countries.shtml (Feels like you just took an international trip with that one, eh!), you can click on market research reports that address export issues or business travel and protocol. Main headings—with individual country data under them—include Western Europe, Eastern Europe/former Soviet Union, Middle East and South Central Asia, Africa, South America, Central America and the Caribbean, plus East Asia and the Pacific. Ladies, the world is literally your oyster!

Back on U.S. soil, Lisa Carlson of Upper Access, Inc., Hinesburg, Vermont, believes, "Being open to creative diversity allows you to be much more sustaining." She and husband, Steve, started as writers. After receiving rejection slips from 26 major publishers, they became intrigued by self-publishing and decided to take the do-it-yourself approach.

Next they saw a need for a mail order bookstore specializing in hard-to-find books. So the Carlsons launched a catalog called Big Books from Small Presses, which specializes in selling works by small publishing houses and self-publishers. They design and distribute 70,000 catalogs a year.

Lisa and Steve looked endlessly for affordable computer software to manage all these book orders and found "there was a crying need." So they spent over $60,000 to develop PIIGS (Publishers' Invoice and Information Generating System). It is an industry-specific program that

---

SPINOFF BUSINESS IDEAS
(continued)

equipment, electronic games—you name it

■ Funeral home that doubles as a wedding chapel

■ Boarding kennel that also offers grooming and obedience training

■ Office supply store in conjunction with a data entry/secretarial service

■ Web site designer who also does brochures and direct mail pieces (or vice versa)

handles everything from invoicing to statements, royalties to mailing lists. It not only solved their problem but adds a whole new tier of profit to their enterprise.

Another add-on is a toll-free phone service that publishers can use to promote their books 24-hours a day via Visa, MasterCard, and American Express credit card orders. "The synergy is wonderful," observes

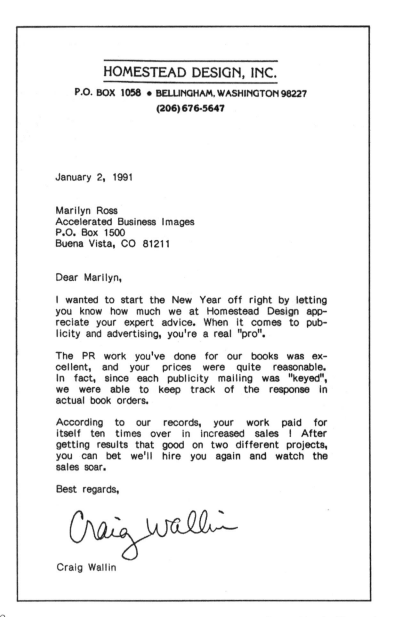

HOMESTEAD DESIGN, INC.
P.O. BOX 1058 • BELLINGHAM, WASHINGTON 98227
(206) 676-5647

January 2, 1991

Marilyn Ross
Accelerated Business Images
P.O. Box 1500
Buena Vista, CO 81211

Dear Marilyn,

I wanted to start the New Year off right by letting you know how much we at Homestead Design appreciate your expert advice. When it comes to publicity and advertising, you're a real "pro".

The PR work you've done for our books was excellent, and your prices were quite reasonable. In fact, since each publicity mailing was "keyed", we were able to keep track of the response in actual book orders.

According to our records, your work paid for itself ten times over in increased sales ! After getting results that good on two different projects, you can bet we'll hire you again and watch the sales soar.

Best regards,

Craig Wallin

Craig Wallin

Lisa. "People who order through our 800 number get the catalog, then come back to us for additional purchases."

Their latest outgrowth is subcontracting shipping for another firm. They pack and ship UPS orders of odd-shaped special contractor tools. "This, coupled with our in-house shipping demands, has given us enough volume to now hire a warehouse foreman," explains Carlson.

Upper Access is an ideal example of diversify to multiply. They watch what's happening, audit consumer trends, then capitalize on complementary new needs. In the process their business has become like the interlocking parts of a chain that, when forged together, form an invincible whole.

You too can think progressively. Inventively. Outrageously. An eclectic approach may be just the touch needed to build your dream. As you resist conformity you reach new heights. By boosting the ingenuity with which you view your organization, it becomes possible to turn niches into riches—to diversify to multiply—to go around roadblocks and discover exciting new profit centers.

Cultivating Testimonials and Endorsements

Testimonials from others are almost as good as money in the bank. Professional practices and service firms sell intangibles rather than something a prospect can see and touch—such as a vehicle, wearing apparel, or garden tools. Selling intangibles is harder; it requires a higher degree of trust on the part of the buyer. That's why third-party endorsements are so valuable. Instead of you saying how great you are, an impartial outsider recites your praises.

When someone compliments you, the first thing to do is write back thanking them and request their permission in writing to use what they've said. We've devised a standard letter for such purposes. A sample follows. Notice it gives you unlimited leeway to do whatever you please with their comments. (Run this by an attorney to be sure it covers all contingencies in your situation.) Only once in the 23 years we've been in business has anyone refused to sign such a release.

After you have their written permission to use the material, think about how to capitalize on it. We've put together a leather notebook of the original copies of letters we've received. When prospective clients come in or we exhibit at a trade show, we invite people to look through the book. This pre-sell technique builds trust and credibility. We also include photocopies with proposals and have added the accolades to our Web site. When prospects get our proposals, they are blown away by the dozens of glowing letters.

People are more likely to compliment you verbally than in writing though. What to do then? Thank them for the kind words, then say something like, "Jim, I wonder if you'd do me a favor? Would you take a couple of minutes and put that in writing for me? Comments like

290   www.BrazenHussiesNetwork.com

yours are very reassuring to prospects who don't know us like you do." Once you've received Jim's correspondence, proceed as above.

But maybe you're not getting a lot of praise from satisfied customers. Be proactive. Ask for it! Write and explain you're developing a new brochure, adding to your Web site, or whatever, and you'd like to include a testimonial from them. Ask for their honest opinions about your product or service. You might also want to include their picture; then they'll feel almost famous.

Also encourage those giving you testimonials to *quantify* the exact results they received. A client saying a direct marketing copywriter *doubled* her response rate is much more powerful than a lot of flowery general words. When a company can say a management consultant increased their annual revenue by *36 percent*, that's heavy marketing ammunition. Or perhaps your accounting savvy saved a company *14 percent* on their taxes. Specificity breeds success. It doesn't matter if you're a car dealership, florist, restaurant, charity, software developer, gift shop, whatever...people believe in testimonials.

The Magic of Referrals

According to a survey of 900 sales and marketing professions conducted by the Nierenberg Group, referrals are the most effective technique for attracting new customers. The message to entrepreneurs and sales professionals is that the shortest path to new business comes from reviewing existing contacts and asking them to recommend you to others. It's a fact the leads that convert to sales at the highest percentage are referrals from current customers.

Although testimonials may be as *good* as money in the bank, referrals *are* money in the bank. Once you've honed your referral approach, I can almost guarantee your bank balance will blossom. A referral is simply one happy client or customer telling another. It is word-of-mouth praise. (To help you stimulate this area, pay close attention to the next chapter on Providing Awesome Service and Customer/Client Satisfaction.)

A Whirlpool Corporation study showed Americans are six times more likely to rely on the judgment of others than on advertising when making a buying decision. By some accounts, a whopping 80 percent of all consumer choices are the result of personal recommendations. The individual who refers once will do it again and again. Because the average person has a sphere of influence of 52 people, these kudos can create dazzling momentum.

Begin today to develop a referral mind-set. You get referrals by *asking* for them. (You have provided business cards to all key associates, right?) Instruct service technicians to give two cards to each customer with the following request: "Would you please pass these along to anyone you know whom we can help?" Ask for the sale. People need to be alerted to your desire for referrals. A physician, architect, or financial planner might post a discreet sign that says "We appreciate your referrals."

Start prospecting for referrals with the folks who gave you testimonials; they're obviously on your side. When they offer positive feedback—let's say Judy is praising the new copier she bought from you because it allowed her to produce a classy customized brochure in one day—inquire if she knows anyone else who might want to create materials with similar efficiency. Without seeming like a homicide detective, try to find out as much as possible about the referral. And ask permission to use Judy's name when you call.

Now think about your existing and recent client/customer base. You know who is especially high on you—and who isn't. Target the accounts where you excelled. Contact them and explain that you find people are reassured when a satisfied client or customer shares a happy experience. Say that you would appreciate their mentioning you to some of their friends or associates who could benefit from what you do.

Don't overlook nonclient contacts. Individuals who are influential in their fields can further broaden your referral program. What about attorneys, accountants, CPAs, association executive directors, insurance agents, bankers, even those who have worked for you previously? Several of these people might be glad to put you together with someone who needs what you offer.

Engaging others to market your services with their clients is a wonderful way to expand your market reach. Establish relationships with other professionals who deliver services to the same or similar consumers or businesses as you, but who are not in direct competition with you. Educate them about why this will be beneficial. You may find trading referrals works well.

When someone gives you a referral, promptly recognize their contribution. This can be done in person, by phone, or via a personal handwritten note. (No e-mail, please.) Notice the adjacent postcard used by some dentists. If it doesn't violate your—or their—professional code of ethics, a small thank-you gift may be in order. We sometimes

send flowers or gift baskets to individuals who go out of their way to do nice things for us.

In some industries, paid referrals (finder's fees) are an acceptable way of doing business. If yours falls into this category, be sure your record-keeping is accurate. No one will shoot you down faster than a contact who gave you a referral, but never received the agreed-upon remuneration.

On the other side of the spectrum is the person or organization that would find financial compensation distasteful. Here's an idea from Adelaide Aitken, a certified financial planner in Cambridge, Massachusetts. She devised a way to boost referrals without seeming mercenary. She simply makes a donation to the favorite charity of people who give her leads that turn into business. That makes everyone feel good.

The Business Breakfast/Lunch/Tea

The days of macho men swilling down martinis, gorging on red meat, and taking three-hour lunches are as extinct as dinosaurs. They have been replaced by women and men who often prefer nonalcoholic beverages, eat grilled chicken and fish entrees, and practice more disciplined time constraints. Today's movers and shakers are more health-conscious, more time-conscious, and more price-conscious.

In many circles the power lunch has given way to the power breakfast. It can be as light as a croissant or as hearty as a breakfast buffet. Even in the priciest spots of New York and Los Angeles, costs hover below lunch. Shoptalk over bagels is gaining ground in several hotel restaurants. Early-morning business powwows can be seen at the Polo Lounge in the Beverly Hills Hotel, the Skyway in Chicago's Hyatt Regency, and the Edwardian Room at New York City's.

Doing business over food and drink is not new. Certain elegant hotel dining rooms or lobbies blossom with laptops perched at full attention each afternoon beginning at 3:00 P.M. They are in sharp contrast to the delicate tea service and clink of wafer-thin china. Yet tea is often the choice of women who shun the old liquid lunches.

If you want to use any of these culinary methods to score more sales or do serious networking, here are a few tips: Act rather than react. *You* do the inviting. If someone you want to know better says goodbye with, "We've got to do lunch sometime," take advantage of the opening. Call in a few days and suggest a couple of alternative dates.

How the conversation is orchestrated varies with different individuals. Sometimes, rather than real conversation, it's nonstop kibitzing. You don't get to the real "meat" of the meeting until you are close to parting company. In some situations, the serious talk is conducted on the way to the parking lot or walking back to the office.

The setting you choose says things about you. If eating out plays a large role in how you develop business, it makes sense to cultivate a close rapport with a couple of outstanding local establishments. Then you will be personally greeted, escorted to a prime table, and your service will be top drawer. This impresses your guests.

Offering Financial Incentives

There are several ways a creative business can use monetary inducements. The restaurant industry pioneered two-for-one dinners years ago. This is a perfect strategy for recreational facilities: Movie houses, theaters, miniature golf courses, amusement parks, bowling alleys, and race track operations could easily employ this tactic to attract new guests. So could a dance studio offer two-for-one lessons, or a museum admit two people for one fee on slow days.

On a similar bent, some places offer family discounts. Currently there is heavy competition among dentists. Because winning patients is like pulling teeth (pun intended) some offices offer family discounts when two relatives schedule appointments. Chiropractors and other health professionals sometimes adopt this plan as well.

Frequent guest programs are the bread and butter of major hotel chains. The business traveler now comprises the hotel industry's largest customer group. Consequently, there is a veritable war to capture corporate business. The financial incentives offered here take the form of points. They are earned for each stay in a hotel and can be redeemed toward free vacation stays, air fare, car rental, even merchandise. There is no reason why an individual motel or B&B could not concoct a similar program to encourage repeat business.

Building customer loyalty can be big business. Consumers will spend as much as 46 percent more with a company that has a loyalty card program, studies show. The average American participates in three such programs. Carwashes already give a free wash after so many paid ones. Airline frequent flyer plans are more popular today than ever before. Smart restauranteurs often reward their neighborhood clientele with a free meal after "X" number of paid ones.

Prepayment alternatives find a place in some industries as well. Innovative funeral directors have long offered prepayment plans. This kind of financing might also work for a health club or spa membership. Forward-thinking owners can often come up with financial incentives when they really concentrate on looking for ways to help customers or clients partake of their services.

Nonprofits Use the Auction Block

The folks at Trinity Lutheran Church in Detroit definitely have a sense of humor. They decided to stage an Ugly Art Show and Auction to raise money for the church's restoration. Over 100 Detroiters paid $25 per couple to inspect and bid on absolutely atrocious pictures and sculpture. (Was there a "Worst of Show" award, I wonder?) In keeping with the evening's theme, refreshments consisted of Cheez Whiz, hot dogs, and Twinkies.

Mile Hi Church of Religious Science took the opposite approach for their expansion fund-raiser. This Lakewood, Colorado, church put on a gala "Fancy Affair." Tickets for the buffet and auction went for $10 each. In addition to international cuisine, there was entertainment, plus free gifts and door prizes. The auction preview began at 4:00 P.M., followed by a silent auction. Items were displayed on tables in rooms around the perimeter of the church. Each room was decorated to represent a country and to organize the objects for sale into logical groupings. Japan had garden items—America, sports. Furniture and household things were displayed in Germany, while Mexico offered a potpourri. Artwork could be found in France; antiques and jewelry were in England.

Those interested in supporting this cause could either place absentee bids using the auction catalog, participate in the silent auction via written bid, or cue the auctioneer during the oral raffle. Items were donated by church members and friends. They ran a wide gambit. There was a wooden icebox, Wedgewood china, valuable coins, a bronze sculpture, an antique quilt, even English Hallmark sterling silver with pearl handles. One of the more inventive things to go on the block was Broncos football tickets for two and dinner with the nationally known head minister and his wife.

Take Your Business on the Road

Want to get your wheels rolling instead of spinning? An old business maxim says *drive* is what gets you to the top. That can be so...literally. Inventive entrepreneurs and professionals are making extraordinary livings by putting their expertise on wheels. They're clobbering the competition by offering the ultimate in service: help at your doorstep. This concept, a lifesaver for harried two-career families, single parents, and mushrooming businesses, involves work performed where and when it is most handy for the customer.

Services such as hair care, massages, video delivery, and auto tuneups are ripe areas for portable profits. Convenience is all important. Busy working women and men patronize service providers who come to them. And innovative business-to-business companies are finding ways to serve the commercial sector as well. Coupled with this public need for better service is the small business owner's desire to avoid hassles and trim overhead. Going mobile offers a galaxy of advantages.

In the majority of cases, your entire operation is in your van, truck, SUV, or car. No longer is there a need for expensive office, store, or shop space. Stranglehold leases and crippling mortgage payments are a thing of the past. The old requirement of "location, location, location" becomes a moot point. Your ideal location is wherever you park! And you bypass zoning problems and bureaucratic red tape for building permits.

Nadine and Tom Manning, thirtysomethings who own the Truly Unique Personal Chef Service in Medford, New Jersey, are slicing and dicing their way to financial freedom. They devise menus, shop for groceries, then drive to clients' homes and prepare restaurant-quality meals of their clients' choice, which can be taken out of the freezer and consumed at will. The Mannings started in 1992 and now earn more than $90,000 a year. "We have enough recipes to make clients a different meal every night of the year," reports Nadine. "They're so appreciative because they're bored with frozen dinners."

George Louser's brainchild is Wash on Wheels. Louser encountered one problem after another when he tried to build traditional carwashes over 25 years ago. His solution was to design a portable pressure washing system that enables the operator to bring the cleaning system to the client. In addition to doing individual automobiles, he expanded to include truck fleets. Initially, Louser even restored buildings and removed graffiti, using a liquid sandblasting technique.

Now Wash on Wheels specializes in servicing the residential market with up to 14 different cleaning services in one visit. With today's "don't move, improve" philosophy, homeowners like the fact his franchisees wash carpets, ceilings, upholstery, drapes, driveways, roofs, pools, patios, even the entire house exterior.

Personal service is a ripe area for portable entrepreneuring. In the Dallas/Fort Worth area, an imaginative bookkeeper has a fleet of mobile computerized offices. More than 300 clients pay from $100 to $1,500 a month for on-site bookkeeping services and tax preparation. Surprisingly, many referrals come from CPAs who don't like to keep books.

Tamara Mattson's slogan might well be "Have Clippers, Will Travel." Mattson launched a mobile animal grooming business in tiny Excelsior, Minnesota. Her van is equipped with water, a water heater, supplies, and equipment. This clever young lady prospects for dogs and declawed cats to groom by blanketing the area with flyers and checking to see who has registered a pet with city hall.

Dr. Jane Summers is carrying on a family tradition. Her grandfather used to make house calls by horse in the early 1900s. Today she rides a red Jeep to the rescue of busy Denver, Colorado, executives who want physicals and sick moms who can't readily get to the doctor. She also offers a less expensive alternative than an ambulance ride. Her practice, Pioneer Internal Medicine, is strictly mobile and very high tech. Until recently, it wouldn't have been possible to offer portable doctoring. But today's technology provides equipment compact enough to fit in a vehicle. With this unique twist, Dr. Summers offers personalized care and a closer physician-patient relationship. She feels seeing patients in their own setting is a real advantage. It gives her a holistic overview of how their condition might be affected by their environment and caregivers.

Jan Robbins, a certified massage therapist, founded Corporate Stressbusters. This San Francisco company provides 15-minute upper body Japanese shiatsu massages to office workers at their desks. "Massage is the only thing that's addicting...and *good* for you," quips Robbins, who followed her vision to help people avoid suffering. When she began, individual workers would hire her at $18 a session, with a discount of $3 for a series of five treatments.

Today she has contracts with several companies who provide her services to employees as "perks." With stress being so widespread, Robbins hopes to get her therapy accepted as a standard health benefit. She is currently breaking ground with the Workers' Compensation Insurance Agency.

Another woman who has turned her personal skills into financial thrills is Caryl Barday. Her Corporate Cuts Unlimited, Inc., provides in-office haircuts for busy Denver executives. The first in the nation to legally conduct such a business, Barday overcame tremendous opposition from the state health department to acquire her cosmetology license. "It took me a year and three months of intense work," she reports. Her average income? Thirty-five dollars a person including the tip. "I make two or three stops in a day and do five to six men at each place," says the savvy stylist.

She sets up in the conference room and makes an appointment on the spot for two weeks hence before she leaves. An assistant carries her customized case, which contains her own chair. He also shines clients' shoes as she grooms their hair. Barday, who has been flown around the country to counsel others who want to get licensed, has been shearing the locks of Rocky Mountain businessmen for several years now. Her best customers are real estate developers, stockbrokers, and county commissioners. When asked why she has been successful, Barday replies, "Professionalism and consistency." These are certainly virtues in any business.

An Olympia, Washington, woman—Yvonne Conway—is another hairstylist who goes to her customers. Rather than operating in the corporate arena, however, she typically calls on local nursing homes, jails, mental institutions, and private homes. With over 100 regulars, Conway has more business than she can handle—sometimes cutting a husband's hair while his wife sits under the dryer.

Clients use her services for one of two reasons: Either they like the convenience or they are in poor health. She has concocted ways to clean and style clients' hair even if they are confined to bed or in a wheelchair. "I find very little competition in offering freelance beauty services," she comments.

Perhaps you can "plus" an existing site-specific business with a mobile unit. By making it easier for customers to do business with you than the competition, you remove their resistance. Additionally, putting a part of your business on wheels often gives you a fresh reason to be news, thus generating valuable publicity.

298

Offshore Sailing School, which is headquartered in Fort Myers, Florida, has 30 new opportunities for such public relations, not to mention a gimmick to increase sales and help their customers beat recessionary prices. They've introduced Learn to Sail vacations in 30 U.S. cities. By taking their 20-hour course on the road, they offer an action vacation minus the hassle and expense associated with long distance travel. Participants can enjoy a weekend getaway close to home.

Bob the Bankwagon enjoys enormous fame in Amarillo, Texas. This bright-red double-decker bus, which was imported from Britain, chases down customers for First National Bank of Amarillo. "It offers full-service banking," explains Jerry Polvado, senior vice-president at First National. "We foresee a lot of benefit," he continues. "There are a number of areas in our city where there are no bank branches." In addition to servicing these locations via an established route, Bob also travels to county fairs, fun fests, retirement homes, hospitals, and company parking lots. Here again, a mobile unit focuses attention on the parent facility. "The PR value is very important," relates Polvado.

California-based EnvirOzone Technologies, Inc., is another example of a business to spin off from an existing enterprise. An environmental engineering firm that specializes in wastewater management, it has won success in a crowded marketplace. To save customers extra expense and hassle, it has developed a mobile unit that can drive to a site and perform necessary clean-up.

It's been said that moving targets are the hardest to hit. But in today's business world, moving targets are some of the biggest hits!

Sales guru Brian Tracy gives us this message in *HomeBusiness* magazine: "Get out from behind your desk and sell. If you cannot meet your customer face-to-face, use the fax, phone calls, and e-mail to make regular contact. Each morning, ask the question, 'What selling action can I take today?' Sales is more than a process. It is an activity where you must constantly interact with customers and prospects. Customer contact is the oxygen to the brain of a small or home-based business."

And to keep that oxygen flowing, we must practice awesome customer service. Spending time to keep current clients or customers satisfied is a wise investment. In this new millennium, there are so many more sales prospects, you'll be tempted to neglect existing business. Don't do it. One third of your energy should be devoted to existing customers. If you keep them happy, they'll make you rich. The following chapter deals with how to keep those already in the fold supremely satisfied.

Web Sites, *Wisdom,* and Whimsey

Coupons help sell products. A recent study conducted by an Ohio State University marketing professor revealed that coupons boost response to advertising—even if unused! "Coupons send more than just a discount signal to consumers," says Robert Leone. "A coupon is a draw for somebody to read the rest of the ad." How can you extrapolate that research to your product or service? Take a look at your ads, promotional brochure, and flyer. Do they include a coupon? Use it to beef up sales. Coupons are also very big on the Web. A recent survey showed 55 percent of women had used e-coupons in the past month.

Invoices as marketing tools? Ever give much thought to your invoices and statements—beyond hoping they will be paid quickly, that is? Maybe you should. They can also serve as a marketing communications tool. You could announce an introductory offer for an upcoming service, run a special on slow merchandise, or tie in to a holiday with a feature promotion. Printing directly on the invoice costs you nothing and ensures your message won't be discarded. In fact, it will probably be seen by several people as most invoices pass through a number of hands for payment approval.

●●●●●●●

I was in a sales meeting the other day and completely forgot what I wanted to say. I had to admit, "I've lost my train of thought." (What I didn't tell them is that it doesn't come by the station nearly as often anymore.)

●●●●●●●

Associations have enormous potential. They can purchase your product, recommend it to their members, or hire you to speak at their annual conference or educational workshops. And they usually have highly targeted mailing lists available.

Seven out of 10 people belong to an association. But where do you find out about these organizations? Well, you could head to the library and consult the three-volume *Encyclopedia of Associations.* Another alternative is the *National Trade & Professional Associations of the United States*. It covers 7,500 associations, professional societies, and labor unions, and is indexed in several helpful ways. You can also go online and do a search by entering the subject you want plus the word "association." Happy prospecting.

Want to "feed" your media contacts or "nourish" your favorite client? This yummy site lets you send a gourmet postcard to favorite people. Is an appetizer of caviar or an entree of game hen or lobster and champagne your style? Maybe you're more the peach crepes or baba with rum type. Or perhaps the standbys of popcorn, spaghetti with meatballs, or chicken soup would be your choice. And who could resist white chocolate mousse? These delicacies—plus dozens more—can be e-mailed to your business colleagues, friends, and enemies by simply going to http://mailameal.com. Enough of this; I'm off to dinner!

Mucho marketing strategies available for the asking. I'm immensely impressed with the generosity of the creators of Idea Site for Business. It features 206 marketing suggestions in such categories as unusual marketing ideas, customer service, prospecting, thanking, fax marketing, signage, marketing materials, Web ideas, etc. You can sign on for their A-Marketing-Idea-A-Day-by-E-mail™ for constant encouragement, or read articles such as "Ten easy steps to creating your first E-zine." And I've enjoyed surfing through the section called "How do you market?" Lots of enterprising entrepreneurs offer suggestions of what works for them. Furthermore, press release access to over 1,800 of the nation's top business newspapers and magazines is just a click away. Find it all at http://www.ideasiteforbusiness.com.

●●●●●●●

The problem with punctuality is that
nobody is there to appreciate it.

●●●●●●●

Prospects are everywhere! As female entrepreneurs determined to succeed, we can't afford to turn off our prospecting clock at 5:00 P.M. And why should we when buyers are e-v-e-r-y-w-h-e-r-e? We've made sales or important contacts at a gas station, standing in line to ship a UPS package, and while waiting (and waiting and waiting) to renew a driver's license. Always have business cards with you!

Save money at the post office. Did you know that Priority Mail cardboard flat-rate envelopes are free and go for $3.20 *no matter how much* *you stuff in them?* You can exceed the 2-pound limit and not pay extra. If you've been spending more, start saving a bundle.

Become part of the ongoing Brazen Hussies Network today! At our Web site we run a clearinghouse for forward-thinking female entrepreneurs. You can find over 100 links to powerful women's business and entrepreneurial sites. Business-related books to round-out your professional reading, a free weekly e-mail tip to help boost your bottom line, money-making articles by industry leaders, a classified ad section where you can promote your business, plus much more. Those who join the Network also receive my monthly e-mail newsletter packed with the same kind of information I've been giving you here. And, because there's clout in numbers, I'm also negotiating wonderful cost-saving discounts on products and services Network members can use in their businesses. For full details, go to http://www.BrazenHussiesNetwork.com. I'd love to welcome you as a member!

Insider information on sales reps can be gleaned on the Manufacturers' Agents National Association (MANA) online forum. Point your browser to the Feedback Chat Room of the MANA Bulletin Board at www.MANAonline.org. This organizations serves 5,500 sales agencies and 1,200 manufacturers, mostly in the field of making and selling industrial products. But repping is repping and their publication, *Agency Sales*, which is dubbed the marketing magazine for manufacturers' agencies and their principals, is often full of useful information. Of course, remember that every time someone gets between you and your customer, it either reduces your revenue or increases your operating costs. It also keeps you from getting close to your market, impeding the communication flow that is often essential to excellent customer relations.

How you say it makes ALL the difference: A sales rep was overheard saying, "You can't return this if you keep it past 30 days." How much more positive the statement would have been had he said, "We stand behind our product and we'll provide a full refund withing 30 days." Be careful you don't shoot from the lip…and get mugged by your own mouth.

●●●●●●●

Sign in store window: "Under New Womanagement"

●●●●●●●

Want an hour on the phone with busy execs instead of a few minutes? Sound too good to be true? Not if you put the slides for your executive briefing on your Web site. Then you can call your prospects or customers, ask them to go online, and talk them through your whole sales presentation. Their computer becomes your visual aid. It's much more effective and efficient than calling, then faxing material, and calling again. You can answer their every question immediately. So instead of waiting passively for someone to hit your site, call them up and lead them there!

Selling made smarter on the Web. Http://www.sales.com is a site created by sales professionals for sales professionals. Here you'll find essential tools and services to maximize your time, productivity, and sales. There goal is to dramatically enhance your sales productivity and effectiveness and they offer some powerful tools to do just that. This is a membership site, though for free you can access a hoard of useful data such as their discussion forums. Topics include selling in the millennium, marketing yourself, calling on customers, notes for road warriors, educating your customers, and a rich archive. Browse and benefit.

●●●●●●●

I'm delighted that the weather service has decided to do away with gender bias. What used to be only hurricanes are now also himicanes! In 1999, for instance, there was Katrina, Harvey, Emily, Dennis, Irene, and Floyd.

●●●●●●●

Be perpetually prepared to pitch. Do you carry product samples or brochures in your briefcase, purse, or trunk? If not, start now. Be ready to pitch your product, show it off, and make a sale anytime, anywhere, to anyone!

Are you a road warrior? If business travel seems as constant in your life as getting up in the morning, here are a couple of Web sites that will make things a little easier. Go to Road Warrior International at http://warrior.com. It boasts a wide selection of products for business travelers and a free e-mail newsletter, *Road Warrior News*. At http://www.city.net, maps and other goodies await you. You can even zoom in and magnify certain areas, thus helping you pinpoint destinations and how to reach them.

Looking for a cheap gift to include with mailings? Plantation Products, Inc., sells customized flower seed packets for three to five cents each in bulk quantities. These little gifts can be used to raise funds, renew memberships, motivate purchases, or say thanks. Since virtually everybody likes flowers, the shipping costs are featherweight, and you can devise all sorts of creative tie-ins, this might help your business "blossom." (I couldn't resist that.) Or your tie-in slogan might be "I can help *grow* your business." Their toll-free fax is 800-SEED-PAK; the phone is 508-285-5800.

●●●●●●●

Some say the two times it's appropriate for a woman to be "pushy" is during a sales call…and in the delivery room.

●●●●●●●

Retailer alert: Visit this Web site! If you run a retail store, a site you should bookmark is www.americanexpress.com/retail. Here you'll find an abundance of strategies to help improve your day-to-day operations and best-practice case studies that serve as models. There are articles on how to drive profits, cut costs, improve operations, increase customer satisfaction, and even industry-specific sections on lodging, restaurants, etc., are included. You can also follow industry trends via timely reports and statistical data. American Express offers a bonanza of learning tools here.

Certification of women suppliers opens procurement doors. When Women Business Enterprise National Council (WBENC) polled 765 companies about their supplier programs for women, the response was dismal. Few answered at all and of those that did, 65 percent spent less than 5 percent of vendor dollars with women. WBENC president Susan Phillips Bari is out to change all that. She launched this organization in 1997 to enlarge opportunities in major U.S. business markets for women's business enterprises. The organization was created to meet the need for a national standard of certification for women-owned businesses. Besides the certification process, WBENC helps women write business plans, obtain capital for growth, and seek out new markets for their products and services. For more information, call 202-872-5515 or go online to http://www.womenconnect.com/wbenc.

Make it easy for prospects to buy. To simplify the sales process, offer your customers various payment options. When you accept credit cards, offer layaway programs, time payment plans, or leasing arrangements, you remove payment as a barrier to making a purchase with you. This also lets customers take advantage of specials or seasonal items even if they don't have the available funds.

Attitude is all. We steal from ourselves and others when we settle for mediocrity. Always strive to be outstanding. Never say "I'm *just* a ____." Adjust your attitude. If you believe you can do it, you can!

CHAPTER 15

Providing Awesome Service and Client/Customer Satisfaction

Did you know that women currently make up 80 percent of consumer spending? We purchase more than half the automobiles sold and make the primary health-care decisions in 75 percent of American households. Of course, we also buy more groceries, apparel, and durable goods than men. So we're primarily selling to our sisters, whom we understand better because they are our same gender. It then follows that we should provide superior service as well.

Simply attracting clients and customers isn't enough. The trick is to turn that first-timer into a loyal repeater. Happy, satisfied patrons are the best publicity a business can have. You want them "blinded by delight." Great service happens between two people. Faithful customers singing your praises are better than all the advertising space money can buy. Revenues mushroom with each person who spreads the good word.

What makes some businesses stand out above the crowd? They are customer- or client-focused. Their single guiding principle is the customer comes first. While every company mission statement agrees that keeping customers happy is priority #1, in reality that often doesn't happen. After taking a close look at 100 companies, the British firm PA Consulting came to a sobering conclusion: maximizing profits in the short term is more important to managers than unswerving commitment to customer needs. Thus, many opportunities to gain a competitive edge are squandered. Please, don't *you* be one of those managers! My fervent desire is to see you become outrageously successful. Giving awesome service is a key component to that success.

Why do the Joneses rave about the Lodo Bristo when there are hundreds of other restaurants listed in the Yellow Pages? What makes customers fanatically loyal to a certain online site? Why do the Smiths drive miles out of their way to take Rover to Samantha's Animal Clinic when there are other vets located much closer to home? What is it about Dr. Reed that makes patients actually *look forward* to seeing her? The answer is a simple yet often overlooked key. The stars of the industry know the main difference between them and their competitors is their level of service. They under-promise and over-deliver! That difference spells client or customer retention and keeps clientele and patients coming back.

This chapter looks at creative ways to provide a quality standard of customer service and maintain a high level of satisfaction—whether you're in retail, e-commerce, or are a service provider. We'll explore vital keys that unlock the doors to superior service. Discover how to defuse customer complaints and transform the "problem" into a valuable promotional tool. We include a sample of a client survey, plus you'll also learn how client perceptions and expectations can be employed to your advantage.

A study by the International Customer Service Association found it costs five times as much to win a new customer as it does to keep an old one. I'll show you how to save precious time and make more money by keeping those clients coming back again and again. Finally, we'll look at some unique tactics for "dismissing" an objectionable client who saps your time and vitality.

Keys to Ensuring Satisfaction

Superior service has always been a bestseller. Walt Disney, Ritz Carlton Hotels, Nordstrom's specialty retailer, and L.L. Bean achieved legendary status for placing the customer first. However, this commitment to quality service was the exception rather than the rule. Few utilized this tool to its full potential. Other marketing strategies claimed top priority; the customer's satisfaction took a back seat. Yet the public has not been fooled.

Unfortunately, the biggest black eye has been dealt to the service industry. According to a study by the National Family Opinion for the Consumer Research Center of the Conference Board, service businesses have a serious image problem. In a survey of 6,000 households, they found the "vast majority of consumers believe that they receive good value for their dollar" when purchasing products. However, there is a "rather pervasive discontent with what they get for the money" when they buy services. The biggest offenders include health-care givers, all categories of repair work, lawyers, dentists, banks, and credit card companies.

The landscape is changing on the customer service scene. Americans are demanding high-quality service as never before. Two-career couples find themselves with more available money—at the expense of time.

Survival in today's crowded marketplace depends on the ability to take the pulse of the consumer then supply the needed prescription. In an economy based on businesses that often perform rather than produce, that Rx is outstanding service. The reward is simple—bigger profits.

So what's the first step in gaining a competitive service edge and ensuring customer satisfaction? Start by defining exactly who your clients or customers are. Ask questions. Listen to them. What do they want? What do they need? Then listen some more.

Next develop a strategy that will meet the expectations of those clients. Be sure you're offering top-quality service with no corners cut. Brainstorm creative methods of adding more *value* for the money than your competitors. Enlist employee input in the creative process. Your associates may surprise you with their innovative responses on going that extra mile.

Brittany's Ltd., a Philadelphia dry-cleaning company, found these "extras" the key to whopping success in an often ho-hum field. This progressive firm targeted the needs of the upscale suburbanites in their area. Brittany's rolls out the red carpet in a world where normal service is usually limited to a hanger, plastic bag, and maybe 24-hour cleaning. Included in their perks are pickup and delivery, drive-in windows, and free minor mending. They charge a little more, but customers gladly line up to pay the prices.

"Providing top-notch service is the only inexpensive way small companies have to really distinguish themselves from their competitors and lift themselves above the pack," states John Tschohl, customer-service expert and president of Minnesota-based Better Than Money Corporation. "Customers expect small firms to be closer to them and to deliver better service."

Now take a good look in the mirror. First impressions are vital and can make all the difference in influencing the first-timer. Businesses need to consider what their "looks" are telling prospects. Walk your premises and observe what your patrons see.

Consider the corner automobile repair shop. The mechanics may be first class, but what do the customers actually see? Is it a grubby waiting area, greasy chairs, and a filthy water cooler? Spruce up the room. Add a few plants and paintings; provide complimentary coffee, tea, cocoa, or cider; and set out some diversified reading material. Customers will find waiting for repairs easier, and their impression of the entire operation will jump dramatically.

Once the service strategy is in place, train the front-line troops in the battle plan. Let employees know the policies and how they will be implemented. Give them the ammunition to do their job effectively. Send them to seminars, do in-house training, provide books or cassette tapes, and (most importantly) set a positive example.

Maryanne and John McCormack own the Houston-based Visible Changes hair salons. They hold motivational classes designed to enhance employees' service-oriented attitudes and build confidence. Periodic refresher training keeps the stylists up-to-date and on top of current trends. John believes if you take care of your employees, they will take care of your customers.

"The first step is setting the standards," he explains. "Then make sure everybody in the company understands those standards. Finally, reward people for achieving your standards and goals. If you reward your associates for superior performance, then your customers are going to get the service you ultimately wish to deliver."

Employee empowerment is crucial. When a customer service rep says, I"ll have to talk to my boss," it's like throwing cold water on a budding romance. Workers need to be knowledgeable about the company; then they can make intelligent decisions and solve customer problems effectively and fast. When your employees are entrusted with insider facts (what it costs to gain a new customer and what actual profit percentages are, for instance) they feel more like partners and will act accordingly.

Firms with only one, two, or three employees may think this aspect is not as important for them. Wrong. In fact, it may be of even greater importance. Those few employees are the only contacts (besides you) the clients have with your firm. The first face a patient sees at a dentist's office is the receptionist. A rude or indifferent attitude sets the tone for the entire visit. The dentist might be topnotch in the field, but the patient only remembers an uncaring experience. The next time dental care is needed the person goes to Dr. Smith down the street. After all, Aunt Betty thinks he's great.

Reward associates who display a strong customer orientation. Positive recognition reinforces their behavior, guaranteeing a happy employee and a satisfied patron. The reward needn't be financial either. A word of praise in front of coworkers, a complimentary handwritten note, or a special lunch after successfully handling a difficult client—these small efforts build team spirit and show you are serious about the customer strategy.

Outstanding customer service delivered by *others* could result in an unusual solution for your personnel needs. Blayne Blowers of the laundry chain, Clean Duds, uses it as a clever hiring tool. Blowers watches for people who are sincere, responsive, have a friendly smile, and enjoy serving. When he finds such an individual, he hands that person a card that reads, "I was impressed by your service. If you're ever looking for a job, please call me." This has proven to be a wonderful way to prospect for those who already appreciate the value of good customer service.

Communicate to Captivate

No, the customer isn't *always* right. But it's easier and more cost-effective to please a current customer than to develop a new one. Those with problems left unresolved will beat a path straight to the competition, bad-mouthing you all the way.

A study by the Technical Assistance Research Programs Institute (TARP) found 91 percent of unhappy customers will never again purchase the services of the offending firm and will tell their tale of woe to at least nine other people! The upside of that study shows 54 to 70 percent of customers who complain will do business with the firm again if the complaint is resolved satisfactorily. If the client feels the problem is speedily handled, the figure jumps to a whopping 95 percent.

No matter what you do and how well you do it, there will be times when people are dissatisfied. Perhaps a Webmaster is slow to make needed changes. Or a person is unhappy with the way a garment washes. Maybe a print job is done on the wrong color of paper; or a service representative is tactless. These are just a few of the problems that plague every business from time to time. Each seems insignificant by itself. Yet they can form an extremely damaging pattern that can erode the profits of your business. If not resolved in a favorable way, not only do you lose the dissatisfied customer, your business will suffer as he or she relates the story of your unfair practices. It's important to fix the problem—not the blame.

Web customer service is becoming a big issue. Just as shopping can be done 7/24, most online consumers expect help 24 hours a day as well. There is a new saying: "It's midnight. Do you know where your tech support is?" Great online service doesn't happen just with money and gee-whiz technology. It's about commitment and establishing trust. While automatic responders can handle some situations, personal e-mails or phone calls are dictated by others. People want customer-service reps who can think and talk…like those super friendly greeters at Wal-Mart. Toy seller Zany Brainy counts on live and capable online representatives to keep its customers smiling. Lands' End also relies on the personal touch to make themselves stand out.

At some sites live human beings personally greet each visitor with a typed offer of help or are on hand to instantly answer typed questions. For those who appreciate a human voice, a few aggressive online merchants have equipped their sites with Internet-telephone capability. Shoppers can look at merchandise and talk to a sales rep at the same time.

If you're an e-tailer, remember that Web shoppers expect good service. During the 1999 holiday season, use of customer support hit record levels with over 27 percent of participants requesting it. Yet the overall customer support experience was dismal. Several major companies were unwilling or unable to deliver purchases in time for Christmas. As cyberspace ventures compete with brick-and-mortar stores, customer satisfaction may be the defining factor in their longevity.

In a study conducted by Consumer Research Network, neighborhood stores were the gold standard when it came to customer friendliness: treating customers with respect and offering good customer service. They received a 75 percent favorable rating; next in line was amazon.com with 65 percent.

310

Handling Objections With Finesse

So how do you handle customer objections? If the complaint is in person or over the telephone, the first rule is to let the person have their say without interrupting. If the incident takes place in a public area, you may want to invite the individual into your office or a secluded area so other customers don't overhear any tirades. Keep the person talking by asking open-ended questions. Use such words as *which, why, what, when,* and *where.* Resist the natural urge to become defensive. Instead, try to really *listen* and understand what the person is saying. Don't offer a solution until the individual has had time to vocalize all his or her feelings.

Employing good communications skills helps assure the customer you are listening attentively. Make direct eye contact, nod occasionally in response to their story, and if seated, lean forward slightly in the chair. This effective use of body language conveys the message "I care about you and your problem." Be sympathetic in your initial reply: "I can certainly understand why you're unhappy, Mrs. Jones. I'd feel the same way in your place." This kind of response will take the angry wind out of most people's sails and make them much more reasonable.

Now continue by asking, "What can I do to make things right with you?" This is a very important question. If you don't find out what they want, you're playing a guessing game on solving the problem. You might volunteer more than you need to! Mrs. Jones may only expect you to repair a ripped carpet seam, so why offer to give her a big discount if that isn't her expectation?

On the other hand, going beyond customer expectations can be a powerful tool. Stew Leonard encourages his employees to go beyond the call of duty when dealing with problems. The spirit of customer service reigns supreme in both his 100,000 square-foot dairy store in Norwalk, Connecticut, and a farmer's market in Danbury. One evening the manager of the market found a note that had been stuffed in a counter suggestion box only a half-hour earlier: "I'm upset. I made a special stop on my way home from work to buy chicken breasts for dinner, but you're sold out and now I'll have to eat a TV dinner instead." As he read the note, up rolled the poultry delivery truck. Five minutes later a complimentary two-pound package of fresh chicken breasts was on its way to the customer's door in an employee's car. This example of going the extra mile did more than soothe an angry customer. It transformed her into a loyal repeater who tells her friends and neighbors what a wonderful place the market is to shop.

As the TARP study showed, the key to customer retention is a *speedy* solution. The moving company that requires weeks or even months, plus tons of paperwork, to settle an insurance claim on a missing box will not win points. Although the customer will eventually be reimbursed, it is unlikely she will dial their number again. Neither will her friends.

Offering the irate customer a choice of possible solutions often solves the problem on the spot. If Mrs. Smith doesn't like her motel room, let her take her pick of two other available rooms. If the flyers have been printed on the wrong colored paper, ask if they would like you to quickly reprint the job correctly or would they rather take the order at a reduced rate?

If you discover an employee was rude, an apology to the customer (preferably by the offender) will create a lot of goodwill. Although everyone can have an off day occasionally, rudeness cannot be tolerated in a firm committed to customer satisfaction. Make sure the employee understands your policies in dealing with the public. If the offense reoccurs, it's time to replace that person with someone who enjoys interacting with the public.

When something has gone badly wrong, never hesitate to apologize. "I'm sorry" are two of the most healing words in the English language. (Did you hear about the guy who crossed a parrot with a pigeon...and got a bird that apologizes for what he does on your car?)

Customer complaints may also arrive via the mail. Again, the emphasis is placed on speed. Consider calling the person immediately rather than responding by writing a letter. It's a sound investment in client satisfaction. Almost everyone has a horror story of a computer billing error and the nightmare of correcting the problem. Phoning the customer with a billing complaint assures him or her that a *real person* is indeed working on the problem versus an endless trip on a computer merry-go-round.

Most people don't expect more than what is fair. They just want "what they paid for" in the shortest possible amount of time. A caring attitude combined with a dash of respect goes a long way in soothing angry feelings. However, there is a small percentage of complainers who are grasping, unreasonable people. You must make a decision about them: Either give in to their demands and pass it off as the price of doing business, or be willing to suffer their ill will and the resulting abuse to your reputation. Weigh the costs before you decide. You may have your fill of dealing with Mr. Brown, but are you ready to risk the unknown number of potential clients he might influence?

The vast majority of customer objections are justified. In fact, complaints should be considered a valuable resource. Handled well, they offer an opportunity to pinpoint problems, make amends, and develop renewed and intensified customer loyalty.

Managing Constituent Expectations

There are times when the old adage "what you see is what you get" isn't worth the paper it's written on. When dealing with the buying public, the truth reads "what I *feel* is what I've got." The client/customer's *perception* is the final factor in how she or he views the quality of service received. Unfortunately, many smaller businesses and professional firms fail to understand that customer expectations and perceptions play a pivotal role in their success. This vital facet of quality service is a basic prerequisite in any well-rounded strategy.

There is a distinct difference between perception and reality, as is pointed out by media trainer Joel Roberts in a story he tells about his Jewish grandmother: The proud grandmother was out with the baby in a stroller. A stranger walked by and commented, "What a cute baby!"

"This?" retorted the grandmother. "This is nothing. You should see his picture!"

Let us look at two situations: Mrs. Smith drops her shoes off at the ABC Repair Shop. The clerk promises they will be ready in two days. When Mrs. Smith arrives to pick them up, she discovers they won't be done for another day.

Mr. Doe leaves his shoes at the XYZ Repair Shop. The clerk promises they will be ready in five days. But on the third day the clerk calls and says, "Mr. Doe, your shoes are ready. You can pick them up anytime."

Both pairs of shoes were repaired with the same level of care and expertise. Both were ready in three days. However, Mrs. Smith is not pleased with ABC. She feels misused and abused. Mr. Doe, on the other hand, believes XYZ is wonderful. He thinks he's been given special treatment. By managing expectations, the second shop appears more professional, more capable, more caring.

If customers expect too much from your firm, satisfaction will suffer when you can't deliver. If your service is promoted as top of the line but turns out to be mediocre, your clients will feel cheated.

Savvy businesswomen use customer perceptions to their advantage. The key is to be realistic. Don't promise more than you can do. Don't sell what you can't deliver.

The bottom line is respect—respect yourself and the customer. Clients don't like delays or problems, but they will deal with them far better if treated honestly. Be up front and as specific as possible. Make sure your actions match your words. Treat your customers the way you would like to be treated in the same circumstance.

Warren Blanding of the Customer Service Institute, a Maryland-based educational and training organization, points out the missing link in service is usually the customer point of view. "The secret of good service is to do things for a customer the way that customer would do them if given the opportunity," he adds.

Lillian Vernon is a prime example of a business leader who really listens to her customers. A few years ago when paper and postage prices went up, she decided to cut back on the number of pages in her Lillian Vernon catalogs and even stopped sending one catalog of sale items entirely. By auditing customer calls, she "realized that our reaction to this setback was all wrong. Neither of our actions was a good decision. I reversed them in short time," says Vernon.

Of even more consequence was a decision to sell more expensive items because the company's overhead had gone up. Customers again signaled their displeasure. "People look to us for practical, hands-on 'happiness' items," Vernon explains. It's these little extras, from $10 to $40, that customers longed for, she learned. So the prices came down and the value went up. It's that kind of attitude and sensitivity to consumer desires that has allowed her to build a $250-million specialty online and catalog business.

How is your firm's "body language" molding client expectations? The environment surrounding your firm correlates directly with customer perceptions. A badly designed office makes one wonder about the capabilities of an architect. An uninformed employee speaks poorly of the art gallery in which she's employed. What person wants to sit in the chair of a beautician with a bad haircut?

Physical criteria can signal either a red or green light to clients. Voice mail that makes it virtually impossible to reach a human being screams "poor service!" Well-groomed employees, an upscale office, and professional attitudes bespeak quality. Customers may not consciously notice the subtle environmental factors, but the unconscious mind reads them loud and clear.

Measuring Your Effectiveness With Research and Surveys

In order to manage expectations, you must first discover how your customers or clients feel about your products or services in the here and now. The only way to do that accurately is through research. Unfortunately, many firms assume they already know what their customers think. This is a "fatal flaw," according to Karen Gershowitz, senior vice president of BAI, a Tarrytown, New York, marketing consulting and research firm. "Often an outsider will see something the company takes for granted."

Resistance to research is greatest among professional service providers. The tradition of protecting client relationships among lawyers, accountants, and others often interferes with the measurement of client satisfaction. The answer is to conduct research in-house.

There are methods for discovering the truth. Focus groups and in-depth personal and telephone interviews are particularly revealing. You bump into problems you didn't know you had. It never hurts to ask the customer, "How do you feel about me? How have I failed you?"

We recently used a written survey to scrutinize the performance of About Books, Inc., and provide our clients with continuous improvement. We had a more than 25 percent return. It not only made us aware of our strengths and areas for improvement, but helped our clients feel as if they're part of the team. You might want to use the following survey as a model for creating one of your own.

The Savings and Loan Network, a small Chicago-based company that markets financial services to savings and loans, recently surveyed about 25 customers by telephone. The hoped-for result was to discover why they weren't getting as many deals as they'd predicted. Those 25 calls were all it took. A few policy changes later, they were back on target.

Surveys can take many forms. Maxine Clark is chief executive bear of St. Louis–based Build-A-Bear Workshop, an interactive retail experience store where kids and adults go to create their own furry friends from scratch. She wants customers to have an un"bear"able experience in the 14 existing facilities. (Hundreds are planned by 2007.) To keep employees customer-focused, Build-A-Bear sends out surveys of employee performance to at least 40 customers in each store every week. Employees who score a rating of at least 80 percent on the five key questions earn a bonus. The forward thinking Clark has applied to her

---

about books inc.

(719) 395-2459 • fax: (719) 395-8374
http://www.About-Books.com • e-mail: ABI@About-Books.com
P.O. Box 1500 • 425 Cedar Street • Buena Vista, CO 81211-1500

How are we doing? In an effort to provide our clients with continuous quality improvement, we'd greatly appreciate your feedback on how you feel about our performance on your book project. Won't you take 10 minutes to complete this brief questionnaire? As a token of our appreciation, we'll send you a complimentary gift book that will be fun to use yourself—or pass on to someone else. For your convenience, a self-addressed envelope is enclosed. Please rank items 1-10 (10 being the highest) or n/a for not applicable. Thanks so much for your help!

Value of project evaluation/manuscript critique _____

Handling of pre-publication functions _____

Effectiveness of editing _____

Caliber of cover design _____

Quality of interior design and typesetting _____

Quality of printing _____

Satisfaction with written promotional materials _____

Effectiveness of national marketing plan _____

Value received for dollars invested _____

Timeliness of turn-around _____

Availability of key personnel to answer your questions _____

Prompt response to your needs _____

Attitude of caring by About Books, Inc. staff _____

Overall satisfaction _____

What you liked best in dealing with ABI: _____

What you liked least: _____

Are there other ways we could be of service to you? _____

Suggestions on how we can improve and serve you better: _____

Name and address (optional): _____

---

venture has earned her the coveted Arthur Andersen Best Practices Award™.

The Applebee's restaurant chain takes its business very seriously. "Our restaurants are about more than food," a spokesperson comments. "They're about inclusiveness, value, comfort, trust, and relationships." To make sure that agenda is being put forward, randomly selected guests get a coupon they can redeem by calling a toll-free number and sharing input on a number of topics: speed of service, taste of food, cleanliness of restrooms, etc. This data helps the company stay on track of big-picture trends and quickly fix specific problems.

Within minutes someone is on the phone trying to right any wrongs. Whenever a "very poor" response is given, a live operator comes on the line offering to connect the guest with a customer-service rep or with

316

the manager of the offending restaurant. Managers are instructed to do whatever it takes to regain a guest's goodwill. (They have been known to give away theater tickets or send flowers.)

American Express mails a survey to customers who have complained. Included are questions concerning courtesy, competence, and whether the problem was handled correctly. Overall service is also measured. Hotels commonly employ the in-room survey, that familiar little card asking questions about the stay. Restaurants likewise poll their patrons. Virtually any firm can tuck a questionnaire in with the monthly billing. (A tip: For a bigger response, offer a small percentage off the bill if the survey is completed and returned with the payment.)

What are the most important characteristics to measure? Researchers with the Marketing Science Institute quizzed customers from a wide range of service business. They found clients of everyone from lawyers to repair firms look for five items to assure satisfaction:

1. *Reliability*. The number one concern of customers is the ability to perform dependably, accurately, and consistently. Always, always keep your promises!

2. *Responsiveness*. Prompt service and a helpful attitude.

3. *Assurance*. Knowledgeable and courteous employees who convey confidence.

4. *Empathy*. Individualized attention and a sympathetic ear.

5. *Tangibles*. Physical facilities and equipment and well-groomed employees.

Now you can conduct surveys online for free! Using the site template and your list of e-mail recipients, you can custom design and deliver your own questionnaires. The results are even tabulated in real time. Zoomerang tallies the responses with percentages and bar charts for each question. To get all the details go to www.zoomerang.com.

Once customer feedback is tabulated, evaluate the results. Is the information about something you can change? Explore creative options. Share the results with the right people. The repair crew can only alter factors under their control. Correct any highlighted weaknesses. Remember, research is conducted to understand customer satisfaction, not to place blame after you have received the results. When you point your finger at someone else, three fingers point back at you!

Want Customer Loyalty? Treat 'Em Like Royalty

Perception is everything. If your clients or customers feel you are going beyond the call of duty, they are much more likely to be loyal. According to research by the Chicago-based International Customer Service Association, fully 68 percent of customers stop doing business with a company due to a perception of poor service. With it being five times harder to recruit a new customer than to please an existing one, we simply can't afford to lose that business! What are some ways we can please and appease?

Consider instituting a frequent buyer program for your consumer or back-to-back customers. On their third purchase, for instance, give them a coupon for a 25 percent discount on their next purchase.

If applicable, offer free gift wrapping. In our busy world such time-saving gestures are noted and appreciated.

Be sure your Web site has a human touch. Include complete contact information so folks can reach you via the method of their choice. People like to know they're dealing with other *people*, not just an impersonal computer. Include personal photos and short bios.

(continued on next page)

The Value of Customer/ Client Retention

I've spent a lot of time in this book showing you how to acquire customers. The other side of the coin is knowing how to keep them. The "once you've got 'em, forget 'em" attitude is financial suicide. Customers are not disposable commodities. Unlike paper plates or napkins, you can't use them once, then toss them aside. That may seem like ordinary common sense, but it's a fact many tend to forget.

The emphasis in many marketing plans is on attracting new clients rather than on retaining the current ones. However, the brightest prospects for future business are present customers. The American Management Association says that 65 percent of the average company's business comes from its existing, satisfied patrons.

It's clearly a smart move to invest company energy into a comprehensive *internal* marketing program. Keeping the current customer happy and satisfied is not always easy but it's certainly profitable.

Hotels offer a prime example. Teri spends a relaxing weekend at City Hotel. The service was excellent, the room a delight, and she couldn't have asked for a friendlier staff. Guess where Teri now stays every time she comes to the city? She sings their praises to Uncle Joe and her business partner and they, too, stay at City

Hotel when in town. What did it cost the hotel? Merely the investment to attract Teri to register that first time.

On the other hand, Pete stays a few days at Town Hotel and is miserable the entire time. The room was too hot, the restaurant was below par, and he couldn't find help when he needed it. Pete will not return. It's back to square one for Town Hotel. They not only lost the chance for a repeat customer, they forfeited any referrals he might have sent their way.

Because service is such an intangible commodity, it is even more important for those within this universe to maintain a close alliance with their clients. Performance ratings are often elusive—unlike the product that either works or it doesn't. How does a client judge the quality of his or her lawyer amidst a bewildering jumble of papers and briefs? That call is influenced largely by the *relationship* between the two. Does the attorney seem to care about me and my problem? Are telephone messages, e-mail, and correspondence answered promptly? Is the lawyer there when I need help? Often, the only difference between lawyer A and lawyer B is common courtesy and service.

By holding the hand of today's customer, you're ensuring tomorrow's success. If you've already installed a topnotch service strategy to keep people happy, you've taken a giant step in the right direction. Developing a strong service culture in itself draws customers back. Regard it as an

---

WANT CUSTOMER LOYALTY? TREAT 'EM LIKE ROYALTY
(continued)

Stay in touch with your good customers. Invest in a software program for creating greeting cards. Then you can even personalize the message. Many holidays lend themselves to a business greeting. For Valentine's Day you could say, "We just *love* to send greetings to our favorite customers!" How about doing something creative for Halloween? Thanksgiving is the perfect time to express your appreciation for their business.

And don't forget your trade accounts. Offering free freight for a short period—and playing on the fact this is because you are grateful for the merchandise they sell for you—will certainly ring a responsive bell.

If you work with an exclusive distributor, they are your biggest customer. Yet you've probably never thought of them in that way. Start right now to look for ways to show your thankfulness for their good work. Then *you'll* be more likely to be remembered fondly.

If you don't have what a customer wants in stock, get it! Place a special rush order. An alternative, if they must have the item immediately, is to refer them to another local merchant. While you'll lose that particular sale, you'll build outrageous goodwill with both the consumer and the other store.

(continued on next page)

Be flexible. While the big guys are locked into airtight "company policies" you have an edge because you can choose to bend the rules. Maybe they want a special billing cycle, an unusual delivery schedule, or some latitude on pricing. By doing things partly on *their* terms, you've invited them to sit at your round table.

When there is a problem, not only meet—but exceed—your customer's expectations. Patiently get a clear picture of what the problem is, ask them what they would like to have done about it, then do anything reasonable (even *un*reasonable) to accommodate them.

Extraordinary customer service leads to additional sales. If you want customer loyalty, treat 'em like royalty. You'll end up ruling over an exceedingly happy kingdom.

investment in future profits. Hyundai does. Before they sold a single car on American soil, they implemented an advance customer communication program.

People buy relationships. That's what service is all about: a caring, serving attitude. Keeping customers content involves maintaining a continual positive association. Loyalty to a brand, store, or vendor isn't the motivating factor it was 20 years ago. Cultivating the allegiance of customers is a high-priority marketing move. The client should feel a close association with your firm even when she or he does not immediately need your services.

Often it's the little things that make the difference. Let customers know they're appreciated. Call or write and say thanks for their business. That's standard practice for a small business in Redwood City, California, that sells shortwave radios. Grundig follows up every sale with a personalized letter that gives toll-free numbers for customer service hotlines, a thank-you for the order, and an offer to buy from Grundig again. To encourage repeat sales the letter's postscript contains a special discount.

It's prudent to acknowledge any large or out-of-the-ordinary orders. Professionals should personally welcome each new client to the practice. Create a list of birthdays, anniversaries, and other important dates and congratulate people on those special days. Forward newspaper or magazine articles that might be of interest. Use any means to *stay in contact* and in the customer's mind.

"Servicing your accounts" is sales terminology, but the technique is viable for everyone in your organization. Call and suggest further service. Would the new mother be interested in an aerobics class held evenings at the hospital? Now that summer's here, does Jane need a pair of prescription sunglasses? Does Steve's will need to be updated since he's remarried?

Encourage feedback. Elicit comments concerning existing services and ways they could be improved. Invite ideas about how your approach might be improved. Thoughts on any additional services could boost your business, because suggestions are truly from the customer's point of view. Tips on what they want or need can open up new profit centers for your business.

So you've sent the thank-yous and clipped and mailed interesting articles. But the client hasn't darkened the door of your establishment in ages. It's time to take the direct approach. Call. Say, "Mr. Smith, we miss you. Is there a reason we haven't seen you lately?" He may have a very good reason—one you somehow overlooked. Perhaps the factors involved are completely out of your control. Whatever the cause, don't lose a customer or client without a good fight.

Going Beyond the Call of Duty

Quality means offering the best service you can possibly render. Half-hearted efforts won't stand a chance with today's smart, sophisticated consumers. Quality, combined with reliability, is the answer. Harley-Davidson discovered this a while back. A variety of problems plagued its motorcycles. At the same time, a wave of reliable machines rolled in from Japan. The company came very close to disaster.

"We learned a painful, but vital lesson: Your product is the most vital relationship you have with a customer," explains Vaughn Beals, former CEO of Harley-Davidson. "If you let anything disturb that relationship, trouble will follow." The company rallied, thanks to customer input and an internal commitment to quality. "But we don't take our comeback for granted," Beals adds. "If we ever fail to deliver what the customer wants, we'll be right back where we started."

Another side to the service coin is follow-up. The shining stars of the industry emphasize its importance. Mini Maid Services contacts every single customer the day after they receive cleaning. All comments are recorded, evaluated, and placed in the hands of the employees who performed the service. Customers are pleased, and employees have a yardstick to measure customer perception of their work.

Home Depot has instituted an in-store "University." This free, hands-on instructional program demonstrates to customers how they can plan and complete various improvement projects for the home. Six subjects are offered, each with four classes. Not only does this generate considerable goodwill, but it also increases the frequency of store visits by quite a magnitude. Additionally, it brings in new customers drawn from friends who participated in the program and recommend it.

Going above and beyond often means taking a critical look at the hiring process. Daniel Krumm, chairman and CEO of Maytag Corporation, points to *people* as the key ingredient in producing quality. "We preach quality throughout the organization, and hire the best people we can," he says. "They understand the importance of quality to our success and to their own job security."

Stew Leonard, owner of "the world's largest dairy store" in Norwalk, Connecticut, interviews 15 to 25 applicants to find the right person for each position. What makes an individual special? According to Leonard, it's attitude. "The main thing our director of personnel looks for is a good attitude—above experience, skills, training, education, or appearance," he explains. "If applicants have a good attitude, we can give them the rest."

Just what does this service cheerleader give his employees? The answer is training. By sending them to seminars, providing tapes and books, and giving in-house training, Leonard molds employees into service-conscious helpers. "But if they have a bad attitude to start with, everything we try to do seems to fail," he adds. What employee traits complement your business or profession? Do you need enthusiasm, empathy, or simply that "right attitude?" Before you read a single resume, make a list of what you (and your customers) need in that new employee.

Take a look at company policies. In fact, take a good look at the word *policy* itself. It's from the same root word as police. Are you servicing your customers or "policing" them? Are you punishing the 99 percent of your clients who are good, honest people simply because of a dishonest 1 percent? Stop and consider each customer on an individual level. If you need a policy, keep it short and simple. Customers don't want a policy, they want a person who listens, cares, and can *do something* about their concerns.

Providing outstanding service also means offering it to all segments of society. Can someone in a wheelchair reach your office or business? Can the elderly master any stairs in the process? The disabled and mature citizens are powerful economic forces who are no longer sitting quietly on the sidelines. Do you want their patronage? Then remember their special needs.

The Greyhound Bus Company targets those requirements in its Helping Hand program. If a handicapped person needs assistance in traveling, a companion may ride free. Wheelchairs, crutches, and walkers are carried in the baggage compartment without extra charge.

Modern technology has boosted expectations when it comes to communications. Customers demand an immediate response to their inquiries, or they'll let their fingers do the walking. From necessity, doctors were among the first to utilize paging devices. Nowadays, everyone from real estate appraisers to interior decorators to contractors use cell phones to keep in close contact with the office or the job and their customers.

A repairperson needn't stop by the office or even be near a telephone to receive instantaneous messages. Have the water pipes burst at Mrs. Remer's? Is the basement rapidly filling with water? Getting your worker to her emergency in record time will ensure a loyal customer. And couriers can receive last minute instructions whether they're walking down the street or picking up a package in a building.

Cell telephones have revolutionized our ability to communicate. Users can drive from New York to Los Angeles with very little disruption in service. According to the Cellular Telecommunications Industry Association, the average charge for the ability to maintain direct customer contact is $97 per month. For those traveling in distant cities, Hertz, National, Budget, and Dollar car rentals offer this option in their autos.

How often do you pick up the phone and dial a toll-free number? AT&T's toll-free directory is now larger than the telephone books in some major cities. Customers have come to expect this method of contacting businesses. They reason that the company should pick up the tab for inquiries or orders, not the customer. Have they got a point? If you deal with out-of-town buyers, this option may be for you. Many companies are realizing that providing a toll-free number for repair and service inquiries also makes sense.

A competitive edge guaranteed to increase customer satisfaction is the fulfillment of rush or special orders. When a frantic client calls asking for air-conditioning repair by 5:00 P.M. because she is having an anniversary party and it's 95 degrees out, opportunity is knocking at the door. Make that repair and appreciation soars. Consider what other arrangements are feasible and how much they will cost. Then inform the client of the charge for this extraordinary service. Whether it's a repair, the advice of a consultant, or a vital machinery part, most customers will gladly pay more to get what they need. And the company comes out looking like a winner.

Whatever your business or profession, take the initiative and go that extra mile. You don't need to be the size of IBM or Maytag to share in their shining reputation for service. Catering to customers and clients fulfills their needs and launches your firm on a steady road to success. Believe in customer satisfaction. Become a fanatic! When you let your enthusiasm for the cause grow, so will your company and your bank account.

Pulling the Plug on Obnoxious Clients

The best way to handle this situation is to avoid it in the first place. By going with your gut and identifying the best prospects, you build a client roster that is a joy to serve. You might try focusing on the *characteristics* of people you want as clients versus their profession. Become comfortable saying "no" to those things you intuit will lead to a loss of vitality or to projects that don't thrill you. If it feels like it isn't a good fit, it probably isn't. The prospect who haggles or is difficult from the beginning only gets worse.

But we all make lousy judgment calls from time to time. Regardless of what business you are in, there will come a time when you need to "fire" a client. It's not always an easy decision, but it often can be the best—and only—way to go.

If you have a client who is disrespectful or abusive to you or your staff, this can cause a lot of stress in the workplace. Good associates don't deserve such treatment. It should be dealt with swiftly and decisively when it does occur. It is the responsibility of the business owner to intervene and advise the client that this type of behavior is not acceptable. Each member of your staff should be treated with respect and dignity.

Then, too, some clients are time-wasters. They call 30 times a day for no reason. They make silly requests that take extra time. If you have a client who needs to be baby-sat, it might be best to simply pull the plug and part company. Perhaps you can suggest another professional with whom this person can work.

In over 23 years and hundreds of clients, we've had to fire three of them. Each was a tough decision to make. But after weighing all options it became obvious to continue working with these people would be counterproductive for both us—and them. It's impossible to do a superior job for someone who is rude or excessively demanding. Better to cut your losses and refocus that energy in a positive direction. A suggested way to end the relationship is to say something like, "It seems we can't give you all the personal attention you deserve. So I think it would be best for both of us if you find someone who can."

Last, but far from least, it's time to look at some other techniques spunky ladies use to magnify their bottom lines. There are no boundaries for today's businesswoman. We can kick butt. Be pioneers. Best the guys who were supposed to be the sharpest knives in the drawer. Go forth and multiply (your methods of marketing)!

Web Sites, Wisdom, and Whimsey

Need a reminder for important follow-up dates, customer birthdays, or prioritized "to do" lists? Then you'll be delighted to learn about eOrganizer, your free personal online electronic organizer. Simply customize it for your needs and this nifty site will nudge you via e-mail on the morning of any must-dos. In addition to providing space for tasks, appointments, and special days, eOrganizer lets you enter names and addresses of key contacts. So if you need access to these people when away from home or office, just bring the site up on your laptop. Find it all at http://www.eorganizer.com.

●●●●●●●

Good enough never is.

—Debbi Field of Mrs. Field's Cookies

●●●●●●●

It's a matter of attitude. The cost of indifference is staggering. A recent survey by the federal government determined why people stopped doing business with service organizations. The primary reason—68 percent—was indifference on the part of the owner, a sales representative, or other employee. Attitude matters!

A fun approach to serious business resides on the Web at http://www.ideacafe.com/. Idea Café started dishing up tasty biz fare in 1995; today they serve it fast, fresh, and friendly. Their menu of biz categories to feast on includes: marketing and sales, starting a business, running one, financing your company, worldwide business information, and lots more. Stop by and see what's cool.

Another site offers solutions for growing businesses. The day I visited, on the home page was a new section called "Women in Business." It included an exclusive lifestyle Q&A, leadership school, divas in residence, and discussions. This site offers roughly 350 downloadable business forms and lots of solid tools. Their "Ask the Experts" section features 14 authorities who dispense worthwhile advice. Check it out for yourself at www.allbusiness.com.

Want a no-cost bonus for good customers? Consider VIP parking. If you have a parking lot anyway, it costs you virtually nothing to surprise good customers, patients, or guests with this perk. Simply prepare a few signs that say "Parking for VIP Members Only." Post them in the most convenient location. Also print small decals to put in car windows that say "VIP Parking." (Include your store name in small letters.) Make a big deal out of presenting these to your customers and watch the grins spread.

●●●●●●●

How many customer service reps does it take to set the clock on a VCR? No one knows because they can never find the time.

●●●●●●●

Combining customer service with shrewd merchandising. Anyone who has driven cross-country has noticed the Cracker Barrel signs along the highway…and probably yielded to the temptation to try one. This chain of old country stores/restaurants encourages travelers to partake of a Cracker Barrel further down the road by renting audio books that are returnable for credit or exchange at any other outlet.

Applaud outstanding customer service with your business card. On the back of my business card I've developed a preprinted mini form that gives accolades to service people who excel. It thanks them for doing a super job, says that their actions show they care about people and take pride in their job. It also suggests that their boss is lucky to have them and to share the card with her or him. I sign the cards before they go to print, then simply add the current date as needed. I've doled them out to servers in restaurants, to saleswomen at boutiques, clerks in stores, employees at home improvement centers, etc. What a joy to sincerely acknowledge a stranger. (And I had one waitress confess to me upon presentation of a second card that the first one resides proudly in her jewelry box.)

●●●●●●●

Have you heard the new word, "Petaphobic?" It describes a person who is embarrassed to undress in front of a household pet.

●●●●●●●

Need professional guidance? SCExperts is a service offered by New York University's School of Continuing Education. Their faculty of 1,300 members consists of professionals who practice what they teach on a daily basis. For more details visit their Web site at www.sce.nyu.edu/dyncon/abus and click on "press kit." Or call 212-998-7070 and ask for SCExperts.

Kick the "but" out of your vocabulary. The advice I give here is something I continue to try and apply. It's sound, but not easy. There are two little three-letter words in our language that, when interchanged, can make a huge difference. They are "and" and "but." When you give a compliment, then connect it with "but" it becomes watered down and negative: "You did a great job on that report BUT I need it sooner next time." How much nicer it comes across if you say, "You did a great job on that report AND I need it sooner next time." If you tell a customer, "I can get that merchandise for you BUT the service charge will be $4" you don't sound like a heroine. Yet if you put it, "I can get that merchandise for you AND the service charge will be $4" you seem to be much more accommodating. It's only one little word BUT it makes a big difference!

CHAPTER 16

Other Techniques
Spunky Ladies Use to
Magnify the Bottom Line

It's rare that a single magic solution makes a person a fortune. It's a process—a lot of ideas that combine to generate colossal cash flow. There are literally hundreds of ways to market a product or service. We've looked at many of them: the unconventional and conventional, the ethical and risqué, the complicated and the simple, the common and the crazy.

In this chapter you'll find an eclectic collection of tips and techniques to make your job easier and your results extraordinary. Discover here why it's smart to make your occupation your preoccupation. What about putting a twist in the same old thing to gain greater exposure? I discuss this, plus details on how to establish a strong board of directors. A grab bag of good ideas is also presented, as are recommendations on how to balance entrepreneurial significance with personal time and pleasures.

Telephone Tricks

For some businesses, the telephone is their lifeline. Even if your enterprise doesn't depend primarily on Mr. Bell's invention, there are

Ross's Rules of Order: 25 Wow! Marketing Strategies

- Find an angle that makes you controversial
- Do radio phone interviews originating from your home or office
- Go after all TV (few can crack Oprah or Letterman)
- Pursue newspaper features about your business
- Write op-ed pieces addressing the subject
- Submit letters to the editor piggybacking on related articles
- Plant news items with local newspaper/magazine columnists
- Provide gratis articles to national magazines
- Solicit plugs in newsletters
- Go after mentions in nationally syndicated columns
- Write articles for corporations' internal publications
- Develop alliances with complementary associations
- Request testimonials from leaders in the industry
- Create a sales flyer and customer order form
- Prepare a "Here's What People Are Saying" flyer of favorable testimonials
- Generate a mailing list of interested professionals
- Create an "event" centered around your service or product

(continued on next page)

many ways you can use a phone to be more successful. For important calls, always have a goal or desired result in mind. Make a brief list of points you want to cover.

When originating sales calls, think through what you will say to launch the conversation. Selecting the right phrase means the difference between coming across as helpful—or obnoxious. After you identify yourself, you have 15 to 30 seconds to convince the other person to stay on the line. Find a way to dramatize your reason for calling, devise a comment that ties your needs into something of interest to the other person. Stress the *benefits*. You may want to write a 30-second script to give you guidance and confidence.

Professional salespeople are masters at knowing how to turn prospects into customers. Their advice is learn to *listen*. After your initial introduction, let the prospect talk. He or she will reveal vital needs, concerns, and objections—which you then can counter with explanations, suggestions, and recommendations for crafting a win/win alliance.

Phone pros also advise scripting your message before you pick up the phone to call a prospect. This helps you know what you want to accomplish and gives you a sense of security. (Scripts are guidelines, however, not straightjackets.)

Also think through what message you'll leave if you get voice mail. This is an opportunity to leave a 45-second uninterrupted commercial. Identify yourself and your company, then let the prospect know what you can do for her or him. Talk benefit, benefit, benefit. And practice this message by saying it into a tape recorder and listening to the result until you sound conversational, energetic, and enthusiastic. By being well prepared you'll get far better and faster results.

Dogged persistence has helped many scale the castle walls. When you realize only 17 percent of business callers reach their intended party on the first try, you know tenacity must play an important role. The higher the person is on the VIP list, the more phone calls you'll need to make. Calling, calling again, recalling—over and

> **ROSS'S RULES OF ORDER**
> (continued)
>
> ■ Establish an award that correlates with your business
> ■ Tie in with special national day/week/month activities and events
> ■ Establish "P.I." (per inquiry) advertising arrangements
> ■ Speak about your topic
> ■ Take out inexpensive classified ads in targeted magazines or newsletters
> ■ Do co-op mailings with others who complement what you do
> ■ Be alert to news events and hot issues you can piggyback on
> ■ Enter any contests for which you qualify

over—will eventually shake loose the desired response. One of two things will likely happen: The secretary will take pity on you and suggest to her boss she take the call. Or the VIP will say, "Oh, her again. Let me talk to her and get it over with so she stops calling."

Here are a few random tips for normal telephone situations. If someone wants to put you on hold, you might counter with, "I'll be happy to hold unless my other line rings. But please jot down my number in case I have to hang up." About half the people will call back *on their dime* if you do hang up. If you have a separate personal phone line, you may want to include the following message at the end of important business correspondence: "To get through to me directly without delay, use this personal number...."

If you do considerable phone business from coast to coast, instruct the receptionist or your secretary to always get the geographic location of the caller when taking a message. Then you can adjust for time zone differences when returning the call.

When your secretary announces callers with unfamiliar or foreign names, ask that the name be written out phonetically. Also consider teleconferencing when you need to get more than two individuals together. This often makes more sense than incurring travel expenses for several people. It is a prudent way to hold a group meeting and save both money and time.

Rather than play an indefinite game of phone tag, if you don't catch up with the proper person when returning a call, consider leaving a *time bomb* message. "Tell John, we'll go ahead with the plans we discussed unless I hear from him by 11 o'clock tomorrow morning." Another alternative is to send a fax or e-mail.

Many companies assure their toll-free numbers are memorable by making them into a word. 1-800-FLOWERS, for instance, isn't just a gimmick. Memory research shows a catchy word or phrase is three to 10 times more likely to be recalled than its number equivalent. Especially if you use extensive TV, radio, or billboard advertising, a phone word tied to your company's service is smart. It is harder to dial, however. People get frustrated translating words into numbers. A way around this is to include the numbers in parentheses in all collateral materials.

With phone area codes multiplying so rapidly these days, you'll often be told a number is no longer in service, when the real truth is the area code has been replaced. To stay abreast of these changes go to http://www.aegisbooks.com/Intro.html. You might also want to consider purchasing this information on disk, adding your logo and a promotional message, and giving it as a business gift.

Suppose you need to get through to an important person—someone who is normally protected by an army of secretaries or assistants who carefully screen all calls. Mr. I. M. Notable isn't a personal friend, not even a business acquaintance. How will you ever penetrate the palace guard?

Using a "familiar" approach might be the open sesame. Say something like, "This is Terri Anderson calling for Ike." Your tone and manner suggest you've known Ike for years. (You never, however, lie and say that!) Chances are the secretary will tell you Ike is not available, whereupon you say, "Just ask him to call me please." Do *not* offer a number. That would blow your cover. Most efficient secretaries will ask you for one to save having to fish it out of the Rolodex or database. You then graciously provide it. This tactic usually gets your message placed in the "A" priority pile.

Another idea is to call after normal business hours. You can sometimes catch a busy executive working late and answering her own phone. Want to outsmart phone jinxes in a voice mail system that never allows you to access a real human being? Dial a number a digit or two off the main number. For example, if the main number is 212-536-2000,

332

try dialing 212-536-2002. You'll probably be connected to an individual's direct line. Then appeal to that person for help.

A further suggestion is to try and track down a home phone number. Occasionally this can be accomplished by looking the person up in *Who's Who in America* or other directories. Some major libraries have street address cross-reference directories that also list phone numbers. If you have your target's address, this might help. Ask friends of friends if they can supply the needed information.

If you do succeed in getting a personal number only to be greeted by an answering machine—leave just your name and phone number. By avoiding any further message, you will pique their curiosity and stand a better chance of getting a return call.

The 7 Habits of Highly Successful Entrepreneurs

Although I have mentioned some of these principles elsewhere in the book, they can make such a huge impact on your bottom line, I want to expand on them here.

1. **Have a passion for what you do.** Uncover your personal "gift" or embark on a business journey you truly love. The hours will seem less, the rewards greater if you get up each morning jazzed about what you do.

2. **Own your niche.** Decide what major area you'll flourish in and concentrate on it exclusively. Know all about it. Join relevant associations, subscribe to all the trade journals and newsletters, get to know the movers and shakers in your industry. Become the *authority*, the place where others turn for assistance or information.

3. **Cultivate word-of-mouth.** Getting a buzz started—people talking about your company—is the result you desire. Do it by soliciting testimonials and referrals; by getting publicity *everywhere*; by tenaciously positioning yourself as THE expert, THE place to shop or eat, THE source for the best merchandise.

4. **Make it easy for people to do what you want.** We live in a frantically busy world. The person who makes it simple and painless for us to accommodate them will probably get their wish. Create a list of interview questions a harried radio host can use to interview you. Put together a panel of experts (yourself included, of course) so a TV producer has a canned show ready to go. Get a toll-free

phone number and credit card merchant status so consumers can easily order your merchandise.

One political candidate distributed promotional videos to people's front porches. A recipient reports watching the candidate on VCR for 12 minutes as she conveyed her persuasive diagnosis of the city's problems, her vision, and qualifications. She even included an office and home phone number in case of questions and ended with a reminder about when to vote. The homeowner noted the date and the woman's name on her calendar. This clever political aspirant made it easy to get informed.

On a totally different level, during a recent trip to Home Depot I was intrigued to notice they now offer pick-up truck rentals. For just $19.00 for 75 minutes customers have no waiting for delivery, no wear and tear on their own vehicles, and no fuel or mileage charges. Home Depot makes it easy to be their customer. Be as flexible as a willow tree. Bend in the wind to accommodate others and you'll experience a rush of goodwill yourself.

5. **Ask for what you want.** Sure you'll be told "no" sometimes, but that's been happening since you were a year old. If you make it clear to others when you desire something, you'll also get "yes" a lot. Take your courage in hand and approach neighboring businesses, catalogs, other professionals, or large corporations. Don't feel like you need to genuflect when you suggest a strategic alliance. Tell them why it's to *their* benefit to partner with you. When you're writing sales material ask for the order—over and over again. During print interviews, request that the reporter include your toll-free number and send you a tear sheet of the published piece.

Just be sure to ask for *exactly* what you want. A stranger entered an apartment building and asked a young desk clerk in the lobby, "Can you tell me where Max Smith lives?" The boy smiled and replied, "Yes, sir. I'll show you." Six flights up, the clerk pointed to a door with the name Smith on it. The stranger pounded on the door for a while, then commented, "Guess he's not here." "Oh, no, sir," answered the clerk. "Mr. Smith was downstairs in the lobby."

6. **Apply the 80/20 rule.** It all started with Italian economist Vilfredo Pareto in the nineteen hundreds. He observed that the wealth in Italy was controlled by 20 percent of the people. J. M. Juran, one of the fathers of the Total Quality Management movement, applied

the Pareto Principle to inventory management in 1950. The rest is history.

This formula applies universally. You'll get 80 percent of your results from 20 percent of your efforts: 80 percent of your orders from 20 percent of your customers, 80 percent of your publicity from 20 percent of your PR contacts, 80 percent of your sales from 20 percent of your merchandise. Your only challenge is to *identify* that powerful 20 percent then concentrate all your energy there! Address the vital few versus the trivial many. Our ability as women to multi-task can be both a blessing and a curse. If we try to do many things at once, our focus—and our results—get diluted. Pick your battles to win the war.

7. **Follow-up, *follow-up*, FOLLOW-UP.** Do you want to call the tune instead of paying the fiddler? Then you'd better be prepared to monitor the progress of your projects. While diligent follow-up increases your odds for success in all aspects of business, it's especially crucial in promotion and sales. Many sound marketing plans flounder for lack of follow-up.

Perhaps the busiest of all recipients are the media, particularly radio and TV producers. They are inundated with literature about prospective guests. No news isn't necessarily bad news. We've had things go astray here more than anywhere else. Follow-up calls, faxes, and e-mail often net big dividends. Be persistent. Stay in touch with the contacts you make at major conventions, trade shows, and regional workshops. Properly worked, connections made at these events can impact your results for years to come.

The importance of this concept was etched in my brain many years ago when I was representing a client's book. It was about raw foods and I strategized that if I could get it carried in health food stores around the country, it would be extremely successful. So I tracked down the primary wholesaler, made my pitch, and was promptly turned down. But I didn't give up. Every time I got a sizeable purchase order, I scribbled a note across the bottom: "This could be coming to you, Dan." Whenever a new review broke, I sent him a copy. This continued for about six months. Then one day, here came a purchase order for a case of the books. Two weeks later he ordered two cases of books. Long story longer, that guide went on to become their bestseller for several years! Plus the author wrote several more books he also sold.

No matter what facet of marketing you explore, the squeaky wheel gets more attention. Be politely persistent. Stopping before you get results—or a firm "no"—is like ordering an ice cream cone, then letting it melt onto the floor. Persistence + passion = success. Don't be like the two cows grazing by the freeway. Stainless steel milk trucks kept whizzing by sporting signs that read "Homogenized." "Pasturized." "Fortified with Vitamin C." The one cow looked at the other and said, "Sure makes you feel inadequate, doesn't it?"

You can accomplish anything you put your mind, and your energy, to! Follow-up will get you across time zones, across borders, across oceans, across finish lines.

Creating a Swipe File

Original ideas can elude even the brightest people; no one can hit the bull's eye every time. But there is a way you can substantially increase your success ratio. How? By mining the treasure trove that surrounds you!

Every day we're inundated with hundreds of good ideas. They masquerade in the form of direct mail packages, commercials, print ads, Web messages, posters, billboards, articles, jokes, quotes, catalogs, newspaper stories, e-mail newsletters, greeting cards—even as conversations. Because they wear such unlikely costumes, however, we often overlook them.

Unmasked, many are naturals for marketing. Why not begin capturing these kernels of wisdom for future use? This is done via a "swipe file"—or more accurately, several swipe files. The term "swipe file" originated because you swipe (read "borrow") an idea from someone else. Naturally, you also give appropriate credit.

I have many such collections. Most reside in file folders. Gen Xers will probably scan them into their computer. One file houses interesting brochure designs and unusual folds. Another contains stunning direct mail packages. Still another is comprised of literature on my competition. And database files hold quotes, jokes, phrases, and sayings I can use for books, sales materials, or speeches. When it's time to develop something new, going through your swipe files adds verve and variety.

Once you tune in to developing swipe files, everything you hear or read, every place you go, every contact you make takes on an exciting new dimension! Ideas for your files are everywhere: at the post office; in the library; over the Internet; watching TV and listening to the radio; chatting with friends. Look for the Wow! Factor. If an eye-catching product makes you pause in the supermarket aisle, or an image stops you as you flip through a magazine, put it physically in a file with other think-outside-the-box concepts. The possibilities are endless. Just be sure to collar the information in written form, then place it in the appropriate archive. By using this technique to cull the best from the rest, you too can excel.

Establishing a Strong Board of Directors

A board can bring in bucks, back you up, and do some smart backseat driving. The ideal time to think about such a group is when you're starting your business. Why not get this wisdom from day one? Adding qualified outsiders to the brain trust relieves you of the sole burden of making decisions. By staffing your board with competent business leaders, you assure your company of strong, diversified advice. Something else you might consider: Many firms are going to boards of *advisors* rather than directors because this removes the risk of personal liability for those who serve proves less costly for the company, and is more practical for businesses or practices under $5 million in revenues.

People in the know suggest starting with a small number of participants, perhaps five. Large groups become mired too easily. You'll probably want to meet quarterly, but have the ability to pick up the phone in between sessions to interact with a board member for advice.

It used to be corporate boards consisted of relatives or company officers—people who willingly rubber-stamped the CEO's wishes. These people were expected to say "aye" or they were told "bye." Often a close advisor, like the firm's attorney or accountant, was also included.

Today the trend is toward including outsiders. According to a survey done by Growth Resources, Inc., two of the five directors on the average small company board now fall into this category. They are CEOs from related industries, professors from business and technical schools, and other professionals. You might also consider adding your savvy Web master to your board of advisors. Look for people who complement, rather than duplicate, your skills.

Aim for the highest caliber individuals. Seek executives who run companies bigger and more profitable than yours. The higher the wattage of your board the more credibility you'll have. The worst they can say is "no." A big name can provide credentials, capital, and influence—not to mention help you land contracts with superstars. That translates directly into dollars. In 1999 when Donna Jensen launched Startups.com, a consulting firm for high-tech fledglings, she recruited a gold-plated board including Guy Kawasaki, the former tech guru for Apple Computer. He brought with him two other top Silicon Valley players.

Before you can decide whom to invite to serve on your board, however, you need to decide what its function will be. Some boards are strictly window dressing to boost the company image; others are operational—involved in day-to-day activities. Then there is the networking board, which is designed primarily to extend the number of contacts available to the firm's owners. More sophisticated companies may want a board devoted to strategic planning. Their main function would be tackling issues such as succession planning and expansion. Perhaps the best approach is an all-purpose board that melds most of the above.

Sixty percent of the companies with boards compensate their directors. One study revealed fees range from $100 to $650 per meeting or structured as annual retainers of $1,000 up to $6,500. If cash is not a possible reward, how about making your directors stockholders? Pay for their services with equity rather than money. Or you might do what a friend of mine did. She is a spa consultant who forged a win/win alliance. When Betsy asked me to serve on her board of advisors, she made a point of saying a free spa weekend was part of the deal.

A strong board of directors based on a one-person, one-vote concept, helps a company stay dynamic. It can turn a business that borders on being a hobby into an aggressive enterprise. Possible candidates to staff your board include a marketing expert, public relations professional, an investment banker, a management consultant, or executives from larger successful companies. For more guidance, contact the National Association of Corporate Directors at 202-775-0509, www.nacdonline.org. And don't overlook adding the names of your list of advisors or board members to your letterhead to reflect status.

Adding a Twist to the Same Old Thing

Oil Can Henry, a Portland, Oregon, quick-lubrication franchise, decided it needed a way to stand out from the crowd. The decision was made to create a different atmosphere, one that presented old-time values and established a feeling of trust. Consequently, customers are greeted by employees wearing clothes reminiscent of early 20th-century Americana. Attendants change their uniforms when they get dirty. Patrons are given a copy of USA Today to read while their cars are being serviced. Or they can watch the process on a TV screen positioned by their car window. Were the results worth the effort? Over a one-year period, business increased approximately 35 percent.

River-rafting, once perceived as high adventure primarily for macho men, today attracts women, families, seniors, even paraplegics. The owners of rafting companies are adding a touch of luxury to this "roughing-it" sport. Some dinners on the river provide better fare than many gourmet restaurants. Western outfitters even offer wine-tasting trips in Idaho and classical music trips in Colorado. That's definitely a twist!

Other businesses join forces with complementary companies to boost their bottom lines. By doubling up you can make more of a splash. The right partner is not a competitor, but rather is after the same type of customer. Be sure you don't lose your own identity in the process.

When a bank sends out monthly statements, what is to stop it from including a promotional flyer about another service? When a management consulting firm mails out data to clients, couldn't it include details about a new peripheral service? A library sending out notices about reserved books being available could seize this opportunity to announce a story hour for children or a special summer reading program. A tax preparation service might mail a flyer about its monthly bookkeeping service with each tax return they do. This kind of back-end marketing builds on the initial front-end sale.

Speaking of building reminds me of remodeling. Perhaps you should consider revamping your services—maybe even *narrowing* them. One of the restaurants in our town prospers because of its limited menu. It thrives because the owner offers just six entrees. That way she only buys what she serves in quantity and doesn't have to cope with waste.

Remember, we're looking at switching the tables now. Maybe it's time to think small. Perhaps your auto repair business would have more profit if you only worked on one make of car, for instance. A janitorial service might specialize in offices rather than doing stores, warehouses, manufacturing plants or whatever comes its way. A temporary service that provided only professionals could easily make a name for itself.

When analyzing your scope, also consider your hours of business. Banks have been very creative in establishing hours that serve their clientele best. If you run a towing service, should you be working a split shift to capitalize on morning and afternoon drive times? Wouldn't a music teacher have more students if she structured classes when children were out of school and adults off work? Likewise, a dating service should open midafternoon and close in the later evening. Doctors, dentists, chiropractors, and other health professionals might do well to stay open on Saturday and take off Sunday/Monday. Altering your hours may be a smart way to fine-tune your operation.

In Rye, New York, an interesting concept has developed. A hair salon located next to a boutique keeps its customers entertained with fashion shows. During slow times, boutique employees don newly arrived clothing and put on an impromptu fashion show for women under the hair dryers.

Only by being informed can you determine if there is a savvy way to add a twist here, subtract there for more advantage. Attack your lack. Educate yourself. Keep abreast of new trends, technologies, and techniques in your field. "Information is the manager's main tool," states business guru Peter Drucker.

A Grab Bag of More Good Ideas

Want to attract customers like bears to a honey pot? Following is a potpourri of ideas for capturing more sales or delighting your patients, customers, or clients.

- **Become active in appropriate trade associations.** This doesn't mean simply join. It means serve on committees, run for office, and generally involve yourself. By doing so you get on the inside track. This gives you access to restricted information. It puts you shoulder to shoulder with the leaders in your industry, people who will prove to be valuable contacts. Larger associations also have unique reservoirs of specialized research facilities. Regularly reading industry trade journals and newsletters is another shrewd move.

- **Work with nonprofits.** Margaret Malsam tells of selling 225 copies of her *Meditations for Today's Married Christians* at the National Theresian Convention, then donating $375 to the organization. She offers prudent advice for dealing with nonprofits: "Don't say 'I will give you 50 percent off.' Instead tell them, 'I will *donate* $5 for every $10 book purchased." For follow-up sales, she makes up flyers so they can mail in orders. Malsam codes her post office box number with the acronym of the organization so they receive appropriate credit. Suggest they sell your product not only at conventions and workshops, but at regional or local meetings as well, and that they promote it in their newsletter or journal.

- **Acquire a brainstorming partner.** Why not approach someone whose opinion you respect and suggest getting together a couple of times a month to bounce around ideas? Done with honesty and tact, this kind of a support alliance can generate meaningful feedback and positive results.

■ **Barter to better yourself**. In 1625, the Dutch traded the Indians $24 worth of trinkets for the island of Manhattan. (Naturally, I encourage more equitable exchanges.) A good trade has balanced merit for both parties. A maid service and a bookkeeping firm might barter their skills. A lawn service could spruce up the yard of a writer, who in turn might create a promotional flyer. An auto mechanic could repair the vehicle of a cosmetologist, who would provide several haircuts.

Or you might contact a local restaurant and cut a deal to bring your clients to lunch or dinner for nothing or at a reduced rate. Sell the proprietor by convincing her that you will be bringing in a new customer. Given normal marketing costs, free meals are cheap advertising. A nonprofit organization was sponsoring a fund-raising golf tournament with a $250 price tag. They gave free registrations to key members of the local media in exchange for plugs in print and on the radio. The possibilities are endless for acquiring cashless customers.

■ **Sell to the government.** The federal government is the nation's largest consumer of goods and services. Every federal agency has been mandated to strive for allotting 5 percent of its business contracts to women-owned companies. (While this seems a ridiculously small percentage, it's a tiny step in the right direction, so let's get on the "Ms. Savvy Goes to Washington" bandwagon.) Learn how to get government contracts and the opportunities available at the Business Women's Network at http://www.bwni.com. Also check out http://www.pro-net.sba.gov, a free service run by the SBA. It's an online database of small businesses seeking state, federal, even private contracts. "Pro-Net can help small business and government make connections, "says SBA administrator Aida Alvarez. Government agencies use the site for procurement, so get listed and you'll have a chance of poking your fingers into the federal pie. The U.S. Chamber of Commerce also offers a free pamphlet on the subject. It is called *How to Sell to the Federal Government* (USCC-2002). You can order a copy by calling 800-638-6582 (in Maryland, call 800-352-1450) or visiting their Web site at www.uschamber.org.

■ *Give* **something away.** That's what a faltering parking-garage management company in Baltimore did. Owner Lisa Renshaw decided to implement a low-cost marketing method to attract new customers from among the business travelers using the nearby Amtrak station. She devised a flyer that contained a coupon good for a free carwash after parking in her garage five times. Renshaw personally distributed them at the train station. Her scheme worked. By the time people parked there five times, it had become a habit. They not only came back to park their cars but began paying for the $6 washes.

The service manager at Gafford Pontiac in La Mesa, California, prospects for business by sponsoring a free environmental and safety check for Pontiac owners. A letter announcing the inspection goes to appropriate car owners. It says the purpose of the inspection is to acquaint them with those conditions that affect their car's performance, efficiency, and safety. Might there be something in this for Gafford Pontiac as well?

- **Know the difference between fads and trends.** Differentiating between them is about as easy and scientific as handicapping the ponies. Fads have included such things as the Hula Hoop, Pet Rocks, Furbys™, and Michael Jackson's spangled glove. Trends, on the other hand have more staying power. You can lose your proverbial shirt by hooking up with a fad. By the time you discover it is a genuine fad, the craze is already on the way out. Aligning with a trend, however, can be an extremely clever marketing ploy.

- **Read the local newspaper as a route to increased business.** Why not read 'em and reap? A diaper service scours the paper to learn of new births. How better to find a fresh list of perfectly targeted clients? A bridal service picks up leads by reading the engagements section. Wiley real estate agents might determine likely people to list their houses by watching the divorce and obituary columns.

- **Give others recognition.** Are you looking for ways to make those you help feel important? A school could give a diploma or certificate of completion—then take a photograph of all graduates and submit it to the newspaper. Speaking of pictures, how about snapshots of your patient? Many clever health professionals have a "rogues' gallery" of beaming patients decorating their waiting room or office walls.

- **Use gimmicky, innovative ways to kindle responses.** KBIG radio in Los Angeles bills its easy-listening format with an "Unwind and Relax With K-BIG" theme. To woo advertising agency personnel, it distributed large, brass, wind-up keys to media buyers. These made attractive paper weights. In addition, the keys were consecutively numbered and packaged in attractive leather pouches. Accompanying each key was an invitation to join the K-BIG Unwind Club. Recipients were not obliged to buy anything, simply complete and return the cards, which entitled them to be eligible for periodic prize drawings. There was a 100-percent response, plus most recipients either called the station to express their appreciation or thanked the sales rep in person!

■ **Consider the often ignored gift certificate.** One of the best approaches is to give your present customers gift certificates for their friends, loved ones, and colleagues. Offer 20 or 25 percent off and let your present customer use one too as a way of your saying "thanks." A dentist we know of increased his business by 15 percent using this strategy. He printed 1,000 gift certificates, which he asked satisfied clients to give to family and friends. "The recipient gets $130 worth of free dental services, and I get to form a relationship with a potential patient," reports Dr. Larry Spidel.

Of course, mention your certificates everywhere: in your flyers, on your Web home page, in consumer catalogs, etc. You want to pique the interest of people scouting for gifts. And you needn't restrict this marketing device to the holidays. A makeover for Valentine's Day, Mother's Day, Father's Day, or graduation opens additional opportunities.

An interesting sidelight is that one out of every four gift certificates you sell are never redeemed! That means you pocket an extra $250 for every $1,000 you sell. This method of merchandising is also nice because you get paid up front and it usually guarantees the next purchase is from your company rather than the competition!

The immediate cash flow can provide an especially satisfying lump sum. One Outback Steakhouse® generated more than $30,000 in gift-certificate sales during a holiday season.

■ **Become part of the ongoing Brazen Hussies Network!** Several of you have told me "Brazen Hussies need to unite!" Well now that's possible. On our Web site we administer a clearinghouse for forward-thinking female entrepreneurs. Here's what awaits you:

■ Over 100 links to powerful women's business and entrepreneurial sites.

■ Business-related books to round-out your professional reading.

- A free weekly e-mail tip to help boost your bottom line.
- Money-making articles by industry leaders that will help you grow your business.
- A classified ad section where you can promote your business.
- Plus much more.

And those who choose to join the Network will also receive my monthly e-mail newsletter packed with the same kind of information I've been giving you here. This guarantees you an ongoing source of shameless marketing strategies! Additionally, I'm negotiating wonderful cost-saving discounts on products and services Network members can take advantage of. For full details, go to http://www.BrazenHussiesNetwork.com. I'd love to welcome you as a member!

Putting Balance in Your Life

Perhaps the best advice I can give you concerns not just your business, but yourself: While making a living, don't forget to make a life. Mellow out occasionally. Rest. Loaf. Let go. According to the U.S. Department of Labor, stress is the #1 problem for working women. De-stress so you're not *distressed*. Small cool downs prevent major meltdowns. To be a consistently effective businesswoman you have to recharge your own personal batteries.

Business Week reports that women who left corporate America to start their own businesses with hopes of achieving a better work-life balance are discovering that finding time for themselves and their children is a bigger challenge than expected. Many female entrepreneurs have difficulty managing a young company and young children simultaneously. This is partly due to the fact that women business owners spend triple the time on childcare and housework as their male counterparts.

So it's imperative we offset all this responsibility with some personal time, some real R&R—and that doesn't mean Run faster, Run faster. Learn to enjoy the little things. One day you may look back and realize they were the big ones.

- **Play—act your shoe size!** It isn't necessary that we behave as business-like adults all the time. Let your little girl out. Lie on your back and watch the clouds. What animal do you see? Fly a kite. Get down on the floor and romp with the dog. Go to the park and swing to your heart's content. Play a game of jacks. Have a pillow fight.

Do keep a sense of humor. In trying times, wit and buffoonery lighten the load. By allowing yourself to see the amusing side of things, you take the sting out of disappointments and obligations. Laughing releases endorphins, those wondrous feel-good hormones. Purposely plug amusing and absurd things into your life: See a funny film, watch *Third Rock From the Sun* on TV, attend a musical comedy theater production.

■ **Turn your bathroom into a luxurious spa.** This is a serene and peaceful time to be completely alone. Close the door and don't allow any interruptions. No telephone. No TV. No kids demanding attention. Tub time offers an escape from everyday chaos, a place to revitalize ourselves.

That's especially true if you set yourself up for pampering. Try to engage all your senses: smell, sight, sound, touch, and taste. Get some aromatic essential oils to create a spa-like atmosphere. (Lavender is wonderfully calming, relieves stress, and softens skin.) Bath salts soothe sore muscles and also soften your skin. Light an assortment of candles. Play lovely music. A common home spa treatment is exfoliating, for which you use a brush or loofah. Invest in a big, extra-fluffy towel for drying and smaller ones for heat treatments. Wet the towels, wring them out, then place them in the microwave for a minute or less. They will keep warm in a picnic cooler for up to 15 minutes. Feel the tension release as you apply them to your neck, shoulders, and aching feet.

To top off your home spa experience sip mineral water with a slice of fruit, have a glass of wine, or herbal tea. Finish up by wrapping your body in a plush bathrobe. You *deserve* to be treated to such luxury.

■ **Let the joy of music into your life.** Listening to soothing music calms the soul. It can be the central activity of the moment, or serve as a background while you accomplish certain tasks. And enjoying music needn't be a passive pastime. Why not sing? You can do it acappella or sing along with your favorite songs on the CD. What about dancing? Whether it's rock or a waltz, get into the movement and rhythm and forget your problems.

■ **Indulge in a fun personal pursuit.** We all need to do something off-hours that keeps us fired up on the job. Bernadette Grey, editor-in-chief of *Working Woman* magazine discussed the diversions of her staff in the February 2000 issue. Here are their hobbies: stand-up comedy, motorcycle riding, singing, drawing, photography, cooking, and tennis. Note that none of their free-time activities mirror anything close to what they do for a living. To refresh your brain cells, escape into something totally different from the day-to-day routine.

■ **Make health a high priority**. While entrepreneurs are highly motivated to build thriving, healthy companies, when it comes to their own health, ironically these high achievers often fall flat. According to *Self* magazine, when women live life at warp speed they become addicted to the adrenaline rush. Yet constantly flooding your body with adrenaline and stress hormones leads to such health problems as hypertension, migraines, hair loss, and weight gain.

Exercise helps to combat such problems. But that doesn't mean you have to struggle working out with weights, run an hour a day, or transform yourself into a jock. Select something you enjoy and choose a location where you won't feel self-conscious. Recent studies show all you need is 30 minutes of moderate activities most days of the week. You can even divide that time up: 10 minutes of yard work, 10 minutes of housework, 10 minutes walking the dog. And remember that you're not trading work time for play time. The few minutes of physical activity will increase your overall productivity. And please ditch the Walkman when you're out on a walk. Participate in life. Focus on the sounds, smells, and sights around you.

There are many relaxation techniques than can also lower your blood pressure and your tension level. Yoga is the preference of many women. Others enjoy tai chi, a Chinese form of movement. Progressive relaxation, in which you lie down and consciously begin relaxing specific parts of your body, starting with your toes and ending at your head, appeals to some. Visualization is also a remarkable way to relax. You see in your mind's eye a divine scene in nature and place yourself within this serene setting.

The old adage, "you are what you eat," rings so true. Pump your body with sugar, for instance, and you'll get a high—then an extreme low. Eat wholesome food in moderation and your body will be better prepared to cope with life's stress. Do yourself a favor: Before the Angel of Success arrives in your life, devote yourself to preparing your welcome for her by eating right.

■ **Give yourself time to think.** In this hectic day, when we often run around like chipmunks on a treadmill, we seem too busy to think. Can you recall the last time you thought deeply about the meaning of life: what you want to contribute to the world, the legacy you hope to leave? Saying you're too busy to stop and think about the way you are living is like saying you're too busy driving to stop for gas. Eventually it will catch up with you.

■ **Choose to be happy.** Sounds like a ridiculously simplistic statement, doesn't it? Yet some women opt for negativism and misery when happiness is just an alternative choice away. We can literally "choose" to change our attitude, to see the good and experience the wonder. This is an exciting, eventful, marvelous time to be alive on this planet. We can interact with people, try new things, and find strengths in ourselves we hadn't known were there. The writer Colette said, "I've had a wonderful life. I just wish I'd realized it sooner." Let's wake up now! Feeling angry, victimized, and retaliatory saps our vitality. Worrying about what *might* happen, dwelling on possible troubles down the road, is a waste of precious positive energy.

Of course we all experience challenges; that's part of life. At times you'll feel like Mother Teresa when she said, "I know God will not give me anything I can't handle. I just wish that He didn't trust me so much." But that too will pass. Dwell in the now. Enjoy the moment. Expect the best.

■ **Learn to say "no."** If you've gotten this far in this book, you're definitely a "doer." And doers are in great demand. Want a job done? Give it to a busy person. You'll be the target for organizing your church potluck, fund-raising for various worthy charities, signing up kids for the soccer league, you name it. Certainly you should be community-minded and help in some way. But not *all* ways! Discover the art of gracefully declining and you've just bought yourself some blessed free time.

Of course, pressure to do more is not just external. Often we ourselves are the greatest offenders. A perfect opportunity to let go of "shoulds" and participate in life around you is the holiday season. For example, several years ago I finally let go of writing individual Christmas greetings and did a general photocopied letter. Last Christmas I gave myself permission to say "no" to the pressure that typically accompanies the season. I did not decorate a tree, a responsibility I typically performed alone and in a resentful frame of mind. I had much more fun decking the *house* with boughs of holly. And instead of my usual huge turkey with all the accompanying trimmings, I served ham to my family and they loved it all the same. Little by little, I'm learning to say "no" to simplify and enjoy my life more. Why not take inventory of what you do and get rid of the time-wasting, energy-draining pursuits that add little to your quality of life?

- **Develop your spirituality.** Open your heart and your mind to the possibility of a Higher Power. Faith sustains us when nothing else can. I choose to let go and let God when the going gets tough. You may decide on a different path. What's supportive is to acknowledge that a Higher Power exists on which we can lean.

- **Let go of guilt.** Don't beat yourself up if you have to leave work early for an important family event. Go with the flow and enjoy it. And if you travel a lot, look for ways to be home even when you're on the road. Make a video or audiotape of your child's favorite story. Leave notes around the house. Cook and freeze a special meal. Call home frequently. And send a letter or postcard. By staying attentive, you needn't feel guilty about being away.

- **Splurge on some extras.** As soon as you can possibly afford it, allow yourself some luxuries. I know so many women who work extremely hard, bring home a nice paycheck, yet still struggle to clean their own houses every week. Hire a housekeeper! Use those hours to rejuvenate yourself and you'll be far more effective on the job, thus earning much more than you'll be paying. As you become more successful, look into engaging a nanny instead of carting the kids off to day care or a sitter. Hire a personal assistant a few hours a week to do grocery shopping, drop off cleaning, take the dog to the groomer, etc. And consider using a personal shopper service. Macy's, for instance, will search their stores for possibilities for you whether it's a gift or an addition to your wardrobe.

- **Vacation to soothe your soul.** You call for Lisa or Pat and are told they are on vacation. How do you feel? Frustrated you can't reach them? Just a teeny bit jealous perhaps? But you know how hard the typical businesswoman works. Don't we deserve some time to rest and refresh? Definitely! In fact, our overall productivity escalates after a week or two of leaving business behind. And therein lies the dilemma: How do we "disconnect"?

There are techniques to master the art of taking time off. Part of the secret lies in timing. Plan your vacation as far in advance as you do attending conventions or other important business events. Then you have time to develop a "countdown to paradise" action plan rather than cramming everything in just before you leave. Manage your workload so no big projects are coming due in the days before you escape. If you have to double up on work the week before you leave, you may be too rundown to really enjoy your holiday.

Make your time off as much of a priority as your time at work. Give yourself permission to set aside your overzealous work ethic, distance yourself, and downshift for a while.

Think about your ideal circumstances. Do you want a razzle-dazzle vacation with lots of excitement and entertainment? (If you choose this option, know that you may come home more tired than when you left.) Or would lying on a sandy deserted beach listening to a gentle surf be more your style? Take along a novel you've been wanting to read and get lost in fantasy land.

About two weeks before taking off, let employees, important colleagues, and key accounts know you are leaving. Then if they have questions or anticipate problems, these things can be handled before you're unavailable. Empower someone to act in your stead while you're away. Train that person in the things that are likely to occur. For emergencies, leave an itinerary and how you can be reached, but stipulate it is to be used *only* in extreme circumstances.

The whole idea is to get away from business completely. Don't take a cell phone, pager, your laptop, professional reading, sales reports to study, or anything else that smacks of your day-to-day requirements. Give your mind a break. Just play! Don't get seduced into checking in with the office. If you do, sure enough there will be things that demand your attention—and your whole mental attitude gears up for stress again. If you insist on keeping in touch, use e-mail. It's easier to control as you are distracted only when *you* choose to bring it up and there isn't the usual give and take that riles one's peacefulness so easily. If you have great trouble letting go, choose a vacation destination were you're virtually unreachable: sailing or a safari perhaps.

If you absolutely can't manage to get away for a good length of time, consider min-vacations. A long weekend every couple of months can be a wonderful respite. Stay in a nice hotel, charming rustic cabin, or welcoming B&B. Or consider camping if you're on a budget. Visiting relatives, however, is taboo. It doesn't provide a busy entrepreneur with the peace and quiet needed to heal and reflect.

In conclusion, getting balance in your life by taking personal time allows you to be a truly effective "shameless brazen hussy" when it's time to again don your business persona. My wish for you is an abundance of professional success spiced with personal fulfillment.

Web Sites, Wisdom, and Whimsey

Here's a proven way to convince people they should do business with you. Begin your letters by quoting the recipient. We all love to be quoted, even in a letter. And it's a compliment to the individual getting the letter that you paid such close attention to what was said. Grab her attention by repeating or paraphrasing some profound statement the person made during your previous conversation. Then play off it in stating your case.

The National Association of Women Business Owners is an organization that offers support and resources to help you grow your business and enrich your life. They are dedicated to helping you balance the things that matter, such as business, community, and lifestyle. To learn about membership benefits go to http://www.nawbo.org.

Extra! Extra! Get your online personalized "newspaper." No time to scour the daily paper to find relevant information? Never fear. Technology is here. There are now a plethora of sites that dish up customized news, delivered to your e-mail address on a daily basis. Some even provide links to the full stories themselves. You simply provide the criteria and they do the work. Busy professionals need a filter to get personalized, streamlined news and information specifically tailored to their requirements. They also need to have access to sites that facilitate a quick and thorough search for tracking down recent articles. If this describes you, check out the following treasures (Be sure to read the fine print, however, as some charge a nominal fee for such services.): http://www.totalnews.com, http://nt.excite.com/, and http://www.infobeat.com/.

●●●●●●●

Office perception gender gaps:
Family picture on HIS desk:
  He must be a solid, responsible family man.
Family picture on HER desk:
  She puts her family before her career.
HIS desk is cluttered:
  He's obviously a hard worker and a busy man.
HER desk is cluttered:
  She must be a disorganized scatterbrain.
HE is talking with his coworkers:
  He must be discussing the latest deal.
SHE is talking with her coworkers:
  She's probably gossiping.

●●●●●●●

Extending credit to a new customer? Selling your goods, then not being able to collect for them is a disheartening experience. If you are opening a major new account, it may be wise to run a credit check even though there is a fee involved. To help you identify risky businesses, you can work with either of the following credit-rating firms: Experian can be reached in California at 714-385-7000 or access their Web site at www.experian.com. Or call Equifax in Atlanta at 404-885-8000. Their Web site is www.equifax.com

"The voice of women on the Web" is the slogan of Bella-Online, a network of women who exchange ideas, offer encouragement, and share advice. They are organized into 14 vertical portals or channels that address all our needs and interests: autos, career, computers, entertainment, family, food and wine, health, home and garden, indulge, money, relationships, shopping, sports and fitness, plus travel and leisure. Find it all by pointing your browser to http://www.bellaonline.com.

Stay in touch over, and over, and over. It typically takes at least five exposures before a person makes a buying decision. Determine who are the top 20 percent of your leads and stay visible to these prime prospects. You can do it with phone calls, faxes, e-mails, letters, notes, postcards, or articles that would interest them with your business card attached. You might even get a friendly colleague to call them and offer a testimonial on your behalf. Be persistent!

●●●●●●●

He's pretty, but can he type?

●●●●●●●

New angle on collecting bad debt. Do you have an account, patient, wholesaler, or other creditor that owes you a substantial amount of money and won't pay? Here's a scheme that might shake loose what is owed you. Convince them to make a very small good faith payment. It isn't the money you really want at this point, it is the *banking information* that appears on the check! (If they won't give you a token payment, perhaps your bank has photocopies of a previous check that would serve the purpose.) Once you have this in hand, you can probably file a suit in small claims court, win, and get a judgment. If they still don't pay, look into having the sheriff put a lien on their checking account! This could cripple their business and serve as an instant motivation to clear their account with you.

Home alone...and hating it? If you work from home, you probably sometimes think your theme song is "Only the Lonely." The feelings of isolation can be overwhelming at times. But I've got some high-tech isolation busters for you: Your computer can open doors to ideas, people, and incredible energy. Via the Internet you can use your own Web site to solicit inquiries and comments from those who visit, then strike up a lively e-mail conversation. You can join chat sessions on topics that pique your interest. Or you could even manage a message board where you run ideas past other professionals and hear about their challenges. If that doesn't do the trick, try slipping into a cybercafe to circumvent the solitude of being home alone.

Use affirmations to overcome your obstacles. An affirmation is a statement of something you want that you repeat frequently. It can be oral or written. (I find writing them morning and night most effective; that serves as another way to reinforce your desires.) "I weight 120 pounds." "My firm has 25 clients." "I'm surrounded by five conscientious, competent associates." Notice these are all in the *present* tense. Not something you long for, but something you already have. They are also specific: 120 pounds, 25 clients, five associates. Affirmations help you focus on your desired results. Believe me, this technique works both personally and professionally! Why not give it a try?

●●●●●●●

Did you hear about the restaurant on the moon?
The food is great, but there's no atmosphere.

●●●●●●●

Five ways to expand your market: If you want to increase your business, here are several strategies you might apply: (1) Relocation: Can you move closer to your customer base? (2) Additional outlets: Could you add more convenient locations throughout your market area? (3) Expansion of present location: Are people waiting too long in lines or do you need more floor/shelf space? (4) New product line: Are there fresh products you can add to boost sales? (5) Grow by acquisition: Can you build market share by buying out your competition?

How do you deal with change? (Not the cash register stuff, the life-wrenching kind.) Well, we can try to change other people. But the only real way to do that is with a lobotomy. So what's left? Us. Here is an exercise you can do daily. It's a gut check to determine what you need to do that will significantly change and upgrade your business. Ask yourself: Do I choose to innovate? Do I choose to imitate? Or do I choose to vegetate? (If your answer is the latter, maybe you should abdicate!) You must become an evangelist for change and growth in your company.

Put some "oxygen" in your day! Online oxygen, that is. This robust new site by and for women offers brain food, chats, play, advice on handling your kids, health and fitness tips—you name it. They also have a nice section on work that covers topics like how to assess your entrepreneurial aptitude, write a business plan, and start your new business. Find it all at http://www.oxygen.com/.

●●●●●●●

Some people never say never. I'm reminded of the woman who called herself "Fatima" and was possibly the oldest performing belly-dancer up until her death at 87. Over the years, she just kept adding more veils and performing before audiences with poorer eyesight. Way to go, Fatima!

●●●●●●●

Being a "spokesperson" can help you reach your audience. Spokespersons Plus Networks (SPN) hooks up experts with well-known companies. Leslie Levine, author of *Will This Place Ever Feel Like Home?*, found a way to reach real estate agents when SPN founder Deborah Durham brokered a deal between Levine and ERA Realtors. Levine sold 15,000 copies to ERA, appeared on major TV shows, and attended realty conferences in their behalf. Durham, whose clients include Hewlett-Packard and Birds Eye, seeks experts in the areas of technology, the home, self-help topics, and cooking. Not only does this provide cash, but also incredible publicity, credibility, and new sales opportunities. For more details, visit SPN's Web site at www.spokespersons.com.

●●●●●●●

The 10 most powerful two-letter words are:
If it is to be, it is up to me.

●●●●●●●

AFTERWORD

My joy in writing this book has been to do a complete mental dump. Everything I know, everything I can imagine, everything I can research—it's all here in my legacy to you. My goal was to write THE definitive how-to marketing book for businesswomen. (Guys, please forgive me for the occasional dig; I truly unabashedly respect and adore men.)

People often come away from my writings and seminars with "information overload." To me that's a great compliment. Because out of all that information, you will surely find a few "aha" ideas to make your own. Ideas to launch a successful new business or to grow the one you already have to more profitable levels.

Educating and inspiring women is my passion. I hope in some measure I've served as a "virtual" mentor for you.

If I can show my sisters how to earn a more substantial livelihood, there will be enormous repercussions. When you succeed, your self-esteem blossoms and your children have a new and better role model. And as your paycheck increases, so does family quality of life. It keeps rippling out: Community well-being is enhanced. Society is transformed when women come into their own power.

So I leave you with one challenge: You go, girl!

Part VI

Sources &
Resources With
More Power Than
a Protein Bar

CHAPTER 17

Marketing Plan Outline

A marketing plan is a realistic assessment of what you are selling, who your clients or customers are (or should be), and how you can best reach your most profitable markets. Developing it draws not only on your knowledge and experience, but also on your intuitive business sense. Here are some practical pointers to help you create an effective plan:

1. Make a list of all your target options
2. Put yourself in your customers/clients' place
3. Define your markets
4. Segment your markets into manageable units
5. Check out your competition

Now go back to the list you created in step 1. Choose the top 10 or 12 options that seem to make the most sense. When prioritizing them, keep in mind their relative profitability, ease of implementation, and if they fit with your current services and price points. Next, review the segments you identified in step 4, matching them with your new list of most promising options. Bingo! You've determined several potentially profitable strategies to use as your marketing bull's-eye.

Your marketing plan is a "working document"—one that is used not only to define goals and plot action to be taken, but also to chart marketing progress. It needn't be lengthy, cumbersome, or unfriendly. Six to 10 pages will be fine. Be sure to include specific costs and the length of time necessary to accomplish each phase. Going through the experience of creating a marketing plan is a wonderful growth opportunity. It stimulates fresh thought. (In addition to being your road map to success, this outline can also be included with your overall business plan if you are seeking financing.)

I. Executive Summary

This is a brief overview of the primary objectives, including planning factors involved in marketing your service or product to the target markets over the next year. (Ideally, a 5-year overall plan is best, with particulars for the next year spelled out in detail.) Describe how the marketing objectives support the future company goals including increase in revenue, projected company size, additional staff, etc.

II. Mission Statement

This is a description of the philosophy of your business, the types of things you do, etc.

III. Market Definition

Define the scope of your target markets. This definition includes as much information as possible about those markets: their size, growth potential, health, etc. It's sort of an industry profile for each target market.

IV. Analysis of Current Situation

Description of the issues impacting your company's ability to compete in the target markets. The issues addressed are:

Internal strengths and weaknesses

Current market position (if any)

Client/customer situation

Economic performance of the company in the past two years

Competitive environment (Who are your rivals and how can you position yourself to compete against them?)

V. Goals and Objectives

A list of the marketing objectives and specific goals to be achieved for the year. For example, you may want to commit to increasing sales revenues by 25 percent. Goals must always be measurable. Don't state something lofty like, "To become the best company in the world."

VI. Action Plans

Taking into consideration all of the information gathered, what must you do to reach your goals/objectives? Each marketing objective should have an action program.

Describe what you're going to accomplish and by when (such as hire two outside sales representatives by December 15th).

Identify all costs connected with each plan.

VII. Budget and Controls

This is your overall budget for costs associated with implementing the action plans. Describe how you will monitor progress (such as sourcing every lead, creating a monthly marketing activity report, etc.) Remember that flexibility is a key ingredient. Review your marketing plan quarterly. Are you hitting your target? Should you make any adjustments or changes? Tweaking your trajectory as you go will keep your marketing plan on track.

CHAPTER 18

Governmental Sources
of Special Interest

General Government Agencies and Information

For your convenience, listed below are phone numbers and Web sites for prime government agencies. Be aware that new area codes are being added all the time. If you hear "that number is no longer in service" when you call, chances are the area code has simply changed. Check with Directory Assistance.

Department	Main Number	Public Affairs	URL
Dept. of Agriculture	202-720-2791	202-720-4623	www.usda.gov
Dept. of Defense	703-545-6700	703-697-5737	ww.defenselink.mil
Dept. of Education	800-872-5327	202-401-1576	www.ed.gov
Publication	877-433-7827		
Dept. of Energy	202-586-5000	202-586-5575	www.doe.gov
Dept. of Health and Human Services	877-696-6775	202-690-6343	www.dhhs.gov
Dept. of Housing and Urban Development	202-708-1422	800-767-7468	www.hud.gov
Dept. of Interior	202-208-3100	202-208-3171	www.doi.gov
Dept. of Justice	800-869-4499	202-514-3642	www.usdoj.gov
Statistics	800-857-3420		www.ncjrs.org
Dept. of Labor	202-219-5000	202-693-4650	www.dol.gov
Dept. of Transportation	202-366-4000	202-366-4570	www.dot.gov
Dept. of Veteran's Affairs	202-205-6773		www.va.gov

Department	Main Number	Public Affairs	URL
Environmental Protection Agency	202-260-2090	202-260-4454	www.epa.gov
Farm Credit Administration	703-883-4056	703-883-4056	www.fca.gov
Federal Communication Commission	888-225-5322	888-225-5322	www.fcc.gov
Federal Information Center	800-688-9889		http://fic.info.gov
Federal Trade Commission	202-326-2222	877-382-4357	www.ftc.gov
Food and Drug Administration	888-463-6332	301-827-7130	www.fda.gov
General Accounting Office	202-512-6000	202-512-4800	www.gao.gov
General Services Administration	202-708-5082	202-501-0705	www.gsa.gov
Government Printing Office	202-512-0000	888-293-6498	www.gpo.gov
Library of Congress	202-707-5000	202-707-2905	www.loc.gov
National Aeronautics & Space Administration	202-358-0000	202-358-1898	www.hq.nasa.gov
National Labor Relations	202-273-1000	202-273-1991	www.nlrb.gov
National Park Service	202-208-4747	202-208-6843	www.nps.gov
National Science Foundation	703-306-1234	703-306-1070	www.nsf.gov
National Transportation Safety Board	202-314-6020	202-314-6144	www.ntsb.gov
Occupational Safety and Health Administration	202-693-1999	202-219-8151	www.osha.gov
Office of Personnel Management	202-606-1800		www.usajobs.opm.gov
Overseas Private Investment Corp.	202-336-8400	202-336-8744	www.opic.gov
Patent and Trademark Office	800-786-9199	703-305-8341	www.uspto.gov

Department	Main Number	Public Affairs	URL
Securities and Exchange Commission	202-942-8088	202-942-0020	www.sec.gov
Social Security Administration	800-772-1213	410-965-8904	www.ssa.gov
State Dept.	202-647-4000	202-647-6575	www.state.gov
U.S. International Trade Commission	202-205-2000	202-205-1819	www.usitc.gov
U.S. Postal Service	800-275-8777	800-562-8777	www.usps.gov

Census Bureau

The Census Bureau possesses a wealth of statistics and information useful in making marketing decisions.

Public Information Office
4700 Silver Hill Road
Suitland, MD 20746
301-457-4608
URL: www.census.gov
(General information and channeling of inquiries)

Census Service Industries (Five-year statistics)
301-457-2800
e-mail: econ97@census.gov (business statistics); pop@census.gov (population and housing)

Department of Commerce

Expert help in navigating the maze of federal government information is available through the Department of Commerce. Call to get general information and the phone number of your nearest district office. Also request their *Business Services Directory*.

U.S. Department of Commerce
Office of Business Liaison, Room 5062
Washington, DC 20230
202-482-1360; 800-872-8723 (reports, markets, and with speak to trade specialists)
URL: www.doc.gov

Small Business Administration (SBA)

The SBA has numerous offices and programs to assist you. SCORE and ACE, for instance, offer free consulting help. Call the number listed here for more particulars on all their activities.

U.S. Small Business Administration
1110 Vermont Avenue, NW
Washington, DC 20416
202-606-4000
URL: www.sba.gov
8:30 A.M. to 5:00 P.M. EST, Monday through Friday

Small Business Answer Desk

800-827-5722
e-mail: answerdesk@sba.gov

This is a new service. You will not necessarily receive an immediate reply. E-mailed questions are answered during SBA business hours, 7:30 A.M. to 5 P.M. EST, Monday through Friday. Staff members try to respond within 24 hours.

Small Business Assistance Office of Minority Enterprise Development

202-205-6412; fax 202-205-7135

SBA Office of Women's Business Ownership

202-205-6673; fax 202-205-7287
URL: www.sbaonline.sba.gov/womeninbusiness

SBA-Net

URL: www.sba.gov

The SBA has established an electronic bulletin board to help small businesses find information and discover resources to help them start, maintain, expand, or operate their business. "SBA-Net" offers SBA information and services, publications, files relating to business, and mailboxes for business-related topics. Many useful files are available for downloading at their Web site.

CHAPTER 19

Entrepreneurial Organizations and Marketing Associations

African-American Women Business
   Owners Association
3363 Alden Place, NE
Washington, DC 20019
202-399-3645 (phone and fax)
URL: www.blackpgs.com/
aawboa.html

American Association of Home Based
   Businesses
PO Box 10023
Rockville, MD 20849-0023
800-447-9710; fax 301-963-7042
URL: www.aahbb.org

American Association of University
   Women
1111 16th Street, NW
Washington, DC 20036
202-785-7700; 202-785-7723
URL: www.aauw.org

American Business Women's
   Association
9100 Ward Parkway
PO Box 8728
Kansas City, MO 64114-0728
816-361-6621; fax 816-361-4991
URL: www.abwa.org

American Home Business Association
4505 South Wasatch Boulevard,
Suite 140
Salt Lake City, UT 84124
800-664-2422; fax 801-273-2399
URL: www.homebusiness.com

American Marketing Association
311 South Wacker Drive,
Suite 5800
Chicago, IL 60606
800-262-1150; fax 312-542-9001
URL: www.ama.org

American Society of Association
   Executives
Information Central
1575 I Street, NW
Washington, DC 20005-1168
202-626-2723; fax 202-371-8825
URL: www.asaenet.org

American Woman's Economic
   Development Corporation (AWED)
216 East 45th Street, 10th Floor
New York, NY 10017
917-368-6100; fax 212-986-7114
URL: www.womanconnect.com

Asian Women in Business
One West 34th Street, Suite 200
New York, NY 10001
212-868-1368; fax 212-868-1373
URL: www.awib.org

Black Career Women
PO Box 19332
Cincinnati, OH 45219
513-531-1932
URL: www.bcw.org

Brazen Hussies Network
PO Box 909
Buena Vista, CO 81211
719-395-8659; fax 719-395-8374
www.BrazenHussiesNetwork.com

Business and Professional Women/USA
2012 Massachusetts Avenue, NW
Washington, DC 20036
202-293-1100; fax 202-861-0298
URL: www.bpwusa.org

Catalyst
120 Wall Street, 5th Floor
New York, NY 10005
212-514-7600; fax 212-514-8470
URL: www.catalystwomen.org

*Center for Entrepreneurial
  Management, Inc.*
180 Varick Street, Penthouse
New York, NY 10014
212-633-0060
URL: www.ceoclubs.org

Business Women's Network
1146 19th Street, NW
Third Floor
Washington, DC 200036
800-48-WOMEN (800-489-6636)
URL: www.bwni.com

Center for Entrepreneurial Studies
Arthur M. Blank Center for
  Entrepreneurship
Babson College
457 Forest Street
Babson Park, MA 02457
781-239-4420; fax 781-239-4178
URL: www.babson.edu/entrep

Center for Entrepreneurship
523 Zane Showker Hall
James Madison University
Harrisonburg, VA 22807
540-568-3027
URL: (under construction)

Council of Better Business Bureaus, Inc.
4200 Wilson Boulevard, Suite 800
Arlington, VA 22203-1838
703-276-0100; fax 703-525-8277
URL: www.bbb.org

Direct Marketing Association
1120 Avenue of the Americas
New York, NY 10036-6700
212-768-7277; fax 212-302-6714
URL: www.the-dma.org

Hispanic Women's Council, Inc.
3509 West Beverly Boulevard
Montebello, CA 90640
323-728-9991; fax 323-725-0939
E-mail hwcla@aol.com
URL: (not available)

Home-Based Working Moms
PO Box 500164
Austin, TX 78750-0164
512-266-0900
URL: www.hbwm.com

366

Home Office Association of America
133 East 58th Street, Suite 711
New York, NY 10022
800-809-4622 or 212-588-9097;
fax 212-588-9156
URL: www.hoaa.com

International Franchise Association
1350 New York Avenue, NW,
Suite 900
Washington, DC 20005-4709
202-628-8000; fax 202-628-0812
URL: www.franchise.org

International Women's Forum
1621 Connecticut Avenue, NW,
Suite 300
Washington, DC 20009
202-775-8917; fax 202-429-0271
URL: www.iwforum.org

Latin Business Association
5400 East Olympic Boulevard,
Suite 130
Los Angeles, CA 90022
323-721-4000; fax 323-722-5050
URL: www.lbausa.com

MIT Enterprise Forum
Massachusetts Institute of Technology
28 Carlton Street, Building E32-300
Cambridge, MA 02139
617-253-0015; fax 617-258-0532
http://web.mit.edu/entforum/www/

Marketing Science Institute
1000 Massachusetts Avenue
Cambridge, MA 01238-5396
617-491-2060; fax 617-491-2065
URL: www.msi.org

National Association for Female
Executives (NAFE)
PO Box 469031
Escondido, CA 92046
800-634-6233
URL: www.nafe.com

National Association for the Cottage
Industry
PO Box 14850
Chicago, IL 60614
312-939-6490
URL: (under construction)

National Association of Home-Based
Businesses
10451 Mill Run Circle, Suite 400
Owings Mill, MD 21117
410-363-3698 or 410-581-0071
URL: www.usahomebusiness.com

National Association of the
Self-Employed
PO Box 612067
DFW Airport, TX 75261-2067
800-232-6273
URL: www.nase.org

National Association of Women
Business Owners (NAWBO)
1411 K Street, NW, Suite 1300
Washington, DC 20005
800-556-2926 or 202-347-8686
URL: www.nawbo.org

National Business Incubation
Association
20 East Circle Drive, Suite 190
Athens, OH 45701-3751
740-593-4331; fax 740-593-1996
URL: www.nbia.org

National Federation of Independent
  Business (NFIB)
53 Century Boulevard, Suite 250
Nashville, TN 37214
800-634-2669; fax 615-872-5353
URL: www.nfibonline.com

National Foundation for Women
  Business Owners
1411 K Street, NW, Suite 1350
Washington, DC 20005-3407
202-638-3060; fax 202-638-3064
URL: www.nfwbo.org

National Small Business United (NSBU)
1156 15th Street, NW, Suite 1100
Washington, DC 20005
800-345-6728 or 202-293-8830;
fax 202-872-8543
URL: www.nsbu.org

National Women's Business Council
409 3rd Street, SW, Suite 210
Washington, DC 20024
202-205-3850; fax 202-205-6825
URL: www.nwbc.gov

The Office for Women's Initiatives and
  Outreach
Room 15, Old Executive Office Building
Washington, DC 20502
202-456-7300; fax 202-456-7311
URL: www.whitehouse.gov/women/

Office of Women's Business Ownership
409 3rd Street, SW, 4th Floor
Washington, DC 20416
202-205-6673; fax 202-205-7287
URL: www.sbaonline.sba.gov/
  womeninbusiness/

Sales and Marketing Executives Int'l
5500 Interstate North Pkwy, #545
Atlanta, GA 30328
770-661-8500; fax 770-661-8512
URL: www.smei.org

Soroptimist International of the Americas
Two Penn Center Plaza, Suite 1000
Philadelphia, PA 19102
800-942-4629 or 215-557-9300
URL: www.soroptimist.org

U.S. Chamber of Commerce
1615 H Street, NW
Washington, DC 20062-2000
800-638-6582 or 202-659-6000;
fax 202-463-5888
URL: www.uschamber.org
(Also talk with your local chamber.)

Women Presidents' Organization
335 Madison Avenue, 4th Floor
New York, NY 10017
212-818-9424; fax 212-818-9423
www.womenpresidentsorg.com

Women's Enterprise Development
  Corporation
235 East Broadway, Suite 506
Long Beach, CA 90802-4431
562-983-3747; fax 562-983-3750
URL: www.wedc.org

National Chamber of Commerce
  for Women
10 Waterside Plaza, Suite 6H
New York, NY 10010
212-685-3454
URL: (not available)

CHAPTER 20

Selected Suppliers

Business Card Printers

Distinctive Cards (color cards)

All Color Cards
PMB 125; 784 South River Road
St. George, UT 84790-2435
888-788-4028; fax 888-788-4028
URL: www.allcolorcards.com

Econocards
PO Box 280981
Memphis, TN 38168
901-753-2900; (no fax)
URL: www.econocards.com

Mitchell Graphics
2363 Mitchell Park Drive
Petoskey, MI 49770
800-583-9401 or 231-347-4635;
fax 231-347-9255
URL: www.mitchellgraphics.com
(also prints brochures, postcards,
and presentation folders)

The Perfect Image Graphics Co.
2429 West 12th Street, Suite 1
Tempe, AZ 85281
800-533-8732 or 480-894-1700;
fax 480-894-0081
URL: www.perfect-image.com

Royal Publishing
PO Box 398
Glendora, CA 91740
626-335-8069; fax 626-335-6127
URL: www.walters-intl.com
(also does Rolodex-type cards)

Standard Cards

Folder Factory
116-A High Street; PO Box 429
Edinburg, VA 22824-0429
800-296-4321
URL: www.folders.com
(Rolodex-type cards)

Parrot Printing, Inc.
3101 NW 104th Street, Suite 6
Des Moines, IA 50322
515-251-6565

The Stationery House, Inc.
1000 Florida Avenue
Hagerstown, MD 21741
800-638-3033; fax 800-554-8779
URL: www.stationeryhouse.com

Walter Drake, Inc.
4510 Edison Avenue
Colorado Springs, CO 80915
800-525-9291; 719-596-3854
URL: www.wdrake.com

Brochure Printers

DeHART's Printing Services Corp.
3265 Scott Boulevard
Santa Clara, CA 95054
888-982-4763 or 408-982-9118;
fax 408-982-9912
URL: www.deharts.com

Tu-Vets Corporation
5635 East Beverly Boulevard
Los Angeles, CA 90022
800-894-8977 or 323-723-4569;
fax 323-724-1896
URL: www.tu-vets.com

Postcard Printers

Modern Postcard
1675 Faraday Avenue
Carlsbad, CA 92008
800-959-8365 or 760-431-7084;
fax 760-431-1939
URL: www.modernpostcard.com

1-800 Postcards
11 East 4th Street, #5F
New York, NY 10003
1-800 Postcards (767-8227)
URL: www.1800postcards.com

Office Supplies

Office Depot
2200 Old Germantown Road
Delray Beach, FL 33445
888-463-3768; fax 888-685-5010
URL: www.officedepot.com

Office Max
3605 Warrensville Center Road
Shaker Heights, OH 44122
800-283-7674
URL: www.officemax.com

Quill Corporation
PO Box 4700
Lincolnshire, IL 60197
800-789-1331
URL: www.quillcorp.com

Staples, Inc.
PO Box 9273
Framingham, MA 01701-9273
800-378-2753
URL: www.staples.com

Viking Office Products
950 West 190th Street
Torrance, CA 90502
800-421-1222
URL: www.vikingop.com

Promotional Products/ Novelties

Baudville, Inc.
5380 52nd Street, SE
Grand Rapids, MI 49512-9765
800-728-0888; fax 616-698-0554
URL: www.baudville.com

Best Impressions Company
345 North Lewis Avenue
Oglesby, IL 61348
800-635-2378; fax 815-883-8346
URL: www.bestimpressions.com

ePromos.com
148 West 37th Street, Floor 3
New York, NY 10018
877-377-6667
URL: www.epromos.com

U.S. Toy Company, Inc.
13201 Arrington Road
Grandview, MO 64030-2886
800-255-6124
URL: www.ustoy.com

Cartoonists

SpeakerNet News
URL: www.speakernetnews.com/
cartoonist.html

Ted Goff
PO Box 22679
Kansas City, MO 64113
(phone unlisted)
URL: www.tedgoff.com

Clip Art Sources

ArtMaster-Art-Pak
112 Harvard Avenue, #296
Claremont, CA 91711
909-626-8065

ArtToday.com, Inc.
3420 North Dodge Blvd., Suite F
Tucson, AZ 85716-1469
520-881-8101
URL: www.ArtToday.com

Barry's Clip Art Server
URL: www.barrysclipart.com

Clipart.com
3420 North Dodge, Suite C
Tucson, AZ 85716
URL: www.clipart.com

Dynamic Graphics, Inc.
6000 North Forest Park Drive
Peoria, IL 61614-3592
800-255-8800 or 309-688-8800
URL: www.dgusa.com

Nova Development
23801 Calabasas Road, Suite 2005
Calabasas, CA 91302-1547
818-591-9600; fax 818-591-8885
www.novadevelopmentcorp.com/

The Printers Shopper
111 Press Lane
Chula Vista, CA 91910-1093
800-854-2911; In CA, 800-522-1573; fax 800-482-8536
URL: www.printersshopper.com

Clipping Bureaus

Bacon's Information, Inc.
332 S. Michigan Avenue, Suite 900
Chicago, IL 60604
800-621-0561; fax 312-922-3127
URL: www.baconsinfo.com

Burrelle's Information Services
75 East Northfield Road
Livingston, NJ 07039
800-631-1160; fax 973-992-7675
URL: www.burelles.com

John P. Stewart Newspaper Clipping Service
9773 LaSalle Boulevard
LaSalle PQ H8R 2N9, Canada
514-366-8410

Luce Press Clippings
420 Lexington Avenue, 2nd Floor
New York, NY 10170
800-528-8226
URL: www.lucepress.com

Press Release Services

Direct Contact
PO Box 6726
Kennewick, WA 99336
800-457-8746 or 509-545-2707;
fax 509-582-9865
URL: www.imediafax.com

eWatch
888-776-0942; fax 800-856-4514
URL: www.ewatch.com

Luce Online
6617 North Scottsdale Road,
Suite 101
Scottsdale, Az 85250
800-518-0088; fax 480-922-3174
URL: www.luceonline.com

Markwatch
800-890-5791
URL: www.markwatch.com

News Index
URL: www.newsindex.com

NewsLinx
URL: www.newslinx.com

Video News Releases (VNRs)

J-Nex Media
5455 Wilshire Boulevard, Suite 2010
Los Angeles, CA 90036
323-934-4356

Medialink
708 3rd Avenue, 9th Floor
New York, NY 10017
800-843-0677 or 212-682-8300;
fax 212-682-2370
URL: www.medialink.com

Reuters Television International
747 7th Avenue
New York, NY 10017
212-603-3300
URL: www.reuters.com

Miscellaneous Vendors

Harrison Publishing Company
624 Patton Avenue
Asheville, NC 28806
800-438-5829; fax 800-645-5909
URL: www.harrisonpublishing.com
(Clever greeting cards for business purposes)

Introknocks Sales Greetings
16 West 36th Street, 13th Floor
New York, NY 10018
800-753-0550 and 877-473-3899
URL: www.introknocks.com
(Specialized business greeting cards)

Jemtech Photo Service, Inc.
3700 Butler Street
Pittsburgh, PA 15201
412-621-0331; fax 412-621-3058
URL: www.jemtechphoto.com
(Black and white and color photo
bulk duplication)

Miller Audio/Video, Inc.
2535 Cloud Spring Road
Rossville, GA 30741
800-426-8399 or 706-861-9602;
fax 706-861-5164
URL: www.milleraudio.com
(Bulk cassettes)

Presentation Folder, Inc.
1130 North Main Street
Orange, CA 92867
800-927-1127 or 714-289-7000;
fax 714-289-7010
URL: www.presentationfolder.com
(Presentation folders)

Traverse Bay Display & Packaging, Ltd.
4366 Deerwood Drive
Traverse City, MI 49686-3810
800-240-9802; fax 231-938-3269
URL: www.tbdisplay.com
(Packaging and display products)

Toll-Free Phone Number Options

To set up an in-house toll-free
phone number, call one of the
following telephone companies:

AT&T: 800-222-0400

MCI Worldcom: 800-888-0800

US Sprint: 800-877-2000

US West: 800-603-6000

RECOMMENDED READING

Abraham, Jay, *Getting Everything You Can Out of All You've Got: 21 Ways You Can Out-Think, Out-Perform, and Out-Earn the Competition*, St. Martin's Press

Applegate, Jane, *201 Great Ideas for Your Small Business*, Bloomberg PR

Ballard, Donna, *Doing It for Ourselves: Success Stories of African-American Women in Business*, Berkley Publishing

Beach, Mark and Elaine Floyd, *Newsletter Sourcebook*, Writer's Digest Books

Bly, Bob, *The Encyclopedia of Business Letters, Fax Memos, and E-Mail*, Career Press

Bock, Wally, *Cyberpower for Business: How to Profit from the Information Super-highway*, Career Press

Brabec, Barbara, *Handmade for Profit: Hundreds of Secrets to Success in Selling Arts & Crafts*, M. Evans & Co.

Briles, Judith, *Woman to Woman 2000: Becoming Sabotage Savvy in the New Millenium*, New Horizon Press

_____, *Gendertraps: Confronting Confrontophobia, Toxic Bosses, and Other Landmines at Work*, Business McGraw-Hill

Brody, Marjorie, CSP, CMC, Allen D'Angelo, MS, CPC, Bill Kerley, Th.D., and Bernard Zick, MBA, CPC, *Power Marketing for Consultants: 142 Insider Marketing Secrets Used by the Nation's Top Consultants*, Archer-Ellison Publishing Company

Business Women's Network Directory 2000, The, The Business Women's Network (BWN)

Business Women's WOW! Facts, The, The Business Women's Network (BWN)

Carnegie, Dale, *How to Win Friends and Influence People*, Pocket Books

Catalyst, Shelia Wellington, *Creating Women's Networks: A How-To-Guide for Women and Companies*, Jossey-Bass Business & Management Series

Chu, Chin-Ning, *Do Less, Achieve More: Discover the Hidden Power of Giving In*, ReganBooks Clark, Sheree, *Get Noticed: Self Promotion for Creative Profes-sionals*, Sayles Graphic Design

Covey, Stephen, *The 7 Habits of Highly Effective People: Powerful Lessons in Personal Change*, Fireside

DePalma, Tami and Kim Dushinski, *Maximum Exposure Marketing System*, MarketAbility, Inc.

Edwards, Paul and Sarah Edwards, *The Best Home Businesses for the 21st Century: The Inside Information You Need to Know to Select a Home-Based Business That's Right For You*, J. P. Tarcher

Evans, Gail, *Play Like a Man, Win Like a Woman: What Men Know About Success That Women Need to Learn*, Broadway

Fererri, Jack, *Knock-out Marketing: Powerful Strategies to Punch Up Your Sales*, Entrepreneur Press

Flesch, Rudolph, *The Art of Readable Writing*, IDG Books Worldwide

Floyd, Elaine, *Marketing with Newsletters: How to Boost Sales, Add Members & Raise Funds with a Printed, Faxed or Web Site Newsletter*, E.F. Communications

Hyatt, Carole, *The Woman's New Selling Game: How to Sell Yourself—And Anything Else*, McGraw-Hill

Kamoroff, Bernard B., *Small Time Operator: How to Start Your Own Small Business, Keep Your Books, Pay Your Taxes and Stay Out of Trouble!*, Bell Springs Publishing

Kawasaki, Guy, *How to Drive Your Competition Crazy: Creating Disruption for Fun and Profit*, Hyperion

Kennedy, Danielle, *Balancing Acts: An Inspirational Guide for Working Mothers*, Berkley Publishing Group

Kennedy, Dan S., *How to Make Millions With Your Ideas: An Entrepreneur's Guide*, Plume

_____, *The Ultimate Sales Letter: How to Boost your Sales With Powerful Sales Letters Based on Madison Avenue Techniques*, Adams Media Corporation

Levinson, Jay Conrad, Seth Godin, and Charles Rubin, *The Guerrilla Marketing Handbook*, Houghton Mifflin Co.

_____, *Guerrilla Marketing: Secrets for Making Big Profits from Your Small Business*, Houghton Mifflin Co.

Lonier, Terri, *Working Solo: The Real Guide to Freedom & Financial Success with Your Own Business, 2nd Edition*, John Wiley & Sons

_____, *The Frugal Entrepreneur: Creative Ways to Save Time, Energy & Money in Your Business*, Portico Press

McQuown, Judith H., *Inc. Yourself: How to Profit by Setting Up Your Own Corporation*, Broadway Books

Recommended Reading

Naisbitt, John, *Megatrends 2000*, Avon Books

O'Connell, Brian, *Gen E: Generation Entrepreneur's Rewriting The Rules Of Business & You Can, Too!*, Entrepreneur Press

O'Keefe, Steve, *Publicity on the Internet: Creating Successful Publicity Campaigns on the Internet and the Commercial Online Services*, John Wiley & Sons

Palder, Edward L., *The Catalog of Catalogs*, Woodbine House

Pierce Zoller, Bettye and Hugh Lampman, *WomanSpeak: The Essential Guide to More Effective Communication for Women (and Men!) In the 21st Century*, ZWL Publishing, Inc., (audio program)

Pinsky, Raleigh, *101 Ways to Promote Yourself: Tricks of the Trade for Taking Charge of Your Own Success*, Avon Books

Ries, Al and Jack Trout, *22 Immutable Laws of Marketing: Violate Them at Your Own Risk*, Harperbusiness

Ross, Marilyn, *National Directory of Newspaper Op-Ed Pages*, Communication Creativity

_____, and Tom Ross, *The Complete Guide to Self-Publishing: Everything You Need to Write, Publish, Promote and Sell Your Own Book*, Writer's Digest Books

Stone, Bob, *Successful Direct Marketing Methods*, NTC Business Books

Underhill, Paco, *Why We Buy: The Science of Shopping*, Simon & Schuster, Inc.

Walters, Dottie, *Never Underestimate the Selling Power of a Woman*, Wilshire Books

_____, and Lilly Waters, *Speak and Grow Rich*, Prentice Hall Trade

Weiss, Wendy, *Cold Calling for Women: Opening Doors and Closing Sales*, D.F.D. Publications Wiener, Valerie, *Power Positioning: Advancing Yourself as THE Expert*, PowerMark Publishing

Yager, Dr. Jan, *Creative Time Management in the New Millennium*, Prentice Hall

_____, *Friendshifts: The Power of Friendship and How it Shapes Our Lives*, Hannacroix Creek Books

Yudkin, Marcia, *Internet Marketing For $500 a Year or Less*, Maximum Press

_____, *Persuading on Paper*, Plume/Penguin

_____, *Six Steps to Free Publicity*, Plume/Penguin

INDEX

Index

O

Obnoxious clients 324–325
Office space needs 30
Office supplies 370
Offshore Sailing School 299
Oil Can Henry 339
O'Neil, Lorraine Brennan 32
Online Women's Business
  Center 39, 42
Op-ed essays 108–109
Outdistance the herd 134–135
Outsourcing 40
Owades, Ruth 209
Own your niche 333

P

Paid presenter, becoming a
  267–269
PartyLine 128
Passion 8, 333
Patents 52
Perception 313
Peripheral revenue centers 283
Permission to quote sample 290
Persistence 123, 219, 248, 331,
  351
Personal power and credibility
  45–49
  body language 47
  dressing 46
  etiquette 47
  feminization of the
    workplace 48
  handshakes 45
  self-introductions 47
  think big 47
  voice 47
Persuasive words 67
Pfeifer, Diane 224, 225
Phillips PR News 128
Photographs 104–105, 122
Play—act your shoe size 344
Plus an existing business 298
Popcorn, Faith 285
Popcorn Report, The 285
Positioning yourself 17–21
  Unique Selling Proposition
    (USP) 17
Postage chart 260
Postcards 119, 204, 262, 279
  printers 370
Potentials in Marketing 231
Power, Dee 201
*Power Positioning: Advancing
  Yourself as THE Expert*
  18
PR/advertising agencies 33
Pregnancy Survival Kit 22
Premiums 223–235
  courting local premium sales
    227

creative matchmaking 224–
  225
customize 225
*Directory of Premium,
  Incentive & Travel Buyers*
  225
discounts 225
do your homework 228
exclusivity 225
Gosselin, Kim 223, 229–231
*Hoover's Handbook of
  American Businesses* 227
hoovers.com 228
how it works 225
IMRA Handbook, The 229
Incentive Manufactures
  Representative
  Association 228
Motivation Show, The 226
Pfeifer, Diane 224
Potentials in Marketing 231
premium reps 228–229
test 225
think big 223
*Thomas Register of American
  Manufacturers* 227
tips from the sage 229–231
trade shows 226
what's hot 224
Prenner, Sue and Bob 254, 259
Preparing for success 7–42
  brainstorming 35–39
  budgeting 27–28
  competition 14–17
  hiring professional help 32–
    34
  location 29–32
  market research 8–14
  marketing plan creation 23
  measurement methods 34–
    35
  niches 21–23, 333
  positioning yourself 17–21
  pricing 28–29
  research: fact finding on the
    Net 10–14
  startup checklist 24–25
Press conferences 106–107
Press kit 105–106
Press release services 371
Price point 247, 252
Pricing 28–29
Product line 284
Professional listings 152
Professional practices 99, 113
Promotional ideas 129–158,
  231
  awards, giving 145
  boards, serving on 150–152
  business socializing 131
  Business Women's Network
    132

cause-related marketing 141
Committee of One Hundred
  154
community involvement
  141–142
computer files 156
consumer education 129–
  131
contests 143–146
directories 152
donating 142–143
governmental recognition
  154
greeting cards 153
industry leadership 148–150
networking 131–138, 156
NUTS! 145
outdistance the herd 134–
  135
products/novelties 370
professional listings 152
promotional schemes 152–
  158
radio 145
restaurants 144
special events 138–140
sports marketing 139–140
store windows 144
surveys, conducting 146–
  147
telephone hotline 153
thank-you 135
trade associations 149, 155
volunteering 142–143, 150
Web site awards 146
Promotional products/novelties
  370
Promotional schemes 152–160
Proprietary information 45
Prospecting 90, 301
PRWeek 192
Psychographics 77, 81
Publicity 99–128, 184–186
  articles and columns 109–
    111, 121–122
  begin locally 124
  broadcast media 118–119
  community newspapers 123
  databases for free 127
  e-mail tips 103, 189–192
  key contacts 119, 123
  letters to the editor 107–108
  media kit 105–106
  news releases 101–104
  newsletter 113–114
  newspapers 126
  op-ed essays 108–109
  photographs 104–105, 122
  press conferences 106–107
  press kit 105–106
  recycle, repeat, reuse 111–
    113, 123

Index

Give the Gift of
Shameless Marketing for Brazen Hussies™
to Your Friends and Colleagues

CHECK YOUR LEADING BOOKSTORE OR ORDER HERE

❏ **YES**, I want ____ copies of *Shameless Marketing for Brazen Hussies*™ at $19.95 each, plus $4 shipping per book (Colorado residents please add $1.39 sales tax per book). Canadian orders must be accompanied by a postal money order in U.S. funds. Allow 15 days for delivery.

My check or money order for $_____ is enclosed.
Please charge my ❏ Visa ❏ MasterCard ❏ Discover ❏ American Express

❏ **YES**, I am interested in having Marilyn speak to my organization. Please contact me about details.

❏ **YES**, I want to hire Marilyn for customized on-site help to launch my business—or for a marketing make over of my existing enterprise.

❏ **YES**, I want to join the Brazen Hussies Network and get Marilyn's advice on a continuing basis. I'll receive a monthly subscription to her dynamite e-mail newsletter and other money-making, cost-saving benefits. (Only $49 annually)

Name _____

Organization_____

Address _____

City/State/Zip _____

Phone _____ E-mail _____ Fax _____

Card # _____

Exp. Date_____ Signature _____

Please make your check payable and return to:

Communication Creativity
P.O. Box 909
Buena Vista, CO 81211

Call your credit card order toll-free to: 800-331-8355

Fax: 719-395-8374; E-mail: Deb@BrazenHussiesNetwork.com